CANADIAN EDITION

WORKING WITH PEOPLE
Communication Skills for Reflective Practice

Louise Harms & Joanna Pierce

OXFORD
UNIVERSITY PRESS

OXFORD
UNIVERSITY PRESS

8 Sampson Mews, Suite 204, Don Mills, Ontario M3C 0H5
www.oupcanada.com

Oxford University Press is a department of the University of Oxford.
It furthers the University's objective of excellence in research, scholarship,
and education by publishing worldwide in

Oxford New York
Auckland Cape Town Dar es Salaam Hong Kong Karachi
Kuala Lumpur Madrid Melbourne Mexico City Nairobi
New Delhi Shanghai Taipei Toronto

With offices in
Argentina Austria Brazil Chile Czech Republic France Greece
Guatemala Hungary Italy Japan Poland Portugal Singapore
South Korea Switzerland Thailand Turkey Ukraine Vietnam

Oxford is a trade mark of Oxford University Press
in the UK and in certain other countries

Published in Canada
by Oxford University Press

Original edition published by Oxford University Press,
253 Normanby Road, South Melbourne, Victoria, 3205 Australia
Copyright ©2007 Louise Harms

Library and Archives Canada Cataloguing in Publication

Harms, Louise
Working with people : communication skills for reflective practice /
Louise Harms and Joanna Pierce. — 1st Canadian ed.

Includes bibliographical references and index.
ISBN 978–0–19–543354–8

1. Communication in human services. 2. Interpersonal communication.
3. Human services personnel. I. Pierce, Joanna II. Title.

HV29.7.H37 2011   361'.06   C2010-907722-9

Cover image: Philip and Karen Smith/Getty

Oxford University Press is committed to our environment. This book is printed on Forest Stewardship
Council certified paper, harvested from a responsibly managed forest.

Printed and bound in Canada

1 2 3 4 — 14 13 12 11

Contents

Contributors

Carolyn Aston is a social worker, educational consultant, and child/adolescent psychotherapist, in private practice, with a background in teaching, community health, and child psychiatry. As founder of the Connect-a-Kid Mentoring Program in 2002 for at-risk middle-school students, she welcomes the opportunity to work innovatively with parents, teachers, and colleagues to maximize the well-being and educational potential of vulnerable young people. A former tutor in the Bachelor of Social Work program, University of Melbourne, and Lecturer in Education, Deakin, she currently lectures in counselling techniques for the Graduate Diploma of Mental Health for Teaching Professionals, Monash University, and is a clinical supervisor in the Master of Child Psychoanalytic Psychotherapy program.

Heather Carmichael has experience in the disability field, quality assurance accreditation consultancy, and has been practising in the alcohol and other drugs field for years in a range of areas including prison, withdrawal, counselling, and supported accommodation. She currently co-ordinates several projects at UnitingCare Moreland Hall, including the Intensive Playgroup, Student Unit, Intensive Support Program, and several youth programs. Her academic background is in social work and psychology and she has a diploma in AOD work.

Louise Harms is a social worker who worked for nine years in hospital and educational settings before moving into social work teaching and research. She has worked full-time in the School of Social Work at the University of Melbourne since 2001, where she is Senior Lecturer and co-ordinator of the entry-to-practice social work program.

Suzie Hudson has worked in the social work field for 10 years in various Australian states and overseas. While her main passion has been clinical work with adolescents and adults in the areas of substance abuse, offending behaviour, and group work, she has also had the opportunity to teach at both Edith Cowan and Melbourne Universities. Suzie completed her MSW at the University of Melbourne and she is currently at the University of New South Wales completing a Ph.D., an ethnographic study in Sydney's Kings Cross area of street-based sex workers who inject psycho-stimulants.

Rebecca Parsons has a Bachelor of Arts (psychology) and a Bachelor of Social Work. She works in Alice Springs, Australia, with children and young people.

Melissa Petrakis has worked in public mental health service provision, management, and research over the last decade. Her Master of Social Work research was in applied solution-focused brief therapy for telephone counselling and referral. Her Ph.D. dissertation is on suicide relapse prevention. Melissa has tutored and been a guest lecturer in the undergraduate program at University of Melbourne School of Social Work for the last six years.

David Rose is a social worker with over 15 years' experience in direct practice and in management roles in the alcohol and drug treatment, offender support, and forensic mental health areas. He is currently in a part-time position as the Chief Social Worker, Forensicare—The Victorian Institute of Forensic Mental Health, while undertaking a Ph.D. in the School of Social Work at the University of Melbourne.

Jane Sullivan is a senior social worker at a pediatric hospital. Her areas of practice include disability, chronic and life-shortening illness, palliative care, and bereavement support. She has qualifications in adolescent and child psychology and theology and an MSW. Jane believes that developing communication skills is a life-long process.

Nicole Tokatlian is a senior social worker and team leader in a pediatric hospital. She has worked in a number of hospital units and is currently working in oncology. She has a particular interest in the impact of trauma on children, adolescents, and families as well as in management and leadership in social work. She has undertaken post-graduate study in Child, Adolescent, and Family Mental Health, and in Family Therapy.

Karen White has worked for over 20 years as a social work practitioner in the areas of child and family welfare and community and mental health. Concurrently, since 1996 she has taught a range of social work subjects at the University of Melbourne. Beginning in 2004, with the support of an Australian Research Council scholarship, she studied children's perspectives and participation within the family welfare sector, the subject of her doctoral dissertation. Karen is an active member of the AASW (Australian Association of Social Workers) with regard to ethical issues and promotes children's rights in practice and policy.

John Douglass Whyte is a social worker who earned his MSW at Michigan State University before completing a Ph.D. at the School of Social Work at the University of Melbourne. He has taught sessionally within the School. He has worked for many years within community development projects in the US, and is currently working as a Research Fellow on an Australian Research Council Linkage Grant examining social work practice with Indigenous communities.

Preface

Who Is This Text For?

Human service work is about working with people. Government and non-government organizations provide services to enhance people's lives and the communities in which they live. These services aim to help people cope better with daily stressors and demands, as well as to prevent the occurrence of these stressors and demands in the first place. The 'territory' of human service work includes work with individuals, group work, social policy, management, leadership and administration; work with families and partnerships; community work; research and evaluation; and education and training (Chenowith and McAuliffe, 2005: 14). Human service workers are committed to making a difference at individual and structural levels.

Workers listen to and respond to the unique stories of each person, family, group, or community. Good communication skills are fundamental to engaging and working with others about their needs and rights. This book aims to explore the place and challenges of communication and interviewing skills within the context of human service practice.

Some Emphases within This Book

This book focuses particularly on:

- *Applying a multi-dimensional approach.* A multi-dimensional approach interprets human experience as arising from inner and outer world influences. A multi-dimensional approach not only acknowledges all these dimensions of an individual's experience (referred to as the biopsychosocial-spiritual dimensions), but it also suggests that any responses by human service workers also need to be multi-dimensional, addressing both cause and consequence, for example, of human adversity and difficulty. A multi-dimensional approach emphasizes the importance of understanding experiences of both vulnerability and resilience, and therefore of understanding both risk and protective factors.
- *Drawing on practitioner experiences and the unpredictable nature of the work.* Much of what is considered to be human service work happens 'on the run' and in diverse and uncontrollable settings, and in single contacts or one-time interventions. This book, therefore, looks at all these dimensions as expected components of practice, rather than as the surprises that interrupt a more controlled counselling approach. Contributions from experienced practitioners in the field ensure that the examples are grounded firmly in the realities of everyday practice.
- *Thinking beyond the first point of contact.* Communication and interviewing skills often are introduced in relation to only the early phases of working with people. While you gain a sense of the skills to begin and (sometimes) end the work, no real sense emerges as to what the actual work 'in

the middle' might be. This book identifies skills across a range of human service work encounters so that you can move beyond the first interview or the first point of contact.

- *Reflecting on how you make decisions.* Many of the frequently utilized microskills of interpersonal communication and interviewing are introduced. Greater emphasis is placed, however, on the critical decisions we make in using these skills in any given situation. It is not just 'what' these skills are but 'why', 'how', and 'when' we use them. Working creatively, critically, and consciously with other people is our focus. The book will not provide you with a 'prescription' for practice, but will instead raise lots of possibilities for you to consider and to practise throughout your career.
- *Paying attention to a multiplicity of factors continuously.* In human service work, we bring together our theoretical knowledge of human beings and the social environment, of adversity and oppression, and of coping and adaptation. At the same time, we bring our practice knowledge and self-awareness to each situation. Given each situation's uniqueness, no 'right' way to communicate exists. The challenge is to develop 'communication sensitivity'. Communication sensitivity is 'the ability to identify circumstances in which communication is required, the nature of that communication, the persons or organizations that should be communicated with, and so on' (Thompson, 2003a: 33).
- *Practising in a critical, reflective way.* You will be encouraged to think about your own communication style: how it has developed over your life course, the ways in which it impacts communication with others, and how it influences the lives of others and the other environments we occupy.

Chapter Overviews

This book is divided into five parts, each dealing with a specific aspect of the communication process in human service work.

Part One: Framing the Relationship

This first part of the book considers the ways in which human service workers conceptualize key practice issues.

Chapter 1 explores why human services are provided and what key values are at the forefront in any professional client–worker relationship. In the final part of this chapter, some ways in which change is thought about are introduced—change through methods of practice, through various stages or phases, and through the use of particular microskills.

Chapter 2 examines current conceptualizations of communication processes. What are the micro-processes that take place within human communication processes and how can they be used to communicate more effectively? This chapter focuses on how change occurs through communication processes, at verbal and non-verbal levels, and from the individual through to collective levels. The chapter also explores subjective perceptions of good communication and why effective communication matters.

Chapter 3 presents theoretical perspectives as ways of informing practice. It looks at the influence of three dominant paradigms—the positivist, constructivist, and critical. Then, a multi-dimensional approach is introduced as a way of understanding human adaptation, as well as providing a broad perspective on intervention. The chapter looks at some theoretical approaches to practice: task-centred, crisis intervention, psychodynamic, cognitive, behavioural, narrative, solution-focused, feminist, and critical approaches.

Part Two: Forming the Relationship

The second part of the book focuses on understanding oneself in the role of worker—your context and the very specific microskills used in communication and the interviewing processes. While they are described individually, they are part of an overall communication process. Therefore, the decisions we make in using these skills at different times for different purposes are vital.

Chapter 4 explores why we need to reflect critically on our personal communication style and experiences. In human service work, the worker is the key 'tool' in the process. Conversation is the means by which most of the work is conducted and we need to understand our role in that process. The focus here is on understanding the client and building empathy. Thus, 'use of self' and identifying the purpose and context of work with individuals, families, or communities are central to the discussion.

Chapter 5 focuses on the essential preparatory work in relation to your self-care and professional development. This preparatory work is as much about your self-care as your skill development. Supervision, debriefing, and critical self-reflection are important maintenance strategies in the ongoing challenges of human service work.

Chapter 6 examines how engagement and rapport with clients can be built. The focus is on preparing to meet, making initial contact, and engaging with people. We also consider issues of confidentiality and your use of self-disclosure.

Part Three: Focusing the Communication

The third part of the book explores how communication can be focused more specifically to explore a person's key concerns and how we might work with them to formulate an assessment of their circumstances and areas for work.

Chapter 7 presents the processes of interpersonal contact through asking questions. Chapter 8 provides an overview of paraphrasing and summarizing skills. These skills are important for clarifying and challenging what you have heard in order to establish what is important to the client. The importance of empathy will be revisited in this chapter.

The final chapters in Part Three focus on forming an assessment of the work to be undertaken. Chapter 9 examines the skills involved in setting specific goals for the work, goals that are mutually agreed to. Chapter 10 then focuses on assessing, and responding to, particular situations of risk.

Part Four: Focusing the Intervention

Part Four looks more closely at the ways in which our practice is informed by theory.

Chapter 11 examines the skills of task-centred and crisis intervention approaches. Chapter 12 presents the skills of psychodynamic and cognitive behavioural approaches. Chapter 13 addresses narrative and solution-focused skills. Chapter 14 explores feminist and critical approaches, and their key skills.

Part Five: Finishing the Work

The final chapter of the book explores how endings are understood. Chapter 15 focuses on the skills of finishing, including dealing with endings that are both anticipated and unanticipated, contracting for further work, and referral. An emphasis is placed on evaluating practice, through evaluations with clients and other stakeholders and through critical self-reflection.

A Map for Your Practice

This book proposes that you use the following task map to think about your practice:

Part One—Framing the Relationship

- the purpose of human service work
- your value base, professional ethics and regulatory guidelines in Canada.
- your theoretical and factual knowledge.
- the purpose of human service work
- your value base, professional ethics, and regulatory guidelines in Canada
- your theoretical and factual knowledge.

Part Two—Forming the Relationship

- your use of self
- your organizational context
- your ongoing support and professional development needs
- meeting the people involved
- opening the communication
- active listening and working with silence
- listening empathically
- using self-disclosure.

Part Three—Focusing the Communication

- establishing the story
- forming an assessment
- goal-setting.

Part Four—Focusing the Intervention

- drawing on theoretical perspectives
- doing the work.

Part Five—Finishing the Work

- ending well
- evaluating the work.

Acknowledgements to the Australian Edition

My deepest gratitude goes to:

- the students of the School of Social Work at the University of Melbourne who continue to teach me so much
- Melissa Petrakis, Karen White, and Chris Daicos, the Communication Skills teaching team
- my colleagues and friends who have so generously contributed stories from their practice and helped to bring this book to life
- the publishing team from Oxford University Press—particularly Debra James, my publisher, and Pete Cruttenden, my editor
- my ever-supportive and loving parents, Glenys and Peter
- Jane Sullivan, who listens, lives, and talks in excellent measure.

Louise Harms

Acknowledgements to the First Canadian Edition

I would like to express my sincere appreciation to everyone who encouraged me through this process: to Louise Harms, for all her work; the students of the School of Social Work at the University of Northern British Columbia, who not only continue to teach me so much, but make the learning process a true adventure; my colleagues who, without hesitation, continue to support me in my academic journey; the publishing team from Oxford University Press—particularly the developmental editor, Kathryn West, and copy editors Richard and Laurna Tallman. Finally, I thank my family, who always support and encourage me unconditionally.

Joanna Pierce

How to Use this Book

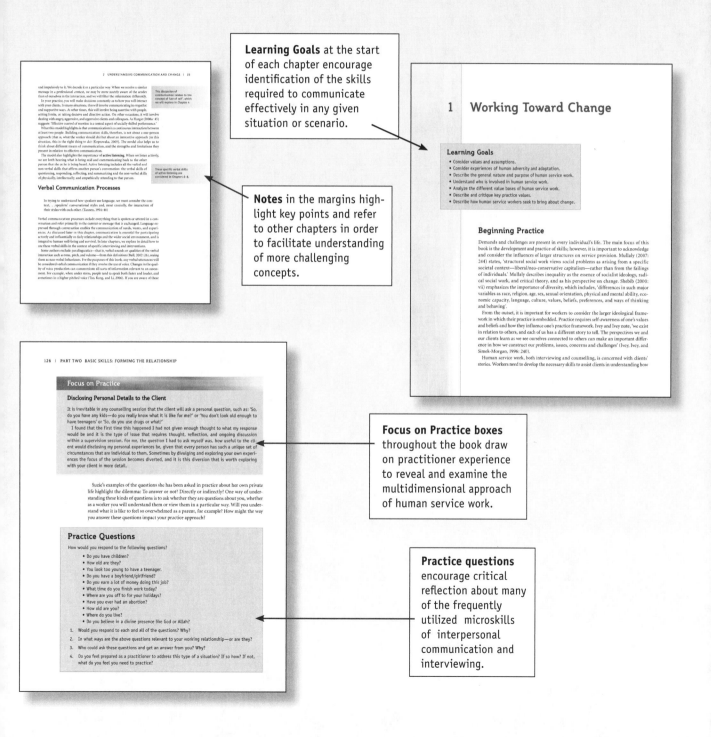

Learning Goals at the start of each chapter encourage identification of the skills required to communicate effectively in any given situation or scenario.

Notes in the margins highlight key points and refer to other chapters in order to facilitate understanding of more challenging concepts.

Focus on Practice boxes throughout the book draw on practitioner experience to reveal and examine the multidimensional approach of human service work.

Practice questions encourage critical reflection about many of the frequently utilized microskills of interpersonal communication and interviewing.

Part One | Framing the Relationship

In this first part of the book, we explore ways in which the relationship between you, as the worker, and your client can be understood. We look at some of the ways in which human service work can be conceptualized, which enables you to think about the ways in which your core understandings, communication processes, and practice theories influence what you will do.

Chapter 1 explores why human services are provided in the first place, and what values and ethics are at the forefront in any professional client–worker relationship. We continue with examining change processes and social justice.

Chapter 2 examines current conceptualizations of communication processes. We look at how change occurs through communication processes, at verbal and non-verbal levels, as well as the individual through to collective levels.

Chapter 3 presents theoretical perspectives as ways of informing practice. It looks at the influence of three dominant paradigms—the positivist, constructivist, and critical. A multidimensional approach is introduced as a way of understanding human adaptation, as well as providing a broad perspective on intervention. The chapter then looks briefly at some theoretical approaches to practice.

Part One—Framing the Relationship

- the purpose of human service work
- your value base, professional ethics, and regulatory guidelines in Canada
- your theoretical and factual knowledge.

1 Working Towards Change

Learning Goals

- Consider values and assumptions.
- Consider experiences of human adversity and adaptation.
- Describe the general nature and purpose of human service work.
- Understand who is involved in human service work.
- Analyze the different value bases of human service work.
- Describe and critique key practice values.
- Describe how human service workers seek to bring about change.

Beginning Practice

Demands and challenges are present in every individual's life. The main focus of this book is the development and practice of skills; however, it is important to acknowledge and consider the influences of larger structures on service provision. Mullaly (2007: 244) states, 'structural social work views social problems as arising from a specific societal context—liberal/neo-conservative capitalism—rather than from the failings of individuals.' Mullaly describes inequality as the essence of socialist ideology, radical social work, and critical theory, and as his perspective on change. Shebib (2000: vii) emphasizes the importance of diversity, which includes, 'differences in such major variables as race, religion, age, sex, sexual orientation, physical and mental ability, economic capacity, language, culture, values, beliefs, preferences, and ways of thinking and behaving'.

From the outset, it is important for workers to consider the larger ideological framework in which their practice is embedded. Practice requires self-awareness of one's values and beliefs and how they influence one's practice framework. Ivey and Ivey note, 'we exist in relation to others, and each of us has a different story to tell. The perspectives we and our clients learn as we see ourselves connected to others can make an important difference in how we construct our problems, issues, concerns and challenges' (Ivey, Ivey, and Simek-Morgan, 1996: 240).

Human service work, both interviewing and counselling, is concerned with clients' stories. Workers need to develop the necessary skills to assist clients in understanding how they think, feel, and act, as they do, towards creating a new way of approaching their story (ibid.). In the Canadian context several terms are used when working with people. For example, human service workers, also called social service workers, are generally people who have obtained a certificate or diploma and, typically, who work in various agency settings. Social workers usually have a university degree at the bachelor's or master's level (BSW, MSW).

For the purposes of this book and to capture the importance of communication skills at all levels, the term 'human service worker' will be applied. Broadly defined, a **human service worker** is someone who provides targeted services, typically within a government, non-profit agency, or community setting, to alleviate human adversity and bring about constructive social and individual change.

The next section provides examples of individual adversity. As you read the case scenarios, consider the larger societal influences that underpin each event.

Experiences of Adversity

People experience **adversity** as a result of many different circumstances. Adversity arises from experiences of poverty and depleted personal resources. Adversity arises from exhaustion, depression and despair; from experiences of hatred, abuse, and trauma. Some adversities are short term and crisis-driven, while others present long-term concerns and difficulties. Demands on the individual arise from the social, structural, and cultural contexts in which he or she lives, as well as from relational and inner-world experiences. Human services aim to alleviate adversity and to promote well-being and health in all of these circumstances. Consider the following four scenarios.

Focus on Practice

Alleviating Adversity

Scenario 1

A child protection worker is going to meet with a parent, against whom allegations of abuse have been made. The worker, on arrival at the family home, notices that the parent is drug-affected and not happy at all about the notification to protective services.

Scenario 2

A housing worker is meeting with a group of concerned tenants to consider writing a letter of protest about the reopening of a road through a quiet neighbourhood where children have been playing. The group includes people from many culturally and linguistically diverse backgrounds. Other actions may be developed after a community consultation.

Scenario 3

An intake worker on a telephone crisis line receives a call from a 24-year-old distressed woman who has been assaulted by her partner, Ann. She asks the intake worker to tell her what she should do—whether to leave or stay.

Scenario 4

A worker has been involved with a separated family for many years, from the time their daughter was diagnosed with cancer through to her death six months ago. The worker wants to invite the siblings to a support group, which will involve contact with both the parents and the siblings.

These scenarios demonstrate how different the life stressors and traumas are for people and how varied the human service workers' responses need to be. In Scenario 4 the worker has an established relationship, whereas in Scenario 3 the worker has had no face-to-face relationship at all. In Scenario 1, the worker receives a hostile reaction as compared with a more sought-after and sustained relationship in Scenario 2. In working with people across such a broad spectrum of experience, human service workers need to develop an adaptable repertoire of **skills** to engage, assess, and intervene appropriately with people. It is important for human service workers to examine the social context in which the above scenarios are embedded.

These four scenarios raise questions as to how you would respond as a worker. In particular, they raise questions about the agenda for change and who is driving that agenda. This chapter is structured around four core questions. First, why are human services provided as a response to these experiences? Second, how do we think about who is involved? Third, what are some of the core **values** that underpin human services? Finally, how is change thought about within the human services, from the perspective of different values, **methods,** and stages?

Why Do We Provide Human Services?

Human services are provided in the belief that resources should be provided in situations of adversity to support and enhance the well-being of individuals, families, and communities. The benefit of people supporting each other through times of adversity is well-documented, whether through practical and instrumental support (Harms, 2005: 38–9; Hobfoll, Ennis, and Kay, 2000; Ife and Tesoriero, 2006) or with emotional support through talking with someone or assisting someone writing about her or his experiences (Lepore and Smyth, 2003; Pennebaker, 1995; Pennebaker and O'Heeran, 1984).

Studies of individual and community experiences of grief, trauma, and stress have consistently identified the availability of resources, social support, secure attachment relationships, and affirmation as key protective factors. A sense of control (Kobasa, 1979) and a sense of coherence (Antonovsky, 1987) are vital protective factors, also. All of these factors can be translated into practical, instrumental, and emotional interventions. Human services are based on beliefs about intervention at two levels. Supportive relationships are a protective factor in their own right, and are also effective vehicles for change in other circumstances—for example, providing resources such as education, skills, information, and other practical resources. A relationship base, therefore, is at the core of human service work. This is reflected within the social work profession's *Code of Ethics* and *Guidelines for Ethical Practice* (CASW, 2005). The Canadian Association of Social Workers (CASW) describes its core values and principles as follows:

> Social work is a profession concerned with helping individuals, families, groups and communities to enhance their individual and collective well-being. It aims to help people develop their skills and their ability to use their own resources and those of the community to resolve problems. Social work is concerned with individual and personal problems but also with broader social issues such as poverty, unemployment and domestic violence. (Canadian Association of Social Workers, at: www.casw-acts.ca)

The outcome of direct social work practice is that needs of clients are met, their potential is developed, and their control over their lives is fostered. This is achieved through mutual engagement and the application of the social worker's knowledge and skill.

To make an assessment of someone's needs and potential and the type of engagement required is an inherently complex process. As Banks (2006: 49) comments:

> Promoting someone's 'good' or welfare is . . . open to interpretation depending on what we think counts as human welfare (happiness, pleasure, wealth, satisfaction . . .) and whether we adopt our own view of what a person's welfare is or the person's own conception of their welfare.

The four scenarios above raise some of these key questions about well-being. For example, how does a society decide what constitutes risk for children within the context of family life? How does a society determine access to resources such as playgrounds in housing estates? How does a society provide the necessary resources for women and children who are separating from family violence? How does a community respond to a family whose child has died? How are these questions translated into relevant and effective human service policies, programs and practices?

Human services are based on notions of well-being, but these notions can become the source of not only of support but of risk. One person's notion of well-being can lead to culturally inappropriate solutions for others and result in generations of damage and harm (Haebich, 2006). The balance between human service workers being agents of social care, change, or control (Howe, 1994) is a delicate one and depends on a continuous review of the values underpinning our work.

Who Is Involved in Human Service Work?

Many people seek support voluntarily as a result of particular experiences of upheaval and crisis in life—experiences of poverty, unemployment, and migration; of violence and abuse; of illness, disability, and death; or of family stress and breakdown. Other people are involuntary users of services, mandated as a result of court orders or legal regulations relating to child protection, juvenile justice, or community treatment orders, for example. They are involuntary **clients** in that they are required to have contact with workers as a result of behaviour deemed to be risky by others. In these instances, human service workers can be an unwanted intrusion into their lives. Other people are somewhere in between the experience of being a voluntary or involuntary client—they experience violence in the context of an abusive relationship or they are admitted to hospital following a fall and consequently have to access human services for support during recovery. Many people are forced by circumstances to become human service clients rather than their choosing freely to access those services.

As illustrated in the above scenarios, language is a crucial influence on how clients are perceived by workers who interact with them. A parent, a group of concerned citizens, a person at the end of the telephone, or a family come to be termed clients, **consumers**, customers or service users—depending on the agency with which they come in contact. From a client perspective, these labels can be experienced as negative and depersonalizing. From the worker's perspective, these terms raise fundamental questions about your perception of the identities of the individuals who are accessing services and how you frame and understand their experience.

The term 'client' is defined by the *Code of Ethics* of the Canadian Association of Social Workers:

> A person, family, group of persons, incorporated body, association or community on whose behalf a social worker provides or agrees to provide a service or to whom the social worker is legally obligated to provide a service.

The term 'client' will be used throughout this book, consistent with this professional base.

The term 'service user' is reflective of many of these assumptions—that is, that they are people accessing services because of neglect, vulnerability, disadvantage, or needs. This term differs, however, in the assumption that they are active users of a service, possibly denoting a voluntary access of the organization or service. In some contexts, the term 'customer' has been adopted, although this has not been done widely in Canada. The underlying assumption here is that the customer has purchasing power, which may be the case only in some situations.

In some specific contexts, such as the Canadian Association of Sexual Assault Centres (CASAC) where a feminist philosophy underlies all dimensions of service delivery, the term 'victim/survivor' is used to demonstrate the status of the person independent of an agency involvement. This emphasizes both the person's risk and strength status.

The use of the word 'client' or 'service user' self-referentially is rare. These terms tend to be used by workers to identify the people they work with, and are not necessarily used by the person herself or himself. One term more readily adopted by the people using the service has been that of 'consumer' (Happell, Pinikahana, and Roper, 2003), adopted by many within the mental health sector as a more appropriate self-referential term.

Each of these terms has particular connotations about the nature of the relationship between the service, the worker, and the person accessing the service. Throughout this book, the term 'worker' will be used for 'human service worker'. Many other terms are frequently used, including 'helping professional', 'social worker', 'community worker', 'child protection worker', 'counsellor', 'practitioner', and 'therapist'. All of these terms reflect different training, emphases, and values in human service work.

Values in the Relationship

Values are central to human service work. As a worker, you rely on processes of personal, professional, and wider cultural beliefs and values to form an assessment that will lead to interventions. According to Banks (2006: 6):

> 'values' can be regarded as particular types of belief that people hold about what is regarded as worthy or valuable. In the context of professional practice, the use of the term 'belief' reflects the status that values have as stronger than mere opinions or preferences.

These strongly held beliefs about what is 'worthy or valuable' also have other qualities: they are recognized as being 'generalized, emotionally charged conceptions of what is desirable, historically created and derived from experience, and shared by a population or a group within it' (Weber, 2006: 18). This definition captures some essential components of our value bases: they can be emotionally charged and, therefore, sometimes fiercely protected; they are developed within a specific historical and experiential context, and may not always be readily transferable; and they are upheld by a group of people as a way of bringing a shared focus and understanding. Values-based practice is complex when uncertainty and unpredictability are prevailing factors in your work. While there are ethical guidelines for practice, even referring to these in times of crisis will not always lead you to a straightforward solution or strategy. You need to revisit and reflect on your value base in an ongoing way.

Professional Value Bases

Extensive and useful discussions in relation to values can be followed in texts by Payne (2006), Reamer (2001), and Banks (2006). Social values do differ across professions and it is important to be familiar with your professional value base. For example, the Canadian Counselling and Psychotherapy Association (CCPA) and the Canadian Medical Association (CMA) both have codes of ethical conduct that highlight ways of relating to the people with whom they are working. These codes have adopted what Payne (2006: 85) describes as a 'list approach' to values: the perceived correct ways of behaving are listed and people are held to account to these behaviours. Social workers generally have university training at the Bachelor of Social Work (BSW) or Master of Social Work (MSW) level. Organizations such as the CASW provide information on the provincial associations' and colleges' regulatory guidelines specific to each Canadian province (www.casw-acts.ca). For example, when you graduate from a social service worker program in Ontario, you are eligible for admission to the Ontario College of Social Workers and Social Service Workers. As a member of this body, you can use the title 'Registered Social Service Worker' (www.ocswssw.org).

The fundamental values of social work practice are 'driven by a mission of **social justice** and change to balance inequities and to create a more enabling society' (Fook, 2000: 129). Others, such as Lynn (1999), identify the values of social justice and personal care as the two core values. Within the CASW *Code of Ethics* (2005: 4–10) six core values are outlined, relating both to views of the client and to the working relationship.

Focus on Values

Core Values of Social Work

In carrying out their professional tasks and duties, social workers strive to act in ways that give equal priority to respect for *human dignity and worth* and the pursuit of *social justice*. This commitment is demonstrated through *service to humanity*, *integrity*, and *competence*, which characterize professional social work practice. Social work principles are derived from the values; together, they underpin ethical social work practice.

Value 1: Respect for the Inherent Dignity and Worth of Persons

The social work profession holds that:

- Social workers respect the unique worth and inherent dignity of all people and uphold human rights.
- Social workers uphold each person's right to self-determination, consistent with that person's capacity and with the rights of others.
- Social workers respect the diversity among individuals in Canadian society and the right of individuals to their unique beliefs consistent with the rights of others.
- Social workers respect the client's right to make choices based on voluntary, informed consent.
- Social workers who have children as clients determine the child's ability to consent and, where appropriate, explain to the child and to the child's parents/guardians the nature of the social worker's relationship to the child.
- Social workers uphold the right of society to impose limitations on the self-determination of individuals, when such limitations protect individuals from self-harm and from harming others.
- Social workers uphold the right of every person to be free from violence and threat of violence.

Value 2: Pursuit of Social Justice

The social work profession holds that each society has an obligation to pursue social justice, to provide maximum benefit for all its members and to afford them protection from harm.

The profession understands social justice to encompass:

- Social workers uphold the right of people to have access to resources to meet basic human needs.
- Social workers advocate for fair and equitable access to public services and benefits.
- Social workers advocate for equal treatment and protection under the law and challenge injustices, especially injustices that affect the vulnerable and disadvantaged.
- Social workers promote social development and environmental management in the interests of all people.

Value 3: Service to Humanity

The social work profession holds service in the interests of human well-being and social justice as a primary objective. The fundamental goals of social work service are:

- Social workers place the needs of others above self-interest when acting in a professional capacity.
- Social workers strive to use the power and authority vested in them as professionals in responsible ways that serve the needs of clients and the promotion of social justice.
- Social workers promote individual development and pursuit of individual goals, as well as the development of a just society.
- Social workers use their knowledge and skills in bringing about fair resolutions to conflict and in assisting those affected by conflict.

Value 4: Integrity in Professional Practice

The social work profession values honesty, reliability, and impartiality in social work practice.

- Social workers demonstrate and promote the qualities of honesty, reliability, impartiality and diligence in their professional practice.
- Social workers demonstrate adherence to the values and ethical principles of the profession and promote respect for the profession's values and principles in organizations where they work or with which they have a professional affiliation.
- Social workers establish appropriate boundaries in relationships with clients and ensure that the relationship serves the needs of clients.
- Social workers value openness and transparency in professional practice and avoid relationships where their integrity or impartiality may be compromised, ensuring that should a conflict of interest be unavoidable, the nature of the conflict is fully disclosed.

Value 5: Confidentiality in Professional Practice

The social work profession values confidentiality in professional social work practice.

- Social workers respect the importance of the trust and confidence placed in the professional relationship by clients and members of the public.
- Social workers respect the client's right to confidentiality of information shared in a professional context.

- Social workers only disclose confidential information with the informed consent of the client or permission of client's legal representative.
- Social workers may break confidentiality and communicate client information without permission when required or permitted by relevant laws, court order or this *Code*.
- Social workers demonstrate transparency with respect to limits to confidentiality that apply to their professional practice by clearly communicating these limitations to clients early in their relationship.

Value 6: Competence in Professional Practice

The social work profession values proficiency in social work practice.

- Social workers uphold the right of clients to be offered the highest quality service possible.
- Social workers strive to maintain and increase their professional knowledge and skill.
- Social workers demonstrate due care for client's interests and safety by limiting professional practice to areas of demonstrated competence.
- Social workers contribute to the ongoing development of the profession and its ability to serve humanity, where possible, by participating in the development of current and future social workers and the development of new professional knowledge.
- Social workers who engage in research minimize risks to participants, ensure informed consent, maintain confidentiality, and accurately report the results of their studies.

Source: Canadian Association of Social Workers Code of Ethics *(2005: 4–10).*

Such a statement as that of the CASW in its *Code of Ethics* immediately determines some particular practice directions. For example, the practice frameworks cannot just be about inner-world change. They must include a focus on outer-world dimensions.

Personal Value Bases

While many practice standards and codes of ethical conduct highlight values that are essential to a particular profession, workers within each of these professions will vary considerably. Your view of social justice may differ from those of your colleagues as a result of different experiences and expectations. While people work under the assumption of a common value base, individual workers will have their own experiences of culture, religion, gender, and class that vary. Personal awareness and self-reflection about these values are important.

Balancing our personal and professional beliefs is important. O'Hagan (2001: 144) describes the ways in which workers may be publicly respectful of, for example, a client's religious value base, while privately in disagreement. Thus, we can differ not only along a spectrum of professional values about a particular issue, but also along a spectrum of personal and professional inconsistencies.

Cultural Value Bases

The above discussion has focused on the professional and personal location of values in practice. Our values also are historically and socially situated. These broader social and cultural attitudes profoundly influence our beliefs, for example, about well-being. The political and cultural values held by a nation or a state influence which services are provided and how they subsequently are delivered. Mullaly (2007: 281) describes a cultural sensitivity model, which 'enables white social workers to better establish a "helping relationship" with members of other races and cultures to make services more accessible and to advocate for the enactment of equal rights legislation.' A major consequence of globalization is that assumptions of a universal value base no longer hold. Mullaly (ibid.) notes that the dominant theory of multicultural social work in Canada, the United States, and Australia is aimed at a cultural sensitivity and focuses on the importance of increasing workers' sensitivity to cultural norms and institutional racism. Different value bases are acknowledged as existing in Indigenous (Lynn, 2001; Connolly, 2001) and non-Western communities (Esteva and Prakash, 1998). For example, Dwairy (2006: 61) provides an overview of how the individual is regarded from an Islamic perspective, which presents some major discontinuities with, if not contradictions to, Western values:

1. The self is not autonomous but is connected to an extended family or tribe. It directs its energy towards achieving group rather than personal goals.
2. The behaviour of the individual is more situational and contextual than dispositional. It is controlled by external factors such as roles and norms rather than internal factors such as personal attributions of behaviour.
3. Priority is given to interpersonal responsibilities rather than to justice and individual rights.
4. More other-focused emotions (for example, sympathy and shame) are experienced rather than ego-focused ones (for example, anxiety).

He argues that, contrary to Western cultures, the main source of suppression of behaviours is external rather than internal. This can lead to major incompatibilities with many of the practice perspectives widely used in the Western context, which focus more on the individual and on liberal understandings of well-being, such as psychodynamic, cognitive, behavioural, and feminist. Dwairy suggests a continuum for understanding work with Arabic or Islamic clients, from individualism to collectivism and from liberalism to authoritarianism (ibid., 5), the two main dimensions on which cultures are spread in his paradigm.

Authors such as Hall (1976), Fisher (1991), and Hick (2005) discuss the importance of understanding cross-cultural communications dynamics. The authors describe the importance of examining theories of cultural screening, collectivism, and constructivism and how these theories underpin successful communication cross-culturally. Cultural screening is described by Hall as the process by which information is taken in by an individual and translated to fit the context of the individuals' cultural group. If information becomes overwhelming or threatens the individual's cultural identity a cultural screen can interrupt the process as a personal safety mechanism. 'The authors explore the notion of understanding a "person's place of knowing". To interact with a client or group on any other level will not be successful' (Pierce, 2007: 20). Further, this cultural connection to communication is significant if the practitioner is attempting to facilitate individual, community, or social shifts.

Brooker (2001) outlines the notion of two languages when working cross-culturally. He examines the need for an individual to negotiate both 'insider' and 'outsider' language. Brooker states this puts pressure on the individual to maintain their collective language style (insider) and carry the responsibility to navigate various language complexities (outsider) when interacting with other groups. For example, a white social worker who resides in an urban area and then becomes employed in a remote Aboriginal community will need to learn the communication style of the Aboriginal community (insider language) and how the worker's urban communication style (outsider language) may impact service delivery.

These cross-cultural issues raise some fundamental questions for you as a worker in a Canadian human service delivery context in relation to shared beliefs about well-being, the nature of relationships, expectations about communication and intervention, and who is the identified client. The following example raises some of these cultural differences.

Focus on Practice

Addressing Aggressive Behaviour

A local school is experiencing difficulties with two young boys who are displaying aggressive behaviour, particularly towards girls. These boys have recently moved from a northern and remote Aboriginal village with a population under 1,000. The teachers have sought assistance because they are concerned about the increase in the levels of aggression and the possible trauma these young boys may be experiencing. The teachers are uncertain if or how the behaviour is connected to their recent move. In consultation with the boys' families, however, a shared concern about this behaviour cannot be found.

1. What would you see as some of the important issues to be addressing in this situation? What is your initial reaction to it?
2. What would you find most challenging in this situation if you were the worker called in to develop a response with the teachers and the parents?
3. What cultural considerations require careful consideration?
4. What education may need to occur for the teachers in this scenario?
5. What education may need to occur for the parents in this scenario?
6. What education may need to occur for the boys in this scenario?

As a worker, you will need to find a common language of rights and responsibilities that can be developed respectfully out of diverse experiences. Discussion and dialogue are critical steps in this process (Furlong and Ata, 2006; Miller, Donner, and Fraser, 2004).

Five Core Practice Values

We will now consider five specific practice values. They are: (1) respecting the human person; (2) promoting social justice and people's right to a good life; (3) privileging the right to self-determination, empowerment, and autonomy; (4) valuing people's strengths and resilience; and (5) being authentic.

Respecting the Human Person

The value of 'respect for persons' is regarded as central to human service work. As Dowrick (1983: 14) states, it is about 'assuming the intrinsic worth of individuals regardless of their attributes or achievements'. How this actually may be achieved is less frequently articulated.

The philosopher Gaita (1999: 17–19) reflects on how this fundamental respect for another human being was shown when he worked in a psychiatric hospital in the 1960s, where 'the patients were judged to be incurable and they appeared to have irretrievably lost everything which gives meaning to our lives' (ibid., 17). He relates the following experience.

Focus on Practice

Treating 'Others' with Respect

One day a nun came to the ward. In her middle years, her energy made an impression on me until she spoke with the patients. Then everything in her demeanour towards them—the way she spoke with them, her facial expressions, the inflexions of her body—contrasted with the behaviour of the psychiatrists. She showed that they were, despite their best efforts, condescending, as I, too, had been. She thereby revealed that even the patients were, as the psychiatrists had sincerely and generously professed, the equals of those who wanted to help them; but she also showed that in our hearts we did not believe this.

1. What do you think were the qualities of her demeanour—the way she spoke to them, her facial expressions, and the inflexions of her body—that demonstrated this respect?
2. What prevents us from demonstrating this respect for others at times?

Respect for another human being, and the importance of an authentic engagement, is described in this brief encounter. The scenario highlights that we can make all sorts of assumptions about our conduct until we witness truly respectful moments and interactions. Organizations can develop cultures around the levels of respect or types of respect shown to clients, which can become firmly entrenched over time to the point where they are no longer noticed, until something like the above situation occurs. This example highlights the ultimate importance of what is communicated in our behaviour and interactions with people, not the espoused value position.

Four important dimensions of respect can be identified (Brown, 1993: 2565). To respect someone or something is to first '[r]egard, consider, taking into account, pay attention to';

second, 'treat or regard with deferential esteem'; third, 'prize or value'; and fourth, 'refrain from injuring, harming, insulting, interfering with or interrupting'. Other definitions of respect refer to 'active sympathy' towards another human being (Downie and Telfer, 1989, 1980, cited in Banks, 2006: 29). The essential characteristics of respect relate to how someone is regarded in an attentive, supportive way, not only in terms of the words that are spoken but also in the whole physical and emotional presence of someone in interaction with another person. Acknowledgement of equality of a shared humanity, although not necessarily of human circumstances, is fully recognized. Another way of thinking about respect is to think about the importance of a love of humanity (Morley and Ife, 2002).

Practice Questions

1. When have you witnessed or experienced respectful interactions?

2. How would you define respect in these circumstances?

3. Conversely, when have you witnessed or experienced disrespectful interactions?

4. What were the features of these circumstances of disrespect?

5. What factors influenced these experiences, thinking particularly of gender, culture, and class?

6. Revisiting Shebib's diversity lens, what factors may influence these experiences, thinking particularly of race, religion, age, sex, sexual orientation, physical and mental ability, economic capacity, language, culture, values, beliefs, preferences, and ways of thinking and behaving?

Demonstrating this respect for all people, 'regardless of their attributes or achievements' (Dowrick, 1983: 14), sometimes can be challenging. It can be hard to respect a perpetrator of horrific abuse or a violent act towards a child or a drug-affected driver who causes a tragic accident. Respect comes to be shown through the understanding of the context of the person and a belief in the possibility of adaptation and change. Many rehab programs, such as those for sex offenders (Adolescent Forensic Health Service, 2007) or for perpetrators of gendered violence (Laming, 2006), are based on a fundamental respect for the person and work successfully towards addressing the causes of violence. The programs are based on respecting the person, not on any implication of approval of the behaviour in which he or she may have engaged.

One student shared her experiences of working in Juvenile Justice for her student placement and the ways in which her view of these young people changed throughout her placement. Respect for them as individuals was a critical dimension of that work.

Using an anti-oppressive practice framework (Mullaly, 2002) as a basis for practice can sometimes seem quite contradictory to work in involuntary settings, where workers can be perceived to be agents of social control rather than of social care. As the examples above highlight, however, the value of respect can be demonstrated in the most difficult or constrained settings.

Focus on Practice

Respect for Involuntary Clients

Working with involuntary clients is a challenge in itself. As workers we are given all the tools and skills to equip ourselves in working with all sorts of people, but when clients are being forced to report to you and they refuse to engage in the process, practice can seem futile. I was working in an area with young men who had sexually offended, who were involuntary clients. Young male adolescents can be difficult to engage in therapy for developmental reasons, but coupled with a history of sexual offending, counselling can seem a difficult road to navigate.

However, given that adolescence is considered a transitional phase, it would follow that their behavioural patterns of offending do not necessarily reflect clients' lasting personal beliefs or attitudes. When working with involuntary clients it is important to separate their offending behaviour from who they are. Unfortunately, many young men begin to identify themselves as defined by their offence, and believe that others will do the same. Just by giving involuntary clients an emotionally safe space to share their side of the story, without judgement, can unlock many doors. In fact, an overemphasis on the individual and his/her offending can hide the fact that adolescents who have sexually offended may be both victim and perpetrator.

Another way of thinking about how to demonstrate respect is to identify when it is absent and to work to counteract these behaviours. In examining the features of inequality, the following discriminatory processes are often used to illustrate the attitude of inequality or disrespect of people.

Table 1.1 Processes of Discrimination

Form of discrimination	A brief description of the process of discrimination
Stereotyping	Filtering and simplifying complex information about people into fixed 'typifications' so that they are not seen as unique individuals in unique circumstances
Marginalization	Pushing people 'to the margins of society' through various behaviours, attitudes, and social structures
Invisibilization	Rendering minority groups invisible 'in language and imagery' in the dominant discourse
Infantilization	Ascribing a childlike status to an adult
Welfarism	Regarding 'certain groups as necessarily in need of welfare services by virtue of their membership in such groups'
Medicalization	Ascribing 'the status of "ill" to someone'
Dehumanization	Using language that denotes people as things
Trivialization	Ascribing a trivial status or no status to issues of inequality

Source: Adapted from Thompson (2003b: 82–92).

Mullaly (2007: 285) views oppression through a structural lens: 'Oppression exists and persists because of the number of positive functions it carries out for the dominant group at the expense of the subordinate groups.'

Focus on Practice

Seeking to Understand the Oppressed and Subordinated

Mulan has recently lost her husband and is struggling in many areas to parent her four children on her own. Her Asian credentials are not recognized by employers as she tries to gain employment. Mulan faces derogatory remarks because English is her second language. She feels professionals (teachers, doctors, bank employees, etc.) perceive her as less intelligent when the reality is language barriers. Currently, Mulan fears losing her family's housing due to being unable to gain employment. What underpins the demeaning treatment faced by Mulan? Practitioners should be aware of the characteristics that make them part of the dominant group. How do these characteristics influence communication and the practice framework in work with clients?

Promoting Social Justice and People's Right to a Good Life

In 1948, in the context of the post-World War II international environment and the atrocities that had taken place, the Universal Declaration of Human Rights was developed. While it has undergone extensive criticism for both its gendered (Division for the Advancement of Women, 2003) and Western (Esteva and Prakash, 1998) biases, it reveals that people were striving for justice and equality of opportunity at a global and universal level. The first article of the declaration, for example, reads: 'All human beings are born free and equal in dignity and rights. They are endowed with reason and conscience and should act towards one another in a spirit of brotherhood' (United Nations General Assembly, 1948).

Many other national and international treaties and conventions have similarly sought to establish ground rules or visions for basic human rights and needs in order to overcome inequalities and oppression. The constitution of the World Health Organization (WHO), established by the United Nations, makes a strong statement about the principles that are 'basic to the happiness, harmonious relations and security of all peoples' (WHO, 2003). These principles are fundamental to how we think about well-being and resilience both locally and globally, and underline many of the common values informing our efforts to build well-being and resilience across global communities.

In Canada, the Canadian Charter of Rights and Freedoms (http://laws.justice.gc.ca/en/charter) describes as fundamental the following freedoms:

- freedom of conscience and religion
- freedom of thought, belief, opinion and expression, including freedom of the press and other media of communication

- freedom of peaceful assembly
- freedom of association.

In addition to the Canadian Charter, provincial codes are in place. For example, in British Columbia the aims of the Human Rights Code are:

- to foster a society in British Columbia in which there are no impediments to full and free participation in the economic, social, political and cultural life of British Columbia
- to promote a climate of understanding and mutual respect where all are equal in dignity and rights
- to prevent discrimination prohibited by this Code
- to identify and eliminate persistent patterns of inequality associated with discrimination prohibited by this Code
- to provide a means of redress for those persons who are discriminated against contrary to this Code. (www.crownpub.bc.ca)

Focus on Rights

Some Basic Rights

1. Health is a state of complete physical, mental, and social well-being and not merely the absence of disease or infirmity.
2. The enjoyment of the highest attainable standard of health is one of the fundamental rights of every human being without distinction of race, religion, political belief, economic or social condition.
3. The health of all peoples is fundamental to the attainment of peace and security and is dependent upon the fullest co-operation of individuals' states.
4. The achievement of any state in the promotion and protection of health is of value to all.
5. Unequal development in different countries in the promotion of health and control of disease, especially communicable disease, is a common danger.
6. Healthy development of the child is of basic importance; the ability to live harmoniously in a changing total environment is essential to such development.
7. The extension to all peoples of the benefits of medical, psychological, and related knowledge is essential to the fullest attainment of health.
8. Informed opinion and active co-operation on the part of the public are of the utmost importance in the improvement of the health of the people.
9. Governments have a responsibility for the health of their peoples, which can be fulfilled only by the provision of adequate health and social measures.

Throughout this discussion is a fundamental avowal of the quality of the human experience (Hart, 2002). If the aim of such interventions is the improvement of lives for individuals, families, and communities, then what is valued in this is some view of what constitutes a good, happy, or healthy way of living. Recent studies in the areas of a strengths perspective (Saleebey, 1996, 1997, 2001) and positive psychology (Seligman, 1992; Seligman et al., 1995), as well as drawing on Indigenous perspectives (Hart, 2002), have given new emphasis to how central a value this affirmation of the quality of the human experience is to practice.

Human service work often occurs at the interface of rights violations, so rights dilemmas are part of the worker's territory. As Banks points out, an ethical dilemma involves 'a choice between two equally unwelcome alternatives relating to human welfare' (Banks, 2006: 8). Remember the earlier scenario, where a child protection worker is making her way to meet with a parent about abuse allegations. In this situation, removing the child from the violent parent may fulfill the child's right to safety, but violate the parent's right to parent as he/she wishes.

Privileging Self-Determination, Empowerment, and Autonomy

Self-determination and autonomy are long-held core values in human service work. For example, nearly 40 years ago, Kadushin (1972: 44–5) provided the key dimensions of the client–worker relationship, emphasizing behaviour that showed:

> belief that the client has the right, and the capacity, to direct [his/her] own life; [they work] with the client in problem solving; [they] communicate confidence in the client's ability to achieve [the client's] own solution and actively help the client to achieve [his/her] own solution in [his/her] own way.

Valuing self-determination acknowledges that people have the capacity to make choices (Dowrick, 1983) about their lives, if they are given the opportunity. What makes it possible for people to influence their environments is an important question for workers to address. Giddens (1991) suggests drawing on their capacity for agency and Kondrat (2002) points towards motivation. In supporting the notion of self-determination, the usual assumption is that self-determination is positively oriented. Workers can support the notion of self-determination only so far as legal and ethical limits apply. In some cases, for example, people express a wish to harm themselves and/or others. At these times, you need to take steps to ensure human safety, over and above a client's right to be self-determining.

Other dilemmas arise in relation to views about how much a person experiencing illness should know about the diagnosis or illness. Again, different cultures regard this information exchange in different ways, with some cultures firmly of the belief that patients should be protected from such knowledge at all times (Duffy et al., 2006). Their right to be fully informed—and therefore potentially self-determining—is overridden by a belief that the patients' health may be negatively impacted by distress if too much information about their health circumstances is revealed.

In other situations, the capacity to realize the value of self-determination is compromised by the person's capacity to participate in decision-making processes or to give informed consent—for example, in situations where a person is living with a severe intellectual or psychiatric disability or is too young to be able to verbalize an opinion. If your underlying value is the promotion of self-determination, empowerment, and autonomy, steps can always be taken to ensure that actions are oriented to the greatest possible extent in the best interests of the person concerned.

A tension arises in practice in emphasizing autonomy. Some authors argue for the client's right to experience a transitional dependence at times, rather than a continuous independence and self-determination (Trevithick, 2005). An example of this tension occurs when a person is in the middle of a major crisis and the usual coping capacity is overwhelmed. Assertive, directive outreach at this time by workers is advocated (Caplan, 1990), consistent with beliefs about the psychological and physiological state of a traumatized person. Within this circumstance, though, the emphasis is still on clients being self-determining within the limits of their capacities at such a time.

You will notice that some cross-cultural practices differ quite significantly as to whether an individual acts autonomously or almost always in the context of community and familial relationships and obligation. For example, recent work within Indigenous communities has stressed that positive change is brought about by emphasizing the individual's location within their community. The use of shame through circle courts is one example of the means of bringing about positive change through explaining the ways a person's behaviour has been damaging not only to that person but also to his/her family and community. While Western approaches with involuntary clients have tended to advocate against the use of 'blame, punish, and judge' strategies (Trotter, 2006), the use of shaming in Indigenous contexts is an age-old tradition that more recently has been revived (Spooner, Hall, and Mattick, 2001), although it is not without its critics (Blagg, 1997).

Valuing People's Strengths and Resilience

If we are to have a positive impact as workers, a core belief needs to be that a client has strengths and a capacity and motivation towards change for the better (Brun and Rapp, 2001). Saleebey (1997: 3) sees strengths-based practice as meaning that:

> everything you do as a . . . worker will be predicated, in some way, on helping to discover and embellish, explore and exploit clients' strengths and resources in the service of assisting them to achieve their goals, realize their dreams and shed the irons of their own inhibitions and misgivings.

A strengths perspective argues that it always possible to find 'constructive ways to meet, use or transcend the problem' (Saleebey, 1997: 47). Other strengths-oriented beliefs include: that unlimited strengths can be found in every individual, group, family and community; that adversities can be both sources of loss and opportunity; and that collaboration works best.

Being Authentic

Genuineness and **authenticity** on the part of the worker have been consistently named as critical to the success of forming a client–worker relationship and being able to facilitate change (Rogers, 1967). Gunzberg (1996: 34) describes authenticity in a therapeutic context as arising in 'the nature of the connectedness that lies between both, within the meeting of both'. How you bring about this connectedness, however, is not easy to articulate. Authenticity, like respect, emerges in the totality of verbal and non-verbal dimensions of your relationships.

Rogers (1987: 38) emphasizes some of the dimensions of this authenticity in reflecting on how he would prepare for an interview with a client. He asked himself: 'Can I be totally present to this client?' 'Can I be with him or her?' 'Can I be sensitive to every nuance of personal meaning and value, no matter how different it is from my own experience?' This captures the importance of an authentic engagement in the client's story and situation. In this sense, the authenticity is about openness to, empathy with, and the understanding of another's situation.

We can be authentic in many other ways when working with people. Authenticity is not necessarily about self-disclosure; an assumption that is often made. It can be about recognizing and articulating the limits of our knowledge, our understanding, or our skills. It can be about expressing our deep concern for someone. It can be about articulating our time limits and our capacity to be present in an interaction with someone. It is fundamentally about our willingness to share our humanness in the context of our professional integrity and our ability to act within the capacities and limitations of what we bring to an encounter.

This value raises many questions in relation to how authentic the relationship can be that is established with a client. The expectations of a professional relationship are different from those of a personal relationship, yet many qualities are similar. Even in a professional context we genuinely like some persons more than others. Some people we genuinely fear. The way we express authenticity emerges in the boundaries we metaphorically and practically create in our work with another person.

How Do Human Service Workers Influence Change?

As a human service worker, you aim to bring about change through your use of skills at both individual and social levels (Payne, 2006: 1). In this section, the ways in which change is thought to occur as a result of methods, phases, and skills will be discussed.

Change is something that is deliberately fostered and worked towards through specific interventions in human service work. Change can occur in our inner worlds, in relation to how we feel and how we think. Change can also occur in our outer worlds, in relation to how we behave and how others behave towards us. In our outer worlds, change can occur in relation to particular circumstances or conditions such as the alleviation of poverty, violence, or unemployment.

There are many different ways of achieving change, from doing very little to bringing about major and radical change. Change as a multi-dimensional concept will be described in further detail in Chapter 3.

Practice Questions

Four client scenarios were presented earlier in this chapter.

1. Revisit each of these scenarios and reflect on what you see as the change agenda you would bring to each of them.

2. How similar or different do you think they would be compared with the clients' perception of the change agenda?

3. What structural influences are present?

The precipitants of change are similarly multiple. Some people change because they have to, as a result of rock-bottom experiences. One study found that change was triggered for women with drug addictions when they realized things could not possibly become worse (Blankenship, 1998). Other people engage in change processes because either they are mandated to or because of some other circumstance; for example, to get their children back from being placed in foster care. Many other people engage in change processes because they want to, recognizing that they need to change to satisfy their own values. Motivations for seeking help with change are often unique and complex.

What influences people's attitudes to change? Change for some people is a terrifying prospect, full of uncertainties and unfamiliar territory. For other people, change is exciting and energizing. Some of the variables that influence our attitudes to change include the perceptions and realities of available supports and resources, the availability of role models, the internal and external encouragement received, and, sometimes, the negative motivational encouragers; for example, seeing someone experience major problems with drug and alcohol abuse and determining never to go down that path. For many people, internal change is possible and motivation can be extremely high, but social circumstances make it extremely difficult to maintain any gains. Working with a change agenda requires constantly asking the question of what change needs to occur and why. Engaging in work as an agent of change means that considerable influence is being exerted.

This chapter now considers some of the ways in which change tends to be conceptualized in human service work. The change process can be conceptualized as involving various methods, stages, and skills.

Change through Methods of Practice

Working with individuals primarily involves interviewing and counselling skills in one-to-one (and typically face-to-face) focused conversation with individuals, couples, or families. The term 'interview' is typically used to define this interaction, being 'any formal or semi-formal discussion between a worker and service user(s)' (Thompson, 2002: 120). While in many settings the interview may not be a structured interaction, others describe the interview as 'the first one or two helping sessions because these sessions are usually for information gathering' (Okun, 2002: 89).

A wide range of terms is used to differentiate this work—interviewing, counselling, or therapy being three common ones. Some practitioners regard these terms as interchangeable, whereas others see them as distinct forms of individual practice. Sommers-Flanagan and Sommers-Flanagan (2004: 8) argue that the key differences between counsellors and psychotherapists is not that they engage in different behaviours but rather that they engage in the behaviours of 'listening, questioning, interpreting, explaining, advising, and so on . . . in different proportions'.

> We will look at how different theoretical approaches influence the use of these responding skills in Chapters 11–14.

In all work with people, interpersonal skills are critical. The vast majority of work occurs at an individual interface—that is, between at least two people engaged in relationship and conversation (Perlman, 1979). Group work, community development, and research methods similarly rely on gathering information through communicating with others, forming an assessment, and undertaking some form of further intervention.

Change throughout Various Stages or Phases

Change is often seen as occurring in stages or phases. For example, Prochaska and DiClemente's (1983) **stages of change** model is the most widely used in Western contexts. Developed from research in relation to addictions, the model proposes people move from a pre-contemplation to a contemplation stage, then to preparation, and on to action. When change is achieved, a maintenance phase begins. Throughout all of these phases, relapse is possible to an earlier phase of change. People can move, therefore, in and out of these phases of commitment to change, depending upon a number of factors. The model is not implying that change occurs in a linear manner. Rather, it is cyclical. The cycle is as follows.

Focus on Change

The Stages of Change Model

Here is a brief overview of the tasks within the stages of change model.

Pre-Contemplation

The client:

- denies that there is a problem.
- is unaware of any negative consequences of the behaviour.
- minimizes any consequences.
- has 'given up the thought of changing because he/she is demoralized'.

Contemplation

The client:

- recognizes the benefits of changing.

- tends to 'overestimate the costs of changing'.
- remains 'ambivalent and not quite ready to change'.
- intends 'to make a change within the next six months'.

Preparation

The client:

- has decided to make a change in the next month or so.
- has begun to 'take small steps toward that goal'.

Action

The client:

- is actively engaged in modifying behaviours or circumstances.
- is developing new, healthy skills, attitudes, and behaviours.

Maintenance stage

The client:

- has 'been able to sustain change for at least six months'.
- is 'actively striving to prevent relapse'.

Source: Levesque, Cummins, Prochaska, and Prochaska (2006: 1373).

Practice Questions

Think about a major change you have been through or would like to make.

1. Does this stage approach to change help you understand what you went through/would go through?

2. Are some stages more challenging for you than others?

3. What habits do you fall back on in each of the various stages of change?

This model of change is useful in helping you to think about what might be the focus of work at a particular point. This model presents some of the unique challenges for workers engaging with involuntary clients. Often the assumption is made that the person is at least at the stage of 'contemplation of change'—in involuntary client situations, however, this may not be the case.

The stages of change model is a way of thinking about how a client changes. Change can also be thought about as a series of stages or phases within your work with your clients. These specific tasks include the tasks of engagement, assessment, planning, implementation, evaluation, termination, and follow-up (Kirst-Ashman and Hull, 2001). Different models are proposed, ranging from three-phase through to five-phase models of intervention.

A three-phase model (Hepworth, Rooney, and Larsen, 2002: 36) proposes that phase one involves the tasks of exploration, engagement, assessment, and planning. Phase two involves the tasks of implementation and goal attainment, and phase three, the tasks of termination. Other three-phase practice models, such as those relating to child protection practices in New Zealand (Connolly, 2004), propose a slightly different prioritizing of tasks: the phases of first, engagement and assessment; second, seeking solutions; and third, securing safety and belonging.

Another model with three phases or stages is that proposed by Egan (2007). In stage one, the question 'What's going on?' is asked in relation to the client's situation. In this stage, the three steps are to explore the story, identify blind spots, and find leverage on the problem. The second stage is about examining the solutions that make sense for the client around the specific area of change that has been identified. The three steps involved in this stage are exploring the possibilities, establishing the change agenda, and establishing a commitment to solution-finding. The third and final stage relates to examining how a client gets what they need or want. Having fine-tuned the possibilities for change, in stage three, possible strategies are identified, the best-fit strategies are sought, and a plan of action is put in place.

Other practitioners use a 'phases of contact approach' (Cournoyer, 2004), which could be applied both within the context of one interview and in the context of the relationship over time. This approach identifies a beginning phase, during which the engagement in the relationship, the availability of the worker and the attuning to the client are established. Empathy is promoted so that an assessment can then take place as to the events, feelings, thoughts, and behaviours experienced by the person. The assessment also includes an assessment of strengths, the establishing of areas of work and subsequent contracting around the specific work to be undertaken. In the middle phase or process, the work focuses on what is being achieved. Some of the relationship issues that emerge are in relation to defense mechanisms and change processes, according to Cournoyer (2005). In the finishing phase, the process is about continuing empathy and assessment but with a move towards evaluation and finishing. The tasks of disengagement and finishing are required. This final phase, Cournoyer suggests, is as unpredictable as the beginning phases.

Other approaches advocate for a greater breakdown of phases in the process. Shulman (1999), for example, advocates a four-phase model, in which there is a preliminary or preparatory phase, a beginning and contracting phase, a middle or work phase, and an ending or transition phase. A five-phase model is proposed by Corey and Corey (2007: 157–77), with stage one establishing a working relationship; stage two identifying the client's problems, including conducting an initial assessment; stage three helping clients create goals; stage four encouraging client exploration of solutions and taking action; and stage five involving the termination of the working relationship.

While different perspectives emphasize and understand these tasks slightly differently, the common tasks are:

- establishing availability and a contract of work with the client;
- engaging with the client in a working relationship;
- expressing empathy;
- exploring the problem or issue through an assessment;
- undertaking work together to resolve or address the problem or issue;
- finishing the work together, often with a process of review.

Many approaches, therefore, recognize that across human service settings these phases are important steps through which the work is conducted. Greatest emphasis tends to be placed on the initial phases, with less emphasis on the last phase—how to ensure safety and belonging, for example, or how to finish the work.

Below, these phases of work are summarized in Table 1.2. The ways in which these phases will be understood throughout this book are presented in the top row: framing and forming the relationship, focusing the communication, focusing the intervention, and finishing the work.

Table 1.2 **Phases of Social Work Practice**

Author(s)	Framing and Forming the Relationship	Focusing the Communication	Focusing the Intervention	Finding Solutions	Finishing
Connolly		Engagement and assessment	Seeking solutions	Securing safety and belonging	
Corey and Corey	Establishing a working relationship	Identifying client problems	Creating goals	Encouraging client exploration and taking action	Termination
Egan		Establishing what's going on	Examining solutions and possibilities	Finding best-fit strategies	
Hepworth, Rooney, and Larsen		Exploration, engagement, assessment and planning	Implementation and goal attainment		Termination
Shulman	Preliminary or preparatory	Beginning or contracting	Middle or work		Ending or transition

Such a table makes a complex, circular, or unshaped process seem logical and linear. In some agencies, you may be able to function in that way. Most workers, however, are in much less predictable environments and relationships, and therefore find that these phases do not typically represent the ways in which the work is undertaken. They do provide a useful map, however, of the tasks involved in change-oriented work.

Change through the Use of Skills

As we explored earlier in the chapter, human services are provided because of the belief that change can occur when workers provide support, in all its forms. You need a skill base to be able to provide appropriate support to others.

The word 'skills' is used throughout human service practice, and for that reason it is important to consider its multiple meanings. Skills can mean, first, knowledge; second, 'the ability to do something well: proficiency; expertness, dexterity'; third, 'an ability to do something, acquired through practice or learning'; and fourth, 'an art, a science' (Brown, 1993: 2882). Each of these dimensions is relevant to developing a base for human service practice.

In relation to *knowledge*, understandings of people and conditions of adversity are essential, as are understandings of human behaviour and development in context. In addition to these forms of knowledge, theoretical perspectives on practice are also important, along with the practice wisdom you will develop over the course of a career. Other forms of knowledge emerge from research understandings—for example, gaining an understanding of what works with whom in what context is crucial, and research provides a useful basis of understanding.

The second dimension refers to the *ability to do something well*; that is, it is not enough to know about the skills of active listening. To use a skill means that the barriers to good communication are removed or that a capacity to apply specific skills at a particular time is developed.

The third dimension, *an ability acquired through practice and learning*, emphasized that learning to communicate effectively in a professional capacity takes practice and application, throughout a career.

The final dimension of the definition—that skills refer to both *an art and a science*—highlights another level of complexity (Connolly, 2001). To contribute effectively to human service work, a sound evidence base for what works is important. But it is also an art to communicate well with others, to support others, and to respond empathically and effectively to those experiencing difficulty and adversity. Connecting with other people and establishing a creative process of working together to resolve situations are skills of a high order.

These four dimensions are all critical in bringing about change. You will need to develop the total package to be effective while making decisions about how to act and what to say in various situations.

Later, we will focus on the **microskills** of communication that are used to direct change. The microskills that we will look at in later chapters help us to:

- establish and maintain empathy
- communicate non-verbally
- establish the context and purpose of the work
- open an interview
- actively listen

- establish the story or the nature of the problem
- ask questions
- intervene and respond appropriately.

Microskills are the building blocks of human communication. They are transferable skills (O'Hara, 2006); that is, they can be used in many contexts and adapted according to the setting in which the worker and client meet. You influence that process through theoretical perspectives. As Howard (2006: 8) states:

> From the most fundamental aspects of the relationship, such as how we greet a client, to the use of advanced therapeutic skills like making interpretations, our whole way of relating to and thinking about our client is driven by the theoretical model we subscribe to.

In the next chapter, we review these microskills before moving in Chapter 3 to how practitioners come to theorize and apply these skills.

Chapter Summary

In this first chapter, we have explored the role of human services in responding to people's experiences of adversity and need. The ways in which your professional, personal, and cultural value bases will influence your perceptions of human service work were also identified. Five core practice values were presented: (1) respecting the human person; (2) promoting social justice and people's right to a good life; (3) privileging the right to self-determination, empowerment, and autonomy; (4) valuing people's strengths and resilience; and (5) being authentic.

We looked at how change can be understood—through using different practice methods; through understanding individual change processes and understanding change in the phases of work you will undertake with your client; and through using particular communication skills.

Questions for Analysis

1. What have you learned about:
   - the value base you bring to your practice?
   - the understandings of change you bring to your practice?
   - the methods of change human service workers use?
   - the phases of change within a client–worker relationship?

2. Going back to the earlier client scenarios, has your view of them changed since reading this chapter?

3. What would you see as the most important purposes of your work?

4. What do you see as the most important values underpinning your practice?

5. What do you see are some of the tensions in those values?

6. How would you go about resolving some of those tensions?

7. What have been some of the major influences on the development of these values?

Recommended Readings

Banks, S. 2006. *Ethics and Values in Social Work*, 3rd edn. Basingstoke: Palgrave Macmillan.

Bodor, R., R. Green, B. Lonne, and M.K. Zapf. 2004. '40 degrees above or 40 degrees below zero: Rural social work and context in Australia and Canada', *Rural Social Work* 9: 49–59.

Brooker, P. 2001. *A Concise Glossary of Cultural Theory*. New York: Oxford University Press.

Delaney, R., K. Brownlee, M. Sellick, and D. Tranter. 1997. 'Ethical problems facing northern social workers', *The Social Worker* 65, 3: 55–65.

DuPraw, M.E., and M. Axner. 1997. *Working on Common Cross-cultural Communication Challenges*. At: www.wwcd.org/action/ampu/crosscult.html. 20 August 2009.

Fisher, D. 1991. *An Introduction to Constructivism for Social Workers*. New York: Praeger.

Hall, E. 1976. *Beyond Culture*. New York: Anchor Press.

Hick, S. 2005. *Social Work in Canada*. Toronto: Thompson.

Ivey, A., B.M. Ivey, and L. Simek-Morgan. 1996. *Counselling and Psychotherapy: A Multicultural Perspective*. Needham Heights, Mass.: Allyn and Bacon.

Mullaly, B. 2007. *The New Structural Social Work*. Toronto: Oxford University Press.

O'Hara, A., and Z. Weber, eds. 2006. *Skills for Human Service Practice: Working with Individuals, Groups and Communities*. South Melbourne: Oxford University Press.

Thompson, N. 2003. *Communication and Language: A Handbook of Theory and Practice*. Basingstoke: Palgrave Macmillan.

Zapf, M.K. 2001. 'Geography and Canadian social work practice', in F. Turner, ed., *Social Work Practice: A Canadian Perspective*, 2nd edn. Toronto: Prentice-Hall, 69–83.

Internet Resources

Canadian Association of Sexual Assault Centres
www.casac.ca/english/home.htm

Canadian Association of Social Workers (CASW)
www.casw-acts.ca

Canadian Charter of Rights and Freedoms
http://laws.justice.gc.ca/en/charter

Canadian Counselling Association (CCA)
www.ccacc.ca/home.html

Canadian Medical Association (CMA)
www.cma.ca

Canadian Psychological Association
www.cpa.ca

Government of Canada
www.canada.gc.ca/home.html

Social Care Institute for Excellence (SCIE)
www.scie.org.uk

Social Justice and Social Change Research Centre, University of Western Sydney
http://sites.uws.edu.au/sjsc/SJSC_Style06.htm

United Nations
www.un.org/Overview/rights.html

2 | Understanding Communication and Change

Learning Goals

- Identify the different ways of understanding communication.
- Understand some of the core verbal and non-verbal skills for human service practice.
- Consider the dimensions of individual and collective communication.
- Understand why communication is so linked with survival, healing, and well-being.
- Reflect on the ways in which communication expresses power.

Understanding Communication

Communication can be understood in many different ways by many different disciplines. Psychology, linguistics, sociology, and anthropology all have contributed enormously to how we think about communication in practice. Here, however, we will consider communication issues thematically rather than through these discipline lenses. In relation to human service work, we can understand communication first as a process (involving **verbal** and **non-verbal skills** at individual and collective levels), and second, as a means of survival, a means of healing and therapy, or as the basis of **power**.

Recall the four scenarios from Chapter 1. Each situation would require different communication skills. You need skills to communicate with clients in altered (drug-affected) states of consciousness; involuntary clients; groups of people rather than individuals; face-to-face communication; and telephone communication where non-verbal cues cannot be experienced; and communication over a long period of time where there is an established relationship. In this chapter, the dimensions of communication in all of these scenarios and others will be explored.

Communication is so fundamental to our **survival** and our well-being that we tend not to think about it as a complex skill that we have acquired across our lifespan. Communication can be defined as: 'The action of communicating heat, feeling, motion etc.; the transmission or exchange of information, news etc.; the science and practice of transmitting information; social context; personal intercourse' (Brown, 1993: 455).

Based on this definition, communication seems to be a straightforward process of the exchange or transmission of information. In order to develop a capacity for 'communicative competence' (Tannen, 1994), however, this process needs to be broken down into its component parts. This helps us to understand how the overall process occurs as a result of the smaller processes inherent within it. Like actors in rehearsal, this breaking down to the microskill level is done (Hargie, 2006a: 554) 'to analyze the overall complex act in terms of simpler component parts, train the individual to identify and use the parts separately, and then combine the parts until the complete act is assimilated'. You can then influence communication processes by adapting these skills along the way as required.

Practice Questions

Think of the many skills you might draw on to raise a difficult relationship issue with a particular friend or partner.

1. What would you do to approach such a discussion?

2. What do you anticipate could happen during that discussion?

3. Share your response with someone else and analyze the points of similarity and difference in your reactions.

Communication as a Process

In understanding communication as an interpersonal process, we focus on the basic skills of talking and listening. This involves the interaction of a sender and of a recipient or receiver. Communication, particularly when face to face, has two major dimensions—verbal and non-verbal. When people are talking, verbal and non-verbal exchanges occur, with ideas being encoded by the sender of the message and decoded by the receiver and filtered through the senses. This process was first proposed by Reusch (1957 as cited by Shulman, 1999: 41). A way of representing this process is provided in Figure 2.1.

More recent analyses of the anatomy of communication (Heath and Bryant, 2000: 75–84) suggest that communication is a process rather than an act of transmission, moving away from the more dyadic and linear notion represented in Figure 2.1. Heath and Bryant (2000) suggest that communication should be understood multi-dimensionally. Similar to the above model, the terms sender and receiver are still used, recognizing the tasks of **encoding** and **decoding**:

> The encoder is analogous to an actor or impression manager, producing and 'sending' the behaviours to be interpreted. The decoder is analogous to an observer 'receiving' the presented behaviours and interpreting them in some fashion. (Gordon, Druckman, Rozelle, and Baxter, 2006: 81)

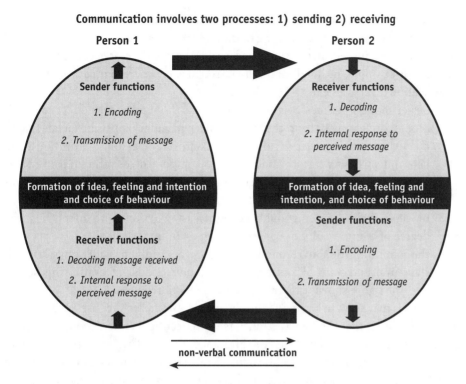

Communication involves two processes: 1) sending 2) receiving

Person 1

Sender functions

1. Encoding

2. Transmission of message

Formation of idea, feeling and intention and choice of behaviour

Receiver functions

1. Decoding message received

2. Internal response to perceived message

Person 2

Receiver functions

1. Decoding

2. Internal response to perceived message

Formation of idea, feeling and intention, and choice of behaviour

Sender functions

1. Encoding

2. Transmission of message

non-verbal communication

Figure 2.1 The Interpersonal Communication Process

In the moment of speaking with another person, however, we also constantly monitor the other person and adapt verbal and non-verbal responses all the time in that exchange. This focus on process is important, particularly when it is recognized that communication is a simultaneous, continuous, and nuanced process.

Some expansion of understanding beyond what is encoded and decoded in language is increasingly recognized. Acknowledged in this process is that the 'receiving system consists of the five senses, the receptors' (Kadushin, 1972: 25). More recent understandings from both Indigenous world views (Lynn, 2001; Hart, 2002) and chaos and complexity theories (Hudson, 2000) would include a sixth sense or receptor: a sense of intuition or 'knowing' at other levels of sensory awareness.

While some of the sender and receiver functions can be objectively verified—through recording verbal and non-verbal exchanges—the *intent* or purpose of what is being conveyed via verbal or non-verbal means is more subjective and is perhaps the most complex dimension of communication. For example, although a person intends to be supportive, their comment may be received by the other person as a critical or patronizing. Irrespective of what was intended, the receiver perceives that message as interpreted through personal, social, and cultural filters.

In processing the verbal and non-verbal messages we receive from an external source, we conduct an internal monologue simultaneously. That is, we cognitively process the information we are receiving through our past and our present structures of understandings. This process produces the meaning of the message (Heath and Bryant, 2000: 76–9). Sometimes a shared intent can be established easily. At other times it needs to be explicitly addressed; for example, in involuntary client settings or where significant cultural or communication diversities exist.

What earlier models perhaps overlooked most was the significance of context (ibid., 84), with context referring both to the individual's particular biopsychosocial–spiritual context and the broader socio-cultural context. Social and cultural influences determine whether certain issues are taboo, important, or valid for conversation.

We will explore understandings of these biological, psychological, social, and spiritual dimensions further in Chapter 3.

Current communication models emphasize interaction rather than transmission and reception. We hold that communication is a simultaneous, reciprocal process, involving interactions between at least two people and their context. The degree of commonality of contexts becomes an important area of focus within the communication, in recognition of how profoundly the wider physical, social, structural, and cultural contexts influence interactions. Integrating this perspective, the figure shown earlier might now look more Figure 2.2.

These models may seem to be stating the obvious. However, they are useful reminders of the depth of analysis that can be undertaken when reflecting on interactions, particularly when they have not gone so well. When we think about these skills in a professional context, the focus is on a more deliberate selection of particular skills at a particular time. For example, when we receive a critical message in a personal context, we might react emotionally

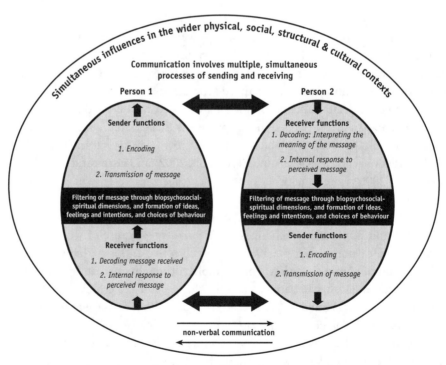

Figure 2.2 Communication as a Multi-dimensional Process

and impulsively to it. We decode it in a particular way. When we receive a similar message in a professional context, we may be more acutely aware of the sender than of ourselves in the interaction, and we will filter the information differently.

In your practice, you will make decisions constantly as to how you will interact with your clients. In many situations, this will involve communicating in empathic and supportive ways. At other times, this will involve being assertive with people, setting limits, or taking decisive and directive action. On other occasions, it will involve dealing with angry, aggressive, and oppressive clients and colleagues. As Hargie (2006a:45) suggests: 'Effective control of emotion is a central aspect of socially skilled performance.'

What this model highlights is that communication is a continuous interaction between at least two people. Building communication skills, therefore, is not about a one-person approach (that is, what the worker should do) but about an interactive approach (in this situation, this is the right thing to do) (Koprowska, 2005). The model also helps us to think about different means of communication, and the strengths and limitations they present in relation to effective communication.

The model also highlights the importance of **active listening**. When we listen actively, we are both hearing what is being said and communicating back to the other person that she or he is being heard. Active listening includes all the verbal and non-verbal skills that affirm another person's conversation: the verbal skills of questioning, responding, reflecting, and summarizing and the non-verbal skills of physically, intellectually, and empathically attending to that person.

> This discussion of communication relates to the concept of 'use of self', which we will explore in Chapter 4.

> These specific verbal skills of active listening are considered in Chapters 6–8.

Verbal Communication Processes

> In trying to understand how speakers use language, we must consider the context, . . . speakers' conversational styles and, most crucially, the interaction of their styles with each other. (Tannen, 1994: 46)

Verbal communication processes include everything that is spoken or uttered in a conversation and refer primarily to the content or message that is exchanged. Language expressed through conversation enables the communication of needs, wants, and experiences. As discussed later in this chapter, communication is essential for participating actively and influentially in daily relationships and the wider social environment, and is integral to human well-being and survival. In later chapters, we explore in detail how to use these verbal skills in the context of specific interviewing and interventions.

Some authors exclude paralinguistics—that is, verbal sounds or qualities of the verbal interaction such as tone, pitch, and volume—from this definition (Bull, 2002: 26), seeing them as non-verbal behaviours. For the purposes of this book, any verbal utterances will be considered verbal communication if they involve the use of voice. Changes in the quality of voice production can communicate all sorts of information relevant to an assessment. For example, when under stress, people tend to speak both faster and louder, and sometimes in a higher pitched voice (Tao, Kang, and Li, 2006). If you are aware of these tendencies in stressful situations, you can manage conversations differently if needed.

Verbal communication can be understood from many different perspectives. This next section examines the ways in which people vary in their verbal communications according to the social context, to emotional expressiveness, and to meaning.

Social Variations

The use of language to convey experiences, emotions, needs, and wants is a fundamental human capacity and skill. Language is the means by which people 'name and evaluate the objects, sensations, feelings, and situations they experience' (Heath and Bryant, 2000: 91). This verbal naming and availability of information enables people to survive and to establish an individual and social identity, as well as a sense of worth, role, and place.

Throughout infancy and early childhood, children acquire rapidly the capacity to apply names in their world and to interact verbally with others (Harris, 1995). What is increasingly recognized is that, from childhood, we learn a particular **conversational style** (or styles), in particular social groupings, with particular 'ethnic, regional, and class distinctions that have so many reverberations in society' (Tannen, 2000: 393). In addition to the ethnic, regional, and class distinctions children also learn gender and age differences.

Some researchers emphasize that children learn not just one overall conversational style, but multiple styles that are adapted according to specific contexts. For example, a study of dying children (Bluebond-Langner, 1978) showed that children do not lack an understanding and a language about their illness and their dying, as was previously thought. Instead, these children make careful decisions as to when and with whom these issues should be discussed; often they protect parents from the knowledge that they know about their imminent death. Similarly, immigrant children very readily adapt to the linguistic context of their peers in order to fit in with them, rather than retaining the accent of their parents (Harris, 1998). Peers are the dominant influence in language acquisition rather than parents, according to Harris and others.

Emotional Variation

Other variations in verbal styles relate to the degree to which individuals and families articulate their emotional experiences. The quality emphasized here is 'emotional expressiveness' (Yoo, Matsumoto, and LeRoux, 2006; Vogel et al., 2006) and it has been a feature of many studies in the mental health area; for example, where both extreme emotional expression and repression have been studied.

These variations become important in client–worker relationships. A conversation that one person may perceive to be reflective may be seen by another as deeply introspective, too emotional, and, overall, inappropriate. These relative depths of experience and expression of experience become important points of congruity or incongruity in the context of conversations.

Language as Signifier: Language Variation

The process of communication is a translation process, which often relies on assumptions— that is, we can think we know what people mean, more or less, by what they are telling us, and by their non-verbal communication (discussed later). Words carry many different meanings, however, and both individual and contextual interpretations are relied on in practice.

In a recent research study at a major trauma hospital, social workers stepped into the role of research assistants, asking people about their perceptions of trauma and about their resources when a member of their family had been admitted to the Intensive Care Unit. In their role as research assistants, the social workers were surprised by some of the information they were told by the family members when they compared it with some of the information they had received in their role as social workers. The 'research assistants' heard some new or quite different dimensions of the 'same' stories. What this example revealed to the research team was that the family members told different dimensions of their story according to differences in what they presumed their roles were at different times. Similarly, the social workers who were research assistants in this instance also found new ways of asking about issues, having stepped outside of their usual psychosocial assessment framework. Stories vary and this circumstance showed that narratives operate differently in different contexts.

Many people report that one of the difficulties following trauma or grief is finding a vocabulary with which to talk about their experiences—that is, finding a way of using words that will accurately convey what has been seen, experienced, and felt (Laub and Auerhahn, 1993; Reiter, 2000). As later chapters on narrative approaches will emphasize, finding the appropriate words to use is an important part of adaptation and recovery.

> This notion of narrative variation is explored in Chapter 13.

In the literature on grief, great emphasis is placed on using very specific language affirming the new reality, consistent with the first task of the grief process: coming to terms with the reality of the loss (Worden, 2003). In the following scenario, Jane, a senior hospital social worker, shows how specific choices of language can be. Words have personal meanings and 'loading' for particular individuals and their experiences in a particular context.

Focus on Practice

Finding the 'Right' Words

Once a year our department holds an afternoon for brothers and sisters who are bereaved through the death of a sibling. As we talk with the children, we feel it is important to use *correct factual* language and not euphemisms. One year, after an introduction to an activity in which I used the terms 'dead' and 'died', a little girl who was seven years old took me to one side and whispered, 'You should say *passed away*, it's much nicer.' A little taken aback, I asked her if this is what she said, 'Of course it is.' I asked her who else said 'passed away' and she replied, 'My mother.' Her point was well made. She knew very well that her sister was dead and didn't need to have this stated bluntly. An alternative response to the little girl might have been to ask her if she could tell me what 'passed away' meant, but I think we both already knew.

Language variation perhaps occurs most fundamentally across cultures. Throughout Canada's history, people have migrated from all over the world, bringing a diversity of languages. **Cross-cultural communication** not only differs linguistically, but also 'involve[s] diverse experiences, worldviews and differential social power and privilege' (Miller, Donner, and Fraser, 2004: 377).

Newhouse, Voyageur, and Beavon discuss the issues in Canada's struggle to come to terms with its Aboriginal heritage. 'It is no wonder that students are unable to articulate Aboriginal contributions to Canada since the dominant idea they encounter, through schools and the media, is that Aboriginal peoples are a problem that needs to be solved' (Newhouse, Voyageur, and Beavon, 2005: 3). The authors acknowledge that more recently a general recognition has developed that Aboriginal peoples have been present in Canada since long before Confederation and that the treatment of Aboriginal peoples in Canada has been unfair and often dishonest. 'We are hopeful that as Aboriginal history becomes more prominent in overall Canadian history, the beliefs of the past can be overcome' (ibid.).

For human service practice, you need to be culturally educated and aware. Debates about cross-cultural competence are complex, however, some authors suggest it is actually impossible to be a culturally competent practitioner outside of one's own culture (Dean, 2001). They argue it is more important to maintain an awareness of this impossibility, which leads to far greater communication sensitivity or focus on building cultural safety.

Practice Exercise

欢迎光临 Kanata

You may or may not be able to read either of these words.

1. What do you notice happens if you cannot understand the word?
2. How do you go about trying to understand it?
3. What would you do if you were confronted with on of these words and you were required to respond, even if you do not understand it?

Focus on Practice

Working with Interpreters

Working with interpreters is a vital skill in working with people from culturally and linguistically diverse (CALD) backgrounds. 'Canada' is derived from *Kanata*, the Huron word meaning 'settlement' or 'village'. The Victorian Interpreting and Translating Service (VITS, 2006: 19–20) proposes the following strategies.

- Introduce yourself and the interpreter to your client.
- Explain what the interview is about and what you hope to achieve.
- Explain to the interviewee the interpreter's role within the interview. Inform the person that the interpreter's role is to assist communication by interpreting everything that is being said, by all parties.
- Maintain control of the interview. You must ask the questions and hear the replies fully. The interpreter's task is to assist in communication, not to conduct the interview.
- Position yourself in a way that permits you to speak directly with the client and allows you to have maximum eye contact with her or him.
- Use the first person when speaking to your client, that is, say 'I' instead of 'Ask him/her' etc. Doing so will encourage both you and your client to talk to each other and use eye contact and body language, which assists in effective communication.
- Keep your questions, statements, and comments short and deliver them in segments, allowing the interpreter to interpret everything you say in stages. Take note of the interpreter's method of signalling to you that your comments or questions are too long and allow the interpreter to do the same with the client.
- Never assume that interpreting is a simple mechanical task of matching the non-English word or expression with an English equivalent.
- It is unreasonable to expect an interpreter to be a walking dictionary.
- Do not assume that because a person appears to have a basic understanding of English, she/he will be able to comprehend specific terms and difficult expressions or jargon, particularly when under stress.
- Do not isolate the client by engaging the interpreter in discussion. If you need to clarify or discuss something with the interpreter, request that this be explained to the client first.
- Allow the client to raise any questions or issues of concern.
- Before the end of the interview, summarize key points for the client.

The Use of Silence

The use of silence—that is, the *absence* of verbal communication—is an important skill. Silence can be regarded as a verbal skill in that it is a deliberate refraining from the use of words to communicate different messages.

Silences can provide extremely powerful spaces in which to reflect and simply 'be' in that moment with another person. The use of silence as a form of protest has been used to bring about major change (Dalton, 1993). On the other hand, silences can be agonizingly long and awkward moments. Assumptions about the appropriateness of silence and pausing are both culturally and individually based. As Tannen (2000: 393) notes about differing assumptions:

> The one who is waiting for a longer pause finds it harder to get a turn, because before that length of pause occurs, the other person begins to perceive an

uncomfortable silence and rushes to fill it, to save the conversation.

John, a social worker who has researched differences between Indigenous and non-Indigenous communication assumptions, spoke with Margaret, a respected Aboriginal Elder, about the use of silence. The following is an excerpt from that interview, reprinted with permission.

Margaret: Nah, they have to fill in every minute with talk, with words. They don't know how to just listen, to just hear silence.

John: [after a pause] How do you mean?

Margaret: It's like they can't stand it when nobody is saying nothing. Silence is important to us. But they don't get that, don't respect that . . . if you don't answer right away they say you're angry or not interested or something . . . after a while, you just say stuff you know they want to hear.

Finding the commonalities and congruities in the content of your conversations is important. You should learn about and consider the use of silence as it is defined by the culture you are working with. Here are some questions to consider when working with silence cross-culturally:

1. How is silence defined within the culture you are working with?
2. Is silence defined as a sign of respect and therefore important to maintain in your working relationship?
3. Is silence part of processing language translation?
4. Is silence a sign of miscommunication?
5. Is silence a reflection of the overuse of professional language or jargon creating difficulties with language translation?

Silence can be defined in many different ways. When working cross-culturally, the worker should consider the cultural context in which silence is defined. Working with silence is summarized by Jaworski: 'on the one hand, silence is useful when one wants to be indirect or to be polite by "leaving options".' The author continues by noting that silence provides time for understanding and to think of a response, which may avoid conflict. 'On the other hand, one's failure to say something that is expected in a given moment by the other party can be interpreted as a sign of hostility or dumbness. This negative aspect of the use of silence becomes especially apparent in cross-cultural communication' (Jaworski, 1993: 25).

Non-Verbal Communication Processes

Equally important is the use of non-verbal communication. The term 'non-verbal' refers to all the cues or skills that emanate from our physical reactions and presence, including, according to Bull (2002: 26–7), 'facial movement, gaze, pupil size, body movement and interpersonal distance. It can refer as well to communication through touch or smell, through various kinds of artifacts such as masks and clothes, or through formalized communications such as semaphore.' Thus, non-verbal cues relate to both the voluntary and involuntary physical reactions and responses we have in the context of a conversation, as well as the messages we transmit physically about our social identity. We rely on these non-verbal cues to indicate that we are listening and being listened to in a conversation.

Each person has a unique repertoire of non-verbal reactions and skills. This understanding is important as many communication texts suggest that up to 85 per cent of communication is conveyed in our non-verbal language. The impact of non-verbal cues on perceptions of rapport has been particularly noted (ibid., 38). Understanding the context of non-verbal behaviour is vital for a number of reasons. First, non-verbal behaviour conveys information for our survival. Recent research has found that we process some information emotionally in the first instance, and then at a cognitive level as a secondary process (Schacter, 1996; Schore, 1994). These understandings have emerged from studying how people process traumatic situations. They contradict some earlier assumptions that a cognitive process occurred first, followed by a physiological response. At a basic survival level, we rely on non-verbal cues to read safety in situations, reacting to stress and trauma with fight or flight reactions (Selye, 1987). Our non-verbal reactions, therefore, convey our immediate physiological responses to situations. In less stressful situations, it is easier to monitor and influence non-verbal reactions.

Second, given that 'negative impressions often result from differences in conversational style' (Tannen, 2000: 394), it is important to think analytically about what we hope is being conveyed and why. Like verbal communication, non-verbal information is 'dependent on a human observer to transcribe and, if necessary, to code the behaviour into appropriate categories' (Bull, 2002: 25).

Practice Questions

1. What non-verbal cues would you rely on to know that someone is:

    - agreeing with you?
    - disagreeing with you?
    - confused by you?
    - understands you?

2. What non-verbal cues did you tend to emphasize in your interpretation?

3. Why did you emphasize these cues and not others?

Increasingly, non-verbal cues are recognized as being highly cultural and gender-specific, as well as context- and age-specific. You can find texts that identify all sorts of cross-cultural differences in eye contact, body language and personal space, and verbal following skills (e.g., Evans et al., 2004, cited in Morris, 2006: 265). The problem with identifying differences on the basis of group membership is that the differences become oversimplified and stereotyped, and group membership is assumed, often wrongly. On the other hand, these important differences can be neglected when they are profound influences. As Clarke, Andrews, and Austin (1999) note, the skill is in asking the client about what is important, and in observing what is important for her or for him. It is about listening to what these gestures or styles of communication indicate—for example, eye contact can be either about respect or indifference, which are two fundamentally different messages.

The following exercise encourages you to play with some of your non-verbal comfort levels by testing out different physical proximities.

Focus on Practice

Your Physical Comfort Zones

In a class or small-group situation, try to keep a conversation going while working from a number of different physical postures. For example, maintain your conversation while you are:

- sitting or standing
- back to back
- shoulder to shoulder
- three metres apart
- ten centimetres apart or toe to toe.

Then, find a comfortable distance and maintain the conversation in that position for a few minutes, noticing the features of this position.

1. What changes do you make in trying to find a comfortable position in which to maintain a conversation?
2. Reflecting on the comfortable position you moved to, how similar or different is that position from your colleagues' positions?
3. What cultural factors or assumptions do you think have influenced your position?

Over many years, the acronym SOLER (Egan, 2007) has been used to promote the optimal non-verbal positioning in an interviewing situation. SOLER stands for sitting **s**quare on (that is, facing the client), with an **o**pen posture (no crossed legs or arms), **l**eaning forward towards the client to express interest, maintaining **e**ye contact, and being **r**elaxed. Egan later changed the acronym to SOLAR, following feedback from a woman who had been working with blind students and found that the **a**im of eye contact, not necessarily eye contact itself in this instance, was of greatest importance (Egan, 2002: 70). This positioning was thought to reflect a genuine and respectful non-verbal orientation to the client. However, as a reflection of cultural changes and particularly shifts in gender relations, this acronym is now heavily critiqued. We will think about these issues of body language more broadly under separate subheadings of facial expression, body posture, and physical proximity.

Facial Expression

Over past decades, a continuing effort has been made to establish whether non-verbal behaviours, particularly facial expressions, are common to all people, regardless of context. Some facial reactions are automatic responses, such as pupil dilation occurring in response to 'stimuli we find attractive' (Bull, 2002: 28), and blushing in the aftermath of embarrassment. All humans seem to express six emotions on their face: happiness, sadness, anger, fear, disgust, and surprise, and they all are 'decoded in the same way by literate and preliterate cultures' (ibid., 29). Cultures vary enormously, however, in the so-called 'display rules' that are developed around the expression of these emotions. Major differences have been found between the extensive use of direct eye contact in Western contexts and more avoidant and hierarchical rules relating to eye contact in Asian and Indigenous contexts (Sciarra, 1999).

Your understanding of cultural influences, therefore, is critical. At the same time, it is difficult to develop such understandings outside of a particular situation. There may be generalizations that can be drawn about specific cultural groups regarding all sorts of dimensions of communication; for example, the use of eye contact, touch, proximity, and emotional expressiveness. Generalizations can also become stereotyped. On the other hand, glossing over cultural differences can lead to misinterpretation of behaviour because of assumptions that do not adequately acknowledge cultural difference. This kind of 'blindness' to issues of diversity and difference leads potentially to further marginalization and stigmatization where difference is no longer acknowledged (Thompson, 2003b).

Practice Exercise

Watch a number of conversations taking place in different contexts—in a workplace, in public, or on television, for example. Observe how people use their non-verbal skills to communicate their message and to respond to other persons.

1. What do you see working effectively and ineffectively in these encounters?

2. What communication differences would you attribute to gender, class, or cultural differences?

In previous decades of counselling training, the emphasis was on the worker maintaining a very neutral facial reaction to the client and the client's story. This neutrality was assumed so the worker was not reacting to the emotional experience of the client but providing a neutral sounding board. Rather than working towards some artificial neutral response, a quality of intersubjectivity is now valued.

One of the opportunities, therefore, throughout any skills class is to learn the skills of monitoring and/or modifying emotional reactions. Four processes of modification have been noted (Bull, 2002: 30–1), including: (1) attenuation, whereby an emotional reaction is weakened in its intensity; (2) amplification, whereby it is exaggerated; (3) concealment, whereby it is hidden by adopting a neutral facial expression; and (4) substitution, whereby a different expression of the emotion being experienced is reflected. For example, it is not uncommon for people to smile while they are telling you about how sad they are feeling. If you have the opportunity to record your use of these skills, you will be able to witness your own reactions to clients and their stories, even if in a role-playing situation.

> This modification of your emotional responses relates to your 'use of self', which we explore in Chapter 4.

Focus on Practice

Analyzing Non-Verbal Behaviour

If you have the opportunity, use a DVD recorder or an observer to map your non-verbal behaviour throughout a role-play interview. A DVD recording, in particular, can provide the opportunity for you to see yourself as others experience you. Often the person on-screen feels a sense of shock when seeing the video for the first time. This sort of viewing links our usually entirely subjective experience with an objective experience of ourselves.

From a British study (Cartney, 2006: 839) of the usefulness of video recordings in developing communication skills in social work training, students had these comments to make:

> During the video you can see your practical skills and then you can analyze yourself and base this in theory and in reading from different books. So you get all parts.
> You see things that you do yourself but you never realized . . . you watch and re-watch and all the time you see new things.

Body Posture

Many different postures have been proposed as the most suitable posture for workers, such as SOLER mentioned earlier. While the absence of clear guidelines about physical **posture** may seem to make the task of interpreting these cues impossible, the quality of the physical alignment between communicators does seem to be the most important factor, referring to 'the way that speakers position their heads and bodies in relation to each other, including eye gaze' (Tannen, 1994: 86). Tannen is echoed in the statement by Egan (2002: 69): 'The point is that your bodily orientation should convey the message that you are involved with the client.' This means a general orientation of your body towards the person is important, but further 'rules' may not be helpful.

In studies of gender and posture, some major differences between boys only and girls only have been identified. As Tannen (1994: 98) notes:

The girls and women are more physically still, more collected into the space they inhabit and more directly aligned with each other through physical proximity, occasional touching, body posture, and anchoring of eye gaze.

This finding raises questions for how we interpret the non-verbal behaviours of men and women, depending on one's own gender.

Perhaps the most important quality of any physical posture is that it conveys respect to the other person. That is, you are available to listen and respond, finding a sustainable posture and one free of distractions. You may need to consider how sustainable your posture is. While it may initially seem a good idea to kneel down beside a child to talk, for example, it can become an awkward position beyond a few moments of conversation and distracting to then shift.

Physical Proximity and Location

Issues of physical space and proximity are similarly important considerations. A conversation too close to another person can seem violating of private or personal space. A conversation that is conducted too remotely can seem impersonal. Again, individual interpretation is influential here. At a recent cross-cultural seminar, two workers had fundamentally different reactions to a photo of two people in conversation. One worker considered them to be very awkward in their posture and disengaged, whereas another worker thought they were two people relaxed in conversation with each other. The only way to know whether or not it was a difficult encounter would have been by asking the participants themselves about their experience.

Another non-verbal dimension in human service work to consider is the use of physical contact with clients. This has been, and remains, a contentious area of practice. On the one hand, a rule of 'no contact' is maintained, primarily to safeguard the client from unwanted touch and intimacy. On the other hand, there are times when physical contact, such as a handshake, becomes an important marker of respect and engagement in work together (Trevithick, 2005). The use of touch raises questions of personal safety, both for your client and yourself.

These non-verbal cues can become the inhibitors rather than the enhancers of good communication interactions. Rather than there being one correct way to physically interact, interactional synchrony, congruence, or alignment within a conversation have been identified as core components of an effective communication. Thus, the over- or under-use of particular non-verbal skills becomes problematic, not necessarily in and of itself but when joined with other incongruities in the conversational context.

Underutilized physical cues tend to leave the talker uncertain as to how the conversation is going. If you receive no response from someone in terms of facial expression, for example, it can be difficult to continue talking. Overused physical cues can similarly leave the client feeling unheard; an overreaction is perceived instead. One person recounted seeing a counsellor whose eyes welled up with tears every time she spoke of her parent who had died some time earlier. The person was seeking help with other matters and felt that the counsellor was involved in her grief rather than with the difficulties she was expected to address.

Other overbearing physical cues can emerge in relation to eye contact that is too intense or a physical presence that is too close or too overbearing, thus overstepping a client's sense of personal space that many consider important. Fidgeting or doodling with a pen and paper can similarly indicate stress or boredom and disengagement. Sometimes we are unaware of our habits—of flicking hair, clicking pens, or playing with jewellery or fingernails, for example. In any of these situations, if you are distracted the client will be left feeling unattended to in the conversation.

Non-verbal cues also are presented through a bodily discourse. Our physical presence tells a story to the client. For example, how you dress and how you present in relation to confidence are interpreted by your clients. In this sense, the 'body can be inscribed with societal norms, values and mores . . . and . . . our actions and behaviours . . . illuminate personal values and ideas' (Osmond, 2005: 892). These worker dimensions can alienate a client or provide reassurance, depending on how congruent they are with the client's world.

Your physical proximity can sometimes be beyond your control. Human service work frequently is done in physical locations other than private rooms where people are sitting together in comfortable chairs. Many significant conversations can be made in corridors standing together, over a patient's bed, or in public places where someone's response to the interview may have as much to do with the overall physicality of the environment as with the immediate conversation. Your awareness of the possible impact of all of these non-verbal dimensions on your capacity to talk together is vital.

Individual and Collective Communication Processes

So far, we have considered communication in relation to at least two people in some form of direct verbal and non-verbal communication contact with each other. Other dimensions of communication complexity in this process include thinking beyond the one-to-one context of communication and beyond a 'five senses' understanding.

Communication Involving More Than One Person

As people are added to the conversation, so the complexity of the communication web grows. As noted in Chapter 1, Western approaches to human services, and interviewing and counselling in particular, have been criticized for failing to recognize communication processes beyond individual interactions. The site of intervention remains primarily the individual, even though family, community, and the broader social context that have such profound influences on well-being are acknowledged. This was illustrated in John's research with a non-Indigenous social worker talking about her experiences with Indigenous clients.

On the one hand, pragmatic realities such as limited agency resources can justify this individual focus. On the other hand, the lack of integration into practice of recent theoretical understandings around communication and interaction leads to a considerable outdatedness of practice assumptions (Whyte, 2005). Seeing the client as an individual rather than as part of a family or community means that the context of the problems, and therefore often the

Focus on Practice

On Communication Skills

Susan: There are two things I wish I'd been taught in school. The first, about how to keep boundaries, how much to reveal—both with clients and co-workers . . . . The second, particularly about working with [Indigenous] clients, is how hard it is to ensure successful communication. In many cases, work is done at the community level or the client attends with extended family. I definitely prefer individual work. I fear missing cross-cultural communication issues and possibly offending the client or sending the wrong message.

solutions, are overlooked. This has been particularly noted by Indigenous researchers and practitioners, who emphasize that because ways of living and thinking are collective and communal (Lynn, 2001), problems should be addressed in collective and communal ways.

Morrissette, McKenzie, and Morrissette(1993: 93) write that 'Aboriginal people do not embrace a single philosophy, there are fundamental differences between the dominant Euro-Canadian and traditional Aboriginal societies, and these have their roots in differing perceptions of one's relationship with the universe and the Creator. . . . decision making was based primarily on sharing, understanding, and the building of consensus.' Such a philosophy requires the worker to consider cross-cultural values, such as a collective, interdependent ways of relating. This standpoint will require the worker to gain skill in working with both individual clients and, when requested, client groups.

Communication beyond the Five Senses

The individualized approach is privileged further within Western discourses in regard only to verbal and non-verbal interactions within the physical realms, thus acknowledging five, not six, basic human senses. Various theorists have tried to articulate understandings of other ways of knowing. Jung (1963: 160) termed one dimension of this extra-verbal communication the 'collective unconscious', referring to the inherited, transpersonal dimensions of communication. Dreams and intuitions are thought to be the ways in which these shared dimensions of communication are transmitted.

Indigenous cultures have always respected the reality of other levels of communication, recognizing conscious and unconscious, individual and collective, physical and metaphysical, and transpersonal ways of knowing (Smith, 2001).

The capacity for human consciousness to effect change, even when people are not physically present together, has been proven in many studies (Hudson, 2000). This research is relatively new and contentious, but it highlights that there are different levels of influence in any communication process. Rogers (cited in Moore and Purton, 2006: 11) identified this when he noted it was not so much the qualities of genuineness or empathy that influenced the process of engagement with another person, but the subsequent transcendent state of being that was experienced as a result of these qualities.

Practice Questions

'I was in London in 2005 in the week following the terrorist attacks in the Underground. On the Thursday after the bombs, at midday, a minute's silence was held. Thousands of people across London stopped to respect this silence.

'During that time, for about 30 seconds, I felt an incredible tingling sensation through my arms and neck. On talking with several other people afterwards, it seems that we had shared this experience.'

1. What is your immediate reaction to this description?

2. Have you had similar experiences?

3. What would you be thinking if a client told you this story?

4. How might you respond to a client who told you this story?

We look now at three major ways in which communication is critical in the change process. Communication influences survival, promotes healing, and expresses power.

Communication for Survival

Communication connects people and facilitates the formation of social bonds and attachments (Koprowska, 2005), which in turn facilitate our very survival. The infant learns to cry when hungry to elicit a response from a caregiver. Over time, they acquire specific words to communicate specific needs. Across the lifespan, we communicate not only our basic physical needs and wants but also our most complex intimate and psychological needs.

We rely also on non-verbal communication for our survival. For example, we experience parataxic distortions (Sullivan, 1953) when we first meet someone, whereby we try to identify whether this person reminds us of anyone else. We scan our memories to see if there is any corresponding cue that reminds us of this person from our experience to date. This is the typification process indicated earlier in Chapter 1 whereby we very quickly group people, determining, for instance, as to whether this person looks safe or threatening.

Communication impacts our survival in other ways. The impact of health professionals' communication styles on patients has been studied, looking at compliance with medication and rehabilitation programs, and reduction of stress and anxiety (Glintborg, Andersen, and Dalhoff, 2007; Yedidia, 2007). Effective communication strategies enhance health outcomes, although, in regard to neuroleptic medications, evidence suggests that compliance with doctors' and workers' promotion of these medications has greatly increased the incidence and degree of mental illness (see, e.g., Whitaker, 2010; Cech, 2010).

This link is emphasized across a wide range of professional guidelines. Rider and Keefer (2006: 626), for example, report on the competencies required of doctors in the US context. They include the capacity to:

create and sustain a therapeutic and ethically sound relationship with patients; use effective listening skills and elicit and provide information using effective non-verbal, explanatory, questioning and writing skills; work effectively with others as a member or leader of a health care team or other professional group.

> Remember Thompson's definitions of the processes of discrimination in Chapter 1, and stereotyping in particular.

Communication generally has been found to profoundly impact mood states and self-esteem, which, in turn, are known to impact physical health states (Goleman, 2006). Positive communications lead to positive outcomes. Thus, communication plays a key role in enhancing or inhibiting well-being.

Communication as Healing or Therapeutic

As a worker, you will be using communication to bring about positive change for individuals and their communities. Thus, communication is both a means and an end in itself. The telling of and listening to human stories is a well-known protective factor for well-being. The **therapeutic** quality seems to be related both to what is said and that someone has listened. Conversations can be healing, therapeutic, relieving, and normalizing.

Some of the therapeutic qualities that we will continue to explore are the importance of 'giving voice' to situations of adversity (Laub and Auerhahn, 1993), of speaking the unspeakable following trauma, of developing a coherent story, and of expressing emotion. For example, one Australian Indigenous man reflects on how sharing stories is healing:

> [M]y medicine is listening to other people, too. The first time I was listening to others talking, I thought they were talking about my life. 'I am not alone' is powerful medicine for people who have felt completely isolated, unheard, unacknowledged in their pain . . . . (Atkinson, 2002: 198)

When working with clients, it is important to identify individual strengths early in the first meeting. It might be acknowledging the initial courage it took to make the appointment and then show up. The strength may appear through the desire to improve parenting skills or the trust in the practitioner to disclose 'a long kept secret', for the first time. Early identification of the client's strengths enhances the engagement process and brings awareness to the client's existing available resources.

A positive impact on emotional intensity and stress and distress levels comes through writing about personal experiences, as has been frequently identified (Kleinman, Das, and Lock, 1997; Pennebaker, 1995; Pennebaker and O'Heeran, 1984). The expression of emotion is seen to enhance a sense of coherence. These findings have been questioned recently (Stroebe, Schut, and Stroebe, 2006), however, suggesting that emotional expression perhaps helps only those with a secure attachment style. This question of who benefits from emotional expression is important, as another study (Ginzburg, Solomon, and Bleich, 2002) found that being an 'avoidant repressor' was more protective in the aftermath of heart attacks, a perhaps counterintuitive finding.

When a person's story is not heard, however, the research conclusions are more straight-forward. When a person's experience is disenfranchised (Doka, 1989), minimized, or ignored, the impact is negative and, in some instances, has been found to contribute more to the ongoing distress than the initial trauma (Holman and Silver, 1996).

The orientation of human service communication, therefore, is towards the promotion of the values discussed in Chapter 1. It is intentional communication towards evoking strengths, positive emotions, and resilience. This can come about in many ways—through the deep listening to the story of the client, through sharing humour (Moran and Massam, 1997), and through breaking down a sense of isolation and alienation.

Communication as Power

Verbal and non-verbal communication is, therefore, the major means of the human work-er's influence. One further way of understanding and analyzing communication is in relation to the power relations inherent in any communication process.

Power is exerted by individuals for many reasons: as a result of unconscious motivations, as attempts to manage uncertainty, or to maintain the social order. Power is exerted through assumptions about ways of being, through hierarchies of interaction, and through language. These forms of power play out whether or not words for particular experiences exist within a particular culture, whether or not recognition is granted to individual constructions of meaning, and whether or not knowledge bases are the privileged ones for power. A major contribution of postmodernist theory has been the raising of awareness of the extent to which dominant constructions of meaning support particular power relations (Fook, 1999: 203). Written and verbal communication can be accepted as authoritative knowledge, maintaining power and social control over the experiences of others (Gordon, 1980: 77; Thompson, 2003a).

Power is exercised by workers in relation to the subsequent flow of information fol-lowing a conversation with clients. For example, client confidentiality is in many ways protected by privacy legislation and codes of ethical practice. At times (and for fam-ily members in particular), the power of workers to withhold certain information from families—even out of respect for the client and consistent with privacy laws—can lead to tensions and frustrations (Deveson, 1991). Not communicating information—the with-holding of information from colleagues and clients, because of legislation requirements and/or personal style—can also be an extremely powerful act. Not communicating ver-bally leaves people unclear, powerless, and unable to ascertain limits and boundaries.

The power dynamics of any relationship, therefore, are important to attend to in the context of professional practice. Often, power dynamics are talked about as if they are something that can and should be removed from a relationship. It seems paradoxical that you become a human service worker to effect change, yet would deny there is any influence or power in that role. For example, if you are the social worker working in child protection, you have the capacity under the legislation to remove a child to safer circum-stances. As a worker, you have the power to breach confidentiality in situations where there are major concerns about the safety of an individual. Another way to think about it is that power dynamics are always functioning in any relationship, along with shifting experiences of influence, interdependence, dependence, and independence.

Legislation and the responsibilities vested in the worker raise all sorts of questions about the degree to which client–worker relationships are 'equal'. Some authors and practitioners emphatically state that client–worker relationships are equal or that the worker should strive to make them equal—for example, 'a radical perspective always assumes equality between the professional and the person being helped' (Fook, 2000: 143; Ife, 1997). Others, just as emphatically, state that a client and a worker cannot be equal in all respects (Brink, 1987). As Burstow (1987: 18) argues, 'the situation is unequal in that [workers] have greater authority, mobility, responsibility for other[s] and power as regards other[s]'. She similarly proposes that the client has power but that it is necessarily less power than that of the worker. For involuntary clients, this is particularly the case.

One strategy for ensuring that this inequality is not a destructive inequality is to develop a consciousness and an articulation of the dilemmas and decisions we encounter throughout a relationship. That is, one needs to recognize the distinction between having power and managing the inequality respectfully and openly. There are ways of minimizing the inequality and the use of power within any relationship. As Tannen (1994: 26) notes, hierarchical relationships can be 'seen as close and mutually, not unilaterally, empowering'. Brink's (1987: 27) distinction is a useful one, even if it is in relation to thinking specifically about therapists rather than about all human service workers:

> Client and therapist are equally meaning-making beings, equally human beings, of equal worth, equally capable of realizing their own unique potential; they may or may not be equal in their coping skills or in their relative comfort in the world.

Another practice skill to ensure equity is addressed by negotiation. 'Negotiation' can be defined as the process of the worker's developing an agreement with the client that clearly defines the working relationship. Deryl's work with Chris, a 17 year old teenager who has not been attending school, offers a practice example of negotiation.

Focus on Practice

Negotiating the Relationship

Deryl: Hi, Chris; what brings you in today?
Chris: My parents are making me come.
Deryl: Why do you think your parents want you to come?
Chris: They are angry because I have been missing lots of school; but it is too much, and I am not going to go back!
Deryl: Tell me about school; what are you taking?
Chris: Well, I have five classes and it's not like I hate school but . . .

Chris explains to Deryl that he has been cutting school because he feels his class schedule is too difficult for him to manage. Chris is dealing with the pressure by not attending.

1. Where might some of the power inequities be in this example?

2. How would you negotiate with Chris to increase his attendance?
3. In negotiating the working relationship what might be some of the initial steps?

Remember the five core practice values, including respect, that were explored in Chapter 1.

This chapter ends with an example, provided by John, of some Indigenous clients talking about their non-Indigenous social worker. It draws together some of the themes that have run through this chapter—the use of verbal and non-verbal skills, the degree to which conversations are therapeutic or not, and the degree to which power is exerted or not in client–worker interactions.

Focus on Practice

Communication and Power

Lee: We'd meet at the hall and she'd have us sitting in a row and she would sit facing us . . . We'd just sit there and she would talk.

Rita: Yeah, she'd tell us what we were there to talk about and stuff. But it's like she wasn't really listening, she just kept on talking even when we didn't answer.

Lee: Yeah, and then she'd talk even more. Once, after [several such meetings] we just sat there, didn't say a word. After a few minutes she just got up and left.

Rita: We broke up laughing, damn near rolled on the floor!

1. What is your reaction to this interaction?
2. Identify the dimensions that you think were problematic in the client–worker relationship.

Chapter Summary

In this chapter, we have explored the many microskills involved in the key dimensions of communication. While communication is regarded as a verbal process, the critical role of non-verbal communication in conveying the emotional and physical components of messages has also been emphasized. We looked at the dimensions of verbal and non-verbal communication processes that enhance or inhibit effective communication.

As a human service worker, you will bring to communication with clients a specialized understanding of the significance of that communication, which constitutes a form of power. We have looked at the impact of communication on health and well-being; the role of communication in healing; and communication as sustaining, reinforcing, or changing power dynamics in individual and social relationships.

Questions for Analysis

1. What have you learned about:
    *   the verbal skills of communication?
    *   the non-verbal skills of communication?
    *   the ways in which communication is integral to culture, survival, health, and power?
    *   the communication challenges within a client–worker relationship?

2. Which points in question 1 do you feel confident applying?

3. Which specific skills do you require more practice with and why?

4. What have you learned about your own communication style from reading this chapter—in relation to both your verbal and non-verbal skills?

5. What are some of the strengths and challenges you experience in your communication style with other people?

Recommended Readings

Heath, R., and J. Bryant. 2000. *Human Communication Theory and Research: Concepts, Contexts and Challenges.* Hillsdale, NJ: Lawrence Erlbaum.

Jaworski, A. 1993. *The Power of Silence: Social and Pragmatic Perspectives.* London: Sage.

Koprowska, J. 2005. *Communication and Interpersonal Skills in Social Work.* Exeter, UK: Learning Matters.

Morrissette, V., B. McKenzie, and L. Morrissette. 1993. 'Towards an Aboriginal model of social work practice. Cultural knowledge and traditional practices', *Canadian Social Work Review* 10, 1: 91–108.

Newhouse, D., C. Voyageur, and D. Beavon. 2005. *Hidden in Plain Site: Contributions of Aboriginal Peoples to Canadian Identity and Culture.* Toronto: University of Toronto Press.

Pennebaker, J., ed. 1995. *Emotion, Disclosure and Health.* Washington: American Psychological Association.

Trevithick, P. 2005. *Social Work Skills: A Practice Handbook*, 2nd edn. Maidenhead, UK: Open University Press.

Weaver, H. 1999. 'Indigenous people and the social work profession: Defining culturally competent services', *Social Work* 44, 3: 217–25.

Internet Resources

500 Nations
http://500nations.com/Canada_First_Nations.asp

Native Social Work, Native Human Services
http://nativesocialwork.blogspot.com

Talking Cure
www.talkingcure.com

VITS LanguageLink
www.vits.com.au

3 | Communication and Change

Learning Goals

- Analyze the influences on our listening.
- Consider the paradigms that influence listening.
- Describe the influence of theory on listening.
- Understand how different practice perspectives influence our practice.
- Apply a multi-dimensional approach to listening.

The Influences on Our Listening

In Chapter 2, we looked at the communication process in some detail, breaking it down into the verbal and non-verbal skills that influence a conversation. As Thompson notes (2002: xviii), 'skill development does not occur in a vacuum—there are also knowledge and values to be taken into consideration.' This chapter focuses on how we can bring together these skills with a theoretical understanding of clients, their particular circumstances, and the events or conditions that require change.

Developing an understanding of the knowledge bases we bring to our practice is essential. Two knowledge bases, in particular, inform human service work—an evidence-based perspective and a reflective practice perspective (Chui and Wilson, 2006: 2; Lewis, 2002). That is, our practice is based on the observed result of the application of knowledge and theory, as well as on the use of an understanding of ourselves as workers.

We can think about knowledge, theories, and skills in a number of different ways. These differences often lead to confusion because a sharp distinction is not made between the level or type of **theory** or knowledge that is being presented (Walsh, 2006). In this chapter, **paradigms**—dominant views held by groups of people at a certain point in time that determine and explain human society or a particular field of knowledge—are described. The chapter concludes with a presentation of a multi-dimensional approach, an overarching framework used within this book.

To focus the discussion, Jahzara's story will be used to show the different ways we might go about thinking about our work.

Focus on Practice

Seeking Help

Jahzara has called your organization and spoken with the duty worker about her concerns that she's going to harm her four children. She's exhausted and depressed following the birth of her baby seven weeks ago. The other three children are all under six years of age, and over the school holidays she has found it increasingly difficult to manage with them at home every day. Her partner Davu is working part-time in the local car factory, but it has been threatened with closure. The financial stress is the worst it has ever been, with the rent in arrears and the bills piling up. If Davu loses his job, she does not know what they will do.

This morning, her eldest son dropped his breakfast all over the floor. His stepfather hit him and he has bruises on his face. He has been withdrawn in his room all morning and she is now feeling so angry and frustrated with him, she thinks she may lash out at him as well. She realizes this and picked up the phone, calling your family service instead. She realizes she needs help before things are more out of control.

1. What is your reaction to this situation and why?
2. Why do you think this situation has arisen?
3. Who would you view as your client(s) in this situation and why?
4. What would you see as your main purposes in working with this situation and whoever you have identified as the client(s)?
5. What would you want to do in this situation to achieve your purpose?
6. What would be your first step?

Jahzara's story raises a lot of questions for your practice: where would you begin in your response to Jahzara and the others in her family? What would be the purpose of your involvement and intervention, along with the other questions raised in the shaded box above? One starting point is to think about the broad paradigms or world views that inform your practice.

World Views and Paradigms

As meaning-making beings, humans 'need to find things out, build and test theories, and take action based on that knowledge-generating activity' (Morris, 2006: xvii). This broad view of the world and how it operates is referred to as a world view. These 'structures of meaning' help us to establish our own personal and social identities, and maintain some sense of predictability, coherence and control in our daily lives (Antonovsky, 1987; Marris, 1993, 1996). We develop a world view or broad understandings from our experiences across our lifespan as we come to form views of the nature of the environment, social realities, and the individual characteristics of people.

World views are often described as differing along continua of beliefs about the nature of human and social realities. Questions about objective versus subjective truths lie at the heart of different paradigms: the patterns of behaviour that may be observed and described, often in terms of models or cause-and-effect principles (Neuman, 1999; Trainor, 2002). For example, some people understand the world in relation to an individual's identity, whereas others maintain more collective notions of identity; similarly, identities can be understood as stable and fixed or as fluid and non-linear. Some people maintain liberal or permissive views of the world and of expectations of other people's behaviour, whereas others maintain conservative and more controlling views; some people combine the two perspectives. Some people see the inner or interior world of the person as the cause of human problems and suffering, whereas others attribute these experiences to outer-world or external causes. Again, both views may be held simultaneously. Each one of these dimensions is part of different world views—overarching ways of thinking about the human experience. In different historical eras and social contexts, different world views dominate. One's religion or non-religion is likely to be a principal aspect of one's world view.

We bring our world views to bear on our understanding of practice. To identify the dominant world view we hold in our mind is an important step towards developing reflective practice. We need to critically appraise our world views for their assumptions. The paradigms within one's world view can be analyzed in turn. As Holloway (2006: 17) points out: 'paradigms, scientific, religious, cultural or political, are all power systems, and the thing you ask about a power system is, "Who are the victims here?"'

Three major paradigms have been identified in social research (Neuman, 1999), which are of direct relevance to practice. They are positivism, constructivism or social constructivism, and the critical theory. The general assumptions of these paradigms have been identified by various authors and some of these are summarized below, although they are by no means neatly segregated concepts and categories. The rationale for providing a brief overview about each theoretical cluster is that they influence the practice theories and related skills we look at in later chapters.

Positivism

Positivism understands social reality as based on 'stable, preexisting patterns' (Neuman, 2006: 105). Thus, experiences can be objectively observed and measured, as Morris (2006: 3) emphasizes: 'The positivist worldview assumes that an objective reality exists outside of personal experience that has demonstrable and immutable laws and mechanisms.' A positivist paradigm, therefore, is based on assumptions of cause and effect (ibid.), whereby it is possible, through the identification of various factors, to identify the causes of problems or difficulties and intervene to alter them. In understanding Jahzara's situation, some of the emphasis might be on understanding the cause-and-effect issues— the impacts of poverty, depression, or abuse on individuals and families.

Constructivism

Many human service workers have embraced a constructivist or social constructionist paradigm (Ife, 1997). This paradigm, in contrast to the positivist paradigm, does not consider that there is one objective truth or reality, but only subjective positions. The construction by the individual—that is, the person's subjective reading or that of the family or the community—is what shapes and informs 'reality'. At the extreme end of the **constructivist perspective** is the view that there is no such thing as 'reality' outside of these subjective perceptions. Thus, Jahzara's circumstances would need to be understood from her point of view as much as from the multiple points of views of the other people involved in her situation. From a practice perspective, the constructionist view does present workers with some challenges—for example, Gambrill (1999: 343) strongly criticizes this approach, given that social work is committed to addressing issues of social *in*equality. The relativism of the constructionist approach equalizes all points of view and thus diminishes the capacity for resolving inequalities of economic and political power, for example, or of violence and abuse. Such issues can be collectively articulated, but the issue remains as to how they can be addressed.

Critical Social Science

A critical social science paradigm has a very different agenda from those described above. In many ways, it enables workers to explicitly address the above criticisms of a constructivist approach. A **critical perspective** is based on an explicit ideological or value base and has an agenda for change. It is critical of the status quo, seeing power, conflict, and oppression as dominant concerns to be addressed. A worker operating within a critical paradigm would interpret Jahzara's situation in structural or outer-world terms, looking at the ways in which gender roles and poverty have disempowered her. An agenda would be drawn up with Jahzara, within the context of an equal client–worker relationship (Bishop, 2002). The focus would be on consciousness-raising and on social action throughout the contact (Blankenship, 1998; Freire, 1996; Ife, 1997).

Table 3.1 on the following page, summarizes the key dimensions of each paradigm in relation to some central themes (Neuman, 2006). While these dimensions are presented here in relation to research, they are of direct relevance to practice. Paradigms provide the basis for theories that inform world views, and directly influence practice (Healy, 2005).

Theoretical Knowledge

While we may be able to agree on what is verbalized in a conversation and demonstrated at a non-verbal level, many interpretations can be made of what the meaning or intention of that communication may be. Theoretical perspectives provide a language and a structure for interpreting information. Theoretical perspectives inform what we ask about in the first interview (Sommers-Flanagan and Sommers-Flanagan, 2004: 9), what we talk about with the client, how we interpret what we hear, and how we respond.

> Remember that in Chapter 2 we looked at how meaning and intent is a major filter on what we hear in a conversation.

For ideas to be called a theory or to provide a conceptual framework for therapeutic work, four main dimensions must be present (Nelson-Jones, 2006: 6):

1. a statement of the basic . . . assumptions underlying the theory
2. an explanation of the acquisition of helpful and unhelpful behaviour
3. an explanation of the maintenance of helpful and unhelpful behaviour
4. an explanation of how to help clients change their behaviour and consolidate their gains.

Table 3.1 Three Dominant Paradigms

	Positivism	Interpretive or Social Constructivism	Critical Theory
Reason for research	To discover natural laws so people can predict and control events	To understand and describe meaningful social action	To smash myths and empower people to change society radically
Nature of social reality	Stable pre-existing patterns or order that can be discovered	Fluid definitions of a changing situation created by human interaction	Conflict-filled and governed by hidden underlying structures
Nature of human beings	Self-interested and rational individuals who are shaped by external forces	Social beings who create meaning and who constantly make sense of their worlds	Creative, adaptive people with unrealized potential, trapped by illusion and exploitation
Role of common sense	Clearly distinct from and less valid than science	Powerful everyday theories used by ordinary people	False beliefs that hide power and objective conditions
Theory looks like	A logical, deductive system of interconnected definitions, axioms, and laws	A description of how a group's meaning system is generated and sustained	A critique that reveals true conditions and helps people see the way to a better world
An explanation that is true	Is logically connected to laws and based on facts	Resonates or feels right to those who are being studied	Supplies people with tools needed to change the world
Good evidence	Is based on precise observations that others can repeat	Is embedded in the context of fluid social interactions	Is informed by a theory that unveils illusions
Place for values	Science is value-free, and values have no place except when choosing a topic of study	Values are an integral part of social life; no groups' values are wrong, only different	All science must begin with a value position: some positions are right, some are wrong

Source: Neuman (2006: 105).

The paradigms described above provide a theory or a grand narrative about behaviour and social interactions. They are theories that provide an explanation for human experience and behaviour. Theories also provide specific explanations for why social events occur and provide broad prescriptions or bases for interventions. To illustrate this point, one theory of human experience is that people need to find meaning or a sense of coherence in order to maintain well-being and function optimally. This observation is based on the understanding that from birth we develop cognitive and emotional sets of internal working models and assumptive paradigms. That is, from infancy, we develop ways of making sense of what goes on in our own internal and external worlds and, increasingly, in the worlds of others. A sense of coherence and predictability emerges for most people, through the development of a story of how the world works and how we are positioned within it, which is integral to our mental health and to our capacity to relate to other people and to function effectively in our daily lives. We develop a sense of meaning, order, and security through these stories.

In the above paragraph, a theory of behaviour and experience has been outlined, drawn from attachment and narrative theories. It provides an explanation of a phenomenon—thus satisfying our need for theory—that has come about following the *observation* of the phenomenon by numerous authors. From that brief *description*, an *explanation* can be given as to how human beings might go about building an assumptive world, and a worker can consider how *predictions* and even *interventions* in a situation with a particular client can be undertaken. These five dimensions are identified by Howe (2002) as ways in which a theory is useful for practice.

If we are working with Jahzara as our client, we need to move from the general issues in her situation first outlined to very specific questions such as: Why have these problems occurred? What can be done about them? How should change be brought about and with whom? We will need to make sense of particular dimensions or priorities in her family situation. Theoretical frameworks provide distinctive maps for the priorities in practice and the directions of any intervention.

Theories have different strengths and limitations. They vary in the degree to which they focus on change in the inner worlds of individuals and families or focus on change in the outer worlds that individuals and families occupy. To illustrate, the 'conservation of resources' theory (Hobfoll, Ennis, and Kay, 2000) contributes to our understanding of grief, stress, and trauma experiences. This theory proposes that there are four domains of resources—condition, energy, personal, and time—and that experiences of grief, stress, and trauma emerge when one or more of these resource domains is affected negatively. Thus, resource losses—that is, impoverishment, the threat of income loss, the physical/emotional stress of recent childbirth—could explain Jahzara's distress reaction. This theory provides a strong and useful explanation for why people may be experiencing stress, grief, or trauma. It provides no explanation, however, of the possible trajectories of reactions experienced by an individual. No theory of intervention at an interpersonal level emerges from this, other than that financial resources are the critical need.

One of the challenges students face when they turn from theories of change to actual practice is that theories of change do not necessarily lead to the details of theories of intervention, or to the particular microskills needed to work in alignment with the theory. For example, while anti-oppressive approaches focus on change beyond the individual—a more equitable society—they do not prescribe practice at the micro-level of interaction with another person. The theoretical focus for change is academic and policy-making groups of people and is not explanatory at the interpersonal level. The problem remains that the interpersonal level is where much of the work actually begins and, indeed, most often is done. Theories of relationship and of communication from a structural perspective do not supply a paradigm of practice at this micro-level. Similarly, theories relating to intrapsychic work do not offer models for practice that relate the worker's interaction with the social realities to the structural dimensions of the theoretical paradigm.

Another challenge of theory is that it is often presented as if in practice we function in a 'pure' way, adhering strictly to all the fundamentals of a particular theoretical perspective.

In practice, we tend to work eclectically, relying on a range of knowledge bases at any one time and integrating them into our practice.

A further difficulty is the extent to which what is espoused as the theoretical perspective is consistently practiced by each worker. That is, someone may declare that they are a feminist or a cognitive behavioural practitioner, but how would someone else know that their practice is actually consistent with that perspective? Banks (2006: 121) observes this kind of gap between theory and practice when she highlights that 'the focus in social work generally is on the individual service user or family and therefore inevitably the stress is on personal change, even if the broader societal context is acknowledged'.

An extreme challenge in relation to the use of theories is that they can be contextually inappropriate or wrong. For example, the practice of removing Aboriginal children from their families was based on theories of well-being current at that time. These theories are now considered ethnocentric and racist for having failed to take into account sufficient appreciation for Indigenous ways of living, and the importance of attachment in child and family well-being. Dominant, colonizing theories have been imposed on many other Indigenous populations around the world with similarly devastating impacts on well-being (Smith, 2001).

Having considered some of the limitations of theory, we acknowledge that theories play an important role, nonetheless, in guiding our practice. The ways in which a number of theoretical perspectives explain some important dimensions of human behaviour and experience illustrate their points of compatibility and points of difference. These theoretical perspectives are examined in greater detail and as they may be applied in practice in later chapters in this book. The key elements for comparison are:

- What dimensions of the human person are considered core?
- What should be the focus of change?
- What is the reason for the human service intervention?
- What are the major or dominant skills used by the worker?
- What are the core beliefs about the helping relationship?
- What are the assumptions about the length of relationship?

The following approaches have been chosen as examples of positivist, interpretive, social constructivist, and critical theoretical paradigms and as examples of common theories of practice, theories emphasized in various agencies. They include task-centred and crisis-intervention, psychodynamic, cognitive behavioural, narrative and solution-focused, feminist, and critical approaches to practice.

Task-Centred and Crisis-Intervention Approaches

Task-centred and crisis-intervention approaches do not fit so easily into one dominant paradigm and cannot be described as 'pure' theories. They are, however, important approaches in practice, and these are included here as a demonstration of more practitioner-led and practitioner-developed theoretical frameworks currently in use.

Crisis-intervention theories arose from work with people during the immediate crisis time of particular critical incidents. Lindemann's (1944) study of grief, for example, identifies that typically, a four- to six-week period following major losses or stressors occurs during which people's usual functioning is significantly reduced, requiring particular supports throughout this change in functioning, both emotional and practical. One of the major emphases of crisis intervention (see Chapter 11) is on assisting people to manage their initial extreme emotional responses, and to return to a more balanced cognitive and emotional state (Caplan, 1990; Granot, 1996). Crisis-intervention approaches are often about initially quite directive and/or assertive outreach, supporting people to make decisions and to vent emotion, while over time these reactions resolve.

A study of family members of a patient in the intensive care unit at the Alfred Hospital, for example, showed that family members were experiencing very high levels of post-traumatic stress symptoms (Harms, Rowe, and Suss, 2006). The implications of this finding are profound for the family's capacity to process the information they are receiving from medical staff and to make decisions on behalf of the patient. One of the major approaches of social work in this setting is to help people to become grounded again through tasks shifting them back into cognitive and practical activities that will help to mediate or settle some of their emotional responses. Emotional containment and support are also key considerations. As Trevithick (2005) notes, the only social work theory developed by practitioners is the task-centred approach (Marsh and Doel, 2005), where the methodology is more about the doing than about theorizing behaviour in particular ways.

These two approaches rely on the rapid establishment of empathy and trust with clients during what typically is a short period of intervention (Healy, 2005: 126). They apply to interventions in both the inner and outer worlds, but view the restoration or the introduction of resources in the outer world as major facilitators of change and adaptation. They also are based on strengths perspectives.

In Jahzara's situation, responding to the immediate emotional crisis and the practical resource crisis she faces would be a major focus of interventions. Intervention would also need to be focused on the rights of the children to safety, and on the legislation relating to child protection practices, which would influence what a worker would do in this situation. Specific interventions within these approaches tend to integrate dimensions of the various theoretical perspectives discussed in the following sections (Walsh, 2006).

Psychodynamic Theories

Of all the theoretical dimensions, **psychodynamic theories** place most emphasis on the client–worker relationship and on the communication processes within that relationship. Psychodynamic theories are primarily concerned with the inner worlds of individuals, and how difficulties arise in functioning because of these past and present inner-world preoccupations. Thus, psychodynamic theories are concerned with human drives or motivations in relation to pleasure, power, conflict, and anxiety. The effects of these experiences are thought to develop across the lifespan, through various psychosocial or psychosexual phases. One of the major arguments within psychodynamic theories is that 'psychopathology arises from early childhood experiences' (Sommers-Flanagan and Sommers-Flanagan, 2004: 41). Relating Jahzara's situation to psychodynamic theory, a worker with this understanding would want to know about conscious and unconscious memories of experiences: Jahzara's own past patterns of being parented and how they are being replayed in her adult context, and the fantasies and drives that motivate Jahzara's behaviour or relationship difficulties.

Psychodynamic theories are intensely focused on verbal and non-verbal communications: messages directed consciously and unconsciously to the worker—these processes behind the telling of the story are to be interpreted as much as the story's content. The client's relationship with the worker is seen as an opportunity to work through and experience a 'corrective emotional' relationship or the 'training ground' (Shulman, 1999: 217) with the worker that may repair or address some of the difficulties experienced in previous relationships, primarily those with parents. Underlying this is an argument that the relationship enables the opportunity for the establishment or re-establishment of a secure attachment. That is, the secure base of the relationship with the worker provides a sense of meaning and coherence that can be carried into other contexts. Transference and counter-transference (Gibney, 2003) are an essential purpose of the work undertaken together. Thus, the experience of connection with the worker, or the therapeutic alliance, is considered to be one of the major change agents (Trevithick, 2005).

These psychodynamic concepts of transference and counter-transference are explored in Chapter 12

Cognitive Behavioural Theories

Cognitive and cognitive behavioural theories usually are located within a positivist paradigm. The early theorists (Ellis, 1995; Beck, Freeman, and Davis, 2004) proposed that a person's difficulties emerged in relation to three domains—the way the person thinks, the way the person feels or reacts emotionally, and the way the person acts. **Cognitive behavioural therapy** is based on this understanding: create change in any of these domains and change in the other domains will follow necessarily. This relationship of reciprocal change is represented in Figure 3.1.

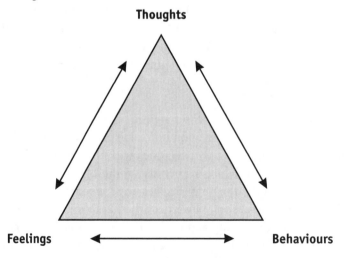

Figure 3.1 **The Reciprocal Links between Thoughts, Feelings, and Behaviours in the Cognitive Behavioural Model**

Source: Harms (2007: 60)

These dimensions are clearly evident in other current interviewing models, such as Egan's problem-management and opportunity-development model (Egan, 2007: 81). He presents these three dimensions as pivotal to what the clients talk about. They talk about:

- their experiences—that is, what happens to them
- their behaviour—that is, what they do or refrain from doing
- their affect—that is, the feelings, emotions, and moods that arise from or are associated with their experiences and both internal and external behaviour.

Others refer to these dimensions of conversation as the 'Think-Feel-Do' framework (Thompson, 2002: xvii). A major criticism of this approach is that many people's difficulties occur within the outer world—for example, Jahzara's poverty or some men's violence towards women—but the therapeutic approach does not address change at these social levels, which affect individuals in society broadly or collectively. Change in the cognitive behavioural model is theorized at the level of each individual's thinking, feeling, and behaviour (Egan, 2007: 7–8).

Cognitive behavioural therapy has tended not to emphasize the client–worker relationship to the same extent as psychotherapeutic approaches, apart from acknowledging the collaboration in which the worker helps the individual to reflect critically on her or his thinking, feeling, and doing.

Narrative and Solution-Focused Theories

As an example of the constructivist paradigm, **narrative theories** place a major emphasis on the way in which an individual constructs and relates the stories of his or her life; and particularly the problem stories. This approach is grounded in the belief that meaning-making, through the formulation of narrative, is integral to well-being because it leads to an integrated inner state: '[T]he establishment of some stability for meaning is an essential foundation to any claim for a meaningful sense of felt subjectivity' (Sharp, 2006: 66).

A particular emphasis on solution-focused or strengths-based narratives is often made, so that the focus is on developing a sense of insight, and control over the narrative. When people experience major adversity, reconstructing a sense of self that is able to influence the environment again is an important process. Thus, unlike psychodynamic and cognitive behavioural perspectives, the self or subjective experience is understood to be a more fluid state of being, rather than constructed across the lifespan through various developmental phases.

Narrative approaches have had wide appeal across a variety of settings and populations. Indigenous communities have used narrative extensively to retell stories of colonization and culture (Smith, 2001; Tamasese, 2000; Wingard, 2001), while Holocaust survivors have used narrative to recount and validate experiences of horrific trauma and torture (Laub and Auerharn, 1993; Reiter, 2000). Bearing witness to a person's experiences of adversity and suffering has been recognized throughout the literature of trauma and grief as a critical process in recovery. It also means that the telling of stories has the power to bring about change at other social levels, such as at program or policy levels.

In Jahzara's situation, narrative work would focus on the ways in which she initially tells her story, and the ways in which it can be co-created to focus more on her strengths and to externalize rather than internalize her problems. The worker is influential in developing alternative narratives that empower Jahzara and her coping capacities.

Feminist Theories

Feminism is a theory located within a critical paradigm. That is, the agenda of feminism is to bring about structural change as a result of women countering the oppression they experience within male-dominated power structures. Feminism focuses its attention beyond the inner world of an individual, arguing that inner worlds are influenced profoundly by the wider social and political context (Dominelli, 2002; Trevithick, 1998).

Like psychodynamic theory, there is no single **feminist theory**; feminists profess a variety of views along a continuum from radical to liberal feminism (Tong, 1998). Within feminism, one of the major variations in these perspectives relates to the extent to which they argue for separatist positionings of women and men. Feminist approaches empower individuals facing adversity to change their circumstances externally, rather than to internalize them as private problems.

Feminist theory grew from critical theory in that it locates oppression and disempowerment within the wider social environment as the major causes of individual difficulty (Ife, 1997; Maidment and Egan, 2004; Pease and Fook, 1999). Critical theory identifies and seeks to challenge multiple sources of oppression—gender, economics, culture, and sex, for example. The primary focus of change is the wider social, structural, and cultural context, rather than the individual. Practice methods range from therapeutic counselling to social action and advocacy strategies.

In feminist analysis, Jahzara's depression might be understood in the context of her structural and social disempowerment (Stoppard, 2000), and its resolution would be anticipated through appropriate social supports and recognition. Similarly, the stressors in parenting might be understood as arising from the privatization of mothering and the unrealistic expectations placed on women to provide care for children and other family members with little social support and acknowledgement.

These theoretical perspectives are summarized in Table 3.2. The major skills associated with these theoretical approaches will be discussed in greater detail in Chapters 11–14.

Factual Knowledge

To work with Jahzara we will need further information to help us understand her circumstances: what she is dealing with and, therefore, how we might respond. Jahzara and her family are coping with many contemporary psychosocial issues. You might identify postpartum (following birth) depression, emotional stress (interior) and duress (imposed by others), impoverishment and financial stress (such as rental arrears), employment uncertainty, poor public housing options for low-income earners, inadequate parenting skills or children with special challenges, the consequences of physical and emotional abuse in at least one of the children, and extreme social disadvantage and disempowerment due to immigrating.

Your knowledge of each of these categories of experience from a broad research perspective is vital. For example, you could draw on recent research into the etiology (cause) of

Table 3.2 Paradigms and Theoretical Perspectives Informing Practice

	Paradigm				
	Positivist	Positivist	Solution-Focused	Critical	Social Constructivist
	Theoretical Perspective				
	Psychodynamic	Cognitive behavioural	Task-centred and crisis intervention	Feminist and critical	Narrative and solution-focused
Dimension of human person considered locus of change	Bringing unconscious thoughts, behaviours under conscious thought and control	Primarily establishing healthy thought patterns, although also feelings and behaviours	Emotional state; restoration of emotional control	Personal functioning and sociopolitical context	Stories we live by, particularly stories that disempower and oppress
Focus of change	Thoughts, desires, impulses: brought from unconscious to conscious	Established patterns of thoughts challenged to produce healthier ways of thinking about self	The immediate tasks associated with the problem as well as the emotional response	Gender and power relations; patriarchal social structures that oppress women and other minority groups	Stories that are empowering and strengths-based, often externalizing the problem
Goal of intervention	Interpretation on behalf of therapist and self-reflection and insight on behalf of client; anxiety reduction	Behavioural and cognitive change	Return to functioning to be able to begin to cope and deal practically with crisis	Externalizing of gender and power problems rather than internalizing	Narrative stories of self and circumstances that lead to healthy, strengths-based ways of living
Dominant skills	Listening, interpreting relationship	Showing the client how thoughts, feelings, and behaviours are connected; challenging patterns of thinking and behaving	Education; resourcing; emotional release	Listening to the story; empowering; externalizing the issue as a political rather than a personal issue; advocacy and social change	Acknowledging problem stories; externalizing the problem; deconstructing negative stories; reconstructing positive ones; living out (enacting) the new stories
Beliefs about helping relationship	Previously seen as 'blank screen'; now intersubjective	Listening for faulty, unhelpful beliefs; not much emphasis on relationship as an essential process	Initially directive and assertive; gradually shifting responsibility to client after initial crisis	Equal, empowering relationship; explicit focus on gender relations and power in client–worker relationship	Helps in constructing a story and in listening to gaps/silences

Source: Harms (2007: 63)

postpartum depression (Pope, 2000). An intervention will vary depending on whether you understand postpartum depression to be a mental illness—in which case you might encourage contact with a general practitioner as a first step—or an outcome of the stress, exhaustion, and loneliness of becoming a mother—in Jahzara's case, for the fourth time. If the latter, you might link her with a mother's group for peer support. Or you might understand her depression to be related to her extreme financial stress, and connect her with a financial counsellor and emergency relief resources.

The information you need comes in many forms—in the form of statistical data, of an evaluation or of stories provided by individuals or families. You need a foundational base of factual knowledge about the phenomena to which you are responding. Issues of child abuse and neglect, disability and chronic illness, poverty, mental and physical illness, and substance use and abuse are issues with which workers need to be familiar. Research knowledge helps you to understand the context in which the lived experience of one person is taking place and the possible effects on that person and on others of such conditions or experiences.

Some disciplines refer to this broad knowledge as a 'social epidemiological' approach, whereby the medical terminology of epidemiology is adapted to understanding social issues. Epidemiology refers to 'the study of how often and for what reasons a health problem occurs in specific groups of people' (Butchart and Kahane, 2006: 17). In an epidemiological approach, issues of etiology (cause), incidence and prevalence, and the effects and/or outcomes (on the individuals both directly and indirectly affected) are taken into account.

Another important dimension of work with Jahzara is a consideration of the broader legal context of practice (Swain, 2002), which influences or controls the decisions we make in practice. These facts include the legislative and political contexts in which you will function—for example, the child protection legislation in Victoria has recently undergone a radical review, meaning that the practice context for working with Jahzara has similarly changed radically.

Refer to the resources at the end of this chapter for the link to the Campbell Collaboration site and others.

Factual knowledge about interventions also is essential. Many outcome studies are available that have looked at what works and what does not work in therapeutic settings (Fonagy, 1999; Hubble, Duncan, and Miller, 1999; Roth and Fonagy, 2005). Online resources such as the Cochrane Collaboration, the Campbell Collaboration, and others provide data about the known efficacy of various interventions.

Randomized controlled trials have some place in human service work, but these cannot be the only ways in which human behaviour, rights, and needs are understood. Many people argue strongly that in human service work it is neither possible nor desirable to apply the rigour of laboratory science because the uniqueness of each person and circumstance must be considered and it is not possible to research the outcomes of each unique intervention (see Duncan and Miller, 2005). Therefore, in the absence of statistical and observational bases for much human service work, some have called for use of the best available evidence (Kessler, Gira, and Poertner, 2005: 247) and others refer to evidence-informed practice (Evans and Benefield, 2001).

You will face all kinds of contradictions, tensions, and complexities in your daily practice. Due to the current risk management environment, never before within the literature, research, and organizations has there been such a push to have practice that adheres to certain standards (Webb, 2006). The emphasis is on workers having a strong, established evidence base for the work undertaken, and clear, accountable boundaries around time and practice with people. In short, a paradigm of positivism governs much practice. On the other hand, never before has there been such an extensive 'evidence base' for the importance and influence of critical reflective practice; an emphasis on practice wisdom; an appreciation for the uniqueness of individual experience and the importance of cultural sensitivity and spirituality; and an emphasis on an authentic, open relationship between client and worker. That is, constructivism also governs much practice.

See Chapter 1 for websites for the Canadian Association of Social Workers, Canadian Psychological Association, and Canadian Counselling Association, where practice standards are available.

Jahzara's circumstances, and the possible courses of action in working with her and her family, highlight how complex human service work is. You are being called on to mediate the unique circumstances of each person, family, or community with your knowledge and skill as a worker.

Client Perspectives

The question as to what works for whom and why in human service work is only one part of the practice. Increasingly, client perspectives are being incorporated into solutions. What would Jahzara want from her human service worker and intervention? It is striking that this perspective is often ignored both by researchers and by organizations.

A research base is emerging in relation to what clients perceive to be of most benefit to them. These studies suggest that the most important factors in interventions are the client–worker relationship or alliance (Hubble, Duncan, and Miller, 1999; Lambert, 2005) rather than specific techniques or theories. This factor is called the 'common factors approach' (Hubble, Duncan, and Miller, 1999: 31), which recognizes that, for clients in psychotherapy, change could be attributed to the following:

- 40 per cent of change arose from extra-therapeutic change
- 30 per cent arose from the therapeutic relationship
- 15 per cent arose from expectancy (placebo effects)
- 15 per cent arose from the techniques used.

As workers, we need to keep in mind the research that suggests lay interventions are just as effective as professional ones or therapeutic ones.

Clients have identified other factors in the relationship in mandated situations (Ribner and Knei-Paz, 2002):

- feelings of closeness
- a working style that creates an enabling atmosphere and an equal stance
- working together on issues

- flexibility in contact—accessibility
- keeping in touch.

Another small-scale study in the field of child welfare (de Boer and Coady, 2007: 35) focused on matched client and worker perspectives and identified similar qualities. These qualities came under two major themes of (1) a soft, mindful, and judicious use of power; and (2) a humanistic attitude and style that stretches traditional professional ways of being.

Focus on Practice

Attitudes and Actions That Build Good Relationships with Clients

A soft, mindful, and judicious use of power:

- being aware of one's power and of the client's fear, defensiveness, and anger as normal
- responding to client negativity with understanding and support instead of counter-hostility and coercion
- conveying a respectful and non-judgemental attitude
- providing clear and honest explanations about reasons for involvement
- addressing fears of child removal and allaying unrealistic fears
- not assuming the veracity of intake, referral, or file information
- listening to and empathizing with the client's story
- pointing out strengths and conveying respect
- constantly clarifying information to ensure mutual understanding
- exploring and discussing concerns before jumping to conclusions
- responding in a supportive manner to new disclosures, relapses, and new problems
- following through on one's responsibilities and promises.

A humanistic attitude and style that stretches traditional professional ways of being:

- using an honest and direct, person-to-person, down-to-earth manner (versus donning the professional mask)
- engaging in small talk to establish comfort and rapport; getting to know the client as a whole person—in social and life-history contexts
- seeing and relating to the client as a person with understandable problems
- recognizing and valuing the client's strengths and successes in coping
- being realistic about goals and patient about progress
- having a genuinely hopeful and optimistic outlook on possibilities for change
- using judicious self-disclosure towards developing personal connection
- being real in terms of feeling the client's pain and displaying emotions
- going the extra mile in fulfilling mandated responsibilities, and stretching professional mandates and boundaries.

Practice Knowledge or Wisdom

A further source of knowledge is the unique store of subjective experience that develops from practice as a worker. Over time, and through various encounters, we come to understand situations through the lens of experience. We can draw on that experience to think about what we did then and what happened as a result, and change our current behaviour as a consequence. This knowledge is referred to as **practice wisdom** (Scott, 1990). As Kessler, Gira, and Poertner (2005: 245) observe: 'Practitioners are expected to be pragmatic, self-reflective, and to learn from their work with clients. The result is practice wisdom, or experientially and inductively derived knowledge.'

Practice wisdom has been defined as 'the accumulation of information, assumptions, ideologies, and judgements that have seemed practically useful in fulfilling the expectations of the job (De Roos, 1990, cited in Osmond, 2005: 891). An understanding of practice wisdom is critical because of the widespread recognition that workers draw more explicitly on their practice wisdom, as well as values and legal parameters, than on theory or research (Chui and Wilson, 2006: 3). Gambrill (1999: 348), however, cautions against the assumption that practice wisdom is necessarily a good thing: 'Experience does not necessarily result in improved performance. In fact, it may have the opposite effect. Experience does not offer systematic data about what works with what clients and what problems.' The crucial distinction to make is between practice wisdom, as distinct from practice experience. One of the challenges in beginning practice is, of course, that one has relatively little practice base from which to draw. At first, every encounter is a major learning experience.

> The development of practice wisdom is explored further in Chapter 4.

How do we bring together these various knowledge bases and integrate them into a perspective or approach for practice? One of the ways is to think about a multi-dimensional approach (Harms, 2005; Hutchison, 2003), which has emerged from an ecological or ecosystemic perspective (Germain and Bloom, 1999).

A Multi-dimensional Approach

Each of the knowledge sources described so far provides a useful guide for practice. The challenge is to be able to access any of them in a coherent way during practice with clients. The difficulty with many of the more overarching practice approaches is that they position problem management entirely with the individual client. Human service workers intersect both the interface of individual problem management and the environmental origins or contributors to these problems. Social work and the human services, therefore, take the additional step of listening to, assessing, and effecting change in outer-world issues, not just the inner-world dimensions of the client's problems. For this reason, human service work and social work have drawn on ecological (Bronfenbrenner, 1979; Germain, 1991) or multi-dimensional understandings of the person in his or her environment.

A multi-dimensional approach incorporates an understanding of the inner- and outer-world dimensions of a person (Harms, 2005; Hutchison, 2003). Some key themes of a multi-dimensional approach are described by Harms (2005).

Focus on Practice

A Multi-dimensional Approach

Theme 1: An individual's inner world is multi-dimensional.

Each person can be thought of as having unique inner-world dimensions. Broadly speaking, these dimensions are biological, psychological, and spiritual.

Theme 2: The outer world or context in which individuals live is multi-dimensional.

Each of these inner-world dimensions of a person in turn influences, and is influenced by, the dimensions of the outer world—the physical, social, structural, and cultural contexts that shape daily experience.

Theme 3: Time is multi-dimensional.

Five dimensions of time—biological, biographical, historical/social, cyclical, and future—influence human behaviour and experience.

Theme 4: Human experience is multi-dimensional.

Human experience is a combination of an individual's unique developmental trajectory and unique life events. An understanding of both the more normative tasks of development and the non-normative tasks provides a more holistic understanding of a person's adaptive capacities and resources.

Theme 5: Adaptation is multi-dimensional.

Just as the causes of adversity are multi-dimensional, so, too, are the consequences—an understanding of the consequences of adversity for individuals, families, and communities needs to incorporate the possibilities of adaptation and maladaptation. This involves understanding notions of risk and protective factors, and notions of vulnerability and resilience. It also involves acknowledging who is making the assessment of adaptation.

Theme 6: Attempts to theorize human development and adaptation should be multi-dimensional.

Human experience, behaviour, and adaptation all can be understood from multiple theoretical viewpoints—theories of the inner world, theories of the outer world, and theories that attempt to bridge the two. Rather than suggesting that human service professionals do not have a firm theoretical base from which to work, a multi-dimensional approach acknowledges that there are many ways of understanding human experience. The task is to discern how we reach understandings and to work towards as good a fit as possible between the identified issues and the possible human service responses.

Theme 7: Human service responses must be multi-dimensional.

Responses by human service professionals must be multi-dimensional, including practices, programs, and policies that incorporate prevention, intervention, and post-intervention strategies.

The relationships between various dimensions are illustrated in Figure 3.2, showing the reciprocal nature of the interactions between them. By focusing on the relationships between them, both the intangible (relationship-centred interactions) and the tangible (entity-centred person and environment targets, such as poverty or violence) can be addressed (Harms, 2005; Ramsay, 2003).

Essential in the assessment and listening process are, first, the inner-world dimensions—the biological, psychological (thoughts and feelings), and spiritual dimensions. In Jahzara's situation, this could mean asking the following questions:

1. What biological dimensions are influencing the current situation?
2. What psychological dimensions are important—feelings, thoughts, other?
3. What is the spiritual dimension in this person's life?

Each of us has a subjective experience of these inner-world dimensions. That is, you are the only one who knows what it is like to be you, to feel and experience your world.

Second, the outer-world dimensions—the relational, social, structural, and cultural dimensions—require consideration. The unique inner identity that each one forms is

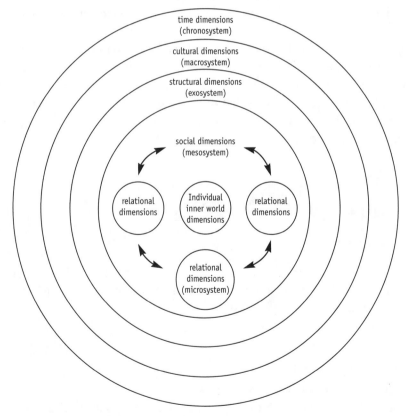

Figure 3.2 **A Multi-dimensional Approach**

Source: Harms (2005: 9).

comprised of experience both past and present including contexts, past and present. Experience shapes one's expectations of the future. One's social and cultural identity is part of one's psychological identity, which needs to be understood when planning for the future. In Jahzara's situation, this could mean asking:

1.   What relationships is the person involved in and what is the influence of these relationships?
2.   How do these relationships interact as a social network, if at all?
3.   What are the wider structural influences on a person's experience?

Thompson (2003b) and others (e.g., Mullaly, 2002) use the 'PCS' model—*personal, cultural,* and *structural*—to take into consideration all dimensions of any given situation. However, one of the limitations of the PCS model is its tendency to underemphasize the relational and social dimensions of any given situation. Giving unique character to Jahzara's experiences are individual, family, and group forces shaping identity (Miller, Donner, and Fraser, 2004). That is, the unique influences of gender, class, culture, and sexual orientation are understood to influence identity, and to influence the experience of problems of social identity. The multi-dimensional assessment and intervention process is mirrored in the Canadian Association of Social Workers' *Guidelines for Ethical Practice* (2005), reproduced in the box below.

The other dimension that has more recently been included in understanding a client's situation is the dimension of the worker. The client's story is constructed in the context of the worker's story—what the worker brings to the relationship. When you tell a story, your audience influences how you tell it—what you tell and what you emphasize or omit in that co-creation. Thus, your inner- and outer-world dimensions are important considerations in any client–worker interaction.

Focus on Practice

Assessment and Intervention

The social work assessment and the intervention taken are appropriate to the client's situation, in keeping with ethical and legislative requirements and directed towards appropriate outcomes reached in agreement with the client wherever possible.

Indicators

1.0 Ethical Responsibilities to Clients

1.2 Demonstrate Cultural Awareness and Sensitivity

1.2.1 Social workers strive to understand culture and its function in human behaviour and society, recognizing the strengths that exist in all cultures.

1.2.2 Social workers acknowledge the diversity within and among individuals, communities, and cultures.

1.2.3 Social workers acknowledge and respect the impact that their own heritage, values, beliefs, and preferences can have on their practice and on clients whose background and values may be different from their own.

1.2.4 Social workers seek a working knowledge and understanding of clients' racial and cultural affiliations, identities, values, beliefs, and customs.

1.2.5 Where possible, social workers provide or secure social work services in the language chosen by the client. If using an interpreter, when possible, social workers preferentially secure an independent and qualified professional interpreter.

1.3 Promote Client Self-Determination and Informed Consent

1.3.1 Social workers promote the self-determination and autonomy of clients, actively encouraging them to make informed decisions on their own behalf.

1.3.2 Social workers evaluate a client's capacity to give informed consent as early in the relationship as possible.

1.3.3 Social workers who have children as clients determine the child's capacity to consent and explain to the child (where appropriate), and to the child's parents/guardians (where appropriate), the nature of the social worker's relationship to the child and others involved in the child's care (see section 1.5.5 regarding confidentiality).

1.3.4 Social workers, at the earliest opportunity, discuss with clients their rights and responsibilities and provide them with honest and accurate information regarding the following:

- the nature of the social work service being offered;
- the recording of information and who will have access to such information;
- the purpose, nature, extent, and known implications of the options open to them;
- the potential risks and benefits of proposed social work interventions;
- their right to obtain a second opinion or to refuse or cease service (recognizing the limitations that apply when working with involuntary clients);
- the client's right to view professional records and to seek avenues of complaint; and
- the limitations on professional confidentiality (see section 1.5 regarding confidentiality).

Chapter Summary

In this chapter, we have explored the ways in which paradigms, theories, factual knowledge, and practice wisdom integrate to form a coherent practice base. We looked at three broad paradigms before looking at the various forms of theoretical and factual knowledge required for practice. We then considered a multi-dimensional approach as one way in which these many aspects of your client's world and your own could be more comprehensively understood.

Questions for Analysis

1. What have you learned about:
   - the importance of understanding paradigms or world views that inform practice?
   - the knowledge bases of practice?
   - the importance of practice wisdom?
   - the strengths and limitations of the theoretical approaches that were presented?

2. Within which paradigm would you locate yourself as a practitioner?

3. What is it about this paradigm that attracts you to it?

4. Which of the five theoretical approaches appeals to you most and why?

Recommended Readings

Boone, M., B. Minore, M. Katt, and P. Kinch. 1997. 'Strength through sharing: Interdisciplinary teamwork in providing social and health services to northern native communities', in K. Brownlee, R. Delaney, and J. Graham, eds, *Strategies for Northern Social Work Practice*. Thunder Bay, Ont.: Lakehead University Press, 45–59.

Faulkner, K., and T. Faulkner. 1997. 'Managing multiple relationships in rural communities: Neutrality and boundary violations', *Clinical Psychology: Science and Practice* 4, 3: 225–34.

Fook, J. 2002. *Social Work: Critical Theory and Practice*. Thousand Oaks, Calif.: Sage.

Germain, C., and M. Bloom. 1999. *Human Behavior in the Social Environment: An Ecological View*. New York: Columbia University Press.

Harms, L. 2005. *Understanding Human Development: A Multidimensional Approach*. South Melbourne: Oxford University Press.

Healy, K. 2005. *Social Work Theories in Context: Creating Frameworks for Practice*. Basingstoke: Palgrave Macmillan.

Internet Resources

Campbell Collaboration
www.campbellcollaboration.org

Canadian Association of Social Workers (CASW) Code of Ethics
www.casw-acts.ca

Canadian Centre for Policy Alternatives
www.policyalternatives.ca

Institute of Health Services and Policy Research
www.acronymfinder.com/Institute-of-Health-Services-and-Policy-Research-(Canada)-(IHSPR).html

National Health and Medical Research Council (Australia)
www.nhmrc.gov.au

Statistics Canada
www.statcan.gc.ca

Part Two Basic Skills: Forming the Relationship

In this second part of the book, we focus on understanding yourself in the role of worker, your context, and the very specific microskills used in communication and interviewing processes.

Chapter 4 explores why we need to reflect critically on our own communication styles and experiences. In human service work, the worker is the essential 'tool' in the process. Thus, your insightful awareness of your 'use of self' and your identification of the purpose and context of your work with individuals, families, or communities are of paramount importance.

Chapter 5 focuses on the essential preparatory work you do before entering into the client relationship and on the differences between your personal self-care and on your professional self-care and development. Supervision, debriefing, and critical self-reflection are introduced as important maintenance strategies for meeting the ongoing challenges of human service work. We approach this examination of self as part of your thinking about *forming* the relationship, rather than considering it in the contexts of problems that could develop later in the client relationship. This precaution is because both personal self-care and professional self-care are necessary parts of your practice that should be part of your skill development from the outset—not an afterthought when you have already experienced burnout or have come to some harm.

Chapter 6 establishes skills for the early stage of forming the relationship with a client. We examine the importance of good engagement skills and rapport-building when beginning work with clients. We also consider issues of confidentiality and your use of self-disclosure as important influences on this formation stage.

Part One—Framing the Relationship

- the purpose of human service work
- your value base, professional ethics, and regulatory guidelines in Canada
- your theoretical and factual knowledge.

Part Two—Forming the Relationship

- your use of self
- your organizational context
- your ongoing support and professional development needs
- meeting the people involved
- opening the communication
- active listening and working with silence
- listening empathically
- using self-disclosure.

4 | Preparing for Practice

Learning Goals

- Understand why the 'use of self' is an important concept.
- Understand the concept of empathy.
- Review the dimensions of your workplace that influence practice.
- Analyze how your practice links with your organizational context.

Why the 'Use of Self' Is an Important Concept for Workers

In earlier chapters we have looked at values and theoretical and factual knowledge bases as key determinants of your practice. This chapter focuses on another critical factor: you. This is an essential difference compared with many other jobs where the worker may be one important part of the matrix, but other technical or mechanical interventions are also involved. The ways you apply yourself in your practice will fundamentally affect what happens.

A discriminating use of self is central to all relationships. Think of how you interact differently with each of your friends. Compare how you interact with your friends as distinct from someone you have just met. You might be wary and self-censoring with the unfamiliar person until you have established a stronger connection. This is 'use of self' in action.

Reflect on the various interactions in your past that have been with individuals unfamiliar to you, such as speaking with a new doctor, being introduced to a new supervisor or instructor, or meeting a friend of a friend. What are your first thoughts or reactions to the new person? Do potential power differences shape your response? Reflect on your internal process in becoming more open in new relationships and what steps occur to increase your comfort level. Is there social diversity or cultural implications in the new relationship that may impact language communication or mutual understanding of what is being communicated?

Another way of speaking about 'use of self' is how you apply your **social intelligence** and **emotional intelligence** in relationships with others (Goleman, 2005, 2006). We will also expand this paradigm to think about your spiritual and physical use of self. Egan and Schroeder (2009: 11) suggest that perhaps 'social-emotional intelligence' is a better term. Goleman observes that this term generates a sense of maturity and defines the entire concept as a 'maturity package'. Egan and Schroeder (2009: 13–14) define maturity—social-emotional intelligence—as containing the following key concepts:

1. *Mature people are self-managers. They know themselves, are in control of themselves, and get things done.* In summary, self-managers are noted as being aware (self-awareness) of their strengths and limitations, aware of their emotional expressions, and having an awareness of self-worth. Self-managers possess self-control through demonstrating honesty, integrity, and decency. Self-control includes keeping impulses in check and managing stress levels in a constructive manner. It also includes being open to new information and ways of doing things and the ability to take responsibility for personal actions. Concluding, self-managers have a bias towards action. They have goals, are assertive not aggressive, strive for excellence rather then mediocrity, develop opportunities, and overcome obstacles.
2. *Mature people handle relationships well. They know how to move creatively beyond themselves.* In summary, mature people understand empathy, communication, interpersonal relationships, and the wider world. They are aware of people's feelings, listen and communicate clearly, anticipate concerns, are able to establish solid working relationships, have a sense of the world in which they live and a sense of social responsibility.

Given that good relationships are core to effective practice, we need to think about what social rules come into play. Social rules exist in all communication interactions, varying according to the context in which we are functioning. As Adams, Dominelli, and Payne (2005: 15) emphasize, the assumption behind much of the discussion about practice is that social workers and other human service workers:

> must form good relationships with service users for productive work to be done. This is fine as long as we recognize that the most productive social work relationship may not have much in common with other relationships such as those with work colleagues, friends and family. In these, the priority may be to maintain good relationships, and, perhaps, intimacy.

In a professional relationship, your **purpose**, boundaries, and behaviour are very different from your personal relationships. The shift to a sense of a professional use of self can be challenging. Furthermore, it is a contentious issue within the human service field. For many students, it feels like giving up important personal traits to become someone else. However, loss of self-identity is not at all the aim of adopting a professional use of self. As Shulman (1999: 26) notes:

when workers or students ask me, 'Should I be professional or should I be my-self?', I reply that the dualism implied in the question does not exist. They must be themselves if they are going to be professional.

Integrating your personal and professional skills is what becoming a worker is about. Decisions emerge on a daily basis as to how you will interact. As Shulman notes, some presentations of the ideal worker are as 'an objective, clinical, detached, and knowledge-able professional' (ibid., 161), while others emphasize the qualities of closeness, flexibility, and keeping in touch (Ribner and Knei-Paz, 2002). Others see the ideal worker as adjust-ing their behaviour along a continuum of qualities, depending on the circumstances (Green, Gregory, and Mason, 2006).

The notion of the 'use of self 'emphasizes a decision-making process—choices about conduct, about priorities, and about responses. The term 'use of self' can therefore refer to the direct use of our own personal 'material' in terms of feelings, views, and experiences, as the content in the conversation. Or it can refer to our more global understanding of how we are central in the client–worker conversation and can make conscious decisions as to how to act in each context. The 'use of self' concept acknowledges that the worker is a critical influence in both the process and content of any interaction. We make choices about how we will be in this particular interaction with this particular person at this par-ticular time. We make the shifts in our interactions and communication skills as a result.

Focus on Practice

An Example of Learning to Use 'Self' Differently

In the early weeks of communication skills classes, students often express feeling overwhelmed by the client's story. How do you listen to it and remember all the details? What do you do to make some sense of it? How do I form the right question? What do I do with silence?

The worker may also have 'solved' the situation he or she is hearing about, as if in a role-play situ-ation, three to five minutes into the discussion. Engaging with the person in a role-play to 'solve' the situation short-circuits the deeper engaging with the person to listen to more of the story. For some students, this hasty response stems partly from feeling uncomfortable with managing silence, and the student's internal focus on what to ask next, instead of realizing questions arise through listening to the client's story. Class exercises provide an opportunity to move towards becoming a listener rather than a solver. Finding solutions *together* is a collaborative work and the goal of the intervention.

How you relate to someone varies. Like personal relationships, we have expectations and experiences of interactions in the professional context. Relationships are not static or passive encounters, however. Your use of self changes over time. It may be about getting to know a person and moving into a more established, trusting way of relating. As a relation-ship develops, different strategies are used to continue the work of change and support.

Some authors emphasize the use of self as more important in the later phases of work than earlier on. For example, Hepworth, Rooney, and Larsen (2002: 43) state: 'As helping relationships become strong during the implementation and goal attainment phase, social workers increasingly use themselves as tools to facilitate growth and accomplishment.' Good engagement, however, in an initial encounter, relies also on a conscious and active use of self as much as in later interactions.

What we are doing here, therefore, is not only thinking about the client's world from a multi-dimensional perspective. Your use of self can be thought about as a biopsychosocial-spiritual process. In this sense, you reflect on your practice, taking into account all these dimensions—how you use yourself psychologically or emotionally, socially, spiritually, and physically in an encounter. You apply yourself differently, according to the purpose of the communication. Each of these dimensions is now briefly considered.

Your Emotional Use of Self

In Chapter 12, we explore the skills of challenging. In these instances, your engagement needs to be high so that you can present other ways of thinking or behaving within the context of a supportive relationship.

What are the differences between the client's and the worker's emotional reactions to the circumstances and what should be the differences? How does your emotional self engage in the work you are doing? Consider the following example. In one of my hospital student placement experiences, another student on placement and her supervisor witnessed the severe physical wounds of a patient's very recent surgery. The student screamed when she saw the wounds, not having witnessed anything like them before. It was her natural reaction to what she saw.

The student's initial reaction was an authentic human reaction to the patient's injury. The injury, however, was not the focus of her intervention. The client was the focus of the intervention and her reaction was certainly not helpful to that person in this situation. Instead, she reinforced the patient's own horror and distress over his physical predicament.

This example is, perhaps, extreme; but it highlights the dilemma as to how we emotionally respond in interactions, particularly when we have an overwhelmingly strong response. Not until we are faced with a very stressful situation do we realize what our authentic reaction will be. While Hepworth, Rooney, and Larsen (2002: 43) state that 'relating spontaneously and appropriately disclosing one's feelings, views, and experiences provide for clients an encounter with an open and authentic human being', where the boundaries lie in practice around an *appropriate* and authentic response is not always clear. Learning to manage any immediate responses and yet to remain client-focused is a critical component in your professional development. This kind of self-control is not about being distant or unauthentic; it is about remaining focused on the client's experience rather than your own. It is also important to be aware that how the practitioner expresses emotion may impact the client. Will your reaction create a situation in which the client becomes concerned for you as the practitioner; thus creating an inability for the client to fully express what she or he is experiencing?

In the next chapter, we will look at the notion of purpose in detail.

Emotional engagement is an important aspect of building rapport. A client and a worker, Christine Simpson and John Merrick, respectively, shared their story in a newspaper's 'Two of Us' column (Stansfield, 2006: 16). Christine, whose daughter had been murdered, said of her work with grief counsellor John, 'I know there are all these theories about professionals not getting emotionally involved with their clients, but I ask, how can you truly help if you're not emotionally connected?' She then said, 'He never tried to push me in any particular direction; he just walked with me wherever I was going, for as long as I needed him. His support is one of the reasons I am still here today.'

The notion of 'walking with' captures the purpose of **empathy**. Empathy refers to the 'power of mentally identifying oneself with (and so fully comprehending) a person or object of contemplation' (Brown, 1993: 808). Empathy is an active skill, and is about 'entering imaginatively into the inner life of someone else' (Kadushin, 1972: 52). This imaginative engagement is not about a strictly psychological process. As Kadushin continues, empathic 'responses have an "I am with you" quality, fitting in with the client's meaning and mood.'

A grieving mother talks from a consumer perspective about what kind of understanding she wants from those around her (Wolterstorff, 1987, cited in Elkhuizen, Kelleher, Gibson, and Attoe, 2006: 281–2):

> What I need to hear from you is that you recognize how painful it is. I need to hear from you that you are with me in my desperation. To comfort me, you have to come close. Come sit beside me on my mourning bench.

Empathy has many dimensions. It can be seen as a skill, a value, or even as an outcome of an encounter. It is considered by many to be the 'glue' of client–worker relationships: the quality that enables advanced insight in hearing the story behind the story and in sharing social empathy.

The capacity for empathy is a skill of 'affect regulation' (Schore, 1994), which means that we mirror a positive attunement to the emotional experience of the client (Koprowska, 2005). Empathy is a trait associated with a secure attachment style (Bowlby, 1984). The argument is that if we have the capacity to monitor our own emotional reactions, and to be secure in our sense of who we are, we are more able to see others where they are at and to appreciate their positions (Schore, 2005; Bandura et al., 2003). This aspect of work is a process of 'goal corrected empathic attunement' (Koprowska, 2005: 48).

Empathy can be seen, therefore, as an outcome of the genuineness, warmth, and unconditional positive regard a worker experiences with the client (Koprowska, 2005). More than this, empathy is the sympathetic connection within a relationship, rather than mere reflecting of feeling: '"Reflection of feeling" can be taught as a cognitive skill . . . Genuine sensitive empathy, with all its intensity and personal involvement, cannot be so taught' (Rogers, 1987: 39). Brink (1987: 33) interprets Rogers's concepts of empathy as a:

> complex cluster of *abilities* (keen awareness and sensitivity), *attitudes* (non-judgemental, open, respectful, flexible, confident, subtle, gentle, caring, willing to articulate the not-yet-spoken, and to be wrong) as well as *skill* in communicating.

Empathy also is understanding 'what it meant for a human being to have fallen into that condition rather than to what it felt like' (Gaita, 1999: xix). This meaning emphasizes that empathy recognizes the worth and dignity of a human despite his or her being in a particular predicament.

Empathy can be conveyed through an attentive presence and attunement with the client. The client needs to hear that you have listening fully to the situation—your empathy must be conveyed verbally as well as non-verbally. This kind of listening is what Egan (2007: 102) refers to as **empathic highlights**. The 'formula' for this active response is:

Worker: You feel . . . [insert emotion] because . . . [insert event, behaviour or condition].

Using the formula, an empathic statement may be:

Worker: You feel confused because what you thought was going on actually turned out to be quite different.

Or:

You feel overwhelmed because no one told you how to prepare for work in a small, remote northern community.

Remember the discussion of respect and authenticity in Chapter 2.

This use of paraphrasing to convey empathy is discussed further in Chapter 8.

A lot of 'bad press' for workers comes from the formulaic use of these statements. We rarely use such formulaic statements in practice. What the formula helps us to do is to think objectively, which is different from how we chat with friends. Whereas with friends we are likely to agree or join with them in some way, this formula keeps us focused on a progressive or directed way of listening and responding to the client. A purpose is maintained while listening to the thoughts, feelings, and behaviours of the client, and while thinking of the connections between these personal factors and the structural and cultural environment of the client. 'Advanced empathy' (Egan, 2007) refers to the skill of being able to hear and convey the underlying or unspoken meanings of a client's story. Karen offers an example from one of her classes, in which the issue of empathy became a focus.

Focus on Practice

What Does the Client Want You to Hear?

If students are required to present and re-present 'real but not current' issues for discussion in a classroom, counselling skills can be developed for emergency situations before such crises are faced during professional work. The opportunity afforded by the 'client' experiencing varieties of styles of questioning, and in giving feedback, can be very informative. One such student had witnessed an injured, possibly stabbed, person while waiting at a bus stop. Her description of the situation provided a classroom scenario that encompassed a range of elements and strong emotions:

- shock at the unexpected and traumatic event
- fear in not knowing what had happened or of the whereabouts of a perpetrator

- anger and frustration about the lack of consideration by the many bystanders
- guilt at not being able to treat the injured person
- worry that her being immobilized in some ways by the event would happen in an even more serious situation at some other time
- fear of accountability around her becoming involved or assisting with the situation
- self-doubt, questioning if she had enough skill to know how to be helpful and not injurious
- feelings of distress around the need to know what she should have done and how.

A number of the student counsellors concentrated on the traumatic event and became engrossed in the detail of the event. The student whose impact was greatest made a point of listening to the meaning of the issue for the 'client', recognizing her sense of helplessness and guilt over her role in the situation. Furthermore, by exploring this situation in detail, the other students were able to challenge the client's view (a blind spot) that she had been completely ineffectual by drawing out more of her story that included other actions she had taken, which included calling an ambulance and staying with the injured person to reassure him until help arrived. In fact, she had been extremely helpful. Subsequent feedback from the student revealed her frustration at the efforts by some to explore the sensational details, and how valuable it had been when the worker listened to the part that mattered most to her. Of course, it should be noted that for some others the 'sensational details' would be the data they would need to have in order to assess what their own reactions would be in a similar situation; the details they would have noticed in her position would have influenced their awareness and decision-making. Also, men and women assess their environment and the details in it differently, which would be a further reason why some of the males in the class would seek different sorts of details from the information sought by females. Cultural (e.g., rural versus urban cultures) values come into play as well.

Empathy is about striking the right balance of focus between the worker and client. As the above example shows, focusing too much on the detail in this instance led the 'client' to feel her experience had not been understood. Similarly, focusing too sympathetically hijacks the client's need to understand his/her emotions and to find emotional release, and can create distance.

Sympathy sometimes is contrasted with empathy. Egan (2007: 118) states: 'Sympathy denotes agreement, whereas empathy denotes understanding.' Sympathy is a joining with or colluding with the client, as distinct from being able to understand their world and feelings without necessarily agreeing, condoning, or participating in that world. Thus, Egan suggests: 'An expression of sympathy has much more in common with pity, compassion, commiseration, and condolence than with empathic understanding. Although these are fully human traits, they are not particularly useful in counselling' (ibid.). Two arguments for not using sympathy are that, first, your response could be misplaced and therefore unhelpful. For example:

Client: I've just left my partner of five years.
Worker: I'm so sorry to hear that.
Client: Oh, no, no, it's such a good thing. It's not that I'm worried about.

In this instance, the sympathetic response has not helped, primarily because an assumption was made about the experience rather than an exploration of it. A sympathetic response can impact the direction of the conversation, depending on the client's reaction to it. In the above example, the counsellor was fortunate that the client clarified the assumption. Furthermore, if you agree with and support a particular emotion and affirm this sympathetically, you may find later that you need to be challenging the same sort of emotional reaction at some point in the process. Again, this scenario highlights some of the **differential use of self**—what you might say to family and friends in such a circumstance may be different from your response with your clients, because your role has a different purpose.

A negative view of sympathy is questioned, however, by Trevithick and others who call for recognition of the importance of sympathy, particularly early on in the relationship during the early phases of engagement.

Practice Exercise

1. Reflect on a conversation or encounter with another person, not necessarily in a formal interview situation, where you have experienced what you consider empathic communication.

2. What occurred during the conversation that made you feel understood?

3. What are the essential qualities, attitudes, and skills that you think were essential in this experience?

4. What words or phrases defined the expression of empathy for you?

5. What specific empathic skills can you identify from the experience?

6. What are your personal skills in which you feel confident in working with empathy and where do you want to improve?

Empathy is predominantly perceived to be a positive skill. A word of caution is raised, however, in relation to working with involuntary clients. Trotter (2006: 26) cites a 1979 study, which found that the use of empathy with incarcerated clients was not always beneficial. Empathy in these instances was found to be counterproductive, as supportive reflections of feeling gave 'some kind of subtle permission or sanction for continuing that behaviour with the result that further offending occurred' (Andrews et al., 1979, cited in Trotter, 2006: 26). The usefulness of even one of the most consistently identified positive skills in communication nevertheless depends on the context in which it is used.

Empathy, as distinct from intimacy or sympathy, is about understanding and supporting someone emotionally, but not being immersed in the same feelings and reactions. Rogers (1980: 137) defined empathy as:

> entering the private perceptual world of the other and becoming thoroughly at home in it. It involves being sensitive, moment by moment, to the changing felt meanings which flow in this other person . . . It means temporarily living in the other's life, moving about in it delicately without making judgments.

Being immersed in others feelings can arouse similar feelings, and this is where self-awareness and self-reflection are useful skills. For example, when talking with someone who is depressed, you can find that you, too, are becoming more sombre in your tone and physical presence. You can begin to mirror their use of self, rather than remain aware of what the client needs in the interaction. In a community health centre context, Karen identifies how she came to manage that in her work with Mark.

Focus on Practice

Dealing with the Unbearable

Sometimes a person's pain is so extreme that you will be affected. A man in his thirties with suicidal concerns attended a first interview. His story related to the recent traumatic event of watching as his small daughter ran across the road, was hit by a car, and dragged a long distance. She had suffered multiple injuries including some brain damage, and he was wracked with guilt as well as with the trauma of witnessing the terrible event. He had left his family and the province, feeling bereft and hopeless.

The telling of his story, in all its graphic detail, together with his projection of his own feelings, was a moving and deeply sad experience, and my way of coping was to ask myself: 'What does Mark need from me in telling me this today?' At such a time, what he needed from me was to be able to bear to hear his pain, in all its detail, without providing either blame or reassurance. By asking myself the question I was able to contain my own feelings, not without a tear, but to the extent that he could feel allowed to move away from believing that he had no other choice than suicide.

This reflection on practice is an important consideration in professional development. In some cases, when the worker becomes over-engaged in a client's story, the client may shut down out of concern for the worker's emotional well-being. The client should always feel safe to express all the details of the story and confident that the practitioner can listen and be present.

1. What is your immediate reaction to this story and why?
2. What do you think could emerge as issues for you personally in working with someone in Mark's situation?
3. How will you manage any issues that arise for you?
4. What skills do you feel you need to develop further so that you could handle the situation in this example?

Your Social and Practical Use of Self

Workers also vary in the degree to which they are involved practically in situations—with and for clients. Sometimes attending to the practical needs, either directly or indirectly, can make an enormous difference—for example, making phone calls on behalf of someone or providing transport. These actions can bring about sheer relief when such basic human needs are not being met otherwise. Maslow's hierarchy of needs (Table 4.1) is a useful reminder of the importance of meeting basic human survival needs, before other growth needs such as self-actualization and self-transcendence can be realized.

Social support, whether emotional, instrumental, or practical, is consistently identified as a key protective factor (Harms, 2005). Sometimes, the direct provision of this social support by the worker is vital. At

Table 4.1 An Adapted Version of Maslow's Hierarchy of Needs

Motivational need	A person at this level
Self-transcendence	Seeks to further a cause beyond the self
Self-actualization	Seeks fulfillment of personal potential
Esteem needs	Seeks esteem through achievement
Belongingness and love needs	Seeks group affiliation
Safety needs	Seeks security through law and order
Physiological (survival) needs	Seeks the basic necessities of life

Source: Koltko-Rivera (2006: 303).

other times, it is more important to link the client to other social support networks for these needs to be met.

Your response as a worker will be determined in part by your views of empowerment and the place of independence, interdependence, and dependence. Some workers view practical needs as critical opportunities to provide support when a client may not have the resources, either practically or emotionally, to attend to such issues. Others view these needs as the vehicle by which some of the other more expressive or therapeutic processes and tasks can be undertaken. Others see these practical tasks as just as essential in the change process as are the emotional tasks—possibly more important, if the client's external environment is seen to be the cause of issues rather than the inner world. Trotter (2006: 8) reflects on his experience in two different organizations and the rationales given for responding differently to clients. In one organization:

> the culture was to see clients as soon as possible even if they arrived without an appointment. This was viewed as respectful. In another organisation the culture was to expect clients to make an appointment for another time. This was viewed as helping clients to be responsible.

Some authors have been highly critical in recent years of the move away from some of the earlier core supportive-task agendas of social work (Specht and Courteney, 1994; Ife, 2001). Ife (2001), for example, urges social workers to redefine their role as rights workers rather than as needs assessors. He maintains that a much clearer basis for action emerges when human rights, rather than needs, form the basis of action.

The example of organizational process given above may not be applicable in other settings, for example, in a northern and remote practice setting. Practitioners need to consider the relevant geographic context and culture. Further, who defines the process and decides whether or not it is appropriate? Northern and remote community practice may place less importance on set appointment times, which are more commonly viewed as essential to service provision in an urban setting. A similar sort of culturally relevant view of time should be taken into consideration for immigrants from particular cultures in which time evaluations and procedural traditions differ from broader cultural norms in North America.

Your Spiritual Use of Self

The spiritual dimension is less frequently discussed as a way in which the worker interacts with their clients, in part because of the diverse ways in which spirituality is experienced and defined. Increasingly, however, clients are identifying this as an important yet neglected dimension of human service practice (Canda and Furman, 1999; Lindsay, 2002).

Coates, Graham, Swartzentruber, and Ouellette (2007) credit four major Canadian social work scholars for their work in capturing spirituality in social work during the twentieth century. E.J. Erwick, Charles Hendry, Reverend Shaun Govenlock, and Reverend Frank Swithun Bowers 'each was a director of a major school for over a decade; each was well published and well regarded; and together they represented a period in social work's history from the 1930s to the early 1970s' (ibid., 29).

Since the 1970s many authors have contributed to spirituality in social work practice (far more than can be summarized in this brief overview). After a decline in the literature during the 1970s and 1980s, spirituality and social work saw an emergence in Canadian publications by such authors as Graham, Ouellette, Al-Krenawi, Coates, Swartzentruber, Moffatt, and McKay. This re-emergence included a cultural perspective with Canadian authors Dei, de Mello, Mandamin, Morrissette, McKenzie, and Tester, all of whom recognize that 'cultures are strongly linked with spiritual and religious world views, and this has consistently been a rationale for the inclusion of spirituality in social work' (ibid., 30). Coates et al. (ibid., 38) emphasize that '[t]he integration of spirituality into our contemporary knowledge base is vital as it assists us in working with increasingly diverse clients and communities.'

Recently Canadian texts have included sections or chapters on spirituality, including Aboriginal theory, holistic practice, meditation, and transpersonal theories (ibid.; see also Cech, 2010: chs 3, 5). Currently, a major contributor to the topic of spirituality in Canadian social work is the Canadian Society for Spirituality and Social Work (http://w3.stu.ca/stu/sites/spirituality/index.html).

What would your response be to the following situation, and how would you answer the questions?

Focus on Practice

Considering the Spiritual Dimension

A client is telling you about his strong connection with spirituality, and the ways in which he knows this connection has helped him overcome so many difficulties. As a way of tapping into your beliefs about the spiritual dimension in practice:

1. What is your reaction to this very brief scenario?
2. Would you feel comfortable continuing with the client?
3. What do you think you would want to know more about?
4. Do you think you would ask more questions? If so, what would your questions be and why?
5. How would you manage a client's spirituality if it is in direct conflict with your beliefs?

6. In what ways do you think your reaction would influence your client's experience?
7. How might you address cultural perspectives or theories, such as meditation, in your discussion?

Your Physical Use of Self

Many dimensions of your non-verbal skills and, therefore, of your physical use of self, were explored in Chapter 2. This discussion raises two further issues: touch and availability. Ethical guidelines across all professions prohibit sexual contact with clients, because of the inherent inequalities in power and control within client–worker relationships. In this respect, professional standards have never been as clearly articulated as they currently are in relation to physical boundaries. Yet, a challenge emerges in that, theoretically, the emphasis on authentic human intersubjectivity has never been as strongly proposed, which leaves a worker

As discussed in Chapter 2, the question of whether touch should ever be used in practice is a complex one.

wondering about some of the more subtle forms of physical interaction that commonly typify human relationships. For example, physical contact occurs at points of greeting or separation, through handshakes or hugs. Workers find themselves in situations where someone may spontaneously embrace them. To reject this embrace could be personally and culturally inappropriate.

Your physical use of self also relates to your physical presence and availability. Punctuality and availability have been identified by clients in many studies as important issues of respect and relationship. If it is not possible to be punctual and available because of other work demands, conveying this to the client is a way of relating respectfully and genuinely. It is important for practitioners to ensure they are aware of how physical use of self and physical presence are defined in an urban agency, in institutional settings, and in the community. The expectations and dynamics likely will be different between urban and rural locations and in work with different cultures.

Your Use of Self in Context

Your agency will set the agenda for much of the work you do. Agencies reflect the wider policy context in which they are established, and the subsequent resources that are provided for service delivery. Agencies make decisions about service delivery models. They develop a workplace culture based on its employees and the work that is undertaken. These are dimensions of your **organizational context**.

At an everyday level, the physical and the service system environmental dimensions of an agency will influence the experience for both you and your clients. These dimensions give strong messages about the underlying values of the work and of the client–worker relationship.

An agency may have unique safety issues relating to health, violence, or location. For example, in 2002, Hong Kong implemented the requirement that all hospital workers, irrespective of profession, dress in surgical 'scrubs' and not wear any civilian clothing because of the ongoing threat of SARS and bird flu epidemics to hospital workers and to the wider community. In this context, clients cannot even recognize their worker when gowned and masked in the intensive care environment.

In 2009, Canada faced the H1N1 influenza, also referred to as swine flu. This worldwide health concern saw institutions developing 'pandemic preparedness policies' to increase awareness of how to manage exposure to the H1N1 virus. For some schools of social work this involved specific policy development in the areas of student practicum aimed at addressing the potential risk for students in placements.

In organizations providing refuge from domestic violence, threats of violence can be common, requiring different levels of security and confidentiality. Workers in international services in zones of war or disaster face unique physical and interpersonal risks. These environments will influence the precautions you need to take in your practice.

The geographical location of the organization, whether rural, remote, or urban, can present other challenges in the provision of accessible services for clients. The provision of services to rural and remote areas is extremely sparse; people may have to travel considerable distances to access services and most people who need service may not even know it exists. Not only is transport accessibility an issue, but accessibility also may be influenced by the visibility of individuals accessing a service. For example, the stigma associated with being seen to access an HIV/AIDS or domestic violence service can become a serious block to use of the service. In rural communities, these difficulties can be amplified by the denser communication networks and reduced opportunity for anonymity (Green, 2003; Taylor, 2004). Many people in these instances do not access services. Traditions of self-reliance or of reliance on institutions that no longer have sufficient resources, such as churches and municipalities, reduce service access, also. Workers in these agencies give careful consideration as to how services can be provided sensitively and anonymously (Bramwell, 2005). A newer form of service delivery is the Internet for the provision of information and online support through group and individual connections that do not involve the same levels of stigma as observable physical access. However, rural and remote settings are less likely to be supplied with computer access. Therefore, the actual interview or work setting (Kadushin and Kadushin, 1997; Weeks, 2004) is important to consider. You may work in a structured setting, with interviews taking place in interview rooms, where privacy and comfort can be assured. Or you may be talking in corridors, at the bedside, outdoors, or in people's homes or at some place in their community. In all of these situations, being mindful of who else can and should hear what is going on is important. Concepts of privacy and the privileged role of the counsellor as confidant in a rural setting may be entirely absent. The exchange of information in some interviews may be broadcast in the community by the client, which, of course, leaves the counsellor who maintains confidentiality with little or no platform for relationship or exchange in that community group. Some clients do not desire anonymity in the community; others, of course, have expectations consistent with the standards of practice assumed by urban clients.

Agencies vary in the resources they have to provide adequate talking spaces. Some agencies are more like comfortable homes where family and community work can take place. Others are more formal and even sterile environments where clients can be left feeling disempowered and alienated. We can become immune to the nature of the physical environment of the organization and no longer see how it may impact the client experience.

Service delivery issues are also major influences on the client–worker relationship. Some considerations are whether services are offered on a short-term or long-term basis, whether there are limitations on the number and nature of contacts with people, and whether services are focused on crisis intervention or on longer-term treatment. Some other considerations that will influence your relationship and client work are:

- What client group does your agency aim to reach?
- How does the agency, as well as specific workers, understand its clients' issues—for example, are they seen to be family issues, psychological issues, or issues arising from the structural context?
- What is the workplace culture? That is, what are the written and unwritten rules in relation to worker practice?
- How culturally diverse and/or sensitive is the agency and its workers?
- Does the agency primarily work with individuals, families, or communities?
- What staffing levels are available within the agency to meet the demands?
- What are the expectations of client caseloads for each worker?
- What budgetary restrictions influence the work you can do (Ribner and Knei-Paz, 2002: 386)?
- Are clients' voluntary or involuntary users of the agency's services?
- How does a client access or connect with your service—through a referral, a drop-in duty system, or a waiting list process?
- How available are you as a worker?
- How structured is your time with clients?
- How private and uninterrupted is your work with clients?
- How do you address issues for clients coming to access your services from a rural or remote community who have limited experience navigating services in urban settings?

Community-Based Practice

Considering concepts that will influence your relationship with clients in community practice can look quite different from urban practice. Zapf (1991: 45) states, 'local control and community empowerment have emerged as key issues in most northern regions in Canada, northern social workers will be expected to use collaborative approaches working with communities rather than simply working in communities'. Delaney, Brownlee, and Zapf (1996, quoting Wharf, 1985: 86) note that 'collaboration suggests "the willingness of professional staff to risk and to share responsibility with members of the community, and to expand their job definitions into new and uncharted territory'. This requirement means shifting away from familiar practices towards a more creative, flexible, non-traditional mode of practice.

- How does community practice look different (setting, case load, needs, individual practice, community level practice) from an urban practice?
- How would you redefine your role and expectations to be effective in community practice?

- How would you address issues of visibility?
- How would you address issues of isolation in practice?
- What system would you put in place to address possible lack of supervision?
- How would you address client confidentiality?
- How would you incorporate the community structure into your practice?
- How would you learn the community culture?
- How would you plan for challenges in geography—access to roads, water travel, severe weather, and emergency accessibility?

Focus on Practice

The Impact of Agency Context

Using the questions above, think about the impact of each of these agency contexts on your practice and how differently you would work if you were located in each of the following four settings.

1. *Remote Mental Health Centre.* You work in a northern and remote area providing mental health service. While you are part of a provincial health service, you work with a small multidisciplinary team to deliver assessment and treatment services to people in their own communities. This involves extensive travel to northern and remote communities, often for weeks at a time. In addition, due to the geographic locations you have limited access to technology and, at times, phone services.

2. *Youth and Homelessness.* You work in an urban agency that works with homeless or street-involved youth. The purpose of your work is to assist youth in gaining safe affordable housing and health care services. Part of your work involves going out to locate youth on your case load. In addition, you are responsible for case planning, locating funding, and bringing community awareness of youth homelessness.

3. *Rural.* You work in a rural shelter for victims of domestic violence. Your agency offers emergency or crisis care, counselling, and support for survivors leaving a violent relationship. You are also involved in research projects, resource development, and community education and training. You work with a small team of counsellors/advocates who are committed to feminist understandings of violence and recovery.

4. *Senior Care and Hospital.* You work in a large, regional public hospital that provides specialist assessment, rehabilitation, advisory, and psychiatric services to older and disabled adults. You are involved in assessments and discharge planning, as well as individual patient and family support throughout the time of an admission. You work within a large multidisciplinary team.

In the following two vignettes, Jane provides insight into how many of the agency issues described above influence work in a hospital parent bereavement group. The group Jane describes is a co-led group, enabling the two workers to support the many tasks and processes involved in such a program. Clients and workers alike can be inadequately protected from some of the agency activities and disruptions outlined above. For example, Jane recounts the impact of workplace interruptions on her work with one particular mother.

Focus on Practice

Coping with Interruptions

Despite the best preparations and intentions in our agency, the phone can interrupt times with parents. Some may say, 'Don't answer it.' Yet long ringing can be very disruptive; ignoring a call could give the message that we don't respond to calls here; and answering even very briefly can imply someone else is more important than you! In any response the worker makes, she has to preserve confidentiality. Additionally, if a call comes through, there is always the possibility (as has happened) that there is an emergency in the worker's own family.

During an interview with a mother who was grieving for her baby daughter, her only child who had died within days of her birth, the phone rang and rang. I apologized to the parent and took the call. I asked our administration worker if she could take a message, saying, 'I'm with someone, a client' [not a term I usually say], then, looking directly at her, I said, 'I'm with a mother.' From the look on the mother's face these words were probably the most meaningful in the appointment. Our choice of language is so important, yet so loaded.

To resume a conversation after such a discussion is difficult; it is helpful to try to hold the last words in mind and then to do a brief summary of what had been said so far:

'You were telling me about . . .'
'You were saying that . . .'

Sometimes this can be hard, especially if the call brings its own issues or tasks to be done. To acknowledge this: 'Sorry, it can be difficult to get back to where we were after being interrupted like that. Where should we pick up/continue?' can restart the conversation.

1. What do you think you would do and say under similar circumstances?
2. How would you reflect on your practice to ensure you are maintaining the key elements (non-verbals, sense of self, rapport) described in previous sections and chapters?

Client interactions impact the work as well the organizational issues. Jane talks about some of the challenges of beginning on time a session of a bereavement group, given the diversity of arrival times and the continuing organizational interruptions.

Focus on Practice

Managing Interruptions

It is supportive to begin on time, especially as some parents may have come early and may find it excruciating to wait for such a group to start. Before the formal commencement of the group, as refreshments are offered, we give a brief description of the group (some of this recaps what has been sent in the letter). We would also consider who is already in the room and then do a round of introductions.

Sometimes parents may arrive half an hour into the group when the discussion, presentation or experiential process is well under way. This interruption may include those coming for the first time who may feel very unfamiliar with the group. A quick welcoming and accepting response is called for; one that does not distract too much from the group or draw undue attention to them or make them feel awkward. We stand up, move to them and quietly do introductions, write out name tags, and ensure there are seats in the circle. We say what has been happening or, if it hasn't been long, 'We've just begun', or 'We haven't been talking for long.' The presenter may also recap what has been going on; however, this cannot be assumed.

Interruptions have come from a security guard opening the door and looking in at us (occasionally, then locking us in, giving new meaning to the expression 'closed group'!), and rowdy staff or students in adjoining rooms or someone turning off the lights in the corridor. These are the realities of the situation. Parents have dealt with much more difficult matters, yet these situations can been distracting; once more a brief reference to this interruption can be helpful, sometimes even gentle humour. Sometimes such *outside world* distractions can symbolize what's being or has been said in the group:

'What were we saying about others not seeing you or your grief . . .?'
'Well, that's how others can be . . .'
'OK we're on our own now . . .'
'That's what they think . . .'
'As impossible as it seems, the outside world keeps going on . . .'

What do you think you would do and say in similar circumstances? It is important to make sure your response is appropriate to the group and all of the participants present. An inappropriate comment may impact participants' willingness to stay or to return. Remember the key components when practicing your response: non-verbal, expressions, and gestures, all of which are part of the message you are sending in your response.

The Purpose of Your Agency

Many communication skills texts focus on skills for work that is primarily oriented towards 'social care'. Your use of self in these instances can be spelled out quite specifically, in that the primary aims of your work are therapeutic. You may also be engaged in work that is focused on social control or social cure outcomes (Trevithick, 2005). This type of work demands that you use different influencing skills. The overarching purpose of your agency and the work you undertake within it is important to articulate and critically review.

The purpose of your work can be thought about at even more micro levels; that is, within the context of individual conversations and interviews. Is the purpose to give bad news, to change difficult behaviour, or is it to challenge the breach of an order with a parent? Kadushin (1972) identified three primary purposes influencing the structure and the conducting of interviews, including informational or social study purposes; diagnostic or decision-making purposes; and therapeutic purposes. Sometimes, all three elements will be operating in the one conversational context.

You will draw on various skills, depending on the different purposes of your relationship and the specific communication situation you are working in at any one time. For example, within the medical interview literature, the tasks are mapped out in relation to the doctor's role in the interview, from being patient-centred at the beginning and shifting to a doctor-centredness by the conclusion whereby the assessment and information phase is guided more by the doctor than by the patient (Smith et al., 2000). The purpose here is to move towards diagnosis and treatment. In an educational or welfare setting, a student may need support and information about coping strategies, so there may be movement from a supportive listening role towards a more psycho-educational role within the communication. These examples demonstrate quite different purposes in a client–worker interaction, and therefore quite different uses of self.

Chapter Summary

In this chapter, we have looked at some of the core ways in which you make use of yourself in your practice. We have explored the ways in which you consciously learn to use this self in practice in different ways—including all your biopsychosocial and spiritual dimensions, depending upon the circumstances. Agency contexts have been identified as defining influences on this 'use of self', both at the macro level of determining the nature of the work that is undertaken within a particular setting and at a micro level of the daily structure of interactions with people.

Questions for Analysis

1. What have you learned from this chapter about:
    • Your differential use of self? (empathy and social-emotional intelligence)
    • The importance and potential impact of agency context?
    • Defining the purpose of your work?
    • Northern and remote considerations?
    • Variations in cultural contexts?
    • Areas you want to learn more about to improve your practice skills?
    • What strengths do you have in this area?
    • Where do you most want to improve?

2. What are some of the unique tensions and questions for you in relation to these issues? How will you address these issues?

Recommended Readings

Coates, J., J.R. Graham, B. Swartzentruber, and B. Ouellette. 2007. *Spirituality and Social Work: Selected Canadian Readings.* Toronto: Canadian Scholars' Press.

Delaney, R., K. Brownlee, and M. Kim Zapf, eds. 1996. *Issues in Northern Social Work Practice.* Thunder Bay, Ont.: Centre for Northern Studies, Lakehead University.

Freedberg, S. 2007. 'Re-examining empathy: A relational-feminist point of view', *Journal of Social Work* 52, 3: 251–9.

Goleman, D. 2005. *Emotional Intelligence.* New York: Bantam Books.

———. 2006. *Social Intelligence: The New Science of Human Relationships.* London: Hutchinson.

Green, R., R. Gregory, and R. Mason. 2006. 'Professional distance and social work: Stretching the elastic?', *Australian Social Work* 59, 4: 449–61.

Rogers, C. 1987. 'Comments on the issue of equality in psychotherapy', *Journal of Humanistic Psychology* 27, 1: 38–9.

Internet Resources

Canadian Society for Spirituality and Social Work
http://w3.stu.ca/stu/sites/spirituality/index.html

Conflict Resolution Network
www.crnhq.org/twelveskills.html

Daniel Goleman's website
(social and emotional intelligence)
www.danielgoleman.info

5 | Sustaining Your Self in Practice

Learning Goals

- Learn about your self-care and professional development strategies.
- Understand the nature of critical reflective practice.
- Review the purposes and tasks of supervision.
- Describe the processes of debriefing and when it is useful.

Self-Care and Professional Development

In human service work, you are working with people who are coping with some of life's most extreme difficulties, challenges, and opportunities. The impact on the worker will be significant—both across the accumulation of experiences and through single, complex incidents that confront who we are and what we are doing. This chapter explores some of the ways in which you can prepare and sustain yourself for this personally confronting and rewarding work. These issues are dealt with early in this discussion, as they are fundamental to preparing yourself as a practitioner and sustaining yourself over the longer term.

Focus on Practice

Protectors Need Protecting, Too

Maria McNamara described her experiences of working within the child protection system:
   Given the unique difficulties of the job, it is possible there is widespread undiagnosed and untreated PTSD [post-traumatic stress disorder] among current and former child protection workers. Researchers have theorized that when protective workers deal with violent families, they are not immune from the violence. Not only are they vulnerable to assaults and abuse, but they can also experience secondary trauma from witnessing the violence and abuse to which children are subjected.

> I was abused [verbally] countless times over the phone and in person, and I was assaulted [physically] once during an after-hours call-out. This happened one summer evening while I was questioning a woman about her young children, who were on a protective court order.
>
> *Source: McNamara (2006: 9).*

Good professional **self-care** skills are essential throughout your career. You need to be aware of the risk and protective factors in your work and your workplace. The risk factors or the 'costs' of caring have been understood in a number of ways.

It is important for practitioners to reflect on the differences between 'professional self-care', and 'personal self-care'. Professional self-care consists of the elements a practitioner puts in place to address workplace stressors. For example, scheduled supervision is a way to debrief and gain support around your role and needs in the workplace. Personal self-care may include participating in a group or sport that is independent from your work.

Some self-care tasks benefit both your professional and personal life. Attending the gym on a weekly basis is one example of a self-care activity that would clearly benefit both professional and personal wellness. In brief, it is imperative that practitioners facilitate a reflexive process to assess how both professional and personal self-care strategies are managed towards their overall wellness. This chapter focuses largely on professional self-care.

Human service work can lead to what is termed compassion stress (or compassion fatigue) or burnout (Jenaro, Flores, and Arias, 2007: 80). Burnout arises in relation to chronic workplace stress. It is characterized by 'negative attitudes and feelings toward co-workers and one's job role, as well as feelings of emotional exhaustion'. These experiences can lead to a pervasive cynicism or a lack of enthusiasm and motivation that can be harmful to your and your clients. **Compassion fatigue** (a term that can be used interchangeably with secondary traumatic stress) refers to the experience of 'a sense of helplessness and confusion, and a sense of isolation from supporters' (Figley, 1995: 12). Unlike burnout, however, compassion fatigue can happen following a single incident. A useful checklist has been developed by Figley (1995) for screening your own levels of compassion fatigue and burnout.

Focus on Practice

Compassion Fatigue Self-Test

Rate yourself on each of the following questions, using the 1–5 rating scale, where:

1 = rarely/never
2 = at times
3 = not sure

4 = often
5 = very often

	Question	Score
1	I force myself to avoid certain thoughts or feelings that remind me of a frightening experience.	
2	I find myself avoiding certain activities or situations because they remind me of a frightening experience.	
3	I have gaps in my memory about frightening events.	
4	I feel estranged from others.	
5	I have difficulty falling or staying asleep.	
6	I have outbursts of anger or irritability with little provocation.	
7	I startle easily.	
8	While working with a victim, I thought about violence against the perpetrator.	
9	I am a sensitive person.	
10	I have had flashbacks connected to my clients.	
11	I have had first-hand experience with traumatic events in my adult life.	
12	I have had first-hand experience with traumatic events in my childhood.	
13	I have thought that I need to 'work through' a traumatic experience in my life.	
14	I have thought that I need more close friends.	
15	I have thought that there is no one to talk with about highly stressful experiences.	
16	I have concluded that I work too hard for my own good.	
17	I am frightened of things a client has said or done to me.	
18	I experience troubling dreams similar to those of a client of mine.	
19	I have experienced intrusive thoughts of sessions with especially difficult clients.	
20	I have suddenly and involuntarily recalled a frightening experience while working with a client.	
21	I am preoccupied with more than one client.	
22	I am losing sleep over a client's traumatic experiences.	
23	I have thought that I might have been 'infected' by the traumatic stress of my clients.	
24	I remind myself to be less concerned about the well-being of my clients.	
25	I have felt trapped by my work as a social worker.	
26	I have felt a sense of hopelessness associated with working with clients.	
27	I have felt 'on edge' about various things and I attribute this to working with certain clients.	
28	I have wished that I could avoid working with some clients.	
29	I have been in danger working with clients.	
30	I have felt that my clients dislike me personally.	
31	I have felt weak, tired, and run down as a result of my work as a social worker.	
32	I have felt depressed as a result of my work as a social worker.	
33	I am unsuccessful at separating work from personal life.	
34	I feel little compassion towards most of my co-workers.	

35	I feel I am working more for the money than for personal fulfillment.	
36	I find it difficult separating my personal life from my work life.	
37	I have a sense of worthlessness/disillusionment/resentment associated with my work.	
38	I have thoughts that I am a 'failure' as a social worker.	
39	I have thoughts that I am not succeeding at achieving my life goals.	
40	I have to deal with bureaucratic, unimportant tasks in my work life.	

When you have completed the survey, you can work out your score by circling these 23 questions: 1–8, 10–13, 17–26, and 29. You then add up the numbers you wrote next to the items for a total compassion fatigue risk score, which is rated as follows:

- You are at extremely low risk if your total score is 26 or less.
- You are at moderate risk if your total score is 31–35.
- You are at high risk with a total score of 36–40 and extremely high risk with a total score of 41 or more.

You then add up the numbers you wrote next to the items not circled to estimate your risk of burnout.

- You are at extremely low risk if your total score is 17–36 or less.
- You are at low risk with a total score of 37–50.
- You are at high risk with a total score of 51–75 and extremely high risk with a score of 76–85.

Other impacts of the work emerge from more acute experiences of distress and trauma, as distinct from the accumulation of stress over time. Certain events in the workplace can lead to experiences of secondary victimization, **vicarious traumatization** (Pearlman and Macian, 1995) or secondary traumatic stress disorder. As a practitioner, hearing or witnessing stories of assault or abuse on a daily basis may create vicarious trauma. This process is subtle as it accumulates over time and often passes undetected by the practitioner. As Pearlman and Saakvitne (1995: 31) describe:

> vicarious traumatization refers to the cumulative transformative effect upon the trauma therapist of working with survivors of traumatic life events . . . it is a process through which the therapist's inner experience is negatively transformed through empathic engagement with clients' trauma material.

The negative transformations include disruptions to your personal frame of reference about self and others in the world; your sense of safety, dependency, and trust; your sense of power, esteem, and independence; and your capacity for intimacy (Figley, 1995; White, 2004). Other trauma reactions include 'feelings of emptiness, desolation, and despair', or as White (2004: 47) describes, it is about becoming 'overwhelmed by a sense of hopelessness and paralysis, and [believing] that there's nothing whatsoever they can do to affect the shape of their life or the shape of events around them.' Janoff-Bulman (1992) describes this process as the shattering of our assumptions—that is, the assumptions we hold that the world is benevolent, the world is meaningful, and that the self is worthy.

For workers and clients alike, the goals of trauma work are often summarized as including three tasks: re-establishing safety, experiencing processes of remembrance and mourning, and achieving an eventual reconnection with ordinary life (Herman, 1992). Strategies to support these processes are critical. Your self-care skills and strategies are usually about maintenance and prevention tasks, but sometimes about intervention; in particular, instances of stress and trauma.

Professional maintenance tasks relate to the ongoing development of knowledge and skills. Personal maintenance tasks focus on care of yourself as a person engaged in demanding interpersonal work. This enables you to continue to develop as a worker and be well supported in that work. Some key professional self-care strategies workers adopt in relation to this include:

- supervision, which will be discussed extensively in the following section
- formal peer support strategies, which include journal clubs, ongoing practice discussion groups, and professional development activities
- continued access to training and workshops that assist a worker in successful practice.

In addition, personal self-care strategies workers adopt can include:

- personal maintenance strategies, such as humour, fitness, sleep, diet, maintaining a good psychological sense of well-being, and maintaining a good network of friends outside of the workplace.
- informal peer support strategies, such as social clubs and activities.

Applying the above professional and personal self-care strategies can assist practitioners in maintaining overall wellness. Intervention strategies relate to the more immediate strategies used at key times of stress or crisis; that is, when something particularly stressful has happened. Some key strategies adopted at these times include supervision and debriefing.

This support for a worker is most typically provided by the agency in which you work. Other support strategies are part of your personal lifestyle. Self-care strategies are relatively straightforward and typically relate to a biopsychosocial–spiritual balance within a worker's daily life. Making them happen regularly as a preventive strategy is typically the greater challenge. Getting caught up in the business of your work can erode your commitment to these strategies. One of the ways in which we can bring about an understanding of these issues is to think through them in critically reflective or reflexive processes.

Critical Self-Reflection

Reflecting on your practice is an important skill. Numerous terms are used for this activity—reflection, reflectivity, and **reflexivity or critical reflection**, to name a few. Reflectivity can be defined as:

the ability to locate oneself in a situation through the recognition of how actions and interpretations, social and cultural background and personal history, emotional aspects of experience, and personally held assumptions and values influence the situation. (Fook, 1999: 199)

Another term often used in discussions of critical reflection is reflexivity, meaning more of 'a bending back onto a self, [which] can encompass many diverse processes, depending on what manner of connection, or relationship, is accomplishing the bending back' (Steier, 1995: 63).

Kondrat provides a useful distinction between three conceptualizations of the self in self-awareness. The first is a simple consciousness, which makes our memory of our experience possible. The second is a reflective awareness, which relies on a growing sense of the self who has the experience. The third is a reflexive or introspective awareness, which is not about standing back, objectively, but knowing because 'I am on more or less familiar terms with the self' (Kondrat, 1999: 468). Through a process of reflexive awareness, one of the questions we ask is, 'What do I (we) do in the agency on a day-to-day basis that might contribute to the structuring of unequal outcomes?' (ibid.).

> If we do not maintain an awareness of this possibility of altering the oppressive structures within society, we can perpetuate the very oppressions we are looking to eradicate. Chapter 14 looks at these issues in greater detail.

Reflection on and in all dimensions of our practice has a number of functions. First and foremost, ongoing critical reflection is one way of ensuring good practice outcomes for clients. As Kondrat (ibid.) states: 'As individuals and as professionals, social workers' daily interactions with clients and others have consequences for maintaining or altering society's structures.'

Ongoing awareness of the effects of these interactions is an essential part of transforming the lived experiences of clients. Second, it enables the impact of the work to be addressed. Human service work often provokes strong physical and emotional responses, such as intense sadness and distress or anger and frustration. Some experiences can be overwhelming and evoke a sense of helplessness or powerlessness.

Your work can bring you into contact with violence or extreme poverty. For some workers this may be their first exposure, for others, it brings reminders of past and present experiences. This type of work will inevitably have an impact on you. Its positive impact is the accumulation of practice experience and practice wisdom. Its negative impact can lead to distress, stress, burnout, or cynicism. Through a reflective process, practitioners can maintain awareness of both positive (practice wisdom) and negative (distress, burnout) events that impact daily practice.

Critical reflection provides an opportunity to assess the effect of these experiences, to integrate them in some way, and to develop assessments and interventions that lead to further change. Reflective practice builds the bridge between theory and practice (Payne, 2006), but also maintains a focus on change. Schon (1987) points out the importance of reflecting not only on what has occurred but on learning to reflect *in the midst of practice* to influence the process there and then. A reflective worker can be defined (Thompson, 2002: 235) as someone:

who is able to use experience, knowledge, and theoretical perspectives to guide and inform practice. However, this does not mean applying ideas in a blanket form, unthinkingly and uncritically, regardless of the circumstances. Reflective practice involves cutting the cloth to suit the specific circumstances, rather than looking for ready-made solutions.

Reflection alone can be an introspective process that may influence our own practice but not influence the outer world in any substantial way. That is, problems in the outer world that lead to inner- and outer-world distress or difficulty for others remain unaltered. Critical self-reflection takes this reflective process one step further:

> Processes of dialogue and self-reflection are important in providing critical understandings of how internalised discourses (particularly those we have internalised ourselves) have created the situation. Processes of dialogue are crucial in reformulating and changing discourses that are relevant across different interest groups. (Fook, 2000: 131–2)

A number of strategies can be adopted to practice reflection and critical reflexive practice. The first strategy is to complete a social awareness exercise, such as the one proposed by Fook.

Focus on Practice

Social Self-Awareness Exercise

A multi-dimensional approach suggests that all dimensions of our experience interact to form a personal and social identity. Reviewing the dimensions of our own experience through a social, structural, and cultural analysis can help us to understand how various dimensions have shaped our life and our life choices.

Reflect on the impact on your life and ways of being of the following dimensions of your life. Fook (2002) has identified the following dimensions and you might add others:

- relationship status
- occupation
- social class (past and present)
- education
- family type and background
- ethnicity
- religion
- membership of groups or subcultures
- gender
- sexual orientation
- health
- age
- particular ideologies.

Source: Adapted from Fook (2002: 156–7).

This exercise raises important questions about what experiences influence us. A further step is to ask yourself how we influence each of these dimensions of our social identity, so that their means of expression and understanding are perpetuated or changed in our wider contexts. This is important in relation to what happens for the individual client, as Sharp (2006: 67) notes: 'In other words, if we are not focused on the factors that influence the "what" of who we think we are, we may find ourselves unwittingly imposing that same sense of being on the client.'

This self-understanding is the essential component of reflexive practice and it raises more questions about how we then respond. A study that explored working with couples in interfaith relationships, specifically Muslim and Christian relationships (Furlong and Ata, 2006: 259), encountered dilemmas pertaining to this kind of self-knowledge. Workers were conscious of the importance of cultural sensitivity and of awareness of difference generally, but the study showed that verbalizing that stance may not be enough:

> As practitioners, we are never neutral and we do not wish to be. Yet, it is naïve to believe that the simple declaration of one's position will always be received as courteous and engaging. Nor is it always the case that such declarations will facilitate the outcome that is desired.

Thus, the first step is recognizing your position, but other steps are involved. Changing existing power relationships not only occurs through becoming aware of the language that is used or declaring a position—it is about developing an agenda for change.

Another possibility is to work with these professional identities very explicitly in a role-play situation, to address such meanings and intentions. This process challenges practitioners through a professional development process.

Focus on Practice

Working in Triads

Use the earlier social awareness exercise to identify an issue for role-play. For example, it may be about how gender has impacted your choice of work or study.

One person is assigned the role of interviewer, one the role of client, and one the role of observer (coach, adviser).

The observer can participate in a number of ways:

1. Watch the interview and provide comment at the end as to what was observed. This can lead to a critical discussion of what happened, what was intended to happen from both worker and client perspectives, and as a way of discussing the implications of the direction of the interview. For example, how was the problem constructed by each person: the client and the worker? Were there ways in which the interview perpetuated the social discourses for the client and reinforced the person's oppression rather than redressing it? If so, how?

2. The observer can choose to intervene at points in the interview where the worker could have directed the interview differently. This action interrupts habits of thinking in the worker and can provide useful new insights. It encourages a process of thinking together by 'freeze framing' certain of the worker's choices for discussion.
3. The worker can call on the observer when he or she feels stuck or realizes the interview is heading in an unhelpful direction. This step relies on the worker's recognition of those moments and leads to reflection on new possibilities for action.

The aim of the role of the external observer is to develop an awareness in the worker of thinking 'outside' of practice. The goal is for the worker to internalize the observer role as a critical interior process so that the worker can have this sort of 'dialogue' reflexively during practice. This skill is referred to as being a participant–observer in your practice; you are simultaneously participating in and observing the conversation during an interview with a client.

Another strategy for developing critical self-reflective practice is to undertake a process record. A 'process record' is a systematic, written analysis of an interview, typically in terms of its content and process. Usually, it is written in columns so that the simultaneous moments of a conversation can be suggested graphically. It includes the transcribed (or approximated) content of the conversation, from both interviewer and client, and then varying amounts of comment or critique (Table 5.1). For example, many process records include a column for what the interviewer was thinking or feeling, or what could have done differently, as well as a column documenting the perceived reactions of the client. Others will include a column for

Table 5.1 The Process Record
Example One

Content	What did you think was happening?	What would you do differently?
Worker: 'So you need to find somewhere else to stay tonight? Have you got someone to stay with?'	I thought the client really needed the housing crisis fixed, and that he didn't want to talk about anything else but this task.	I asked two questions without waiting to hear the answer to the first question. The second question might have seemed a bit accusative.
Client: 'Nah. Nowhere to go tonight. Nowhere to go after what I did last night. Nobody will have me.'	I think the client is more depressed than I'd originally thought. My questions seemed to have reinforced the lack of solutions rather than giving him a chance to talk further about what had happened last night.	Now I felt I needed to understand what had happened last night rather than move too quickly to the solution of housing for tonight.
Worker: 'Can you tell me a bit more about what happened last night?'	I invited the client to talk more about the original issue.	This was where I should have stayed with the story from the start rather than rushing to 'fix' the housing problems with him.
Client: [tells more of his story]		

Example Two

Content	What did you think was happening?	What would you do differently?
Worker: 'So you were not prepared for living and working in a northern and remote community. Have you looked for another job?'	I thought the client felt that living in a northern and remote community was too much and wanted out.	I asked two questions, and in the process assumed the client was looking to move and/or could not handle northern living.
Client: 'No, I just was not prepared for how different it is working in a small community. It is very different from what I expected.'	I think the client is more overwhelmed than I'd originally thought. My questions suggested the solution was for the client to get another job, instead of talking more about what the client is experiencing.	I need to gain an understanding of where the client is living and what he finds overwhelming about his new environment.
Worker: 'Can you tell me a bit more about where you have moved to work?'	I invited the client to talk more about the original issue, which was the move to a northern remote community to work.	This was where I should have stayed with the story from the start rather than rushing to 'fix' what I thought the issue was.
Client: [tells more of his story]		

comments about why, from a theoretical perspective, something was or was not said, in an attempt to bridge theory and practice. The opportunity for critical reflective practice takes another column in which the client–worker relationship can be analyzed as to whether it is reflecting, perpetuating, or challenging broader structural issues.

A process record gives insight into the interactions at the interface of a conversation, and, in particular, where change can be identified. From this exercise practitioners can reflect on their process when engaging with clients. In addition, it provides practitioners with the opportunity to self-evaluate and maintain a critical awareness of their skill levels relating to practice competencies. Practitioners may also want to consider keeping samples of their transcriptions to compare to future examples as part of an ongoing professional development strategy.

A more extensive analysis of a conversation or a particular incident can be done using a **critical incident** analysis framework (Cleak and Wilson, 2004: 73–5).The practice exercise below shows how a formal analysis, written or verbal, can assist with this process of reflection.

Practice Exercise

Consider a critical incident that occurred in your practice and reflect on why it happened and why it was critical.

First, retrieve the memory.

1. What was the first image you recall?
2. Where were you in relation to your first image?

3. Who was closest to you?

4. What sounds, smells, and tactile sensations do you recall?

5. Which people, comments, or practices stand out in your mind?

Next, consider the affective domain—reflect on how you felt.

6. What was your first reaction?

7. What was the high or low part of the incident?

8. Were you surprised, delighted, angered, elated, curious, confused, frightened, or depressed by anything in the experience? Describe your mood and feelings.

9. What do you think others around you were feeling?

Now, interpret the events.

10. What have you learned from this incident?

11. From this experience, what can you conclude about your understanding of and skills in assessment or analysis? What are your strengths and what areas require practice?

12. What was your key insight or learning?

13. How does this relate to your framework for practice?

Finally, consider your decisions.

14. What skills and areas of understanding do you need to develop further as a result of your reflection?

15. What would this development entail?

16. What methods does this experience reinforce as valuable for future practice? Why?

Source: Cleak and Wilson (2004: 79).

Overall, processes of reflection and reflexivity are highly valued by workers as they enhance learning and insight, develop personal and professional skills, build theoretical knowledge bases, and, most importantly, lead to better client outcomes (Crawford, 2006: 139).

Supervision and Other Supports

One of the practice arenas where critical self-reflection most commonly occurs is within the context of supervision.

One of the major supports typically available to you in your workplace is **supervision**. Supervision has different meanings in different professions. For human service workers, a supervisor is someone who takes responsibility, typically within the context of your agency, for you, your learning, and your practice. A supervisor assists you in developing your practice and practice wisdom through direct modelling, support, and intervention as an experienced worker.

Three key functions of supervision are administration, education, and support. In relation to other sections of administration, supervisors provide accountability to the organization and to clients by monitoring caseload issues and worker issues. The educational focus is on providing opportunities for learning and discussion, as well as exploring professional development needs. The support function relates to providing staff care, through the provision of an opportunity to reflect critically on practice and to receive support and encouragement (Kadushin, 1972). Thompson (2002: 146) has added a fourth dimension: mediation.

Carroll (1996: 53) expands these three tasks of supervision to seven specific tasks:

1. to set up or create a learning relationship
2. to teach
3. to educate
4. to monitor professional ethical issues
5. to counsel
6. to consult
7. to monitor administrative aspects.

Thus, supervision has preventive and supportive functions, which are important for the worker *and* the agency, and therefore ultimately to the benefit of clients. Many people have noted, however, the very limited research evidence base for supervision (Holloway and Neufeldt, 1995; Carroll, 1996; Carroll and Gilbert, 2006).

Optimally, supervision can provide a safe learning environment; a place to test out new ideas and integrate them into practice. It can provide a place to integrate theory and practice, and the personal and the professional. Workers have someone who can help them to deal with the ongoing accumulation of work issues, as well as provide support around particular crises.

Supervision varies according to the agency, to the theoretical and personal orientation and skill set of the supervisor, and to the expectations and skills of the supervised worker. In many agencies, supervision and support are offered regularly in a structured format and are valued dimensions of the agency's functioning (Renzenbrink, 2005). In other agencies, supervision tends to be overlooked or undervalued. Some agencies structure individual supervision relationships according to management hierarchies within the organization. A senior worker provides support and mentoring to a junior one. Others run with peer models and/or group supervision models.

Heather works in a drug and alcohol treatment service, where a group model of supervision operates. She describes her experience.

Focus on Practice

Group Supervision

I was having a conversation in our supervision group with several clinicians about the difficulty of establishing a good rapport with a client who has been reluctant to engage due to past trust issues. Some of the feedback I received from the group was:

- This can increase the difficulty when the clinician is in a situation where they are mandated to notify protective services about a client.
- This can amplify the conflict that this scenario can place a clinician in, and often the clinician is wishing to retain the hard-fought therapeutic alliance with the client, but is also well aware of risk issues requiring notification.

After, we highlighted the importance of consultation and debriefing when facing these dilemmas, especially in long-term therapeutic work.

1. What do you think Heather gained from this group supervision?
2. What are some of the key practice considerations for Heather?
3. What do you think would be different in individual supervision?
4. How do you have supervision organized in your work?

Practicum placements are a good opportunity for students to initiate active supervision. Consider the guidelines on the following page when developing your learning contract for a student practicum.

The usefulness of the supervisory experience depends on the agenda and the combined skill set of the supervisor and supervisee. As in any relationship, unrealistic or unclear expectations can inhibit a supervisory relationship (Bucknell, 2006: 45; Reid and Westergaard, 2006), as can major differences in opinions about how practice should take place or, for example, what are the important skills to demonstrate. Some other challenges or barriers have been identified as personality or value clashes, issues of hierarchy and management, and issues of trust given the inherent risks of disclosure, both personal and professional (Carroll, 1996). Supervision relies on a high level of trust for it to be successful (Dyregrov, 1997). Sometimes, the expectations of either the supervisor or the worker can be unreasonable. Supervisors can be busy and stressed, working under similar agency demands as the supervisee, but often with higher management responsibilities. All of these dimensions can influence the availability, quality and effectiveness of the relationship.

Like other professional relationships, having an initial discussion about the mutual expectations of supervision is important. Difficulties in the supervisory relationship occur when these expectations differ or when needs cannot be met within the context of the relationship. It is important to assess whether supervision can be an effective learning space or not. Sometimes a change of supervisor is possible and necessary. In other circumstances, an assessment as to what can be gained from supervision and what cannot, and what part each person plays in that situation, is needed.

Focus on Practice

Establishing a Supervisory Relationship

Here are some questions that workers have found useful to discuss with a prospective supervisor.

Questions relating to the structure of supervision:

1. When and where will you meet, including time, day, and length of time?
2. How frequently will you meet—weekly, twice per month, monthly?
3. What should happen in relation to phone calls, pagers, and other interruptions?
4. If so, who will document it? Will a record of supervision be kept?

Questions relating to the process and function of supervision:

1. What are the expectations and goals of each of you in supervision? for example:
   - How will the agenda be set and revised?
   - What should the worker bring to supervision; for example, case material, workplace/team issues and personal issues?
2. What are the learning and communication styles of each of you?
3. Are there possible incompatibilities in the ways in which each of you works?
4. What measures, if any, can be in place should the supervisor be away for an extended period? For example, is there an alternate senior person who could be available to consult?
5. How should conflict or disagreement be managed?
6. What review processes will take place?

Other possibilities for ongoing professional development include using supervision that is external to the agency. A major benefit of this arrangement is the ability to step outside the politics of the workplace and to have someone as a more objective sounding board who is an independent support for you and your work. The loss is the potential for bringing about change within the organization through direct consultation and negotiation with your work-based supervisor.

Outside of the forum of supervision, learning, reflection, and self-care can take place through numerous strategies:

- recording yourself in an interview (either audio or audio visually, and with the consent of the client) for review and critique
- undertaking joint work with a colleague, which provides the opportunity for critical feedback and discussion
- formalized mentoring with senior staff
- undertaking a process recording
- maintaining a personal journal, in which you critically reflect on your work
- maintaining reading of professional journals and texts.

Debriefing

Critical Incident Stress Management (CISM) has been increasingly recognized as an important dimension of workplace support, in the aftermath of specific events or critical incidents. Recognition of critical incidents came from emergency services work, and in this context was defined as: '[A]ny situation faced by emergency services personnel that causes them to experience unusually strong emotional reactions which have the potential to interfere with their ability to function either at the scene or later' (Mitchell, 1983: 36). This definition has also been applied to incidents involving a wider range of work contexts. It does raise the question as to whether it is the worker or the organization or the wider community that identifies the risk situation, an issue to which we will return later.

The tasks of CISM, as identified by Poindexter (1997: 125), include:

- offering an immediate response
- giving support
- providing focused problem-solving
- aiding in the enhancement of self-image
- setting limited (short-term and attainable) and specific goals
- identifying and getting access to resources
- initiating new modes of thinking, feeling, and coping.

A formal **debriefing** is one process that can be used to address these factors. The aim is to reduce distress, to educate and provide support around reactions, and, in many instances, to review workforce strategies.

Debriefing provides an opportunity to emotionally ventilate and psychologically process what has occurred. It can occur in dyads or in larger groups, and usually occurs between the first 24 hours following an incident, up to three days afterwards. It is used in many different practice contexts, such as schools, hospitals, and the community, particularly in the aftermath of distressing or traumatic incidents. In the context of human service practice, this could include a wide range of events such as natural disasters, deaths, accidents, and violent incidents.

Since its implementation, extensive debate has continued as to the effectiveness of debriefing and additional support interventions that make up CISM (Deahl et al., 2001; Dyregrov, 1997; McNally, Bryant, and Ehlers, 2003; Mitchell, 1983). The Mitchell Model, the debriefing model developed for firefighters in the US, follows a facilitated six-stage group structure, moving from the incident details to issues of personal reactions and education around self-care strategies (Everly, Flannery, and Mitchell, 2000; Mitchell, 1983, 2004).

The introductory phase includes introductions of everyone in the group, an introduction of the purpose of the meeting, and the establishment of group rules, particularly in relation to confidentiality. The fact phase invites participants to give their account of what occurred, including their roles and responsibilities. This account includes 'where they were [and] what they heard, saw, smelled and did as they worked in and around the incident' (Mitchell, 1983: 38). The intention is to re-create the incident from as many perspectives as possible.

The feeling phase involves asking questions relating to emotional reactions, such as:

- How did you feel when that happened?
- How are you feeling now?
- Have you ever felt anything like that in your life before? (Ibid.)

The emphasis is on hearing all emotional reactions and privileging no one over another. The symptom phase focuses on reactions through asking such questions as:

- What unusual things did you experience at the time of the incident?
- What unusual things are you experiencing now?
- Has your life changed in any way since the incident? (Ibid.)

This phase focuses on possible disruptions to functioning as a result of stress reactions. The teaching phase provides an opportunity for the facilitator to discuss normal stress and/or trauma reactions with the group and to educate around possible future reactions. The final phase of the debriefing session, the re-entry phase, draws the session to a close through review and careful planning about next steps, including what people might do immediately after the meeting, both individually and as a work group.

A follow-up debriefing is often included as a seventh stage. This provides an opportunity to review how people are coping and to implement other coping strategies as required.

Some research has found that this intervention can effectively assist 'emergency service workers return to work, reduce sick leave, and aid in trauma recovery' (Robinson, 2003). Supporters of debriefing argue that a stress response is normal and usually follows a regular pattern among the majority of individuals and it is this pattern that debriefing addresses. The major criticism of debriefing efforts is that they are not effective in reducing the longer-term posttraumatic stress impacts of traumatic events. The studies that critique such debriefings suggest that positive results attributed to debriefing interventions might have occurred spontaneously anyway, particularly when emergency workers typically informally debrief among colleagues in the workplace (Gordon, 1995a). They also maintain that debriefing alone does not necessarily assist in the prevention of traumatic stress, a finding supported by a number of studies (Deahl et al., 2001; Gordon, 1995a). Others have gone so far as to argue that debriefings may be harmful processes in that they interfere with an individual's usual coping processes in the early phases after exposure to a traumatic event (Gist and Woodall, 1999; Arendt and Elklit, 2001; Campfield and Hills, 2001).

After years of offering debriefings, a more cautious approach is now being recommended. For example, Rose, Bisson, and Wessely (2003) recommend restricting 'across the board' immediate psychological debriefings, but add that it is important to ensure early practical support and to notice those with possible acute stress disorder, an important predictor of PTSD. Mitchell's work, however controversial, has radically altered people's thinking about psychological first-aid responses, and has enabled a far greater awareness of the immediate and potentially devastating effects of critical incidents.

A significant issue influencing the efficacy of any CISM effort is the overall work environment. For example, if tensions or low levels of trust exist among work colleagues, the literature indicates that debriefings may not be beneficial; indeed, they may be counterproductive (Dyregrov, 1997). In negotiating complex workplace dynamics, adequate training of those who are to conduct a debriefing is essential. The status of the debriefer as either an insider or an outsider is an important consideration (ibid.). These dimensions are presented in Figure 5.1 on the following page and provide a useful checklist to think

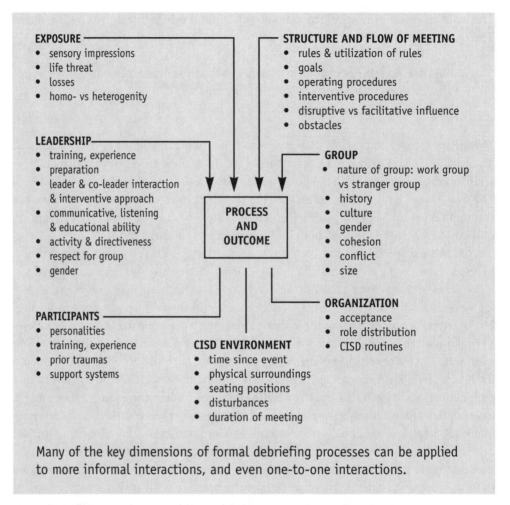

EXPOSURE
- sensory impressions
- life threat
- losses
- homo- vs heterogenity

LEADERSHIP
- training, experience
- preparation
- leader & co-leader interaction & interventive approach
- communicative, listening & educational ability
- activity & directiveness
- respect for group
- gender

PARTICIPANTS
- personalities
- training, experience
- prior traumas
- support systems

STRUCTURE AND FLOW OF MEETING
- rules & utilization of rules
- goals
- operating procedures
- interventive procedures
- disruptive vs facilitative influence
- obstacles

GROUP
- nature of group: work group vs stranger group
- history
- culture
- gender
- cohesion
- conflict
- size

ORGANIZATION
- acceptance
- role distribution
- CISD routines

CISD ENVIRONMENT
- time since event
- physical surroundings
- seating positions
- disturbances
- duration of meeting

PROCESS AND OUTCOME

Many of the key dimensions of formal debriefing processes can be applied to more informal interactions, and even one-to-one interactions.

Figure 5.1 Workplace Conditions for Debriefing to Occur

Source: Dyregrov (1997: 592).

about as to whether a debriefing process is appropriate or whether a smaller-scale strategy is warranted. As discussed earlier in this section, the question of who decides whether an incident has had a significant impact and whether debriefing is required is important.

Chapter Summary

In this chapter, we have explored some aspects of your ongoing learning and support needs. These have been raised early in the text to emphasize that they are core preventative skills for your practice. Using supervision preventively, and debriefing when required, minimizes the impacts of stressful and traumatic events, often preventing vicarious traumatization and burnout. We also explored the processes of critical self-reflection, supervision, and debriefing as three ways in which you can be sustained in your practice.

Questions for Analysis

1. In thinking about your readiness for practice, what strategies do you have in place in for professional self-care?
   - self-care strategies aimed at your professional work?
   - critical self-reflection processes; in particular, what supervision or mentorship structures do you have in place and when do you use them?
   - How would this differ in more northern and remote practice settings?

2. What strategies do you have in place for personal self-care?
   - self-care strategies aimed at your personal wellness outside of work?
   - critical self-reflection processes; in particular, what personal support networks do you have outside work and when do you use them?
   - What would be the implications for personal wellness in rural or northern settings?

3. What have been your experiences of supervision or mentoring in other contexts, and how do you think they will influence your current expectations?

4. What do you see as some of the challenges of engaging in critical self-reflection?

5. What is your understanding of debriefing?

6. What are the arguments for and against formal debriefings?

7. What are your thoughts on debriefing the debriefers?

8. If you are working in isolation, what system do you have in place to address professional self-care?

Recommended Readings

Dyregrov, A. 1997. 'The process in psychological debriefings', *Journal of Traumatic Stress* 10, 4: 589–605.

Figley, C., ed. 1995. *Compassion Fatigue: Coping with Secondary Traumatic Stress Disorder in Those Who Treat the Traumatized*. New York: Brunner/Mazel.

Fook, J. 1999. 'Critical reflectivity in education and practice', in B. Pease and J. Fook, eds, *Transforming Social Work Practice: Postmodern Critical Perspectives*. St Leonards: Allen and Unwin, 195–208.

O'Donoghue, K. 2003. *Restorying Social Work Supervision*. Annandale: Federation Press.

Internet Resources

American Academy of Experts in Traumatic Stress
www.crisisinfo.org/articles.htm

Canadian Centre for Emergency Preparedness
www.ccep.ca/ccepadvi.asp

Canadian Centre for Victims of Torture
www.ccvt.org/declaration.html

Canadian Mental Health Association
www.cwhn.ca/en/crisis_enan

Canadian Red Cross
www.redcross.ca/article.asp?id=000005&tid=003

International Critical Incident Stress Foundation
www.icisf.org

Mental Health: Canadian Women's Health Network
www.cmha.ca/bins/index.asp

Psychoz Publications—Resources for Effective Psychotherapy and Counselling
www.psychotherapy.com.au/link_search.asp

Trauma Care Network
www.trauma.ca

6 Establishing a Good Working Relationship

Learning Goals

- Describe what you need to think about before meeting with someone.
- Know how to open the communication process.
- Understand the processes involved in engaging with and actively listening to your clients and their stories.
- Analyze the concept of confidentiality.
- Critique the notion of self-disclosure, understanding why it is such a controversial skill.

Preparing to Meet

Chapter 4 outlined many of the questions you could consider prior to your contact with any client in your organization, including questions about the physical environment and the type of service delivery. This discussion focuses more specifically on preparing for an initial contact with your client, and highlights three particular issues.

Remember Carl Rogers's statement (1987: 38) about the importance of being psychologically available to someone: 'Can I be totally present to this client?' 'Can I be with him or her?' 'Can I be sensitive to every nuance of personal meaning and value, no matter how different it is from my own experience?'

The first relates to who it is you will be seeing. The initial engagement process needs to be thought through. For example, in working with Indigenous clients, thinking about who you will meet with and whether Elders need to be approached before contact with the client can be initiated are important considerations (Clarke, Andrews, and Austin, 1999; Rigney and Cooper, 2004). Working with family members first may be more appropriate. For survivors of torture and trauma, working with a support person present may be more appropriate (VFST, 2004). Working with children may require parental consent or the accompaniment of independent adult support. Work with some clients requires an interpreter, with whom the guidelines of the interface must be understood and agreed on beforehand.

The second issue is whether you are able to psychologically attend to this person or these people. An attitudinal readiness is vital. Many factors will impact your attitudinal readiness. For example, your contact with someone will be influenced by what has immediately preceded it, and what you might be anticipating afterwards. Being fully present in a conversation with another person is difficult if you are distracted by other issues. Part of being present with clients includes the verbal, non-verbal, and listening skills outlined in chapters 2 and 3. Meeting people involves a biopsychosocial–spiritual attentiveness and, if for some reason it is not possible to be attentive, discussing the options with your supervisor is an important step.

The third issue relates to what you already know about this person, if anything. Someone in your organization may have been working with this client and an extensive case note history may be available to you. Or this person may never have had contact with a worker or an agency before. This history, or lack thereof, is important for you to be aware of prior to any contact. The history can convey important details, such as risks to be aware of that may affect your new involvement with the person. For example, if someone has a history of aggression when she perceives her needs not to be met, you may want to consider where you meet with her and, indeed, whether you meet alone or with a co-worker. On the other hand, a case history can maintain a particular story about a person that has never been verified and could lead to the perpetuation of incorrect labels being imposed on the person. Equally important in this interaction will be what the other person knows about you and what she brings in terms of expectations and attitudes, drawn from knowledge of you or other workers.

The issue of prior knowledge can be complicated in rural or remote practice. Often, the turnover rate of professionals is higher then in urban settings; therefore case histories may not be available. Issues of consistency in planning also may be interrupted by changes in workers. In many such cases, the worker will be faced with clients who appear frustrated or aggressive, which may be due to fear or to a lack of trust that accompanies explaining their needs repeatedly to new workers.

Making Initial Contact

Whether in an involuntary client setting or a voluntary one, welcoming skills ensure that 'the welcome people receive is warm and respectful' (Trevithick, 2005: 150). Introductions and welcomes aim to help people feel at ease and to break down some of the initial anxiety or **anomie** that many people experience in unfamiliar relationships. Typically, people approach new relationships with some tentativeness, until trust and familiarity are established. Common questions clients have in mind are, according to Shulman (1999: 94):

> What is this going to be all about?
> What kind of worker is this going to be?
> What trouble can she/he cause me?
> What will the agency try to make me do?

The initial phase of work together should address these questions. These four questions influence the possibility of **engagement**, as a major choice the client makes early on is 'whether or not [he or she] will engage with the worker in a meaningful way and begin to develop what has been called "the therapeutic alliance"' (ibid., 95). Equally, important is for the worker to acknowledge the first question in his or her initial reaction to the client and the client's story. We make choices about the information we will reveal about ourselves early on in relationships with others, depending on what we read into the other person, and whether we feel the worker is a safe confidant, interested, and neutral or non-judgemental in attitude. The establishment of a client–worker relationship is similarly influenced by these factors. Creating a mutually safe environment is a priority during the initial contact.

Suzie, a worker in a drug and alcohol treatment service, describes some of the steps she takes to create such an environment for her clients:

> One of the things I noticed early on that helped me and the client(s) to relax on the first session was to be very aware of the environment and how it might feel for them on their first visit. I would make sure they knew where the toilet was should they need it and offer to make them a tea/coffee or get them some water. Ask if they found the office location okay. This initial exchange enabled a type of 'settling' time before anything more formal had commenced. I also find it useful to establish the amount of time you both have to avoid interruptions and, more importantly, to be able to create a safe place where there is some type of wrapping up or setting up of the next session before the time runs out. It is also important to leave time for the client to ask questions so you can be sure they understand the guidelines you have jointly created. This all helps to provide that safe environment for you and your client.

The 'settling in' process may vary according to where the conversation is taking place. In some instances, this will not be in an organization but in the client's home or community. Respecting the practices and space of another's world is critical. Suzie highlights the importance of a 'settling' time before any formal work has commenced, as well as the importance of being clear about the boundaries of the contact. These are important steps in engaging with another person.

Another decision point relates to the role of 'small' talk in engaging with people—the term even implies that there is 'big', important talk and trivial talk. The beauty of small talk is that it puts us all at ease—and sometimes this aspect of the process is the most important in engaging with someone in a working relationship. It connects again with how we regard our role and what kind of relationship we want to establish with people.

Introductions are part of this process. We typically need to hear a new person's name a minimum of three times to connect it into our memory. The name is an important dimension of a person to remember. If we are not named properly, we can feel misunderstood or isolated. Getting to the end of an interview with someone and realizing that you cannot remember her or his name can be embarrassing. It is better to spend time at the start of any contact ensuring that names are remembered by both client and worker, and that other introductory issues are attended to, such as the worker's role and reason for contact.

Whoever is present should be engaged directly in the conversation, as individuals. In many family meetings in hospitals, for example, the person who is the patient can be referred to as 'he' or 'she', as if somehow not present in the room and not part of any decision-making process. To speak this way immediately disempowers and silences people, as the denial of his or her basic right to recognition as a human being is implied.

A special moment or question may not be needed to shift the focus of the discussion onto the issues at hand. If someone is presenting for structured counselling at a set time in an agency, however, there usually will be a moment of transition into the work of a session. Some ways of getting started are suggested below:

Ways of opening an interview are considered in more depth in Chapter 7.

Focus on Practice

Getting Started

Some ways of opening an interview include:

> Worker: What's been happening, Tim? Are you still living at your dad's place?
> Worker: Last week you planned to reconnect with your grandmother. How did that go? Or, is there something else you would like to talk about, Susan?
> Worker: You did well to get through the holiday traffic, Jamal. How can I help you?
> Worker: Are you comfortable, Andy? What would you like to discuss today?
> Worker: You mentioned in your phone message that the storm kept you away Tuesday. What brings you here today, Joanna?
> Worker: Now that you've changed your address, tell me about what's been going on, Dawn?

As discussed above, it is important to refer to a person by name, when appropriate, to model recognition of the person, as a person, not as a label or gender (he, she).

1. What do you see as the risks and benefits of each of these different questions or invitations?
2. How would you open a conversation with a person you have just met?
3. What do you feel you would avoid saying? Why?
4. Can you reflect on a time when you felt uncomfortable starting a conversation with someone? Why was it uncomfortable? Did things improve? How?

Engagement

'Engagement' refers to the process of entering into and establishing a positive working relationship or alliance with people. As explained in Chapter 1, the client–worker engagement or alliance is fundamental to good work being accomplished together. While engagement is acknowledged as fundamental to engagement in a therapeutic context, Gibney (2003: 81) questions the prevailing assumption that all clients 'engage in the process with a full and genuine intensity'. Davis (2006: 191) claims practitioners must to some extent, accept where the client 'is at' for engagement to be successful.

Engagement varies in its intensity and also in how it can be negotiated between the worker and the client in tandem with external factors. Engagement begins with the practitioner's first contact with the client and evolves throughout the working relationship. Egan and Schroeder (2009: 57) describe some of the key components of engagement, starting with the premise that clients can change if they choose and followed by: don't see clients as victims; don't be fooled by appearances; share the helping process with clients; help clients see counselling sessions as working sessions; use each helping interaction to promote client engagement in problem-solving; and become a consultant to clients. Additionally, skills such as probing, active listening, and appropriate paraphrasing all assist a successful client engagement.

The concept of engagement should be considered from a community perspective, also. 'Community' can be defined in many different ways. Al-Krenawi and Graham (2003: 50) cite an early study that:

> found ninety-four separate uses of the word. Yet, most definitions include four components: people, location in a geographic space, social interaction, and common ties . . . . Hence, the term 'community' may be used to identify a First Nation of Plains Cree living in Saskatchewan, a group of Vietnamese refugees who settled in Halifax 20 years ago, or a group of Bosnian refugees dispersed across southern Ontario.

There can also be communities within a community. Briskman and Flynn observe that 'a community-embedded framework provides a different way of looking at rural practice—a new angle on where the practitioner, and practice, fit within a community' (cited in Cheers, 1999: 93). Wilkinson expands this notion stating, 'this process is perhaps more vivid in rural than urban communities for, in a rural locality, the limited pool of people produces a particular community through daily interaction across arenas—culture, social structure, economy, politics, religion, and other natural environment' (Wilkinson, 1991: 16).

In a study conducted by Brownlee and Graham (2005: 7) the authors quote a participant who explains, 'comminutes cocoon themselves and become self-protective and wary of outside influences'. In this context, a practitioner must view the process of engagement from a community perspective. It would be helpful for the practitioner to consider: the size of the community, geographic location, service limitations, community structure, current internal roles of community members, and what the appropriate method for engagement specific to the community would include.

Corey suggests the following practical guidelines towards increasing effectiveness in engagement with diverse client populations. Consider how these suggestions (adapted from Corey, 1996: 30–1) may influence the engagement process:

- Learn more about ways in which your own cultural background has an influence on your thinking and behaving.
- Identify your basic assumptions—especially as they apply to diversity in culture, ethnicity, race, gender, class, religion, and lifestyle—and think about how your assumptions are likely to affect your practice as a counsellor.
- Where did you obtain your knowledge about culture?
- Learn to pay attention to the common ground that exists among people of diverse backgrounds. What are some ways in which we all share universal concerns?
- Realize it is not necessary to learn everything about a client's culture or background prior to working with that person. Allow the client to teach you about her/his culture.
- Recognize the importance in being flexible in the methods you apply.

- Remember practising from a multicultural perspective can make your job easier and be more rewarding for both you and your clients.

Corey and Corey discuss the broad range of counselling groups. Group engagement tends to become shaped by the participants and while the group structure varies (for example, open or closed groups) Corey and Corey (1997: 13) maintain all groups share the following goals:

- Helping people develop more positive attitudes and better interpersonal skills
- Using the group process as a way of facilitating behaviour change
- Helping members transfer newly acquired skills and behaviour learned in the group to everyday life.

Bitter (2009: 40) remarks that 'before we can know the richness and diversity of other families, we must come to know our own heritage'. Below, Jane talks about some of these dimensions in the parent bereavement support group discussed in Chapter 4.

Focus on Practice

Initial Engagement

Unexpected processes also happen when we hold our evening support group for parents who are be-reaved. As it is an open group and no reply about attending is asked for, it is difficult to know how many people are coming. The room in which the group is held is located deep within a non-clinical area of the hospital, and lost visitors or parents or staff looking for other groups or meetings does happen from time to time.

From the outset it is critical to establish in a welcoming, respectful way that those coming are for the appropriate group. Signs along the way and on the door of the room are no guarantee of this, as we have found. Returning to the hospital and/or coming to the group for the first time may confront or overwhelm parents with powerful memories, images, or emotions. If couples are coming, one may have agreed to come for the sake of the other and bring their own reluctance. Some may find it hard to speak.

Jane then describes some of the ways in which she goes about the actual introduction and engagement processes with group members.

Focus on Practice

Meeting a Bereavement Group

Our greeting and the process of engaging takes place outside the door. 'Hello, are you here for/ looking for the parents' group? I'm Jane. Welcome.'

We extend our hand for a handshake—there may be some instances when this is not appropriate, perhaps with some members of certain faith and cultural communities, and again a quick decision may need to be made, and assumptions about CALD [culturally and linguistically diverse] citizens may be incorrect. Despite the context a small smile may add to the sense of welcome, but sensitivity is needed.

Parents mostly volunteer their names, and the name of their child who has died. If, however, they are too distressed, it may be impossible for them in that moment to speak and we need to acknowledge this—a gentle nod and some brief words may help: 'It can be very hard coming to the group for the first time.' 'Many parents who have come to the group have found it difficult, too.' We may add, 'See how you go tonight.'

Depending on how the parent responds, it may be sensitive to ask the name of their child (if not already given) and how long it's been since the child died. There have been times when a parent is coming for the first time, several years after the child's death. At such times we would ask 'What brought you tonight?' or 'Is there something about tonight's topic?' A fine line has to be trodden between introductions and moving too far into their story. Sometimes it may be appropriate to say 'Perhaps we'll be hearing more about [their child's name] or just more through the night'. We then encourage the parents to write out a name tags and their names and their child's in the book (placed just inside the room) and offer refreshments and gesture to the seats.

The assumptions we make about who a person is, based on momentary contact and 'first impressions', profoundly influences the initial engagement. Studies have demonstrated that information about another person's gender, sex, ethnicity, and age is processed within seconds of encounter. From a survival perspective, this makes sense. This instant survey enables us to make quick decisions as to whether this new person is 'safe', based on our 'typing' of them according to previous encounters with others like them. In psychodynamic terms, this process is referred to as a 'parataxic distortion' (Stack Sullivan, 1953), where we draw on our past knowledge of people from the same (*para*) group (*taxis*) to make sense of the present person. The drawback of this process is that typing can become stereotyping, and prohibits us from seeing individuals as individuals, outside of 'labels' (Thompson, 2003b: 2006).

Egan and Schroeder (2009: 118–19) refer to this as 'stereotype-based listening', and provide an example of overhearing someone being referred to by a doctor as 'the hernia in [room] 304'. They continue: 'to use terms borrowed from Gestalt psychology, make sure that your client remains "figure"—in the forefront of your attention—and that models and theories about clients remain "ground"—knowledge that remains in the background and is used only in the interest of understanding and helping this unique client.'

Engaging or bonding with another person can happen very quickly under some conditions. Working intensively as a small group over a weekend, for example, can build a very strong sense of cohesion, particularly if contact with others outside of that group is discouraged and intense time is spent together talking about emotional issues. Some groups rely on this process to form rapid and seemingly strong bonds. The phenomenon of 'speed dating' is based on this process of quick assessment and engagement with another person. Within a matter of minutes, people have decided whether they wish to continue to engage with a person.

These decisions, nevertheless, are complex processes, and different theoretical perspectives understand this complexity in very different ways.

Focus on Practice

Finding Commonalities

In a small group, form pairs and talk for one minute with that person before moving around to talk for one minute with other group members. Find as many points of commonality as possible.

1. How did you gather the information from the other person? For example, did you ask questions or did you talk with each other in a non-questioning way?
2. When did you realize that there were points of commonality—or not?
3. What did you notice about your style and other group members' styles of gathering information?
4. Did you incorporate any of the engagement techniques (listening, non-verbal, verbal) discussed in previous chapters?
5. What did you find most effective?

Gibney (2003: 81–2) proposes that four levels of engagement occur in a therapeutic context. Level one refers to the negotiation around whether therapy 'is required, wanted or needed or is even appropriate at this time, in this place, between these people in attendance.' Level two refers to a form of problem-solving or solution-focused therapy: '[T]hey perceive something is wrong that they want fixed, and they have no particular wish for understanding or insight' (ibid., 83). Level three refers to engagement when the therapeutic relationship is seen as the 'nexus of change' by both the therapist and client. Level four refers to a deep engagement in the relationship that is regarded as transformative, and the therapist is 'an implicated witness' (ibid., 86). While specific to psychotherapy, this typology reveals that even in the most highly mandated of client–worker relationships, it may be possible to achieve level three or four engagement, returning to the arguments of Chapter 1 that the client–worker relationship can be positively influential in and of itself.

Nicole, a social worker at a children's hospital, wrote about her experience of engagement with Mrs B., a client whose story has been de-identified.

Focus on Practice

Initial Engagement with Mrs B.

Mrs B. is the mother of an eight-year-old son diagnosed with a treatable but life-threatening condition. I received the family's file at the point of her son's diagnosis and Mrs B. spent two formal sessions with me discussing the impact of the diagnosis on her, her son, and their family. Mrs B. did not attend a subsequent appointment, but was informed by me that she could have ongoing sessions with me and that I would also make contact with her during her son's subsequent outpatient appointments.

In the introduction, notice the process of establishing a relationship. Nicole was given the file to the family as their worker. This often occurs through weekly team meetings or daily intake reviews of clients. It raises important questions about the goodness of fit or the compatibility between the worker and the client. A poor fit can limit engagement, strain relationships, and influence both the worker's practice and the client's opinion about the value of the service provision. Nicole describes what happened next.

Focus on Practice

Working with Difficulties in Engagement

After two months of no contact from Mrs B., and little contact in outpatients due to my feeling that Mrs B. did not want to further engage with me, I heard via a colleague that Mrs B. was not happy because I had not spent enough time with her. I organized a session with Mrs B. to discuss her support needs. I began by inquiring about Mrs B. and her family's current situation. I then stated that I would like to discuss openly the concerns that Mrs B. discussed with her colleague. I said that the purpose of the discussion was to ensure that Mrs B. and her family received the support that was needed. I had discussed this strategy with my supervisor and attempted to ensure that I was not defensive of my actions during my sessions with Mrs B.

Mrs B. stated she felt that other parents saw their social workers on a more regular basis and that she would like another social worker who could spend more time with her. I said that it was very important that Mrs B. have access to the level of support that she felt was necessary. I commented that Mrs B. had given me the impression that she was not comfortable receiving support from social work and that she seemed reluctant to engage in anything more than discussion about practical issues. Mrs B. disclosed that she did find it difficult to trust people and that she felt that some of the material discussed with me in the first two sessions was 'more than I've discussed with most people'.

In this interaction, Nicole and Mrs B. have been able to discuss the situation openly. Nicole framed the discussion in terms of supporting Mrs B. She was open to critical feedback from Mrs B. about why the engagement process had gone the way it had. This enabled Mrs B. to talk about the difficulties both between them and in relation to the ongoing issues with which Mrs B. was grappling. In this example, despite the difficulties in initially engaging, good engagement and rapport between Nicole and Mrs B. seem to be beginning, as demonstrated below.

Focus on Practice

Moving on with the Work Together

Mrs B. stated that she knew that she had given me the impression that she didn't want to speak to me but was angry that I did not persevere. Mrs B. and I spent a session discussing the difficulty

Mrs B. was experiencing with a number of intense and sometimes conflicting emotions and how difficult it was for Mrs B. to access help. Mrs B. disclosed that she was concerned that she may have said something to me that may have changed the way that I perceived her. Mrs B. decided that she wanted to continue seeing me for assistance and that it was helpful that I was able to 'take the criticism without getting angry at me'.

1. At what level of engagement would you see Mrs B. and Nicole engaging?
2. What would you have done in Nicole's situation?
3. What key points stand out for you in this example?
4. What practice skills are important in this example? (reviewing plan and roles, expectations)
5. How do you receive disagreement or dissatisfaction from clients? Do you take feedback personally or do you see this as an opportunity to reflect on practice?

These engagement difficulties illustrate that clarifying the initial reason and ongoing basis for contact is critical. In some settings, clients can be bewildered by the sudden arrival of a worker, for example. They may not know why a referral has occurred, what is known about them, and what the role of the worker is all about. In other situations, as in Mrs B.'s case, her own assumptions, needs, and expectations strongly influenced what occurred. These are all important introductory clarifications that may need revisiting throughout the length of work together.

Each theoretical perspective would understand these interactions differently. These understandings of Mrs B.'s situation will be revisited in Chapters 11–14.

The discussion of engagement so far has focused on working with clients who choose to engage in the process. Some clients, however, will not want to talk with you at all, and the process of engagement becomes more challenging. Trotter (2006: 1) identifies some of these questions:

How do you help someone who has no interest in being helped? . . . How do you counsel someone who does not even recognize they have a problem? How do you work with someone who has a totally different set of values from yourself?

In these situations, role clarification and contracting are even more important factors in the establishment of a working relationship. Role clarification refers to the process of establishing clear understandings of purpose. That is, to answer as clearly as possible why it is you are meeting together. In some instances, this will involve explicitly addressing the lack of interest or free will in the contact; for example: 'I doubt you want to be here, talking about what's happened. What if we agree on talking for 10 minutes about some things the court is going to need to know to make their decision?' It also involves talking very explicitly about the purpose of the contact and what the outcome or next step may be:

This section explores the initial contracting of the relationship. In Chapter 9, we will look at the processes involved in contracting around specific goals once an initial assessment has been done.

Worker: Hi, Brandi, my name is Joseph. I'm a social worker with the Ministry for Children and Family Development. I'm here because concerns were raised about your daughter being home alone and we need to understand what's going on. Given that a notification's been made, we will need to assess whether there are ongoing concerns about your daughter's safety.

Other issues that may need to be addressed in the initial contracting phase include:

- The length of time in this contact and ongoing contact
- the purpose of the conversation
- the purpose of the conversation from the client's perspective
- any concerns or questions the client has at the onset
- what will happen with the information discussed—that is, what are the limits of confidentiality?

This initial conversation is about establishing the when, where, why, and how of the work. A respectful and empowering strategy is to have an explicit discussion about the anticipated contact (Trotter, 2006). Sometimes making this agreement is more possible than at others. However, to make an assumption that our mandate as a worker—our theoretical orientation or the limitations of confidentiality, for example—are immediately understood by a client can be very wrong. These parameters may need to be outlined in detail so that the client is empowered to make decisions within that conversation.

One central tenet of the process of engagement is to begin where the client wants to begin. As Marsh and Doel (2005: 13) propose: 'From the very start of the work, the expressed views and preferences of people are central. Finding ways to help people express them as clearly as possible is a prime practitioner task.'

Starting 'where the client is at' is illustrated in Karen's work with Myrtle and the setting of the priorities for their work together. An initial priority may seem to be the grief issues, but another priority emerges.

Focus on Practice

Engagement Is about Starting Where the Client Is

A single, 80-year-old woman, Myrtle was referred for a social work assessment following the death of her sister. The two women had lived together for their whole lives, and cared for their mother who had died when the sisters were in their sixties. Myrtle was, not surprisingly, distressed at the death of her sister, but her worry on the first day of our meeting was what to do with the sister's body, as the two had both decided that their bodies should be donated for use by medical science. Ensuring that this occurred brought her significant relief.

Subsequently, over some years of contact, we explored her loss and revisited much of her life story. Myrtle wrote little notes to herself to remind herself of what she wished to discuss with me on my regular visits. On one such occasion the note revealed the question 'When I go [she had no fear of dying, now that her sister was gone] who is going to turn off the fridge?' I viewed this question as having multiple meanings, and in answering her practical question was able to begin also to deal with the larger question of what will happen to what remained of herself and her sister.

Starting with 'where the client is at' sounds like a relatively straightforward positioning. Some challenges, however, include:

- cultural differences—how does the worker know where the client really is at? Is the outset of relationship sometimes more a matter of where we *think or assume* the client is at?
- communication barriers—how do we ensure that the client's perspective is heard and understood when communication barriers are present, such as language differences or hearing impairments or audio-processing deficits?
- disagreements with where our client is at—how do we ensure this positioning of where they are at actually respects his or her humanity, when it may be so fundamentally opposed to our own world view, as in the case of a perpetrator of violence or sexual assault?
- What are the first steps to engage the client in the direction of a plan that includes the above points, is ethical, and facilitates the best interests of the client?

This is where some of the skills we will look at in Chapters 7 and 8 come into play as ways of exploring these dimensions and ensuring, as much as possible, that the client's views and preferences remain central.

People's unique communicative styles should be attended to, either directly or indirectly, in this time of relationship formation. Koprowska (2005) identifies experiences of deafness, visual impairment, learning difficulties, and dementia as influencing communication. The engagement process is about finding ways to work with these dimensions and establish a working relationship.

The degree of cultural congruence (Dean, 2001) is an important consideration in initial contact. As Jane mentions in her experience with the bereavement group, sensitivity in relation to culturally safe practices is important. Decisions about initial interactions may consider whether to engage in a formal handshake, or who to address in the group. These issues can always be enquired about in the initial encounters. For example: 'I would like to talk with you, but I'm wondering if we should have someone else here with us from your community?'

Cultural identities also influence engagement experiences; for example, when a female worker is engaging with a male client and the client's cultural background does not permit contact with women. Other differences will be more fundamental, but perhaps more subtle, in relation to different world views and beliefs. Furlong and Ata (2006) were cited in the previous chapter in regard to naming cultural diversity and how this naming may not be enough.

The Canadian Association of Social Work (CASW) *Practice Guidelines* contain a section titled 'Demonstrate Cultural Awareness and Sensitivity', which states that social workers must, 'strive to understand culture and its function in human behaviour and society, recognizing the strengths that exist in all cultures'. Further, the practice guidelines affirm that 'social workers acknowledge the diversity within and among individuals, communities, and cultures' (CASW *Practice Guidelines*, 2005). The practice guidelines review the need for the social worker to take account of his or her personal beliefs and heritage and how they influence practice with clients. Perhaps most important is a commitment to obtain the training required to maintain competence pertaining to diversity issues in practice.

Confidentiality

Maintaining the confidentiality or privacy of a person's information is an important professional requirement, essential to creating a 'safe' space for the client to talk about concerns. Agencies will have different practices, however, in relation to expectations of reporting and accountability around client information. Agencies involved in writing court reports, for example, have different recording and reporting arrangements compared with therapeutic and voluntary agency settings. Being aware of your agency's requirements and talking with your clients about mutual understandings of confidentiality from the outset are two practices of paramount importance.

Melissa provides an excerpt from a presentation based on her doctoral thesis, which examined people who had been engaged in suicidal behaviours and the impact of an intensive support program on their behaviour (Petrakis, 2004). She describes how the worker's decision might be influenced by the legal and agency context, as much as by the immediate client–worker situation.

Focus on Practice

Acting on Client Disclosures of Risk

Confidentiality is a cornerstone of professional social work practice. Note in the CASW *Code of Ethics* that 'Social workers demonstrate respect for the trust and confidence placed in them by clients, communities and other professionals by protecting the privacy of client information and respecting the client's right to control when or whether this information will be shared with third parties' (CASW, 2005). With a client at risk, a therapist needs to use careful professional judgement about the balance between potential harm to the client by either disclosing information or maintaining confidentiality. A disclosure in the absence of a strong belief that the client presents an immediate risk to him/herself and/or others potentially creates a situation in which the therapist could be sued by the client for breach of confidence (Bond, 2000); however, failure to disclose when there is a strong belief that the client presents an immediate risk to him/herself and subsequently takes his/her own life may lead a therapist to having to defend him or herself in court against the accusation of failure in duty of care (Daines, Gask, and Usherwood, 1997; Jenkins, 2002).

Increasingly, therapists and clinicians are concerned with the risk of litigation (Reeves and Seber, 2004). The risk of clients harming themselves can debilitate the therapist from acting creatively and collaboratively, making their actions defensive and focused 'solely on risk assessment rather than therapeutic change' (Sharry, Darmody, and Madden, 2002). Understandably, then, in an under-resourced system, focus shifts to at least keeping these clients safe. The focus shifts to risk assessment.

Using Self-Disclosure

Establishing a good relationship relies to a large extent on the client's willingness and capacity to engage in it. Degrees of disclosure (Burstow, 1987: 18) vary enormously between workers and their clients, as this example from a therapeutic context illustrates:

Therapists, certainly, disclose now and then. Therapists sometimes make themselves very vulnerable indeed. Clients, however, do not just do this 'sometimes'. The clients' ongoing job is precisely to do this disclosing, to make themselves vulnerable, to uncover, live, and embrace those parts of self that we generally hide.

It is taken for granted that clients in most situations will disclose extensively about their life circumstances. The degree to which a worker should self-disclose, however, is more controversial. To self-disclose is to explicitly talk to the client about your own experiences. **Self-disclosure** is 'loosely defined as what individuals verbally reveal about themselves to others (including thoughts, feelings and experiences)' and is seen to play 'a major part in close relationships' (Derlega et al., 1993: 1). We are always revealing things about ourselves through both our verbal and non-verbal interactions, but our use of self mediates these decisions and provides a boundary around some information. Bitter (2009: 428) defines self-disclosure as simply 'sharing part of oneself or life with a client' and notes that it is '[h]ighly valued in feminist family therapy'. In addition, it involves 'a judgment on the part of the therapist: that sharing some aspect of the therapist's life will directly benefit the client' (ibid.). Self-disclosure, then, refers to your explicit use of your own circumstances, either past or present, in ways that overstep the usual boundaries, as the following example illustrates:

Client: I'm just not coping anymore. I don't go out; I can't go out. I sit at home and cry and eat. That's all I do. I can't see how this will ever change.
Worker: When my Dad died, I found it really hard to go out, too. It felt much safer at home. But I found if I forced myself to go out, I'd sometimes have an OK time. Gradually, it just got easier.
Client: So I'm not going crazy? This will change?

In this example, the worker is emphasizing the skills he found helpful in overcoming a similar situation. Such disclosure *may* help the client feel less alone and overwhelmed, as the response in this example implies. It may provide some modelling as to how someone else coped with a difficult and distressing time. On the other hand, the client may feel resentful that the worker is saying the pain will lessen, when that is not how he feels right now, and that the worker has been able to adapt to something the client feels he will never be able to adapt to. The use of self-disclosure is controversial because it highlights some of the major differences in expectations of the boundaries and purposes of helping relationships. It draws a much more complex set of assumptions about similarities and differences between interviewer and client into the interaction.

Some workers are adamant that self-disclosure should always be avoided, whereas others are just as adamant that it is one of the most powerful, equalizing skills of practice. This diversity of points of view raises questions as to why the field is so divided and whether an absolute position is possible to maintain over time and in all situations.

Consider the situation Suzie found herself in, in her work with clients with drug issues.

Focus on Practice

Disclosing Personal Details to the Client

It is inevitable in any counselling session that the client will ask a personal question, such as: 'So, do you have any kids—do you really know what it is like for me?' or 'You don't look old enough to have teenagers' or 'So, do you use drugs or what?'

I found that the first time this happened I had not given enough thought to what my response would be and it is the type of issue that requires thought, reflection, and ongoing discussion within a supervision session. For me, the question I had to ask myself was, how useful to the client would disclosing my personal experiences be, given that every person has such a unique set of circumstances that are individual to them. Sometimes by divulging and exploring your own experiences the focus of the session becomes diverted, and it is this diversion that is worth exploring with your client in more detail.

Suzie's examples of the questions she has been asked in practice about her own private life highlight the dilemma: To answer or not? Directly or indirectly? One way of understanding these kinds of questions is to ask whether they are questions about you, whether as a worker you will understand them or view them in a particular way. Will you understand what it is like to feel so overwhelmed as a parent, for example? How might the way you answer these questions impact your practice approach?

Practice Questions

How would you respond to the following questions?

- Do you have children?
- How old are they?
- You look too young to have a teenager.
- Do you have a boyfriend/girlfriend?
- Do you earn a lot of money doing this job?
- What time do you finish work today?
- Where are you off to for your holidays?
- Have you ever had an abortion?
- How old are you?
- Where do you live?
- Do you believe in a divine presence like God or Allah?

1. Would you respond to each and all of the questions? Why?

2. In what ways are the above questions relevant to your working relationship—or are they?

3. Who could ask these questions and get an answer from you? Why?

4. Do you feel prepared as a practitioner to address this type of a situation? If so how? If not, what do you feel you need to practice?

The usual argument for the use of disclosure is that, in a professional context, self-disclosure helps to build trust and authenticity in a relationship. That is, the worker joins with the client through self-disclosure as another human being, facing similar challenges or successes. This sharing reduces inequalities in the relationship by reducing the sense that the worker is somehow outside of life's problems and challenges. The norms of reciprocity that operate in many relationships are considered to be enhanced by mutual disclosure and intimacy levels. Shulman's (1978) study of perceived worker effectiveness found that the 'worker's ability to "share personal thoughts and feelings" ranked first as a powerful correlate to developing working relationships and to being helpful.'

The argument against the use of self-disclosure is that it detracts from the focus on the client's story. The purpose of the relationship is to hear and support the client's story, not to hear and support the worker's. Some argue that self-disclosure not only shifts the focus onto the worker, but also burdens the client with the worker's issues and with personal values that perhaps should not enter the agency arena. Another argument is that self-disclosure can place the worker at risk in certain situations. Clients may find out where you live or if you have children, and use this information to threaten you or to intrude into this private space. Once this information is known, it can neither be retracted nor controlled, and can lead to serious breaches of privacy and safety. The consequences of self-disclosure are in some ways 'independent of what the teller might intend' (Derlega et al., 1993: 9). Managing self-disclosure is about managing privacy and vulnerability—dimensions that differ from individual to individual, as well as cross-culturally. As with other relationships, over time, the capacity to tolerate or trust different levels of vulnerability or reciprocity within the context of a client–worker relationship can increase.

Melissa, a social worker in the mental health field and teacher of communication skills, recounts a discussion of self-disclosure in one of her classes, which shows how she resolves these issues in practice. These conversations are presented with the permission of the students. Melissa was working with, a group of students who were about one month into their first field placements. She presents her experience below.

Focus on Practice

Issues in Self-Disclosure

We watched a video showing a counsellor opening an interview. The counsellor stated her name, asked the client in an open-ended manner what the client hoped to gain from the interview, and then explained the types of questions that would be asked in counselling and the rationale. The counsellor had described the *process* of counselling, but had not disclosed anything about herself, her qualifications, or her life. I reflected on this with the students. Exchanges with two students were particularly instructional regarding the issue of self-disclosure:

Student Situation 1—Wanting to Disclose

> Student: I know I shouldn't self-disclose, but . . .
> Melissa: It feels as though self-disclosure would help with rapport?
> Student: Yes.

Melissa: What was the context?

Student: I am working in a mental health setting. We go out on home visits to families with a member with a mental illness. My brother has bipolar.

Melissa: It feels as though it could help to share this information.

Student: But I know I shouldn't.

Melissa: It sounds as though you know there is a rule but your gut is telling you something else.

Student: I guess so.

Melissa: I'm a big believer in following our gut in counselling, but when we start out, our gut isn't trained yet to how counselling is different from everyday conversations. In everyday conversations we assume two equal parties who can contribute confidently and assertively. Counselling is not like that. One party is feeling very vulnerable and is being asked to reveal something he or she has tried to resolve, and often with the help of family and friends and even other professionals, yet the person is still very troubled. Such people will feel embarrassed about sharing and unsure what we will think of them if they tell us everything they are thinking. If we talk about ourselves the client will gladly let us, relieved to be off the hook, at least for a while, and out of the spotlight. This is not good, because we have missed this early opportunity to show our curiosity and concern and to indicate that we can focus exclusively on the client in this space because we consider her or him and their experiences important.

Student: Yeah, I don't want to make it about me.

Melissa: There's just one other thing, too. It might be that, if the family's experience is similar to yours, they *do* feel a quicker rapport established by your self-disclosure. However, it will become evident quickly that yours and their experiences are not exactly the same. The gender of the family member with bipolar may be different; that age of diagnosis probably was different; the level of chronicity also will be different; your family and theirs may differ in financial resources or social supports available . . . . Suddenly, as these differences come out in conversation, the family can feel betrayed that they thought you understood, when you don't understand at all.

Student Situation 2—Not Having the Experience to Disclose and Share

Student: My situation is different. My lack of experience makes me feel less skilled to help my clients.

Melissa: Tell me how self-disclosure would help with feeling less skilled.

Student: I am working in a women's health service where all the clients are pregnant. My supervisor has two children.

Melissa: So it feels like your supervisor has legitimacy or expertise because she has been pregnant before, like these clients, while you have not?

Student: Yes. I feel like I don't have that knowledge to offer.

Melissa: You feel that the knowledge isn't something book-learned or learned through your work in the service, that you need to have gone through it yourself?

Student: Yes.

Melissa: This situation is not so different from the first one we looked at.

Student: How do you mean?

> Melissa: Your colleague is feeling that in her setting, rules prevent her from disclosing when it would be helpful. You are feeling that in your setting rules would support disclosure and it would be helpful, but you have no material to disclose.
>
> Student: Yes.
>
> Melissa: The dilemma is the same, though. Our self-disclosure shifts the focus away from the client and is personal and specific, therefore, limited. Even your effective supervisor, who uses her self-disclosure incidentally as part of her genuine use of self, will get into trouble sometimes because the client will note the differences in their experiences: that the gender of their babies is different; that their experiences of labour were different; that one did have and the other did not have postpartum depression; the involvement or lack of involvement by their partner/spouse and extended family was different; they were affected differently by cultural beliefs surrounding diet, child-rearing practices, the question of circumcision, and by difference in beliefs around religion and faith and rituals, such as baptism and naming rites. We need to be very careful not to fast-track rapport at the expense of real empathy.

The following questions may assist you in deciding whether or not to self-disclose:

- Is change in the client possible without self-disclosure?
- Is the disclosure client-centred and client-focused or does it shift the focus to you and your circumstances?
- Is it a necessary condition of practice? Or is it always contextual?
- How does your use of disclosure change as you practice and what determines those boundaries?
- What do you want to disclose and, more importantly, why?
- Is it possible or desirable to generalize from your experience or to distance yourself by offering a useful story without creating the burden for the client of its being your story? For example, 'Some women have found . . . ' or 'Some people have found . . ..'
- What are your beliefs about the comparative values of book-knowledge, work experience, and lived experiences? How do your beliefs impact your choices around self disclosure?

Chapter Summary

In this chapter we have explored some of the skills in establishing a client–worker relationship. This has included the skills of creating a safe and supportive environment in which to meet, the skills of an initial contact, and the skills of active listening. In looking at engagement, the use of minimal encouragers, empathy, and self-disclosure, it is apparent there is no one right way to be using these skills. Rather, they need to be thought about in context.

Questions for Analysis

1. What have you learned about:
   - empathy?
   - engagement? In both urban and remote practice setting?
   - minimal encouragers?
   - self-disclosure?

2. Which skills of engagement do you find relatively easy to apply and which not?
   - Provide specific examples.
   - How will you practice in areas you identify as difficult?

3. What do you notice about people's reactions to emotion in:
   - your family?
   - your work place?
   - your community?

Recommended Readings

Bishop, A. 2002. *Becoming an Ally: Breaking the Cycle of Oppression*. Crows Nest: Allen and Unwin.

Bitter, J.R. 2009. *Theory and Practice of Family Therapy and Counselling*. Belmont, Calif.: Brooks/Cole.

Briskman, L., and M. Flynn. 1999. *Community Embedded Rural Social Care Practice*. Geelong, Australia: Deakin University Press.

Brownlee, K., and J.R. Graham. 1997. *Violence in the Families*. Toronto: Canadian Scholars' Press.

Corey, M., and G. Corey. 1997. *Groups Process and Practice*. Belmont, Calif.: Brooks/Cole.

Egan, G., and W. Schroeder. 2009. *The Skilled Helper: A Problem-Management and Opportunity-Development Approach to Helping*, 1st Canadian edn. Toronto: Nelson Education Brooks/Cole.

Gibney, P. 2003. *The Pragmatics of Therapeutic Practice*. Melbourne: Psychoz.

Goleman, D. 2005. *Emotional Intelligence*. New York: Bantam Books.

———. 2006. *Social Intelligence: The New Science of Human Relationships*. London: Hutchinson.

Scales, T., and C. Streeter, eds. 2004. *Rural Social Work: Building and Sustaining Community Assets*. Toronto: Nelson.

Schmidt, G., and R. Klein. 2004. 'Geography and social work retention', *Rural Social Work* 9: 235–43.

Wilkinson, K.P. 1991. *The Community in Rural America*. New York: Greenwood.

Internet Resources

Canadian Association of Social Workers, Practice Guidelines *(2005)*
   www.casw-acts.ca

Canadian Counselling and Psychotherapy Association (CCPA)
   www.pacfa.org.au/scripts/content.asp?pageid=ETHICSPAGEID

Daniel Goleman's website, Social and emotional intelligence
   www.danielgoleman.info

Social Care Institute for Excellence
   www.scie.org.uk

Part Three | Basic Skills: Focusing the Communication

In the previous chapters, we have explored the ways in which workers might approach practice and begin to think about the process or relationship into which we are entering. In this next part of the book, key verbal skills are identified in order to establish the client's particular situation and to identify a working agenda. Typically, this phase of work involves, first, using probes such as useful and relevant questions (Chapter 7) and, then, seeking further clarification and understanding of the situation through inviting, reflecting, paraphrasing, and summarizing (Chapter 8). This process adds another dimension to the framework: focusing the communication.

Part One—Framing the Relationship

- the purpose of human service work
- your value base, professional ethics, and regulatory guidelines in Canada
- your theoretical and factual knowledge.

Part Two—Forming the Relationship

- your use of self
- your organizational context
- your ongoing support and professional development needs
- meeting the people involved
- opening the communication
- active listening and working with silence
- listening empathically
- using self-disclosure.

Part Three—Focusing the Communication

- establishing the story
- forming an assessment
- goal-setting.

7 | Establishing the Story

Learning Goals

- Understand the purpose of minimal encouragers.
- Describe and use a range of probing skills.
- Differentiate the types of questions and their purposes.
- Understand the skills involved in using statements and making requests.

The Task of Establishing the Client's Story

As Chapter 1 outlined, your focus will be on building a multi-dimensional understanding of the client and the client's story. This means understanding the client's story in relation to both inner and outer worlds.

Specific verbal skills are used to support and encourage the client's telling of her or his own story. We look at minimal encouragers and probing skills in this chapter.

Using Minimal Encouragers

In Chapter 2, we looked at the verbal and non-verbal skills that enhance or inhibit a conversation. In order to keep talking in a conversation, we need some feedback from the other person that it is all right to continue speaking. The verbal and non-verbal cues we give to another person are often **minimal encouragers**. That is, they are minimal in the sense of not being major statements or questions or reactions, but they encourage the person to continue talking. Minimal encouragers can be verbal or non-verbal. Verbal minimal encouragers include:

Yes!
Uh-hunh . . .
Mmm . . .
Right . . .
Sure.

Non-verbal minimal encouragers include all the facial and postural reactions we give—nodding, smiling, or the raising of eyebrows; leaning back, leaning forward, making a gesture—that inform the speaker you are listening attentively and that she should continue. Minimal encouragers are regarded as a way of keeping the conversation going. They are part of the conversation, too, however, and their impact can be significant, both in intended and unintended ways. The following example highlights the unintended impact, when a minimal encourager was experienced by the client as the end of a conversation rather than as an affirmation to continue.

Focus on Practice

A Need for Minimal Encouragers

At a cross-cultural seminar, a woman from a severely war-torn part of the world spoke of the impact for her of minimal encouragers when she encountered professionals. When she advised them of her nationality, she was often greeted with a response of 'oh'. She said she did not want that as a response to her communication, because she did not know what it meant. She was left wondering what the person was thinking and meaning by 'oh'. Did it mean they assumed she'd been raped, that she'd been directly affected by the war, or that it was too hard to speak about? She wanted to know more of what the other person meant by 'oh' rather than feeling as though she was on the end of someone else's assumption about her.

In this example, the meaning to the client of the minimal encourager was not clear. Similarly, if the minimal encourager 'right' or 'sure' is used, a very specific meaning as well as a general meaning can be conveyed. People can be affirmed unintentionally in what they are saying, whereas the use of the minimal encourager is intended only to affirm the continuation of the conversation, not the meaning of it. Minimal encouragers should be well-timed, appropriate, and sensitive to the situation.

Focus on Practice

A Need for Sensitivity

A woman of Aboriginal ancestry required a medical assessment that involved extensive arrangements to travel from her community to the urban centre where the assessment could be completed. Riya was very nervous, as she had not travelled outside her community often and was worried about talking with a new doctor. In my role as community wellness worker, I reviewed the process with Riya and suggested that she share her concerns with the doctor when they met. Upon Riya's arrival she told the doctor she was scared about what was going to happen and the doctor responded with, 'I'm sure you're scared . . . .' What Riya heard was 'You should be scared.' Riya completed the assessment and returned to share her story; and I wondered how accurate the assessment could be, given how it began.

The above example highlights how misunderstandings can occur unintentionally. The doctor's statement was meant to support Riya, by acknowledging that he understood that it must be frightening for her having travelled so far and not to know him. Unfortunately, Riya interpreted his words differently, raising questions around the accuracy of her assessment outcomes.

How would you ensure appropriate communication, considering the above example? Gilliland and James (1997: 14) cite Belkin (1984: 527), who 'points out that cross-cultural counselling does not have to be negative; that it may provide effective resolution of client problems as well as serve as a unique learning experience for both the client and the helper; and that the main, "barrier to effective cross-cultural counselling" is the traditional counselling role itself, which is not applicable to many cross-cultural interactions.' Belkin concludes his discussion by observing that perhaps the major unearthing is the realization that humans everywhere are more similar than different.

Using Probes

Another set of skills is termed **probes**, because they are an active way of encouraging the client to relate the many dimensions of a problem situation. The verb 'to probe' means to 'examine or look into closely, especially in order to discover something; investigate; interrogate closely' (Brown, 1993: 2362). This definition brings to the forefront both the strengths and the risks of these skills—the strengths being about discovery and investigation; the risks being that a client can feel violated in the interrogation.

Egan and Schroeder (2009) state that practioners should 'use probes to help clients engage as fully as possible in the therapeutic dialogue.' They describe the key components of probing as the use of prompts, statements, requests, questions, and single word phrases (ibid., 150). Probes are one of the major groups of verbal skills that enable us to follow the client's story and get to the details. As Hepworth, Rooney, and Larsen (2002: 155) state, focusing an interview is a complex skill, requiring three distinctive tasks. The first is selecting the topics for exploration; the second involves exploring the topics in depth; and the third involves maintaining a focus and keeping on topic. The use of probes is one way of moving through each of these phases. These skills enable us to stay with the client's story and where they want to head with it. At the same time, we use these skills to diverge from the seemingly dominant story to expand the focus of the interview. Therefore, probes are as critical for following the details of what the client is telling us as for exploring the unspoken dimensions of the experience; for asking about the history of an issue, or to explore the range of impacts of a situation in terms of feelings, actions, thoughts, and contexts.

Some scenarios were presented in earlier chapters for general discussion. Consider the ways in which each of these conversations would require very different opening statements or questions, and probing skills.

Practice Questions

1. How would you open discussions under the following circumstances?
   a. A child protection worker is going to meet with a parent, against whom allegations of abuse have been made. The worker, on arrival at the family home, notices that the parent

has blood-shot eyes, drooping eyelids, speaks slowly, and moves slowly with a stooped gait. The parent stares angrily indicating she is not happy at all about the notification to protective services.

b. A worker in a seniors' centre is assisting a client 80 years of age who has recently lost his spouse. The man expresses that losing his spouse of 60 years has created feelings he is not sure what to do with. With tears on his cheeks he continues by saying that he can't wait to be with his spouse again.

c. A duty worker on a telephone crisis line receives a call from a young, distressed woman who has been assaulted by her partner. The caller doesn't know what to do—whether to leave her apartment or to stay.

d. A worker has been involved with a separated family for many years, since the time when their child was diagnosed with cancer right through to her death six months ago. The worker wants to invite the siblings to a sibling support group, which will involve contact with both the parents and the siblings.

2. What would be the first question you would ask and why?

3. Share your response with someone else—how different are your questions?

4. Did the different questions result in different answers? If yes, how?

5. Was your interpretation of the situation different? How?

6. What questions would you want to ask to assess the situation? Why?

7. What are some of the key points to consider in each of the above examples?

What Questions Will I Ask?

The skilful use of questions is a potent device for initiating, sustaining, and directing conversation (Dickson and Hargie, 2006: 121).

In Part Two, we looked at the importance of understanding the agency context and the worker's role. Your context and role will strongly influence where, when, how, and why you work with your client, and will inform the ways you go about asking particular questions. How we ask and what we ask is inextricably linked with the purpose of the contact.

Questions can be very intimidating—they can ask people to think about things that they have never thought of before or to recall traumatic issues and events. They can stigmatize and blame, inadvertently. If people are questioned continuously, they may feel interrogated rather than heard—that it is more important that the facts be established than it is for the individual to be heard. In the next chapter, we will explore the skills of paraphrasing and summarizing as ways of minimizing such an outcome.

This discussion brings together some of the current thinking about the nature of questions in general. Questions can be effective in opening up an interview and gathering the necessary information, or they can alienate, marginalize or disempower people even further. Knowing how to ask effective, empowering questions is an essential skill.

Asking Open-Ended or Closed Questions

Questions can be open-ended or closed in their structure, influencing the kind of response that is elicited. An **open-ended question** invites the client to provide further elaboration of the details of the story. Questions beginning with the words 'how', 'what', 'why', 'when', 'who', and 'where' are open-ended because they invite some kind of descriptive, expansive response, not mere confirmation of information that has been provided by the person asking the question. For example:

> Worker: When did you first notice these difficulties?
> Worker: How many children do you have?
> Worker: What do you think is the most important issue to work on right now?

Closed questions, by contrast, seek confirmation or negation of information—with a simple 'yes', 'no', 'maybe', or other singular word response such as 'never'. They do not call for further elaboration on detail:

> Worker: Have you spoken with anyone about this?
> Worker: Can you get another job?
> Worker: Do you think it will happen again?

Some authors suggest that any question eliciting a short answer is also a closed question—that a closed question is one where the topic is defined and the client's response is restricted to a few words or to a 'yes' or 'no' response (Hepworth, Rooney, and Larsen, 2002: 142). A question as to how far someone had travelled could similarly be seen as a closed question, although this is moving to a different interpretation of confirmation or negation of information, which is typically considered to be the defining feature of a closed question.

Some questions, while structured as closed questions in a grammatical sense, can function as open-ended purely through your vocal intonation: 'Can you tell me about that?' can be understood as an encouraging **invitation** to talk more about a problem situation rather than as expecting a 'yes' or 'no' response.

Closed questions can lead to more detailed, descriptive responses, but they rely on the client taking up the intent of the question and initiating further response. To illustrate how a closed question can lead to further elaboration, notice the responses here:

> Worker: Have you spoken with anyone about this?
> Client: No.
> Worker: Do you think you should speak with someone, perhaps at work?
> Client: No.
> Worker: Isn't there anyone else?
> Client: Maybe . . .

In this instance, the conversation was not getting very far. Closed questions can present a number of risks—the risk of getting the question 'wrong' or becoming too directive, and the risk of having to negate the other person's position, as well as the risk of lapsing into an interrogation, or of limiting the options.

The first risk, where the onus is on the interviewer to get the question 'right', means that the interviewer can become too directive of the agenda—if the asking of closed question after closed question is not working to open up the discussion. In using closed questions, try to find the right lead. It can become a hunt for the right question—looking for a point of engagement. At these times, it may be more useful to reflect on what is not being heard in the situation or to pause to summarize what has been stated to that point in the conversation. It may be that the story has been difficult to establish because the client is not forthcoming—and why this is so should be reviewed. The client may not wish to talk to you or to trust you, he may not perceive you as competent, she may not be confident about her view of events, or they may not have the words to express what they think and feel.

Persistent questioning in the face of little response can result in the client becoming reluctant or resistant to the process. In some cases, reluctance and resistance are developed by the client as a personal safeguard measure based on fear, previous experiences, or the belief he or she has been wrongly accused. Egan and Schroeder (2009: 231) explain that 'defense mechanisms are unconscious processes that serve to maintain our self-esteem and keep our sense of self intact. They may be adaptive or maladaptive. Adaptive defenses lower anxiety. Maladaptive defenses prevent development of insight. Reluctance and resistance may stem from the unconscious use of defenses to protect the self.'

Resistance can be particularly difficult when working with mandated clients. Consider the following example.

A young male client is forced to attend sessions with an alcohol and drug worker due to having breached his probation and sustaining a second charge of possession of drugs. The counsellor is faced with the client's resistance to attending his appointments.

> Worker: Can you tell me what brings you here today?
> Client: My probation officer says I have to come.
> Worker: What would you like to discuss?
> Client: Nothing . . . I don't want to be here.

In this example, the client clearly states not having a choice in attending. It is important that the practitioner have the skills required to work with resistance. The practitioner needs to work from where the client is at, which in the above example is the fact of forced attendance. Here are some examples:

> Worker: You said your probation worker is making you attend?
> Client: Yes.
> Worker: Can you tell me a bit about why you think he is making you come?
> Client: I guess because this is my second time.
> Worker: Second time with what?

As the conversation continues it increases the opportunity for engagement and leads to a decrease in resistance and reluctance. Additional engagement skills or statements may include:

Worker: I am not sure I would like someone making me attend, and I can't force you to stay. [pause] How about if we meet for two sessions and decide from there how to proceed?

Is there a time when you felt resistant? How did you react? It is important that practitioners recognize that some level of resistance and/or reluctance from clients is normal. Further, it is the practitioner's role to assist the client in working through these feelings and to find an incentive to follow through with the process. What are your skills in working with resistant or reluctant clients?

If the question is poorly chosen, the client is put in the situation of having to negate the person who has asked the question. For example:

Worker: Are you waiting to see me?
Client: Uh, no; I'm waiting to see Doug.

However, asking an open-ended question—'Who are you waiting to see?'—would have led to the person asking to speak to a particular person. This may seem like a trivial example, but when a closed question is asked with more serious implications, the issue of having to negate another person becomes significant. In disempowering situations, the client is less likely to have the confidence to negate someone else's statement.

Worker: So, your partner didn't give you the support money?
Client: [Who knows he did but she spent it on drugs.] Yes.

Closed questions can be coercive and manipulative, either intentionally or unintentionally. A closed question such as 'Are you going to leave?' presents only one possible line of action to the client. There may be many other options to consider, so an open-ended question such as 'What do you want to happen?' may not exclude these options.

Closed questions, however, have a very important role in assessment and intervention processes. They enable the clarification of the intensity of mood states or intentions of the client, for example, or details of a past history that may be critical to an understanding of the current circumstances. The use of open-ended questions tends to be encouraged in practice over closed questions as the more exploratory and less presuming style of the two forms of questioning.

Focus on Practice

Interrogation and Human Service Work

Watch any of the nightly television programs showing courtroom scenes or police investigations and observe the way questions are framed to force particular answers. In these situations, the answer is anticipated—a 'leading question' has been asked. One of the major differences between police interrogation and human service work is that we want to ask questions that will not assume the answers but instead encourage the client to discuss surrounding circumstances as openly and fully as possible.

> What are the key differences between these two approaches? Why is it important not to presume to know the answers?

Asking open-ended questions, however, can also present challenges. Some workers, for example, propose that 'why' questions should be avoided, on the basis that asking people for explanations of situations is too difficult and that these questions can be experienced as 'accusatory and blaming' (Trevithick, 2005: 163). Others argue that 'why' questions should be avoided because they tend to encourage the client to look for a preconceived response, which may even include 'excuses or rationalizations' (Geldard and Geldard, 2005: 74). The other reason that 'why' questions may be difficult to answer is that when we are caught up in personal difficulties it can be very difficult to answer issues of causation or reason—that is, to understand why we are facing difficulties in the first place. Other schools of thought see open-ended questions and issues of explanatory power as a fundamental part of a person's story, which we will explore later in Chapters 11–14. For example, psychodynamic theory looks at the connections and interpretations we make as to what is happening in the present. Similarly, narrative approaches emphasize the importance of what meaning we are making of particular situations.

Safer and more adaptable questions to ask are questions beginning with 'what', because they are 'consistent with a systemic perspective that stresses that no one person is responsible for a problem or a difficulty that exists' (Trevithick, 2005: 163). For example:

Worker: What do you think led to the argument?
Worker: What was happening before the argument began?
Worker: What is your reaction to that situation?

These open-ended questions using 'what' are particularly useful in the narrative approaches, which emphasize externalizing the problem.

Asking the Opening Question

An open-ended question is often used to start off a conversation—and it is the one question with which you can be relatively prepared. It is useful to think of the opening questions that appeal to you and why. Beginning with the very vague and open-ended question:

Worker: How are you?
Client: Not good at all. I've had some tests recently and it looks like I have cancer.

The question has worked as a vague, open-ended question to engage the client around the issue to discuss. At other times, though, the question can be seen to be a social question we ask as a greeting rather than an authentic question about the client's well-being. As an open-ended question, it is too vague and too socially anticipated. So the reply can be:

Client: Fine. How are you?

And the conversation has not gone very far in relation to the specific issue. A further open-ended question is required to get to the specific issues. Some other opening questions could be:

> Worker: What's been happening?
> Worker: What's going on?

These questions imply that something has occurred to trigger the contact with you as a human service worker, but they do not imply that the person needs or wants help in the way that other opening questions do:

> Worker: What can I help you with?
> Worker: What brings you here today?

The questions about what has been happening or going on also do not imply that the person is the one with the 'problem'.

The opening question you ask will not only influence the initial information the client shares but can impact the level of client engagement. What would be your response to the above opening questions? Which question feels the most comfortable for you to work with and why?

Asking Succinct Questions

A succinct question is a brief and concise one. Lengthy, imprecise questions can confuse both the worker and client. The worker can lose track of what the 'trigger' was for asking the question and the client can be left wondering what is being asked. For example, how would you answer this question if you were the client?

> Worker: Why do you think, I mean, what caused him to be so angry, or if not
>   angry so frustrated when you spoke last with him, um, or was it, um,
>   when he called you?

Notice that in the question above, the worker has not hesitated in order to gather thoughts about what the question should be. The extraneous language used, such as 'I mean' and 'um', also breaks up the flow of the communication. Lengthy questions also can become multiple questions, where a client is asked:

> Worker: Do you talk with anyone about this? I mean, have you spoken with your
>   family? Or your friends? What do they think?

In this 'question', there are now three different questions all wrapped up in the one delivery. It is as if the worker has found a flow and is rolling out all those thoughts in one go. The dilemma for the client becomes which of these questions to answer first. As a general rule, one question at a time should be asked.

Worker: Have you spoken with anyone else about this?
Client: Yes, my sister.
Worker: What does your sister think about what is happening?
Client: She is worried about me and . . .

Short, specific questions provide clearer focus to the interview, even if you have to pause to work out exactly how that question should be framed. A momentary pausing and gathering of thoughts is often better than rushing headlong into a series of questions.

Asking Relevant Questions

Your agency context and purpose will determine what questions are relevant to ask. Even in a specific setting, however, each one of us will ask different questions. What we think is relevant is, therefore, a question of our subjective and objective positioning.

Focus on Practice

Group Task

In a role-play, one 'client' is interviewed by a number of 'interviewers' (other students in the class) for about 10 minutes. The other students each take a turn at asking a question, and participants come to realize how differently each is thinking about the situation. It is a good opportunity to reflect on why you wanted to know about certain issues and what you saw as relevant in this interview.

1. What questions were asked that resulted in gaining insight into the client's story?
2. What did you learn from this exercise?
3. What areas in your interviewing skills do you want to improve?
4. Where are your strengths?

In our time-limited client contact, we need to be quite selective about what we ask and why we ask it. Armstrong (2006: 19–20) states:

When we know another person . . . there are often large blank spaces in their history . . . . We may have only a sketchy—and probably one-sided—grasp of what occurred over substantial stretches of that person's life. And yet our encounter with them is not puzzling or missing something.

Armstrong is highlighting a fundamental process of engagement with another human being—that engagement is not necessarily a matter of knowing the client's whole story, but about the narrative that is established together. Working with a client to establish her story is about building up an understanding of what has occurred in relation to specific events or experiences. It may be a sketchy picture, but the work together is about building as relevant a picture as possible, even though it is not complete.

The narrative picture that is created should be understood to be a result of co-authoring by the client and the worker. Payne (2006) explains that note-taking is a collaborative process in which the counsellor takes notes and scripts them for the client's review or invites the client to script the session. Corey (2008) suggests one technique for consolidating the gains a client makes is by writing letters. Narrative therapists have pioneered the development of therapeutic letter-writing. These letters that the therapist writes provide a record of the session and may include an externalizing description of the problem and its influence on the client, as well as an account of the client's strengths and abilities that are identified in a session. Letters can be read again at different times, and the story that they are part of can be reinspired.

Thus, to facilitate narrative counselling effectively and ethically, the counsellor must ensure that the client is part of the note-taking process so that it is the client's narrative being documented and not the counsellor's viewpoint of the client's narrative. It is a collaborative effort, and this means the client having access to session notes or participating in the documentation of session notes as part of the therapeutic process.

Given that we gather selected information, the question of relevance is paramount. Important questions to keep in mind throughout all your practice are:

- Why am I asking this question?
- Who am I to this person and therefore is it valid that I ask these questions?
- For whom is the information important and/or relevant?
- Am I listening to the client's story?
- Which elements of the story need to be clearly established, and which ones do not?
- What other sources of information are available—for example, through case file notes—rather than repeatedly asking the person the same questions?
- How would I feel about answering that question?

A major dimension of relevance is cultural relevance. What cultural dimensions of this person's experience may impact whether this question is relevant or not? For example, in many cultures, providing information about mental and physical health experiences is taboo. As Youssef and Deane (2006: 5) draw to our attention, 'Social reputation (soma) is a valuable asset in Arab culture and great efforts are made to avoid any shame that may threaten or compromise the family reputation.' An awareness of all such issues is fundamental to sensitive and focused communication. Discussing these issues first may be more important than trying to move into a conversation that will be experienced as culturally insensitive.

Relevance can be considered not only in relation to the nature or breadth of issues that are discussed but also in relation to the depth of questioning that occurs. One comment made frequently by students in debriefing after role-play is: 'I wanted to ask that question but I thought it might upset them.' Clearly, this is an important consideration in all of our conversations—the intention is never to cause harm and distress. This highlights the importance of checking the client's comfort level with such questions and the direction of the conversation, as well as us checking your own comfort levels and knowledge bases. What this hesitation may mean, however, is that if a worker avoids some questions for fear of upsetting a client, a client may not have the opportunity to tell the story. We live daily with the issues and preoccupations of our own lives, so telling a sad, tragic, or otherwise painful story is not necessarily distressing to the client, who may welcome the opportunity to talk. It may seem overwhelming to the worker, but it may not be a new or 'out of control' experience for the client. Similarly, if the question does upset a client, inviting her or him to explore a part of the story perhaps not verbalized previously may not *necessarily* be a bad outcome, but rather a step in the process of establishing the story and those experiences.

Relevance can also be a point of engagement. For example, inquiring about a client's cultural background creates the opportunity for the client to share personal and expert knowledge and at the same time assists the practitioner with understanding the client's background. When used correctly, this opportunity can engage the client in the process.

In considering the depth of questions and their relevance, it is also important to consider some of the assumptions we carry as workers about the ease of answering questions. Working in the human services, we can become very familiar with a language of emotions and of the inner world, and of valuing self-disclosure and self-reflection. These ways of being are not ways in which all people are comfortable, and yet we can expect answers to the questions we ask. The question of relevance remains crucial in determining whether or not we need to ask these types of questions.

Asking Specific Questions

As the worker in the situation, you have the responsibility for keeping a sense of direction and purpose; for avoiding a sense of 'drift' (Trevithick, 2005: 170). Drift emerges when the direction and purpose of the conversation disappear and either the client and/or the worker is left wondering what the conversation is about.

The aim is to elicit specific information in relation to a client's story, not generalities. We need to know the detail of a client's experiences, which can then lead on to specific interventions. If we do not know how unhappy someone is, for example, we are not going to know enough about that person's current mental health to adequately undertake a **risk assessment** of him/her. If we do not know how difficult the person's financial circumstances are, we may not make the referrals or seek the assistance the situation requires.

In exploring stressful situations with clients it can be useful to think about the dimensions of events that make them stressful. Martin (1997) highlights the duration, timing, predictability, and controllability of events as the important dimensions to explore. For example, a client reports spending a great deal of time in his room, but until an assessment of duration, timing, predictability, and controllability of this behaviour is undertaken, it is very difficult to discern what kind of situation this is from the client's point of view or from the point of view of normal or understandable behaviour. It may be the extremely problematic behaviour of self-isolation accompanying drug abuse or bipolarity or schizophrenia, or it may be entirely functional behaviour in the client's context as it gives him time and space to work out issues or to avoid conflict in other areas of the family home.

The following scenario shows how important it is for you to think about all of what is implied when you are listening to a story. Taking the response at face value, as all the information you require, could be a serious mistake. With the person who is spending a lot of time in his room, further questions are required, such as:

> When did this start?
> How often does he go to his room?
> How long does he stay in his room?
> What happens prior to his going to his room?
> Why do you think it is a problem?
> Is this new behaviour?
> What concerns you about it?
> What does he say or think about it?

Only after asking some of these more specific questions can we begin to establish genuine understanding of how significant this behaviour is and whether or not it is a problem.

Asking specific questions can also mean raising taboo or difficult issues. Sometimes just asking a question gives a client permission to discuss a previously taboo issue or even, in some instances, the elements of language to discuss it. In a recent conference presentation, Dora Black (Black and Trickey, 2005) from the Tavistock Clinic in London spoke about her work with children recovering from experiences in family situations where one parent has murdered the other parent. Black's own therapeutic training had been within the psychoanalytic model, where specific questions were not asked. Interpretations of free associations or thoughts of the client were made, but questions rarely asked. In working with these children, and particularly in discussing the art work they created about what they had witnessed, she has discovered that because of their developmental stage at the time of the murders, these children did not actually have the language to name the experiences they needed to talk about. Thus, asking specific questions as well as commenting on the drawings was one way of bridging this gap in the client's story.

For many people, some specific questions can be highly culturally and personally inappropriate. As individuals, we have different levels of tolerance for questions affecting privacy. Similarly, as families and communities we have spoken and unspoken rules in relation to information that is public and that is private. For some families, saving face and not airing private problems is a primary value, whereas for other families, the boundaries of family extend to the community, and nothing is private. In asking questions, we can be intruding across the boundaries of another person's private world. When questions are experienced as intrusive, it is important that opportunities to decline questions are provided. How will you ensure you understand the spoken and unspoken rules mentioned above? In rural and remote settings issues of isolation, small populations, and community structure play an important role in how information is shared. The practitioner will need to be aware of the existing boundaries, social structure, and process for community decision-making.

In addition, Gilliland and James (1997: 13) outline multicultural perspectives revealing that a large majority of the world's population lives by a non-Western viewpoint. The authors continue by noting it is the practitioners' responsibility to evaluate their processes and emotional attitudes from a multicultural perspective to work towards addressing issues of institutionalized racism, ethnocentrism, ageism, sexism, and other forms of cultural and personal bias that clients may encounter in their workers.

Building an understanding of the specifics of a person's situation is critical. What we do with the responses to questions, therefore, requires careful consideration so that we continue to develop detailed understandings of what the client has said. Sometimes we might ask only one question and regard that as having explored the issue. For example:

Worker: How does that leave you feeling?
Client: Oh, I'm just so disappointed.
Worker: What do you think you'll do now? Look for more work?

In this scenario, the worker has asked about the emotional state and has been told one specific dimension of this experience, but on hearing an answer, has not explored it any further. The worker has moved on to the next issue, having spent only a moment focusing on the emotional response the client has expressed. One person's disappointment is very different from another's—one person might be very depressed and make that statement but another might be quite recovered and be expressing a manageable feeling. One answer does not necessarily provide the depth of understanding that might be required.

So, revisiting that situation, a follow-up question begins to provide some further elaboration on the disappointment:

Worker: How does that leave you feeling?
Client: Oh, I'm just so disappointed.
Worker: Tell me some more about that?
Client: Well, I thought the money stress was going to go away with these extra
         hours of work, but I'm still behind. It just isn't fair. Every time I try to get
         on top of things, they just keep on collapsing around me. I'm just useless!

Now the worker has a sense that the client is possibly feeling both angry about the situation and disappointed with herself. A lot more exploration of this situation is required to really understand what is going on. Alternatively, the worker could have just used the word 'Disappointed?' to indicate a question and similarly encouraged further elaboration on the emotional experience of the client.

In many settings where you work, specific psychosocial or risk assessments will be used by your organization to focus the information that is considered crucial. One of these specific assessment frameworks is a Mental State Examination (MSE; Bloch and Singh, 2007). An MSE is designed to assess the cognitive status of a client in many different settings. It is included below as an example of a very specific set of questions that can be asked. Other agencies may have standardized psychosocial assessment questions that are used—they ask specific questions so that specific issues of risk and protective factors can be addressed.

Chapter 9 explores assessment further and presents more of these assessment frameworks.

Focus on Practice

Folstein Mini-Mental Status Examination

Orientation

What is the year?
Season?
Month?
Date?
Day?
Where are we?
Province?
City?
Community?
Hospital?
Floor?

Registration

I am going to name three objects and I want you to repeat them after me. [Interviewer: give one point for each correct answer. Repeat the objects until the patient can name them all—six trials maximum.] Number of trials?

Attention and Calculation

I am going to ask you to do some subtraction. Think of the number 7.

I want you to subtract 7 from 100. Now subtract 7 from that and keep on going. 100, __, __, __, __, __. Stop.

Alternatively, spell 'world' backwards.

Recall

Please name the three objects that I had you repeat after me just a short while ago. [Interviewer: give one point for each correct answer.]

Language

Please name these for me [interviewer: show client a watch and a pencil].

Now please repeat the following: 'no ifs, ands or buts.'

Now I am going to ask you to do something for me. Take a paper in your right hand, fold it in half and put it on the floor. Now I want you to read this and do what it says. [Interviewer hands the client a card that says 'close your eyes'.]

Now please write a sentence for me on this blank piece of paper. [Interviewer gives the client a blank piece of paper and asks him or her to write a sentence. Do not dictate a sentence. It must be written spontaneously. It must contain a subject and verb and be sensible. Correct grammar and punctuation are not necessary.]

Visual Motor Integrity

Please copy this design. [Interviewer: on a clean piece of paper, draw intersecting pentagons, each side about 1 inch, and ask him or her to copy it exactly as it is. All ten angles must be present and two must intersect to score 1 point.]

Total score (30)

Interviewer: assess client's level of consciousness along continuum:

alert   drowsy   stupor   coma

Source: Adapted from Coulehan and Block (2006: 222–3).

Davis (2006) provides an example of a self-assessment focused on relapse prevention/ crisis plan adapted from a model created by Eric Macnaughton of the Canadian Mental Health Association:

Signs that suggest I am doing well:
Events or situations that triggered relapse in the past:
Early warning signs that I experienced in the past:
Effective ways that I can cope if I experience early warning signs:
What early warning signs indicate that I need help from others:
Who I would like to assist me (names):
What I would like them to do:
If in crisis:
Ways I can manage stress, regain balance, or claim myself:
People I can call and their phone numbers:
Resources that I can use (agencies, support groups):
Things that I or other people can do that I find helpful:
Medications that have helped in the past:
Medications that have not helped or that have caused an adverse reaction:
Medications that I am currently on:

Specific questions, however, can be used to manipulate responses or they can also mean we miss out on critical information. In asking about 'x' and not 'y', we may then not realize that 'y' is the problem. Being too specific can mean that, because we do not ask the 'right' particular question, we do not establish what is going on or a particular detail of the circumstances. Again, using open-ended questions and clarifying responses further can help in avoiding some of these difficulties.

Asking Neutral Questions

Questions can be very loaded; that is, questions can carry very strong assumptions within their wording or expectations about the answer. Particularly in the early stages of a working relationship, minimizing these assumptions is important, and asking questions that are more neutral in their language is a way of building the relationship and finding out the necessary information.

As discussed in earlier chapters, language can marginalize and stigmatize people. Questions need to be framed as inclusively as possible so that a client's story can be explored with as few barriers as possible. Assumptions about relationship status and sexuality, about financial capacities, about abilities and capacities, about beliefs and culture, about normative world views and a range of other dimensions of our lives can be made through the questions we ask or are asked. Rather than illustrate a whole range of possibilities, the reflection task below encourages you to think about the underlying assumptions that may be present in those questions.

Practice Questions

1. What underlying assumptions could be present in the following questions?
   - Have you talked to your friends about that?
   - What does your wife think?
   - Why didn't you write to them to lodge your complaint?
   - Are you going away for Christmas?
   - Can't your children help you?
   - Why didn't you move out?
   - Why don't you get Home Support Services involved?
   - Can you tell me about why you've been so upset lately?

2. How would you reframe each of these questions so that some of the assumptions in each question are minimized?

3. How would you reframe the closed questions above as open-ended questions?

Some questions are very 'leading' in their intent; for example: 'Don't you think it really would be important to tell them what's going on?' In this type of leading question, the answer that the worker wants to hear is present in the question. Leading questions such as these have either the intention or the outcome of trying to 'coerce the other person into agreement' (Koprowska, 2005: 84). For all these reasons, framing questions as neutrally but as specifically as possible is important.

Another way to address these issues is to clarify with the client whether the process of asking these questions is appropriate.

> Worker: Is it OK to be asking these questions?
> Client: Actually, I feel really uncomfortable.

Or alternatively, asking an open-ended question:

> Worker: How do you feel about me asking these questions?
> Client: It's fine. I just find it difficult to talk about these things.

Either of the answers could have been given to those questions—again, it is a matter of judgement as to whether you frame the question in terms of your role with the client or more as a question of how the client is feeling in the situation. Depending on the reasons for the human service contact, this situation could be re-contracted so that a mutual understanding of why such questions are being asked, and whether they are essential or not, can be reached.

Asking 'Difficult' Questions

In some areas of practice, very difficult questions need to be asked. They are difficult questions because they relate to extreme human situations and, often, ethical dilemmas. Many of these questions emerge in medical and legal contexts, such as the question as to whether or not a patient is consenting to resuscitation, whether a family is consenting to an organ donation of a deceased family member, or whether a child is a victim of abuse within a family. In these situations, some general principles (see, e.g., Evans et al., 2006) include:

- taking time to prepare in your own mind what the purpose of the conversation is about
- finding the optimal time to talk with the key people
- speaking clearly and slowly about the issues, even considering the possibility of using a warning or preface to what you are about to say
- being aware that on breaking bad news, very little is heard and remembered subsequently, so repeating and revisiting issues is essential
- checking in with people as to what they have heard, so that you can affirm that the message has been accurately conveyed.

In addition, the practitioner should feel prepared to state things clearly and not use words that are less clear but easier for the practitioner to say. For example, phrases like 'she is no longer with us' and 'he has gone to another place' are ambiguous, and can be confusing and create additional crisis if the statement is initially misunderstood. See the following example.

A mental health intake worker was recently assigned a file of a young woman presenting with high anxiety and depression issues. During the first meeting, the practitioner discovered the woman had been assaulted. This caused intense fear, which had resulted in the client not being able to go to work, sleep, leave her room, or talk with family for over a month. During the discussion the practitioner wondered if the client was suicidal, when the practitioner approached the topic with the client, the client responded with . . . 'I am so relieved you said the word . . . I was afraid if I said the word "suicide" my family would be angry at me for thinking that way.' This was the beginning of the client being able to address her situation openly from where she was at.

Asking Questions at an Appropriate Time

Sometimes a question may be an excellent question to ask, but the timing is wrong in the context of either the working relationship or the session itself. For example, we may not have established enough rapport with the client or we may be at a point in a conversation where it is inappropriate to ask such a question.

Carolyn identifies timing as a key issue in reflecting on her psychodynamically oriented practice, as outlined below, in the context of complexity, too.

Focus on Practice

Helping Clients Face Painful Truths about Themselves

One of the tasks of the psychodynamic therapist is to take in the verbal and non-verbal communications of their clients and to try to understand unconscious thoughts, imaginings, and feelings about themselves, their relationships, and their difficulties.

As some of our clients are struggling with experiences of lifelong losses, trauma, and rejection, or painful realities such as disability, terminal illness, or complicated mourning, our timing and way of making the 'unthinkable' thinkable is crucial.

With the therapist's support, their capacity to explore and integrate this aspect of themselves (and the attitudes of others towards them, which is arguably more difficult) will strengthen them and free them up to engage more with life. However, this may be a highly painful and confronting experience.

Discussing her clinical work with adults presenting with intellectual disability on a background of trauma, Sinason (1992: 319), describes this well: '[S]ome of their histories and life stories are extremely harrowing, and the process of recovering them has made me understand why their authors numbed their memories and minds for so long.'

Within the counselling literature, in particular, a great deal of emphasis is placed on the experiences of reluctance and resistance (Shulman, 1999; Egan, 2002). Reluctance, as in a hesitation, is seen to emerge when a client knows that 'managing their lives better is going to exact a price' (Egan, 2002: 163) and thus is related to hesitating in the face of change. **Resistance** 'refers to the reaction of clients who in some way feel coerced' (ibid., 165). A strengths-based approach is to understand these processes more positively as processes of timing and readiness—to focus on why a person might be able to look at change at one point as distinct from another.

Specifically regarding the timing of questions, some important questions to ask in relation to reluctance and resistance are:

- What's going on here?
- Am I as the worker adequately addressing the issues with this client?
- Are there barriers to good communication within the relationship in relation to effective engagement?
- Am I asking appropriate questions?
- Are there other problematic dimensions of this communication process—that is, not so much the focus of the interview but the way I am talking about issues or the language I am using?
- What is it about the timing of these questions that may be contributing to this reaction?

Asking Questions that Lead to New Insights

We seek assistance primarily for new insights—to manage situations or emotions differently, to gain information or to understand situations more fully, or to learn new skills and behaviours. Talking with someone else or in a group is an opportunity to see things differently. Below, Karen describes her work with Max and a moment of new insight.

Focus on Practice

Challenging with Creativity

It is sometimes important to have clients see the other person's viewpoint in order to recognize their own.

Max presented at the community health centre at age 50, referred by his doctor for 'support'. With a recent acrimonious marriage breakdown and estrangement, avoiding his role as bank manager, and a serious health issue, Max was in need of much more than support. Max was suffering situational depression, sleeping problems, poor nutrition, and financial difficulties. Over a number of sessions, Max reassessed some of his previously insignificant relationships and was able to regain some feelings of happiness from a sporting interest, a daily walk, and a 'cooking for one' class.

His relationship with his adult children remained strained by his former wife's bitterness, leaving him feeling embarrassed and belittled by the experience. This was compounded by a lack of status, and hence self-esteem, associated with the recent loss of his job. He felt unworthy of his son and daughter's offers of support and consistently refused them, although his ill health meant that he was unable to complete some tasks himself.

No amount of challenge regarding reciprocity in family relationships was effective in budging his view that, 'I am the father, I should be providing for my children and I don't deserve their help', until one day I asked him about his own role with his parents. He told me that for many years before they died he had maintained their house and garden.

Karen: So how was it that you did this for your Mom and Dad?

Max: They weren't well, I am their son, and I wanted to help them stay in their home.

Karen: What would it have been like for *you* if he had refused your help, because he felt he should have been able to cope?

Max   [hesitates, then bursts into tears]: My pride has got in the way of letting my kids be my kids!

While we will look at these issues in greater detail in Chapters 11–14, this section raises the importance of questions that open doors for clients. Questions that lead to new insights can be oriented around previous perceptions and experiences of coping so that a client begins to reflect on her/his strengths and capacities. People can become oriented around what they think the future could be for them and what would need to change in order to bring that about. It is an important emphasis to maintain throughout a communication process, as questions so frequently focus on risk, problems and difficulties, rather than on exploring protective factors, successes, and strengths.

Suzie's example from her practice highlights the use of these sorts of questions.

Advocates of a strengths perspective suggest asking the following types of questions (Saleebey, 1997: 52–4):

Focus on Practice

The Change Process Requires Small, Manageable Steps

Mac: Would you like to see some of the new pictures that I have done?

Suzie: Yes, that would be great.

[Mac shows his drawings.]

Suzie: They are excellent, I like this one in particular . . . you have a real talent there.

Mac: I was asked to do a whole set of murals by this shop the other day—they have seen my stuff before, but I just can't. I think that's why I am an addict; I just think I am afraid of success.

Suzie: What does success mean to you?

Mac: Like doing something and then being expected to be able to repeat it again and again.

Suzie: Can you give me an example?

Mac: Like giving up H [heroin]. I have stopped before but that doesn't mean that it will last.

Suzie: What if, with your drawing, you could do one wall or one section of the shop? Is it possible to negotiate doing something smaller, with no commitment to do any more—just that one piece of work? Is it possible to draw it first on paper until you are happy with it then show it to the shop owner and, if they like it, replicate it on the wall?

Mac: Hmm, I am not sure. I never thought to ask them about that.

Suzie: Sometimes it is helpful to take the things that have worked and replicate them in different situations, start with smaller steps and build up.

Suzie says of this interaction: 'Concrete examples of problem-solving can provide opportunities from which to draw parallels with other, more complex issues such as addressing substance use that a client is finding problematic.' This process allows the client to identify success in smaller pieces and how to transfer success into other areas of his life. The client can then determine what success means in his life and how to build on each smaller success. This is particularly important in this example as the client identifies success as being 'all or nothing', thus creating feelings of being overwhelmed.

1. Survival questions: for example, 'Now that you have testified, can you tell me what you mean by feeling free?'
2. Support questions: for example, 'Your friend seems to care a lot about you, can you tell me a bit about your relationship?'
3. Exception question: for example, 'Tell me about a point in your life when you weren't stressed?'
4. Possibility questions: for example, 'You have created three different times what will work for you to take a walk. Which one do you want to try?
5. Esteem questions: for example, 'How did it feel to meet your goal?'

These questions will be looked at more closely in Chapter 13. The following exercise encourages you to think about how you use questions.

Practice Exercise

1. Conduct a 10-minute role-play with a 'client', having an observer present. Debrief around the probing skills you have used throughout the interview.

2. Try to conduct the interview again using:
   • only open-ended questions
   • only closed questions
   • no questions—only comments or statements
   • only problem-focused questions
   • only strengths- or problem-focused questions.

This exercise helps you to identify your preferred questioning style—for some of us, asking questions is easy, whereas highlighting and reflecting back emotion is more challenging, and vice versa. This exercise highlights that we can use different questions to explore different dimensions of a situation. There is no one right way, but there are a lot of choices throughout an interview as to where we head with the conversation. It can be helpful to have a very active observer who will call a halt to an interview when certain skills are being demonstrated or are not present. This can be a useful way to begin to identify your style and skill preference.

Additional Verbal Skills

Questions are clearly not the only verbal skills used in exploring a story. Questions or comments using single words or statements also keep the conversation flowing. Without being formally structured as questions, by using tone of voice and non-verbal encouragers, the following can be used to establish further the details of the client's situation:

Worker: You're angry?
Worker: It was due on Monday?
Worker: Confused?

Another type of probe is a request—an invitational or encouraging way of asking the client to explain more about the situation, in a genuinely interested way:

Worker: Tell me more about that.
Worker: Go on . . .
Worker: What do you mean by . . .
Worker: Say more about when she . . .

Carl Rogers, the founder of person-centred counselling, appears in a well-known video interview with a client called 'Gloria' (Rogers, Ellis, and Perls, 1977). One of the striking features of this interview is that throughout the half-hour interview Rogers rarely asks a question. The rest of the interview is conducted using the skills of empathy, paraphrasing, and summarizing via which he clarifies Gloria's story and works with her towards a deeper understanding of her predicament. This interview highlights that questions are not always needed—that information can be shared through an engagement in a different form of dialogue. This is an important point. While many human service interactions are not going to be in the therapeutic context in which Rogers was working, many people tell their stories through means other than the more interrogative style of prompting. In the next chapter, we will explore the specifics of these skills of paraphrasing and summarizing, again looking at their strengths and limitations.

Chapter Summary

In this chapter, the key verbal probes for exploring a client's story have been described and analyzed. The ways in which asking open-ended or closed, succinct, relevant, specific, neutral, well-timed questions that may lead to new insights have been explored, highlighting both the strengths and limitations of each of these styles of questioning. We then focused on the options of not asking questions but instead using other forms of verbal probes to achieve some similar outcomes. It depends on how the conversation moves as to whether a further question is needed or whether an empathic observation is made. Conversation is created between people. Egan (2002) suggests that an empathic highlight should follow a question, but there is no rule. In a therapeutic context, more weight is given to empathic reflections and observations.

Questions for Analysis

1. What have you learned about:
   - some of the risks involved in asking questions?
   - the differences between an open-ended and a closed question?
   - some of the key considerations in asking effective questions?
   - the various types of probes?

2. What is your preferred style of questioning?

3. How do you think you will go about opening an interview or point of contact with someone?

4. What assumptions have been evident in some of your questions to date?

5. What are some of the key challenges for you in asking questions?

6. How will you challenge or improve your questioning skill?

ESTABLISHING THE STORY | 155

Recommended Readings

Davis, S. 2006. *Community Mental Health in Canada*. Vancouver: University of British Columbia Press.

Egan, G., and W. Schroeder. 2009. *The Skilled Helper: A Problem-Management and Opportunity-Development Approach to Helping*, 1st Canadian edn. Toronto: Nelson Education.

Gilliland, B.E. 1997. *Crisis Intervention Strategies*. Pacific Grove, Calif.: Brooks/Cole.

Hepworth, D., R. Rooney, and J.A. Larsen. 2002. *Direct Social Work Practice: Theory and Skills*, 6th edn. Pacific Grove, Calif.: Brooks/Cole.

Shulman, L. 1999. *The Skills of Helping Individuals, Families, Groups and Communities*. Itasca, Ill.: F.E. Peacock.

Trevithick, P. 2005. *Social Work Skills: A Practice Handbook*, 2nd edn. Maidenhead, UK: Open University Press.

Internet Resources

Breaking Bad News website—for strategies and guidelines
www.breakingbadnews.co.uk

Health Canada Best Practices
http://hc-sc.gc.ca/hc-ps/pubs/adp-apd/bp_disorder-mp_concomitants/eval-eng.php

Montreal Cognitive Assessment
www.mocatest.org

Skills Cascade
www.skillscascade.com/index.html

Wadsworth Curriculum Connector—online tutorials
www.wadsworth.com/ connector/ ViewConnector.do?connectorId=1&categoryId =13&resourceTypeId=2

8 Paraphrasing and Summarizing

Learning Goals

- Describe reflecting skills and their use.
- Understand the structure and function of summarizing skills.

Building the Dimensions of People's Experiences

In the previous chapter, we explored the use of questioning skills. Questions help to probe further into a person's story and to more fully understand some of the specific dimensions of thoughts, feelings, events, and behaviours. However, you will need other skills to support people in the telling of their stories. If you only ask questions, the conversation can become an interrogation, as if running through a checklist. You need other skills to open up the story further; specifically, you can encourage someone to elaborate on the story through the use of paraphrasing, reflecting, and summarizing skills.

In facilitating paraphrasing, reflecting and summarizing skills, it becomes important to reflect on how this occurs culturally. As a practitioner, it is your responsibility to be sensitive to and familiar with multiple cultures and world views. Bitter (2009: 415) defines cultural sensitivity as: 'An awareness of cultural issues in families and a willingness to make these issues a central part of family practice, including an understanding of different values and beliefs, different levels of acculturation experiences, and the need to consider the marginalization, discrimination, and oppression of some cultures by the dominant culture'. Bitter (ibid.) defines culture as: 'Shared experiences, language, and ways of being based on ethnicity, nationality, gender, age, ability, sexual/affectional orientation, and/or location'. As a practitioner, if you are engaging in an attempt to assist the client in elaborating his or her story you must consider the lived experience of the client in your working relationship.

Paraphrasing and summarizing are the skills we use least in our everyday conversations. We tend not to actively reflect back to someone what we think we are hearing. Instead, we pick up the threads of a casual conversation and ask questions. In a professional conversational context, paraphrasing and summarizing skills are a useful way of ensuring a number of things are occurring. In reflecting and summarizing, you can confirm the details of the story with the client. In doing this, you can confirm that you are hearing the story as she or he wants and needs you to hear it. This confirms that you are listening, and, in particular, listening to the key dimensions of the experience.

> Remember the model of communication presented in Chapter 2, where messages are encoded by the sender and decoded by the receiver. The skills of paraphrasing and summarizing enable these messages to be confirmed or represented.

Reflecting Skills

Reflecting skills are used in many ways—to affirm, challenge, clarify, or normalize a person's situation. Bitter (ibid., 226) notes that 'the solution-oriented practitioner often will reframe problems as normal, everyday occurrences when the family or family members have been pathologized or have begun to self-pathologize their situation. Normalizing problems implies that because it is not so extreme, it can be addressed and solved.'

Summarizing usually occurs at the end of a session or at a pivotal point in the conversation in an attempt to ensure clear understanding. Bitter (ibid., 225) states, 'the summary lets the client know what the therapist(s) has heard and understands about the family's problem, and seeks to clarify anything that the interviewer might have missed.' This summary includes recognition of the emotional burden the client or family is facing.

Generally speaking, 'reflecting' is a process of 'mirroring back to the interviewee what the interviewee has just said, as grasped by the interviewer' (Dickson, 2006: 167). The term **paraphrasing** is similarly used to describe this process of relating back, in your own words, what you think you have heard the other person say. The risk in using the term 'mirroring' to define these processes is that it implies a static echo of what has been said, which is not the aim of the skill.

A distinction sometimes is made between the two types of responses—reflecting and paraphrasing: 'while paraphrases are restricted to what is actually said, reflections concentrate upon less obvious information frequently revealed in more subtle ways' (ibid., 2006: 171). Paraphrasing is seen by others to be reflecting of 'cognitive aspects of messages rather than feelings' (Hepworth, Rooney, and Larsen, 2002: 141). However, these distinctions are not maintained by everyone, and the terms are often interchanged.

Gilliland and James (1997) state that most practitioners would agree that they would like to increase their accuracy in communication. The authors suggest this requires two steps, restatement and reflection. Restatement of ideas involves making simple statements back to the client to ensure you are 'on the same page'. Reflection of feelings involves sending the client a message that you understand what the client is feeling emotionally. During this process if miscommunication has occurred or clarification is required, it provides the client with the opportunity to provide the practitioner with additional information.

Egan (Egan and Schroeder, 2009: 143) provides tactics for communicating your appreciation of important facts and feelings, thus:

- Give yourself time to think.
- Use short responses.
- Gear your response to the client but remain yourself.

Being empathic and engaged in a story involves actively conveying that you are hearing how the person feels, as well as understanding the 'facts' of the story. The 'formula', as presented in the earlier chapter, for this active response is:

You feel . . . [state emotion] because . . . [state the event, behaviour, or condition].

Applying this, a conversation may go as follows:

Client: I'm exhausted. He's terrifying. He's so controlling of my every move, and any attempts I've made to break out of the situation, he's right there. When I moved out, he tracked me down and made me move back in. He threatened to beat the crap out of me if I didn't. And he would have if I hadn't returned. When I changed my phone number, he got it by tricking my best friend that there was an emergency.

Worker: You feel controlled and trapped by this guy because he's right there, wherever you turn in your life.

Client: Yeah, that's it. I'm trapped by him. It's useless trying to escape him.

In most situations, however, the essence of this formula is applied in a more abstract way. That is, we listen for the feelings and events that are at the heart of what is going on for the client, but we actively convey this using other responses; for example, in more abbreviated forms:

Worker: So, he's trapping and controlling you, wherever you turn?

Alternatively, a more extended form would be:

Worker: And what I'm hearing is that while you're really trying to deal with this situation with this guy, whenever you do, he's able to get back in your life, and that's why you're feeling so tired and controlled.

'Owning' the reflection as the worker listens is achieved through the use of such expressions as 'What I'm hearing . . .', 'It seems like . . .', or 'I wonder if . . .' and gives the client the opportunity to respond by refuting, correcting, or agreeing with the view. If a reflection is correct, it is often greeted with the response: 'Exactly!' But the client needs also to be able to say, 'No, that's not what I meant' or 'Well, he didn't actually say that . . . .'

Egan and Schroeder (2009: 142) discuss the importance of expanding this topic to include empathetic highlights as a way of bridging diversity gaps. Interacting with clients who differ significantly from you can create the opportunity for you to be the learner. Scott and Borodovsky (1990) refer to empathetic listening as 'cultural role taking'. In this instance, it is important for the practitioner to understand the client's cultural background to avoid assumptions based on the worker's personal beliefs.

In Deborah's discussion with a student about self-disclosure, notice her very natural integration of paraphrasing skills in her conversation:

Student: I know I shouldn't self-disclose, but . . .
Deborah: It feels as though self-disclosure would help with rapport?
Student: Yes.
Deborah: What was the context?
Student: I am working in a mental health setting. We go out on home visits to families with a member with a mental illness. My brother has bipolar.
Deborah: It feels as though it could help to share this information.
Student: But I know I shouldn't.
Deborah: It sounds as though you know there is a rule but your gut is telling you something else.
Student: I guess so.

In most instances, a reflection should move the conversation in some way. Notice the lack of movement in the following conversation:

Client: I'm absolutely fit to be tied about this whole situation.
Worker: You're feeling fit to be tied about this situation.

This worker is merely repeating or mirroring directly, not reflecting what has been said. In some instances, however, mirroring might be useful, depending on the tone of voice and the intent—it might help the client hear how angry he is in a particular situation. The risk is that the person may feel mimicked, and that the conversation has gone nowhere. In fact, the client could feel more frustrated and unheard:

Client: I'm absolutely fit to be tied about this whole situation.
Worker: You're feeling fit to be tied about this situation.
Client: That's what I just said.

It raises the question as to what conditions in the client–worker relationship enable us to feel best heard. It is rarely about repeating the story or echoing feelings, but more about what kind of purposeful response we give and receive.

In some instances, however, reflecting is helpful to just 'sit' with the emotion or the experience that has been described and share it for a moment. Rather than finding out more detail through the use of questions, or challenging perceptions through reflections and summaries, sometimes reflecting back the emotion—be it heartache, exhaustion, or excitement—is a way of sharing in the reality of the client's experiences. Returning to the case of the harassed partner, this sort of response would be:

Client: I'm exhausted. He's terrifying. He's so controlling of my every move, and any attempts I've made to break out of the situation, he's right there. When I moved out, he tracked me down and made me move back in. He threatened to beat the crap out of me if I didn't. And he would have if I hadn't returned. When I changed my phone number, he got it by tricking my best friend that there was an emergency.

Worker: It sounds really tough, and exhausting, and frightening.

Client: It is. It's lonely, it's frightening, and I can't see it ever ending.

Here, the worker does not draw out the events or the feelings of the client in any extensive way. An affirmation of how the client may be feeling is reflected in a short, empathic statement. This type of response is a normalizing response. In this case, it draws out the client's fear that she has no alternatives.

Normalizing is a skill of affirmation. Typically, it draws on a wider pool of knowledge or experience to place a person's experience in context. For example, in grief situations, many people report that they feel as if they are going crazy, based on their experiences of auditory or visual hallucinations or disturbances to their sleep or capacity to function as they had prior to the loss (Raphael, 1983: 40–3). Normalizing is used in these instances to reassure people that these experiences are shared human experiences. Normalizing can focus on these grief experiences, or on coping strategies. For example, this conversation shows how the focus is on normalizing the experience following the death of a child:

Client: It's just stupid, stupid stuff. I hate feeling so disoriented. I feel as if I'm losing my mind. It's as if she's right there beside me and it drives me crazy. Am I crazy?

Worker: You're feeling like you're crazy because of these different experiences. Many people who have been through a major loss, like you have, experience similar things and find that they ask themselves these questions. It seems to be part of the 'making sense' of it. They're not crazy, nor are you.

Normalizing provides a useful reflection and reminder that people are not alone in their distress and difficulty. For some people, however, this is not what they need or want to hear. Their experience feels unique to them and any attempt by other people to presume to understand it is deeply offensive. Workers have different competencies and inclinations in using normalizing skills. The potential for the *least* authentic interaction is high in paraphrasing, as is the potential to offend with normalizing. The potential to deepen understanding and empathy, however, is also high and that is why these skills are encouraged.

Multicultural perspectives require further consideration when utilizing normalizing skills. It is imperative that the practitioner understand the world view of the client's cultural background to work effectively. If the worker does not understand the values and beliefs of the client, miscommunication can occur and damage the working relationship. How will you know what is 'normal', when working with diverse populations? How will you determine when this concept of normal is appropriate to the context of your work?

In using reflecting skills, thinking about why you are using these skills is important. A major argument for the use of these skills is that they actively convey that you have understood where the person is coming from. These responses do more than simply clarify (Hargie, 2006a). These responses can lead to new insights because people:

1. can feel heard, respected, and affirmed in what they are experiencing.
2. may not have thought about the situation in that way or may never have listened thoughtfully to what they themselves were saying. Listening clients can hear a different account of events because of additional new experiences, their listening to the worker or to themselves more insightfully, or because their emotional distance from their troubling situation has improved, which is so often why a counsellor is sought out as a listener.
3. may not realize the full implications of what they were saying about their problems.
4. may not realize the levels of contradiction and complexity in their situation, which can be hard to hear or to articulate. Reflecting or paraphrasing often normalizes these complexities of emotions and experiences, through naming them and recognizing them as significant dimensions of the overall situation.

The worker's listening skills in these situations are primarily about acknowledgement and provide a way of actively demonstrating to the client the values discussed in Chapter 1.

Sometimes you will be aware of the other layers of experience through the client's conversation or interaction. For example, someone describing feelings of sadness, both verbally and non-verbally, seems to you also to be feeling helpless or angry or ambivalent. It is important for the worker to be able to 'read' the total communication message in any conversation—the message involves both the verbal and the non-verbal in fundamental ways.

As with questioning, reflecting and paraphrasing are your means of influence—of your own opinion and world view—in the interview. Your choice of response will depend on what you are listening for, as the following exercise demonstrates.

Focus on Practice

A Group Role-Play

A group role-play or discussion can be a useful way to explore how you use particular responding skills and what connections they may have with your initial effort to learn the client's story and assessment from the start of an interview.

One person can role-play the client. Alternatively, you could watch a short piece of a DVD conversation where a client is describing her or his situation. The whole group, with the exception of the student playing the client, becomes 'the worker' and each person is invited to say what she/he would reflect back to the client.

1. From the client's perspective, which response did s/he prefer and why?
2. How varied are the responses your group has formed?
3. What was the type or category of the responses?
4. What are the consequences of each kind of technique in terms of the direction of the interview, the impact on the client, and the theoretical assumptions behind this focus?
5. What did you learn about your responding skills? Are there things you were not aware of?

Overusing paraphrasing can convey that you are listening, but may also mean that you have established few of the 'facts' of the story, leaving you without the information you need to assess the client's situation. Again, it depends on your context and purpose as to whether you need to be probing for details or adopting a more reflective approach.

Summarizing Skills

Summarizing skills are used in a conversation to draw together the various issues that have been discussed. While reflecting and paraphrasing are used throughout an entire interview, the use of summarizing is connected to some important timing issues. A summary can be used after the initial overview of the issues with which someone is grappling:

> Worker: So you're saying you've been into Child Services, you've spoken with the duty worker there, and she referred you to me to follow through on your complaint?
>
> Client: That's right.

It can also be used when you feel the conversation has come to a standstill or if you want the client to know exactly how you have heard what has been discussed. It enables the client to clarify your summary.

> Worker: So you're saying you've been into Child Services, you've spoken with the duty worker there, and she referred you to me to follow through on your complaint?
>
> Client: No, that's not what I said. I spoke with someone on the phone and she said I have to go into Child Services, *after* talking with you, to put in my complaint.

This summary establishes the details of a complex sequence of events, which the worker had misunderstood. Had he or she not summarized at this early point in the conversation, the misunderstanding could have caused major confusion. Clarifying statements like 'Let me see if I have this right . . .' can also be added to actively seek the client's view on what you are summarizing (Trevithick, 2005: 166).

A summary also can be used as a way of setting the direction of the next stage of conversation. It can close off some issues, too, and enable a focus to be agreed on for the rest of the discussion:

> Worker: So, we've talked now about what's going on with your drinking and how it is impacting your family. You have said how urgent you think it is for you to attend treatment, but you are feeling unsure of the process and about leaving home. What do you think we should focus on now?

A summary can also be used at the end of a meeting to bring together the essence of the conversation:

Worker: We've talked about a lot of things today—your relationship and whether or not you will leave, and your current level of stress, which is affecting your ability to focus at work. We have decided that a good step for you is to focus on applying stress reduction skills so you can begin to feel clearer. You stated then that you would like to discuss your relationship further. We'll talk again in a few days to see how things are going and if coming back to discuss your relationship is something you'd like to do.

In general, a summary should be short. A long or mistimed summary can seem laborious. A long summary can sound as if it is just repeating what the client has said or is presenting a 'shopping list' of issues. A summary should aim to pick up the complexity of issues to date and, typically, to open the next phase of the discussion. In addition, conveying accurately the language and emotional intensity of the client is important. A mismatch to the client's emotional intensity can leave the person feeling very misunderstood or misrepresented:

Client: [having discussed in detail her sexual harassment case and the need to access legal representation] So I'm a bit concerned about what this is all going to cost.
Worker: So with the hassle of finding a lawyer, the ongoing complications at work where you are enduring this person each day, your ongoing stress at home, you're now also really overwhelmed by the enormous cost of the lawyers.

In this instance, the worker has used unnecessarily intense emotional language—the client said she was a 'bit concerned' and the worker has said 'really overwhelmed'—and the client has been inundated by all the issues they have discussed, when in fact she only asked about the issue of legal costs.

Summaries are particularly important in situations where cultural or linguistic misunderstandings can occur. For example, when working with interpreters, it is sometimes difficult to know what the interpreter has communicated to the client, both from the standpoint of what the interpreter heard you say and from the standpoint of what the client has said to you through the interpreter. Regular summaries by both the client (through the interpreter) and the worker (likewise) can mediate some of this communication difficulty as to what has been heard and understood.

Chapter Summary

This chapter presents an overview of some of the skills you can use to consolidate the details of a person's story, with an emphasis on reflecting and summarizing skills. These skills help to establish a mutual understanding of a conversation, and of the overall work. They are skills that we tend not to use much in our everyday conversations, but they are one way of ensuring that the client's story is heard accurately and from his or her point of view.

Questions for Analysis

1. When would you use reflecting and summarizing skills, and when would you not?

2. When have you experienced the effective and/or ineffective use of these skills?

3. How is active listening important in summarizing and paraphrasing?

4. What potential miscommunication may occur in summarizing or paraphrasing?

5. What skills do you need to develop further in this area? Provide some examples.

Recommended Readings

Bitter, J.R. 2009. *Theory and Practice of Family Therapy and Counselling.* Belmont, Calif.: Brooks/Cole.

Egan, G., and W. Schroeder. 2009. *The Skilled Helper: A Problem-Management and Opportunity-Development Approach to Helping,* 1st Canadian edn. Toronto: Nelson Education.

Hargie, O. 2006. 'Training in Communication Skills', in Hargie, ed., *The Handbook of Communication Skills.* New York: Routledge, 553–65.

Gilliland, B.E., and K.R. James. 1997. *Crisis Intervention Strategies.* Pacific Grove, Calif.: Brooks/Cole.

Rogers, C. 1967. *On Becoming a Person: A Therapist's View of Psychotherapy.* London: Constable.

———, A. Ellis, and F. Perls. 1977. *Three Approaches to Psychotherapy.* Video produced and directed by E.L. Shostrom. Corona del Mar, Calif.: Psychological and Educational Films, 1986.

Schmidt, G., and L. Jarrett. 2000. *Mental Health and Northern Aboriginal People: An Annotated Bibliography.* Prince George, BC: Northern Interior Regional Health Board and UNBC Social Work Program.

Internet Resource

Person-centred links, University Counselling Service, University of East Anglia
www.uea.ac.uk/menu/admin/dos/couns/training/person_centred.htm

9 Forming an Assessment—Setting the Agenda

Learning Goals

- Understand the purposes of assessment.
- Consider some of the inherent challenges in assessment.
- Understand the focus of assessments.
- Describe the process of setting goals for the work.

In the previous chapters, we have focused on some of the ways in which you can meet with people, engage in conversation, and begin to explore the circumstances that have led to your contact. Each time you ask a question or reflect back to someone what you have heard you are making decisions about what to respond to, what to hear (but not actively address), and what to remember from the conversation, and perhaps address at a later point. You are beginning to focus more on particular dimensions of this individual's situation. You are forming an assessment of someone's circumstances and how he or she is placed within those circumstances. The example below highlights that an interview or conversation will need to move to a particular focus after an initial period of exploration of the issues and concerns.

Focus on Practice

Moving from the Story to an Assessment

Your client, Mohammed, has described his difficult transition to life in Canada. He arrived several months ago on his own, after 14 months in a refugee camp adjoining his home country. He has some distant relatives living in Canada, but not locally, and contact has been difficult. His wife and two children are still in his home country and he is working towards bringing them to Canada, but it is not an easy process, especially given the language barriers and financial resources required.

Mohammed has found accommodation, but is experiencing great difficulties in adapting to Canadian life. He has come to your service for assistance with a number of urgent issues:

- his housing circumstances, which are temporary accommodations
- his health—given both his lack of financial resources and therefore inadequate nutrition—and his traumatic memories, which combine to keep him from sleeping
- his difficulty finding employment
- fear for his family and the need to bring them to Canada.

1. What else would you want to know about Mohammed and his situation?
2. What would you see as some of the major issues to address and how would you go about setting the priorities?
3. Are there other issues you would want to explore and possibly focus on in your conversation?

Remember the values, knowledge bases, and theoretical perspectives explored in Chapters 1–3. These provide the basis for your assessment.

The term **assessment** is very broad, meaning different things in different professions. In Chapter 1, we looked at the general purpose of human services: working with people to alleviate adversity and oppression, and to promote well-being and health. Assessment, therefore, focuses on exploring how people are functioning and how optimal functioning and well-being can be enhanced through the provision of specific resources for their inner and outer worlds.

The type of assessment required from the worker varies according to your agency context. In work that is oriented towards a social care agenda, where change is a mutual goal, the assessment process focuses on setting goals for the work that will be engaged in together. Where you may be in a position of imposing a change agenda, assessment may be driven more unilaterally by you. You will be making judgements and decisions about coping capacities, about risk, and about resources. This work will still focus on change as the outcome, but it may not be so mutually determined.

Davis (2006) discusses the early phase of any intervention as including working with the client to define and set goals. Where necessary, this can include a formal assessment to assist with the recovery process. Davis describes a clinical assessment as, 'an ongoing process, one that involves interviews, gathering collateral information, using psychometric instruments, and in some cases laboratory tests as well as scanning and imaging techniques' (Davis, 2006: 191).

A self-assessment on individual professional practice is discussed by Bitter (2009: 360), who proposes a continuous process of reflection in practice. Part of professional development is to be aware of professional strengths and limits in all points of practice. One method of understanding what works best for you as the practitioner is to revisit a video tape of yourself and 'reflect and connect'. 'Reflection is largely an internal assessment . . . . You also will begin to see that you connect your personal and professional patterns to one or more models you have already studied. You won't so much adopt a model as you will arrive at it'. Bitter suggests asking yourself the following:

Based on the video tape of your work—what thoughts, feelings and reactions were triggered? Were there things you did well and made you feel competent as a professional? Were there things you had wished you had done differently? What interventions do you rely on to form relationships? Do these assessments create meaning or promote change? By facilitating this self-assessment, the practitioner will become aware and connect to the patterns of your work. (Adapted from ibid.)

The processes and purposes of an assessment are filtered by the influences we have discussed in earlier chapters: your values, knowledge bases, skills and organizational context. You can see in the following scenario that you would be dealing with a number of different points of view throughout the assessment process and would need to juggle these.

Focus on Practice

Mr and Mrs Willis

Mr and Mrs Willis are in their late seventies and have been living in their own condo for 32 years. They have strong connections with a number of neighbours, and with their local Rotary Club. Mr Willis fell last week when he got up to answer the phone. He is currently in the local hospital with a fractured leg and wrist and diagnosed osteoporosis. Since his admission, the nurses have become very concerned about his memory and have organized an assessment for him, which has confirmed that he has dementia. The worker is to talk with Mr and Mrs Willis about a range of home-care options, including the possibility that he move into a supported living arrangement. Mrs Willis is distraught about the dementia diagnosis and the possibility that he might move out of their family home, where they have lived for so long. She has made it very clear that she wants her husband to come back home and live there. In her mind, this hospital admission is only about his physical recovery from the broken bones and she is terrified of any suggestion that he should no longer live with her.

1. What would you see as some of the immediate issues that would form part of your assessment?
2. How would you go about exploring these issues with the people involved in this situation?
3. Who is the client?
4. What strengths and risks are present?

In this scenario, the focus has moved from the initial presenting problem or concern—Mr Willis's hospital admission—to establishing some underlying concerns. In this instance, the presenting and underlying problems are quite different, depending on who you talk to about the situation.

Who Is the Assessment For?

Ideally, an assessment process enables the establishment of a mutual agenda for future action. In exploring the story with the client, the assessment process provides the step towards establishing the basis for further work and the ongoing purpose of the relationship. It is about moving from 'starting where the client is at' to working towards where the client wants to be, or, in mandated circumstances, where others consider the client should be.

The different formats and requirements for assessments raise some major challenges in the assessment phase, depending on who the assessment really is for. For example, the following assessment formats are identified by Lloyd and Taylor (1995, cited by Trevithick, 2005: 130):

- third-party assessments
- investigative assessments
- eligibility/needs assessments
- suitability assessments
- multidisciplinary assessments.

In addition to these are assessments within the context of a more therapeutic client–worker relationship, where the assessment is conducted to ascertain what should be the focus of the work together. Some of these challenges raised in the assessment process are described now, before moving into an exploration of assessment frameworks.

Challenges in the Assessment Process

Forming an assessment is a challenging task. An assessment needs to capture the diversity of a client's life and the complexity of their unique and current situation. An assessment can have a profound impact on a person's life; for example, if it denies them eligibility for a service, or concludes that their child can no longer live with them. In the scenario outlined above, an assessment may lead to a strong recommendation that Mr Willis not return to his home. A comprehensive assessment, therefore, is critical. Some major challenges inherent in the process of assessment are briefly discussed, including the focus of the assessment, the adequacy and accuracy of the information gathered, the fluidity of assessment, who sets the agenda, and cultural diversity. Davis (2006) cautions practitioners to consider that the initial assessment may occur at a time of crisis for the client, and therefore may influence the accuracy of the information being gathered.

Assessing for Risks or for Strengths?

In the context of resource limitations and a focus in Western society on risk management (Webb, 2006; Lupton, 1999; Giddens, 2002), many assessments remain risk assessments, adopting a primarily pathogenic approach to understanding of people and their circumstances. Morley (2004: 127) defines a risk assessment as a 'process of categorizing and recording particular information about clients to make predictions about the likelihood of particular future events occurring'. Examples of 'risk' may include reckless actions, neglect involving personal health or safety, or suicidal thoughts.

Assessment is, therefore, about highly subjective predictions being made by someone who may not have gathered all the relevant information (Webb, 2006; Lupton, 1999; Giddens, 2002). A focus on capacity-building, both within the person and within their wider families and communities, is an essential component of an assessment. A comprehensive assessment should incorporate not only a risk but a strengths perspective.

Adequate and Correct Information

In some situations, a systematic, detailed assessment may be possible. This enables an in-depth discussion of many dimensions of a person's life. Assessments, however, are often conducted quickly with people under less than optimal conditions. The available time and place can impact, therefore, quite profoundly on the outcome of an assessment. Similarly, what clients know of you—and what the information they give you will be used for—influences willingness to disclose, or even the perception that disclosure of certain information is relevant or required.

> Remember the example of the research conducted at the Alfred Hospital where people told very different dimensions of their story to the researcher because of the perception of her role as researcher rather than as social worker.

Gathering adequate and correct information with diverse populations requires that practitioners consider a client's cultural background and world view. The practitioner should consider any possible barriers the client is facing throughout the process and take steps to ensure the client understands purpose in gathering the information required.

Issues related to northern and remote locations also require consideration when gathering information. If the client is from a remote community, her or his experience in a larger urban centre may be limited and therefore, overwhelming. The client may require assistance in understanding what the purpose of the assessment is and how the process is designed. Bitter (2009: 368) suggests the following multicultural questions to consider in practice:

- What cultures are in the family background of each of the family members?
- In what culture or region is the family currently living?
- Is immigration or migration a recent family experience?
- How do economics, education, ethnicity, religion, race, regional affiliation, gender, and age affect family process?
- How is the fit between the therapist and the family with regard to economics, education, ethnicity, religion, age, race, majority/minority status, and regional background?

Fluidity of Information

People and circumstances change over time, sometimes very rapidly and sometimes more slowly. For example, someone with great enthusiasm for life who is developing dementia may become preoccupied with thoughts of suicide and appear to recent acquaintances as severely depressed. Poverty is another experience that, in Western contexts, often shifts for people across their lifespan, rather than remaining a constant (Room and Britton, 2006). People acquire different coping capacities or different stressors. Assessments can be written up and placed in client files, and become the source of information about the client over many years, without ever being revisited or verified. Details of a client's life can be handed on as 'fact' when it may long since have changed yet again.

As a worker, too, you will change over time as you develop your knowledge base and practice wisdom. Perceptions of risk, for example, may change the more you are confronted with people in a particular setting. You may realize you were more cautious or liberal in an assessment of a client situation a few years ago than you would be now. The information gathered in any assessment process therefore necessarily changes over time.

The monitoring of changing needs and issues is important in situations where ongoing contact is maintained. Thus, assessment is both a single process done in a first interview and an ongoing process throughout the length of any contact with workers.

Howatt (2000: 31) suggests the following procedure for an initial interview:

- Introduce yourself: *Hello, I'm (title) (name). And you are ————?*
- Explain what an assessment is for, or ask what they are expecting.
- Explain what your role is, or ask the client to define what your job is, and then clarify.
- Explain the concept of choice, and that the counsellor cannot make or fix a person; the work is to help the client work through areas of concern.
- Explain any orientation information the client may need to know.
- Explain how long the interview will be, and that a break for any reason (for example, restroom) is OK.
- Explain that the assessment process is ongoing, and that all decisions are made in a collaborative manner. Also, that the cleint's goals can change or be fine-tuned at any time.
- Explain that this is a helping process, and that at any time (unless court ordered) the client can terminate the process.
- Explain, if applicable, that you have already read any reports; however, the emphasis for today is on what the client has to say and wants to do.
- Explain your qualification.

Who Sets the Agenda?

Your aim is to set a mutually agreeable agenda for the work to be done together. At another level, you as the worker, and as part of a particular agency, influence that assessment and agenda, either implicitly or explicitly.

Reflect back on Mohammed's situation earlier in this chapter, and on the ways in which your assessment may be influenced by an agency's resources.

Remember the diagram reflecting the communication process in Chapter 2. In any assessment process, the worlds of the worker and the client are present.

Depending on the context, you and your client may disagree in your assessments of a situation. For example, in acute psychiatric service settings different perceptions often arise as to whether someone requires an involuntary hospital admission; disagreement may arise as to whether or not a parent should be allowed to continue living in the family home following allegations of sexual abuse; or questions may occur as to whether a young person's non-attendance at school is indicative of more serious underlying problems at home or at school.

Making an assessment with clients in involuntary circumstances is a more fraught process. Important information is likely to be missing if a strong engagement and rapport has not been established. It is also critical to explain why the assessment process is important—that is, clarifying the role accurately (Trotter, 2006: 18). This can be done through ongoing, honest discussion. People's experiences of trust in both personal and professional relationships may have been poor, and so this is an opportunity to promote collaborative problem solving (ibid., 21).

An organizational context will also profoundly shape what assessment can be made and what subsequent interventions can occur. Thus an assessment may be limited by what resources are available rather than what the person actually needs or has a right to access (Ife, 2001; Trevithick, 2005: 130).

Diversity

Assessment processes have the potential to amplify all sorts of assumptions about world views. Assumptions about consent, agreement, and commonality of goals can be imposed without a worker realizing it. Similarly, assumptions about ways of living and perceptions of coping and adaptation (Rigney and Cooper, 2004; Smith, 2001) can be imposed. You can build optimal understanding by asking open-ended questions about the meaning of events or actions and by using paraphrasing. Workers have a professional responsibility to develop and sustain cultural awareness in relation to all diversity issues—including sexual, religious, and cultural diversities—and to their own prejudices and assumptions. As Miller, Donner, and Fraser (2004: 380, citing Goodman, 2001) note: 'Most people with agent status do not view themselves as having power and privilege.'

Davis (2006: 299) notes, 'in considering the mental health needs of Canada's culturally diverse population, one can identify a number of potential barriers to establishing and maintaining a constructive relationship between service providers and minority clients. These barriers include language, different world views as to what constitutes mental disorder and mental health, stigma, distrust, and how services are designed and allocated.' In addition, it is important to go beyond defining culture as solely linked to ethnicity. Some groups may define the term 'culture' to include contextual variables such as, rural, urban or suburban settings; language, age, gender cohort, family configuration, race, ethnicity, religion, nationality, socio-economic status, employment, education, occupation, sexual orientation, political ideology; migration, and stage of acculturation (Falicov, 1995).

1. How do you define the term culture?
2. What are some of the ways you have experienced culture being defined?
3. In a small group discuss how culture could be defined from the above list, for example, family configuration, or sexual orientation.

Corey (1996: 30) suggests, 'effective multicultural practice demands an open stance on the part of the practitioner, a flexibility, and a willingness to modify strategies to fit the needs and the situation of the individual client.' Corey continues: 'it is important to realize that it takes time, study, and experience to become an effective multicultural counsellor. Multicultural competence cannot be reduced simply to cultural awareness and sensitivity, to a body of knowledge, or to a specific set of skills' (ibid., 31).

Mussel, Cardiff, and White (2004: 7), define cultural competency as, 'a specific set of values, attitudes, knowledge and skills that sensitize and improve sharing of information and assistance between people of different cultural orientations'.

What Assessment Frameworks Are Used?

As we listen to someone speak, we begin to form an assessment. In this sense, assessment begins as the work begins. Typically, though, after an initial exploration of the client's story, the communication needs to become focused in a purposeful way around specific issues of concern and action. Given the diversity of the specifics of each particular context, no single assessment framework exists. Many agencies have standardized intake and assessment forms and procedures, reflecting the assessment of the particular dimensions they focus on in service delivery.

Why we come to emphasize some dimensions and not others within these assessment processes is an important question to reflect upon. The theoretical dimensions we privilege as a worker and/or as an organization profoundly influence the listening we are capable of. As Fook (1993: 74) states, assessment is 'the phase of casework helping where a theory is formed about the particular causes of a particular person's particular situation'. This knowledge returns our discussion to some of the earlier chapters, when we noted that theoretical perspectives influence what we hear and why.

Many assessment frameworks focus primarily on a client and the client's inner-world dimensions. Their personal stories and circumstances are understood as follows (Egan, 2002: 77): 'Stories tend to be mixtures of clients' experiences, behaviors, and emotions. Traditionally, human activity has been divided into three parts: thinking, feeling, and acting.' From this theorizing of human experience, a framework for listening includes the following questions:

1. What are the main points?
2. What experiences are most important?
3. What themes are coming through?
4. What is the client's point of view?
5. What is most important to him or her?
6. What does he/she want me to understand?
7. What decisions are implied?
8. What is he or she proposing to do?

This way of thinking about assessment focuses primarily on the individual and his/her inner world. Other assessments consider outer-world dimensions that impact these experiences, taking into account such factors as poverty and marginalization. Later chapters will elaborate on these themes in greater detail.

This framework will enable you, the worker, to listen to the things you consider priorities in the client's story as well as the client's evaluations of priorities. It provides an insight into clients' inner world by linking their thinking, feeling, behaving (both in the past and the future), and events. These dimensions begin to provide the basis of 'what' to listen for.

Often underemphasized at this point is a sense of clients circumstances in relation to their outer-world connections—their relationships, their social and cultural contexts, and the nature of their **structural contexts**. As Fook (1993: 75) notes: 'The structural element will always interplay with personal factors such as biography, current life events, emotional and psychological characteristics, genetic inheritance, physical health, and so on to create a unique personal situation.' This appreciation for the client's context shifts an assessment from focusing only on thinking, feeling, behaving, and events to include the mediating dimensions of social context.

A Multi-dimensional Assessment Framework

A multi-dimensional framework includes the other dimensions of individuals' lives: the social, structural, and cultural contexts. The ways in which the environment enhances or inhibits the person's coping become part of the assessment. Frameworks that assess behaviours, thoughts, and feelings place the individual at the centre of the construction of the problem, as opposed to frameworks that position the person as having been acted upon by external forces or circumstances. Assessment within human services involves inquiry about these external dimensions as much as about the client's internalizing of situations and events.

As outlined in Chapter 3, a multi-dimensional approach seeks to understand both the inner- and outer-world dimensions of a person's circumstances. The inner-world dimensions include the biological, psychological (thoughts and feelings), and spiritual dimensions. The outer-world dimensions include the relational, social, structural, and cultural dimensions. A broad, multi-dimensional assessment framework should include, then, each of these specific dimensions (Anglem and Maidment, 2004; Fook, 1993: 153–5; Harms, 2005; Hepworth, Rooney, and Larsen, 2002).

Exploration of each of the dimensions in the box below includes an assessment as to whether they are significant sources of stress and vulnerability or are significant sources of protection and resilience. In some instances, you may need to ask very direct, closed questions to establish an understanding. In others, you may develop your understanding from a more descriptive conversation, so that specific questions do not need to be asked. Each of these dimensions can become the focus of further exploration and intervention.

Focus on Practice

Exploration of the Client's Physical Dimensions

In what ways do the following dimensions impact a person's current circumstances and coping capacity:

- age?
- sex?
- family configuration?
- general presentation and appearance?
- general health or medical status—drug and alcohol use?
- housing environment?
- physical changes and their impact on well-being?
- sources of physical stress?
- physical coping strategies and resources?

Depending on the circumstances, a range of other questions about specific dimensions may be relevant. Within the physical dimension, for example, specific assessment tools are available to assess drug and alcohol use and abuse or general health (Goldberg, 1978).

At the end of this chapter, links to specific websites with assessment tools are provided.

Thousands of scales have been developed to assess a person's psychological functioning. For example, scales are available to measure intelligence; emotional intelligence; the impact of trauma, stress, and grief; and personality traits. *The Diagnostic and Statistical Manual of Mental Disorders* (APA, 2000) is a major resource, a collation of psychological assessment guidelines, used in many mental health settings (although some theorists and practitioners take a strong stance against this tool because of its misuse in practice and its shifting, ever-expanding view of what constitutes mental illness; see, e.g., Cech, 2010: 12–14, 18, 22–3, 27, 226). For any psychological phenomenon, a scale seems to be available.

Focus on Practice

Exploration of the Client's Psychological Dimensions

In what ways do the following dimensions impact a person's current circumstances and coping capacity:

- intellectual capacity?
- language capacity?
- self-image, self-esteem?
- sense of agency and motivation?
- mental health status?
- subjective perceptions of the problem situation?
- psychological changes and their impact on well-being?
- sources of psychological stress?
- psychological coping strategies and resources?

Similarly, spiritual dimensions of a person's life can be measured using a range of assessment tools, such as Fowler's faith development framework (Parker, 2006), as described below.

Focus on Practice

Exploration of the Client's Spiritual Dimensions

In what ways do the following dimensions impact a person's current circumstances and coping capacity:

- importance of spirituality?
- spiritual practices?
- importance of religion?
- religious practices?
- spiritual changes and their impact on well-being?
- sources of spiritual stress?
- spiritual coping strategies and resources?

Many dimensions of a person's social network also can be analyzed, using a range of available tools.

Focus on Practice

Exploration of the Client's Social Dimensions

In what ways do the following dimensions impact a person's current circumstances and coping capacity:

- qualities of relational networks with partners and family?
- qualities of social networks with neighbours, friends, colleagues, clubs, church groups, etc.?
- perceived and received social support?
- significant power relationships?
- qualities of social roles the person engages in: occupation, education, schooling, university, or paid/unpaid work?
- major family and life events and history?
- sources of social stress?
- relationships with social institutions (past or present)?
- social changes and their impact on well-being?
- sources of social stress?
- social coping strategies and resources?

A comprehensive assessment of a client's social dimensions or environment networks can be undertaken by talking through and drawing an eco-map, for example. In an eco-map, you document each relationship a person has with those in his/her immediate networks, according to its particular qualities or resources. You can also show the interconnections between people in a person's network. Each relationship can be illustrated by using different connecting lines, according to the legend in Figure 9.1.

An eco-map can also identify workers in various organizations who may be contributing to a particular situation. In this sense, they are the front line of the structural dimension; that is, the broader systems that profoundly restrict a person's coping capacity, and indeed, often create the difficulties in the first place. Thus, it is equally important to assess the structural and cultural dimensions of people's lives.

The assessment tools for the structural dimensions are less utilized in many organizations, and are often more the focus of discussion than of formal assessment.

Cultural assessment tools are also available, and address a range of issues within this critical dimension. For example, the checklist of social dimensions (Fook, 1993), cited earlier, provides a way of reflecting on the dimensions not only of your social identity but also those that may be influencing your client's experience. Other possible areas of assessment are outlined on the following page.

> Remember, in Chapter 7, a Mini-Mental Status Examination was presented as one example of an assessment tool.

Focus on Practice

Exploration of the Client's Structural Dimensions

In what ways do the following dimensions impact a person's current circumstances and coping capacity:

- financial circumstances?
- legal circumstances?
- socio-economic status and roles?
- political circumstances?
- gender roles?
- occupation and education level?
- structural changes and their impact on well-being?
- structural sources of stress?
- structural resources?

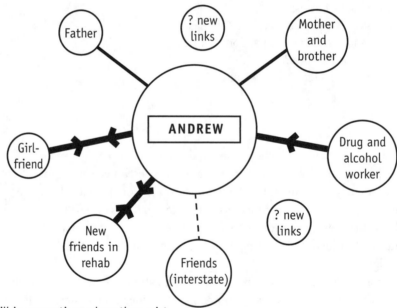

Fill in connections where they exist.

Indicate nature of connections with a descriptive word or by drawing different kinds of lines:

████ strong   ──── tenuous   – – – stressful

Draw arrows along lines to signify the flow of energy, resources, etc.
Identify significant people and fill in empty circles as needed

Figure 9.1 Mapping a Client's Social Network Using an Eco-map

Source: Harms (2005: 37).

Focus on Practice

Exploration of the Client's Cultural Dimensions

In what ways do the following dimensions impact upon a person's current circumstances and coping capacity:

- culture and ethnicity?
- culture and sexuality?
- subculture or cultural minority status?
- socially held beliefs and myths?
- cultural changes and their impact on well-being?
- cultural sources of stress?
- cultural coping strategies and resources?

A sound assessment should focus on the risks and on the strengths in a client's circumstances. Listening for strengths is paramount in any assessment process. While such a focus by no means diminishes the difficulties a person has been encountering and may be facing (Saleebey, 1996, 1997, 2001), your understanding of how someone is addressing or coping with other demands or similar demands is an extremely important evaluation to include in an overall view of how the person can change and adapt in regard to the main problem.

Focus on Practice

Unexpected Strengths

Many practitioners within prenatal care services have been concerned about women's non-attendance at clinics when substance abuse issues have been identified. However, a study (Tobin, 2005: 7) of 23 women attending a major women's hospital, combined with a data analysis of 1,250 hospital records, found that:

- Contrary to popular opinion, less than half (47 per cent) of the women identified that a lifestyle preoccupation with drug and alcohol issues posed a barrier to attendance for pregnancy care.
- The overall attendance rates for women with substance abuse issues . . . do not differ greatly from those without substance use issues.

These findings have enabled workers to rethink their understandings of women's efforts to attend prenatal care while they also are dealing with drug and alcohol issues.

Focus on Practice

Addiction Assessment Tools

The CAGE is widely used in emergency rooms because it is quick and simple to administer. CAGE is an acronym using key words from each question as follows:

(a) Have you ever felt you should **C**ut down on your drinking?
(b) Have people **A**nnoyed you by criticizing your drinking?
(c) Have you ever felt **G**uilty about your drinking?
(d) **E**ye opener: Have you ever had a drink first thing in the morning to steady your nerves or get rid of a hangover?

A score of 2 or 3 on the CAGE is recommended as a cutoff for identifying individuals with alcohol-related problems.

Source: Adapted from http://counsellingresource.com

Additional assessment tools commonly used in addiction assessments are the Michigan Alcohol Screening Test (MAST) and Drug Abuse Screening Test (DAST). The MAST is a self-test consisting of 22 questions which may assist clients in becoming aware of their alcohol misuse. Similarly, the DAST is a self-test consisting of 20 questions, which may assist clients is becoming aware of their drug misuse.

An assessment process can vary from a very brief discussion and assessment of needs or rights, through to a planned assessment period over a specified time period or number of sessions. For example, the Metta Youth Psychotherapy program (Harms and McDermott, 2003), which provides intensive psychotherapeutic support for at-risk young people for up to three years, has a four-session assessment period, at the end of which both the client and the worker discuss the continuation or cessation of therapy.

Assessments are often a part of client intake or referral for specialized services. Tools for assessment can include depression scales, anxiety scales, Attention Deficit Hyperactivity Disorder (ADHD), and other specific mental health disorders. This may involve a practitioner facilitating the initial assessment as part of determining the best plan of care for a client and the most appropriate referral.

An example of problematical suicide assessment is pointed out by Davis (2006: 194), where he stated, 'a study of a large Canadian community mental health program found that the forty-three documented completed suicides over a three-year period by clients of the program represented a rate twenty-five times higher than that seen in the general public'. Davis notes that it is imperative that practitioners regularly consider clients' 'thoughts and intentions concerning suicide, a process that involves assessment, documentation, and consultation with colleagues and supervisors'. Risk factors for suicide completion can be categorized as follows (ibid., 195):

1. *Vulnerable populations:* includes males, persons with a mental illness, youth, First Nations, the elderly, widowers, and those suffering from a painful, chronic, or terminal physical illness or condition.

2. *Historical factors:* previous attempts, history of suicide in the family or among friends, history of abuse or trauma, history of impulsivity, the proximity of anniversaries of significant events, such as the birthday of a child who was taken away.

3. *Current risk factors:* current symptoms of mental illness, such as 'command' hallucinations or delusions that support suicide, loss of job, social standing, or relationship (or anticipation of same), living alone or in isolation, recent death by suicide of another significant person, rigid 'black-and-white' thinking, perfectionism, recent discharge following hospitalization for psychiatric reasons, use of substances that are depressive or disinhibiting (such as alcohol).

4. *Current thinking:* A sense of hopelessness, thoughts of suicide that are frequent, persistent, and specific, having a plan and a means to carry it out.

What Interventions Are Used?

At the end of an assessment process, possible interventions typically are discussed. A 'contract' is sometimes formally undertaken, in that there is agreement around the problem areas or difficulties, and the ways of addressing some or all of these issues. Typically, you will discuss:

- the perceived areas of work for change
- how that may be achieved
- your mutual responsibilities and commitments as the worker and the client
- the time limits on your work together.

From this, a plan for intervention emerges. Interventions can address resources in the inner and/or outer worlds of the person. For example, inner-world interventions can help clients develop new ways of coping with behavioural or belief restrictions that they impose on themselves, or others impose on them. Intervention strategies include counselling, **psycho-education**, social support strategies, and group work. Outer-world interventions can help clients manage and change the structural restrictions in their worlds, and may involve very active worker action to bring this about with the client. Intervention strategies include resource provision, referral, liaison, advocacy, capacity-building, group work, and community development.

How Do We Set the Goals for the Work?

Whereas the assessment process establishes the overall problem and strengths areas in a client's circumstances, and resource requirements, contracting and **goal-setting** are important processes in establishing the priorities for intervention, both from the client and worker perspectives. That is, when you have explored with your client the

Remember Mrs B.'s work with Nicole in Chapter 6 and their ability to reset the goals of their relationship.

key themes of their difficulties, priorities need to be set as areas for work. It is not possible to address everything at once, and a process of goal-setting enables a plan to be developed around the tasks and timelines.

The goals for the kind of intervention need to be articulated and ultimately, even if only in a small way, mutually satisfactory. In the following box, Burstow (1987: 21) recounts her own experience of encountering a therapist who worked in such a different way from what she was wanting and needing by way of intervention at a particular point in her life.

Focus on Practice

Mutual Goals

From a client's perspective, Brian said: 'I was in the process of making a major move and found myself panic-stricken. The therapist I sought help from was client-centred. He was very empathic, very kind, very respectful, but he gave me nothing on which to hold. He offered no clue about what I might do in a situation that demanded that I act almost immediately and in which I was paralyzed. I emerged from the session more terrified than ever and by now markedly suicidal. Eventually, I did what I should have done in the first place. I sought help from someone who would offer me what was missing in myself, who half-gave-me, half-helped-me-find some preliminary sense of direction. I sought help, that is, from a helper who did not ask me to be an equal at a point where I clearly could not be.'

Reflecting on this experience, Brian suggests that the therapist 'failed' because:

1. He did not acknowledge or understand how vulnerable he was.
2. He assumed that everyone at all times was equally able to get their needs fulfilled, as long as the therapist is empathic.
3. He did not take an active leadership role when such a role was required.

One possible explanation for why Brian's situation occurred was that the client and the worker did not explicitly discuss the goals of the work. An opportunity to discuss goals together is vital.

Goal-setting occurs in a number of ways, depending on the context and the theoretical orientation of the worker. Goal-setting is also influenced profoundly by the client's engagement in the change process. Some general views on the nature of the goal/s that are set are expressed by Marsh and Doel (2005: 117):

> In common with the selected problems, the chosen goal should be one which is feasible and desirable for the person to achieve within the agreed time limit, relatively specific, something he or she feels motivated about, and a clearly understood link between the problem and how the goal will alleviate it.

Breaking this process of goal-setting down further, an emphasis is often placed on developing SMART goals (Marsh and Doel, 2005: 36), where the well-known acronym SMART stands for specific, manageable, achievable, realistic, and timely.

1. *Specific*—Goals should be focused on particular issues, not generalized states of being, for example. This may involve transforming the following statements, where the worker is talking with his client about his goals in moving in with his new partner and her two children from another relationship:

    Worker: What would your goal be with these kids?
    Client: I really want to be a good dad to these kids [goal statement 1].
    Worker: How will you know when you're being a good dad?
    Client: I'd be doing things that would be natural, like taking them to the park that's just around the corner, and those things that I know we already share. But I'd also be able to be clear with them when they start fooling around and not having to worry that they're 'not mine' [goal statement 2].

    The first goal statement is global and it may be hard to know when it has been achieved. Notice that the second goal statement is much more specific to certain situations, so the client will know when he has, by his criteria, met his goals.

2. *Manageable*—Notice the goals set in the above scenario are manageable goals, in that they involve some small steps about the kinds of changes he wants to see. Many people set unmanageable goals, in a number of different ways. They may take too long, or require resources that are unattainable, for example. Goals need to be manageable in the sense that adequate resources are available—be they time, energy, condition, or personal resources (Hobfoll, Ennis, and Kay, 2000).

3. *Achievable*—The client in this scenario can probably easily achieve the goals; he has specified two ways in which he can make immediate, tangible changes in his interactions. Many people set unachievable goals that are incompatible with where they are at. The goal may be too ambitious or may require too much of a major change in too many dimensions of the person's life. For women leaving situations of violence, a major barrier is often the prospect of leaving so many dimensions of their lives—including, sometimes, children—to ensure their own safety.

4. *Realistic*—This client is talking about realistic goals; visiting a park is probably possible in a local community during the course of a week. Realistically, he recognizes that differences in parenting style may be a source of difficulty in the new family arrangement. He is not setting ambitious goals, for example, by promising a trip to Disneyland or that he is always going to be able to maintain his commitment without fail.

5. *Timely*—His goals seem to be appropriate in terms of timing in that he is anticipating moving into a new situation. If he was presenting in the midst of a high-conflict situation around parenting issues, these goals may not be so timely. They may be too late! The timeliness of goals is an important determinant of their success.

Practice Questions

1. Think of a time when you have wanted to change a specific dimension of your life. What was your goal?

2. In retrospect, would you describe it as a SMART goal, using the definition above?

3. What were the challenges or barriers to making the change in the first place?

4. How did you go about trying to make the change?

5. Did it work? Why or why not?

6. What would you do differently if you wanted to make that change again?

Focus on Practice

The Egan Model

Egan's problem-management and opportunity-development model has been used internationally as a framework for an interview or series of counselling sessions with clients. It is based on a process of goal-setting, and includes the following questions within each stage of the model.

Stage 1—Problem clarification and ownership

What's going on? What are the problems, issues, concerns, or undeveloped opportunities I should be working on?

-   Help clients to tell their story.
-   Help clients break through blind spots.
-   Help clients choose the right problems/opportunities to work on.

Stage 2—Goal-setting and commitment to goals

What solutions make sense for me? What do I need or want?

-   Help clients use imagination to spell out possibilities for the future.
-   Help clients choose realistic and challenging goals that will equal real solutions (agenda for change).
-   Help clients find incentives—what am I willing to pay for what I want?

Stage 3—Strategies for accomplishing goals

What do I have to do to get to what I want?

-   Help client see possible actions—many ways to achieve goals.
-   Help client choose best fit.
-   Help client to craft a plan.

The Egan model is a very structured way of working and, in some settings, can be applied fully. Processes like these enable us to talk through goals with clients or to even write them down on paper or on a whiteboard or flip chart so that they are clear and can be easily remembered.

One way of further opening up the goal-setting process is through brainstorming. 'Brainstorming' involves either verbally or in writing proposing every possible solution or course of action even vaguely relevant to the current situation. The important feature of a brainstorm is that it is done without any censoring of ideas. Brainstorming enables the opening up of new possibilities. In some situations, the lack of new coping strategies is part of the problem. As a discussion between the client and worker, brainstorming enables a pooling of resources, without any pressure towards a particular option at that point in time.

Worker: Let's think about what the possibilities are here, without putting any limits on our imaginations at this point. What have you thought about doing?

Client: I'm stuck. I can't think of anything.

Worker: OK, that's one option. To stay stuck, to keep things as they are!

Client: [laughs] I hadn't thought about that! No way, I couldn't bear that. You know, when I felt more on top of things, I did half wonder about going back to school and finishing that.

Worker: And what would you then do?

Client: Well, I'd be able to work, you know. Get a job. Get out of the house, get some money. Have some time out from my kid who drives me nuts sometimes.

Already in this scenario, six different goals have been identified as possibilities, all of which would need some further exploration:

1. not doing anything
2. going back to school
3. seeking a job
4. seeking a job after a further educational experience
5. getting out of the house—either through employment or through other options like community involvement
6. time out from the children.

'Not changing' is a goal to explore equally with a client, when so much of the emphasis is on changing. It provides a safe place to explore why change really is so often necessary, and emphasizes that any change beyond staying the same brings new challenges and possibly new territory.

Some goal-setting will require negotiation and possibly compromise, where the goals with clients are not mutually agreeable. Some actions will be imposed on clients, as a result of court orders, and in these situations the goals that need to be met are not always mutually agreeable. Working through the SMART dimensions of goals, however, can go a long way towards finding mutually agreeable grounds for continuing the work together.

Chapter Summary

In this chapter, the assessment process has been explored, highlighting its usefulness in focusing the client's story on intervention and action. A multi-dimensional assessment framework was presented as a very broad way of understanding a client's situation and resources. The risks inherent in assessment have also been examined, particularly in relation to perpetuating fixed and assumptive assessments of people and their circumstances. The chapter briefly outlined some of the interventions human service workers use in relation to both outer-and inner-world change for clients. The chapter concluded with an exploration of the process of goal setting, often used in practice to set the agenda for action and intervention.

Questions for Analysis

1. What have you learned from this chapter about:
   • assessment processes?
   • interventions?
   • goal-setting?

2. What are the dimensions you find relatively straightforward to ask about in an assessment process and what do you find more difficult? Why?

3. What are the risks in an assessment process?

4. How often do you consciously use goal-setting processes to work through issues? What impact do you think this has on your practice?

Recommended Readings

Anglem, J., and J. Maidment. 2004. 'Introduction to assessment', in J. Maidment and R. Egan, eds, *Practice Skills in Social Work and Welfare: More Than Just Common Sense*. Crows Nest: Allen and Unwin, 112–26.

Bitter, J.R. 2009. *Theory and Practice of Family Therapy and Counselling*. Belmont, Calif.: Brooks/Cole.

Brownlee, K., J. Graham, and P. Dimond. 1997. 'Strategies for community assessment', in K. Brownlee, R. Delaney, and J. Graham, eds, *Strategies for Northern Social Work Practice*. Thunder Bay, Ont.: Lakehead University Centre for Northern Studies, 113–28.

Corey, G. 1996. *Theory and Practice of Counselling and Psychotherapy*. Pacific Grove, Calif.: Brooks/Cole.

Davis, S. 2006. *Community Mental Health in Canada*. Vancouver: University of British Columbia Press.

Egan, G., and W. Schroeder. 2009. *The Skilled Helper: A Problem-Management and Opportunity-Development Approach to Helping*, 1st Canadian edn. Toronto: Brooks/Cole, Nelson Education.

Hepworth, D., R. Rooney and J.A. Larsen. 2002. *Direct Social Work Practice: Theory and Skills*, 6th edn. Pacific Grove, Calif.: Brooks/Cole.

Mussel, B., K. Cardiff, and J. White. 2004. *The Mental Health and Wellbeing of Aboriginal Children and Youth. Guidance for New Approaches and Services.* Report prepared for the British Columbia Ministry for Children and Family Development.

Trotter, C. 2006. *Working with Involuntary Clients: A Guide to Practice.* Thousand Oaks, Calif.: Sage.

Internet Resources

American Psychiatric Association and the DSM IV
www.psych.org

Canada Drug Information
www.canadarehab.ca/drug_information_canada.html

Canadian Resource Centre for Victims of Crime
www.crcvc.ca/en/services.php

David Baldwin's Trauma Information Pages
www.trauma-pages.com

Health Canada Mental Health Depression
www.hc-sc.gc.ca/hl-vs/iyh-vsv/diseases-maladies/depression-eng.php

National Drug and Alcohol Research Centre (Australia)
www.ndarc.med.unsw.edu.au

National Native Alcohol and Drug Abuse Program
www.hc-sc.gc.ca/fniah-spnia/substan/ads/nnadap-pnlaada-eng.php

Published International Literature on Traumatic Stress database via the National Center for PTSD (USA)
www.ncptsd.va.gov/ncmain/index.jsp

World Health Organization: International Classification of Diseases (ICD)
www.who.int/classifications/icd/en

10   Assessing Risk Situations

Learning Goals

- Understand the dimensions of situations of conflict.
- Review your safety and appropriate responses when you are threatened by others.

Working with Conflict

In Chapter 4, we looked at the concept of your 'use of self'. The focus in that discussion was primarily on how you engage as a worker in empathic and supportive work. In many situations, this is the case. For many workers, the work is characterized by frequent or occasional incidents of physical and/or verbal abuse. You need to respond to these situations with some additional priorities, using some different communication skills.

To this point, the examples we have looked at have been interventions where a relatively positive engagement is possible, even if not in the initial stages of working together. Below, David describes one such practice experience where initial engagement seems to be progressing relatively smoothly.

Focus on Practice

David Works with Conflict

When I was working in a prison mental health unit, I was the case manager for a client with an acquired brain injury who spoke English as a second language. He was charged with a serious offence and was distressed about a discussion he had with his lawyer regarding whether he should plead guilty or not guilty at court. He asked to see me and I decided to see him in an open area rather than an enclosed office, as he appeared quite agitated. We talked through his concerns for some time and he gradually became less distressed.

1. How do you think David approached this conversation to help reduce his client's agitation?
2. What concerns would you have?
3. How would you feel about seeing this client?
4. What do you think you would do in this type of situation?

At this stage, David and his client have managed to engage together in conversation. The client seemed to be experiencing a highly agitated physical and emotional state, influenced not only by his stressful circumstances but likely through the communication difficulties and cognitive difficulties created by his brain injury. Some of the skills David may have used at this time include:

- Speaking slowly and calmly, avoiding getting caught up in the emotion of his client's agitation.
- Speaking clearly and in plain English so as not to compound his client's disempowerment through use of his second language.
- Emphasizing an alliance or joint problem-solving relationship, alleviating the isolation that the client may have been experiencing—for example, focusing on statements like: 'Let's see what we can sort out together.'
- Containing the emotion, through not mirroring the distress and agitation of the client but mirroring a calmer state that may reduce the client's agitation; and, in some instances, maintaining a distance so that the client does not feel enclosed or trapped, and maintaining steady eye contact to help engage him in a different mood state.
- Establishing an appropriate and structured agenda for the conversation. If someone is feeling overwhelmed by circumstances, remember the goal-setting tasks outlined in the previous chapter, where goals are SMART. In this instance, a very small goal may need to be set in discussion to establish a focus among the chaos.
- Using repetition: the 'broken record' technique encourages the use of one message until it finally is 'heard' by the other person. In David's situation, he may say something like: 'Let's just sit over here and talk.' And he would repeat that one statement calmly until that can happen. In some situations, this technique would be inflammatory, but in others it helps restore focus and agreement on the next step in the conversation.

It is important for practitioners to know the safety procedures of their workplace and of agencies they work with that require an 'on-site' presence on a regular basis, such as prisons. Here are some questions to consider:

1. What is your agency's policy for working with potentially aggressive or violent clients?
2. Does the agency have a safety committee?

3. When are the specific steps in place to address a potential incident?
4. Is there an alarm system, or how do you gain assistance?
5. Are the numbers for police posted?
6. Do you have experience working with potentially aggressive or violent clients?
7. If not, how do you know you are prepared should an incident arise?

All of these skills are examples of **smoothing skills**. They aim to reduce agitation and the escalation of emotions that can make communication difficult to sustain. David also took steps to ensure his physical safety and, potentially, that of his client. It is not always appropriate to move into private spaces if you have concerns for yourself and/or your client. Thus, his responses were active, assertive responses. Despite all of David's efforts, the situation escalated into a more violent one. We will return to this situation in the next section for further discussion.

> In Chapter 12, we explore containment skills more fully.

The situation to this point, however, highlights the differences between passive, aggressive, and assertive responses. Workers need well-developed assertion skills, particularly in response to aggressive encounters. The advantage is that assertion:

> unlike aggression, respects the other person's rights and dignity through the use of non-hostile verbal content and verbal attributes. Assertion is expected to produce strong relationships and relatively few negative emotions, whereas aggression is predicted to result in a strained, emotionally charged relationship. (Rakos, 2006: 348)

Rakos (ibid., 350–1) identifies four behavioural components of what he terms 'conflict assertion'. Related to the above situation, these components include:

- The content of the conversation—that is, what David says in response to his client's distress and agitation.
- Paralinguistic elements or how the communication sounds to the other person—that is, does David speak loudly, warmly, or gently?
- Non-verbal behaviours or how people appear to be physically reacting—does David bear in on his client's personal space or step back and allow him some space?
- Social interaction skills—Rakos (ibid., 351) identifies 'the timing, initiation, persistence and stimulus control/skills that enhance the impact of the verbal behaviour'; what does David choose to do by way of focus in the conversation, for example?

Assertive feedback is characterized therefore by: (1) 'I' statements—as the worker, you clearly own your feelings, beliefs, or thoughts. The other person can disagree with your view. (2) Behaviour-focused statements—you provide feedback or criticism of the behaviour, not the person. Behaviour can be changed. (3) Seeking a response back from the person—through asking, for example, 'What do you think?'

Other strategies can be used to deal with criticism and feedback that is directed towards you, as indicated in Table 10.1.

Table 10.1 Dealing with Criticism

If it is accurate	Accept it.
If it is clearly wrong	Disagree and affirm yourself.
If it is unclear	Clarify it.
If it is about you rather than your behaviour	Accept the behavioural part if it is true but reject the personal label.
If it is nagging, too frequent, or destructive; if you are stunned, overwhelmed, or confused by the criticism	Use fogging techniques; delay your response.

Source: Adapted from Kotzman (1995).

In managing conflict, it is important to consider what the best strategy may be. If the situation is too confronting or unexpected, it may need to be dropped and dealt with at a later time. Opportunities for direct conversation about a conflict normally should be offered; however, one way of de-escalating tension is to deprive people of opportunities for open, albeit difficult, communication. Clients have often experienced major disadvantage and oppression in prior circumstances, and the opportunity for them to be heard and for a solution to be worked towards is critical. Intense emotions can be compounded through a lack of resolution mechanisms. Mediation, in some instances, can facilitate a resolution.

Threatening Behaviour

As mentioned above, David's situation with his client escalated further. The scenario continues here.

Focus on Practice

David's Next Step in Work with a Client

David reflects on the next steps in his contact with his client: 'We talked through his concerns for some time and he gradually became less distressed. We started to discuss if it might be useful to arrange for the lawyer to visit again, when—as part of a stream of conversation—he focused on my use of the word 'guilty'. He became highly agitated, believing I was now accusing him of being 'guilty', and he started to become aggressive and threatening before storming off. The situation was becoming quite tense and I decided to remove myself from the area to avoid it escalating any further.'

This example reinforces how factors such as a disability and limited language skills can inhibit clear communication, and the importance of assessing potential risk from both verbal and non-verbal cues prior to and during work with distressed and agitated clients.

1. What is your immediate reaction to the situation David and his client were in?
2. What do you think you would do in a similar situation?
3. What cross-cultural issues could be influencing this situation?

David's example is one where finding common ground was not possible. David's safety, the client's safety, and the safety of others in the environment became the most immediate issues of concern. In reviewing the situation, some conclusions may be that:

- It was an unsafe situation to stay in and physical evacuation was needed. In some instances, police or guards may need to be called.
- The client's agitation was indicating something very important about what was going on for him—the disempowerment, frustration, and anger he was experiencing.
- He had a low frustration tolerance—in this case, as a result of the brain injury.

In this instance, the client returned later and smashed furniture in the reception area, and the police were called to manage the situation.

People considering social work as a profession should realize that human service workers often may face circumstances of **violence**, stalking, or threatening behaviours (Ogloff, 2006; Warren, 2006). Some key principles or skills for potentially threatening situations include:

- maintaining a high alertness for your own safety, both physical and emotional, and trusting any of your own intuitions about a lack of safety, even if not immediately manifest in a situation; the situation may rapidly become physically unsafe and you may need help or you may need to leave
- reporting and accountability requirements, including *always* alerting someone in your organization as to your whereabouts
- high levels of proactive planning; supervision as a preventive strategy for your safety and well-being.

Community Outreach

Practitioners who work in community settings may find themselves isolated and detached from a formal agency environment. In outreach practice it is important for the worker to take time to ensure their environment meets personal safety needs. The following example highlights the importance of safety.

Focus on Practice

Working Outside the Supervised Office

A worker travelled away from her agency for community outreach two days per week. Her outreach office was located in the basement of a designated professional building in a remote community. One day, a client came in very angry at someone else and became violent, threatening to hit someone in the reception area while pounding his fist on the counter. In that moment the worker realized she was in the basement and the only way out was blocked by the angry client. In addition, she was alone.

What are the important questions to ask yourself when you are working outside a supervised agency setting?

Risk and Confidentiality

In thinking about the worker's situations of risk, it is important to revisit the issue of confidentiality. Remembering Mark's situation and his expressed thoughts of suicide (Chapter 4) and considering David's client who was threatening violence and became violent, some additional considerations come into play in confidentiality. It may be necessary to breach the confidentiality standards we usual adhere to with low- or no-risk clients when the risk level escalates. Within the ethical guidelines of various human service professions, this 'duty to warn' is identified as follows:

- Social workers uphold the right of society to impose limitations on the self-determination of individuals, when such limitations protect individuals from self-harm and from harming others, and
- Social workers uphold the right of every person to be free from violence and threat of violence. (CASW, 2005: 5)

In becoming aware of a public safety risk, social workers, in this instance, 'will be excused from breaching confidentiality where they disclose information about the risk in order to protect the public.'

At times when you have concerns about a client's safety, or the safety of others because of what the client is saying, a careful consideration of whether to breach confidentiality is required. If possible, this breach should always occur with the support of a supervisor or manager, and, if it seems safe to do so, the client can be advised of your intended actions. For example, you might have a conversation with Mark about his suicidal thoughts and feelings and then discuss with him your concerns for his safety before contracting together on a safety plan. The safety plan may involve discussions with other significant people in his environment, or it may involve a hospital crisis assessment and treatment team if the danger of self-harm or suicide is high.

Some of the myths surrounding suicide include:

Myth 1: Suicide occurs without warning.
Myth 2: People who talk about suicide are not serious about killing themselves.
Myth 3: Bringing up the topic gives people the idea.
Myth 4: People who try suicide are just trying to get attention.
Myth 5: The best response to a threat is to say 'Go ahead.' (Shebib, 2000: 269)

If suicidal thinking is suspected, bringing up the topic of suicide has proven to relieve the client of the stress of hiding his or her intent. Practitioners should take specialized training to competently assess if a client is suicidal. A suicide assessment includes the following questions/considerations:

1. past attempts
2. physical and mental status
3. presence of a viable plan

4.   a means to kill one's self
5.   talk about suicide
6.   personal losses
7.   efforts to put affairs in order
8.   substance misuse.

In addition, practitioners need to assess the client's access to means of suicide, such as prescription medication or firearms (Shebib, 2000).

Further information about suicide risk assessment and managing physical or verbal violence is available, and some useful links are included at the end of this chapter.

Chapter Summary

In this chapter, we have looked at some of the main strategies for dealing with high-risk situations. These strategies are not prescriptions for success; rather, they provide some points of departure for thinking about what to do in certain situations; all have been found to be effective in situations in the past. The risk situations of suicidal behaviour, threatening behaviour, and conflict have been explored here only very briefly and you are encouraged to expand your reading, supervision, and awareness in practice in relation to these experiences. Risk cannot be eliminated in the work that we do—people in stressful situations often respond unpredictably, and that applies to ourselves as much as our clients. Good ongoing support and supervision are two ways of working preventively, but they are also critical buffers in the aftermath of high-risk encounters.

Questions for Analysis

1.   What have you learned about assessing risk situations?
2.   What are some of the personal and professional dilemmas that such risk situations raise for you?
3.   What are some of the essential skills required in dealing with risk situations?
4.   Reflect on situations of conflict or risk that you have been in and on the ways you responded. Do you respond well in crisis situations? If not, what will you do if you find yourself in a crisis with a client?
5.   What further training do you require to work with clients who present risk?

Recommended Reading

Brownlee, K., and J. Graham, eds. 2005. *Violence in the Family: Social Work Readings and Research from Northern and Rural Canada.* Toronto: Canadian Scholars' Press.

Cutcliffe, J. 2005. 'Toward an understanding of suicide in First Nation Canadians', *Journal of Crisis Intervention and Suicide Prevention* 26, 3: 141–5.

Laming, C. 2006. *A Constructivist Approach to Challenging Men's Violence against Women*. Melbourne: University of Melbourne Press.

Morley, C. 2004. 'Conducting risk assessments', in J. Maidment and R. Egan, eds, *Practice Skills in Social Work and Welfare: More Than Just Common Sense*. Crows Nest: Allen and Unwin, 127–45.

Ogloff, J. 2006. 'Advances in violence risk assessment', *InPsych* 28, 5: 12–16.

Shebib, B. 2000. *Choices: Practical Interviewing and Counselling Skills*. Needham Heights, Mass.: Allyn and Bacon.

Tranter, D., and J. Vis. 1997. 'Flexibility, sensitivity and timing: A comprehensive trauma debriefing model for the north', in K. Brownlee, R. Delaney, and J. Graham, eds, *Strategies for Northern Social Work Practice*. Thunder Bay: Lakehead University Centre for Northern Studies, 187–216.

Trotter, C. 2006. *Working with Involuntary Clients: A Guide to Practice*. Thousand Oaks, Calif.: Sage.

Internet Resources

Australian Government—Mental Health and Wellbeing publications
www.health.gov.au/internet/wcms/publishing.nsf/content/mental-pubs

Beyondblue National Depression Initiative
www.beyondblue.org.au

Canadian Association for Suicide Prevention
www.casp-acps.ca

Domestic and Family Violence Resources
www.vaonline.org/dv.html

Domestic Violence and Incest Resource Centre
www.dvirc.org.au

Part Four | Applying the Skills: Focusing the Intervention

In this next part of the book, we explore briefly some of the specific tasks and skills of human service practice. This book is not primarily about theoretical approaches to working with people; however, we will examine some of the specific skills emerging from the eight theoretical approaches that were introduced in Chapter 3.

In Chapter 9, human service interventions that target change within the inner and/or outer worlds of people are identified. Change strategies that focus on people's inner worlds—strategies of counselling, psycho-education, social support, and group work—can help clients develop new ways of coping with behavioural or belief restrictions that they impose on themselves or that others impose on them. Change strategies that focus on people's outer worlds—strategies of resource provision, referral, liaison, advocacy, capacity-building, group work, and community development—can help clients manage and change the structural restrictions in their worlds, and may involve very active worker intervention to bring about changes with the client.

Each theoretical approach has a long tradition informing its current understandings and uses of skills. It is beyond the scope of this book to explore the rich tradition and the developmental processes that inform that tradition, but resources are provided at the end of each chapter for you to follow up with your own reading on these topics. The aim here is to provide you with an introduction to some of the skills used in practice.

The emphasis throughout these next four chapters is on how these skills can be applied in different settings. Some workers adopt a 'purist' theoretical approach; that is, the worker self-identifies as a psychodynamic worker or as a feminist worker. Most workers, however, incorporate a range of skills into their practice—drawn from a range of theoretical perspectives—using an eclectic theoretical base. That is why skills are presented in relation to their particular theoretical paradigms rather than under the design of a single, overall approach. The aim of these four chapters is to illustrate how to choose among these skills those that will positively impact the work you do.

Part One—Framing the Relationship

- the purpose of human service work
- your value base, professional ethics, and regulatory guidelines in Canada
- your theoretical and factual knowledge.

Part Two—Forming the Relationship

- your use of self
- your organizational context
- your ongoing support and professional development needs
- meeting the people involved
- opening the communication
- active listening and working with silence
- listening empathically
- using self-disclosure.

Part Three—Focusing the Communication

- establishing the story
- forming an assessment
- goal-setting.

Part Four—Focusing the Intervention

- drawing on theoretical perspectives
- doing the work.

11 | Task-Centred and Crisis-Intervention Skills

Learning Goals

- Identify the core skills of task-centred and crisis-intervention approaches, particularly in relation to the establishment of the relationship between a worker and client and specific interventions.
- Understand the strengths and limitations of these approaches.

Core Skills of Task-Centred Practice

The Ahmed family arrived at your agency seeking assistance with their multiple stressors. Depending on what agency the Ahmed family chooses, the focus of the work will differ. Some agencies are focused on outer-world or practical tasks associated with living in a new country, whereas others are focused on inner-world tasks of adapting to life in a new culture.

Focus on Practice

Immediate Needs

Two years ago the Ahmed family came to Canada from Somalia. They have five children—three attending school, a three-year-old, and a one-year-old infant. They are living in shared housing with another family, all of whom have been granted refugee status. They have been able to connect with the local school. They miss many aspects of life back home, specifically their rural village, traditional foods, and less extreme changes in seasons. They have been able to build connections with some other members of the Somali community. They feel emotionally torn about their migration. They have left behind family and many friends. They are learning English but find it very difficult to fit into Canadian culture. Being unemployed, they are also finding it difficult to afford the expenses of daily life.

Mrs Ahmed has found their situation much easier than her husband. She enjoys being in the shared house situation and sharing the cooking and domestic duties with the other family. Mr Ahmed is frustrated by his difficulties finding work. He sees himself as solely responsible for earning the family's income, and feels deep shame that he has not been able to do this so far. He has become very withdrawn and depressed.

Source: Adapted from Harms (2005: 68–9).

Establishing and Sustaining the Relationship

From a task-centred perspective, your engagement with your client is established through the focus on task- and goal-setting. Given the multiple concerns for this family, this may need to occur in a culturally empathetic space for exploring the needs and goals, with adequate time and space for a full exploration of their circumstances (Marsh and Doel, 2005: 115). In order to engage in problem-solving, which is the main goal of task-centred practice, a worker typically engages using emotional warmth, optimism about finding solutions, and, in some situations, considerable **assertiveness**. Engagement is with the details of the person's circumstances and the possibilities for solution.

A major criticism of task-centred approaches is that they fail to acknowledge the importance of rapport in the client–worker relationship. This imbalance is considered to be a misrepresentation of the centrality of relationship to positive change, as Marsh and Doel argue (2005: 119), with the relationship emerging:

> from the doing, rather than the doing arising from the relationship. We believe this mirrors what happens in our everyday lives, just as a complete stranger can feel like a lifelong friend if you happen to find yourselves mutually dependent in a short, intense crisis.

Nevertheless, the task-centred relationship is seen primarily as an active and 'doing' relationship, in contrast to some of the other approaches described in the next few chapters. Thus, the knowledge of potential resources you bring to this interaction is just as important as your interpersonal engagement skills.

Specific Interventions

Task-centred practice has evolved from a more pragmatic approach to human service delivery. It is a time-limited, contracted, and highly structured approach, and therein rests both its strengths and limitations. Interventions focus on 'doing'—on activities, either within the context of the contact itself or outside, as 'homework' (ibid., 38).

The skills of task-centred practice relate to the Task Planning and Implementation Sequence (TPIS), first outlined by Reid and Epstein (ibid., 78; Tolson, Reid, and Garvin, 2003). As seen below, once the client's circumstances have been explored, six steps are followed, drawing on the exploration and goal-setting skills we have looked at in previous chapters. Using the example of the Ahmed family, task-centred practice proceeds as follows.

Focus on Practice

The Six Steps of Task-Centred Practice

1. Task Selection

Drawing on the probing, paraphrasing, and summarizing skills discussed in Chapters 7 and 8, you work with the Ahmeds to identify a key task to work on—you ask the question: 'What do you think you might be able to do about this issue?' This question then begins a brain-storming exercise to find possible solutions. In this instance, it could be to connect Mrs Ahmed with a local food bank and to address Mr. Ahmed's isolation and lack of income possibilities, linking him with more prosperous members of the community who are willing to help other newcomers to get started.

2. Task Agreement

Talking with the Ahmeds about a number of possible goals, you then discuss each goal to arrive at one task that you all think will be the most achievable.

3. Planning Specifics of Implementation

An implementation plan is then discussed—'how, who, where, when, and why' are often important questions to explore during this phase.

4. Establishing Incentives and Rationale

In this phase of exploration, you look together at why the change should occur—what are the motivations, and why is it necessary?

5. Anticipating Obstacles

In this exploration, you turn the focus around from that above, to look at all the potential barriers to the successful achievement of the goal. Both inner-world and outer-world barriers are important to explore. This is about exploring the 'what if' questions (Marsh and Doel, 2005: 78).

6. Simulated and Guided Practice

Exploring a process thoroughly is important—the technique of role-playing prepare us to put into practice new skills and helps us to experience some of the potential new emotions we may experience in a situation. We can learn how we might react to a number of different dimensions in an experience.

7. Task Review

A further seventh step might happen in another session: task review. Review and evaluation are critical in a task-centred approach. What worked and what didn't work? Why? It enables a review of goals and whether or not they were SMART goals.

Healy (2005: 113–15) outlines eight practice principles related to this structured approach, which translate further into the skills you could use. Each of these is applied to understanding the Ahmeds' situation.

1. *Seek mutual clarity with service users.* Explore the story extensively, and come to understand the story fully from the Ahmeds' perspective and your own, using the skills we have looked at in Chapters 7 and 8. Shared concerns would be raised and a particular emphasis on cultural empathy would be required. A cultural consultant may be a very useful ally for the Ahmeds and also for you in this situation, so that solutions are culturally sensitive and appropriate.

2. *Aim for small achievements rather than large changes.* With the Ahmeds, so many needs are being expressed by them as requiring change that it could feel overwhelming both to them and to you as a worker. Achieving small steps helps to build a sense of efficacy and accomplishment (Bandura et al., 2003), thereby building the confidence and capacity to continue to make changes.

3. *Focus on the 'here and now'.* A major difference from other approaches is that the problem is seen to be in the present, not in the past, or even the future, as other approaches might locate issues. Change is brought about in the present to enhance current coping and functioning, and to build coping capacity for the future. In this sense, a way of coping is being taught or developed further with the client.

4. *Promote collaboration between the worker and service users.* You can establish a sense of collaboration with your client through sharing the solution-focused process; using collaborative language such as 'we' or 'when we have done that'. The solution becomes shared so that a sense of isolation can be somewhat reduced for people in overwhelming situations. The collaboration, however, must be authentic and viable, rather than becoming a series of false promises.

5. *Build client capacities for action.* As Healy (2005: 114) notes, '[w]hile acknowledging that the problems may have their origins in other "causes" such as "deeper" psychological problems or unjust structural conditions' these are not the focus of task-centred interventions. The focus is on dealing with an identified problem and targeting immediate practical or psychological resources to solve them. Capacities for action emerge from the provision and receipt of resources (Hobfoll, Ennis, and Kay, 2000).

6. *Plan on brevity.* Task-centred approaches are short-term and time-limited approaches, not extending beyond 15 sessions. You may even focus on task-centred work within the context of a single session with a client. The Ahmed family would be advised of this in your initial contact, and a close scrutiny of these time limits would be maintained, once the goals for the work have been set. This approach is consistent with a strengths perspective, which sees people as capable of influencing their own lives and functioning adequately when adequate resources are in place.

7. & 8. *Promote systematic and structured approaches to intervention, and adopt a scientific approach to practice evaluation.* These last two principles highlight that the model outlined above gives you and your clients a very clear map of how you

will work together and what you will aim to achieve. In this sense, the Ahmeds are empowered in the process as they are informed of the process. Healy (2005) identifies the mutual clarity and the 'external accountability' of applying a standardized practice model as two of the approach's major strengths. In contrast to the less structured and arguably less measurable interventions outlined in the following chapters, this approach is seen to use and provide ongoing evidence for practice.

In summary, the skills relied on extensively in task-centred practice are:

- exploring, probing, and clarifying skills
- contracting and problem-solving skills
- task-focused, strengths- and solution-focused, goal-setting skills teaching, advising, and directing around resource use
- resourcing and referral skills.

> We explore the process of making a referral in Chapter 15.

Core Skills of Crisis-Intervention Practice

Recall the Willis family, presented in Chapter 9, who are experiencing difficulties of a different nature after Mr Willis suffered a fall and had to be hospitalized, where the staff recognized and diagnosed his dementia and suggested a radical change in living arrangements. As Mrs Willis is facing an immediate **crisis**, task-centred skills could be successfully used, but crisis-intervention skills may be more appropriate.

Crisis-intervention skills are based more on an understanding of the mood and cognitive state of the person at the time of the intervention; that is, the immediate context or state of the person determines the way of thinking and intervening at that time. As a result of this focus, your intervention is about enhancing the immediate functioning of people affected by the crisis, both practically and emotionally.

A crisis is typically defined as:

> an upset in a steady state (state of equilibrium) that poses an obstacle, usually important to the fulfillment of important life goals or to vital need satisfaction, and that the individual or family cannot overcome through usual methods of problem-solving. (Hepworth, Rooney, and Larsen, 2002: 382)

A crisis state is a temporary state 'during which a person has the potential for heightened maturity and growth or for deterioration and greater vulnerability to future stress' (Poindexter, 1997: 125). This understanding is vital, as Caplan (1990) and others have argued that crisis presents an opportunity for the development of new coping skills, as well as the threat of loss.

Davis (2006: 141) notes, 'a more common method of psychiatric crisis response in Canada is the mobile crisis team, which generally is a seven-day-a-week service with some after hours capacity that provides brief crisis intervention through telephone contact or home visits.' Davis describes the team as including trained nurses and clinicians who have access to an on-call doctor.

Examples of mobile crisis teams include: Vancouver's Mental Health Emergency Services, which offers a crisis line that clients and other citizens may access and which can provide home visits with a nurse, sometimes with a plainclothes police officer as back-up; the police officer provides more security for evening calls in higher-crime areas and can also invoke a provision of the Mental Health Act whereby persons can be taken to hospital for an assessment.

Gilliland and James (1997) offer a basic crisis intervention model, as outlined in Table 11.1, that focuses on 'ongoing [assessment] throughout the crisis' in terms of such factors as the client's coping ability and threat factors, so that the crisis worker can judge the 'type of action needed' throughout the course of the crisis.

Table 11.1 Basic Crisis Intervention Model

Listening: attending, observing, understanding, and responding with empathy, genuineness, respect, and caring	Acting: becoming involved in the intervention at a non-directive, collaborative, or directive level, according to the assessed needs of the client and the availability of environmental supports
1. Define the problem: Explore and define the problem from the client's point of view Use active listening, including open-ended questions. Attend to both verbal and non-verbal messages of the client.	4. Examine alternatives: Assist client in exploring the choices he or she has available to him or her now. Facilitate a search for immediate situational supports, copying mechanisms, and positive thinking.
2. Ensure client safety: Assess lethality, criticality, immobility, or seriousness of threat to the client's physical and psychological safety. Assess both the client's internal events and the situation surrounding the client, and, if necessary, ensure that the client is made aware of alternatives to impulsive, self-destructive actions.	5. Make plans: Assist client in developing a realistic short-term plan that identifies additional resources and provides coping mechanisms—definite action steps that the clients can own and comprehend.
3. Provide support: Communicate to the client that the crisis worker is a valid support person. Demonstrate (by words, voice, and body language) a caring, positive, non-possessive, non-judgemental, acceptant, personal involvement with the client.	6. Obtain commitment: Help client commit himself or herself to definite positive action steps that the client can own and realistically accomplish or accept.

Source: Adapted from Gilliland and James (1997: 29).

Establishing and Sustaining the Relationship

Like task-centred approaches, crisis-intervention approaches do not typically focus on understanding the nature of the relationship between the worker and the client to the extent that other approaches do. It is fundamental to the success of the work, however, and therefore is still regarded as being the 'glue'.

Intense and strong bonds often form during crisis, from a sense of the shared experience, and from (as others argue) the psychological regression and dependence that can occur in the midst of a crisis. The regression and dependence, however, are viewed as temporary, resolving typically within weeks of a particular crisis.

Early in the crisis period, particularly in disaster situations, the worker fosters a highly directive and assertive role, expressing warmth and a highly empathic engagement. Over time, as individuals resume their pre-crisis levels of functioning, the worker is no longer as directive or assertive.

Focus on Practice

Confronting a Crisis

You have been assigned to work with the Stewart family. Mr and Mrs Stewart, who both hold professional positions, have one child Melissa (age 16). Melissa, who had been struggling with addiction issues, recently disclosed to her parents that she is confused about her sexual orientation and has been seeking counselling supports. This resulted in Mr and Mrs Stewart throwing Melissa out of the house. That evening, distressed by her parent's reaction, Melissa went drinking with a friend and ended up being critically injured in a car accident. Both Mr and Mrs Stewart feel responsible but refuse to see Melissa.

1. How might you address the immediate crisis state of Mr and Mrs Stewart?
2. How would you address the immediate crisis state of Melissa?
3. How would you establish a working relationship?
4. What might you identify as immediate concerns in assessing this situation?

Specific Interventions

Crisis-intervention skills support people, helping them to cope in the immediate aftermath of traumatic or stressful situations. Based on understandings of how people cope in crises, they focus on an immediate restoration of cognitive and emotional control, as well as on resuming normal functioning as quickly as possible, through the re-engagement with daily tasks and defusing of mood and emotion. Some of the key skills required by the worker include the following.

1. *A rapid assessment of functioning.* As a worker, you need to assess very quickly how well someone is functioning. This is important because, often, in the midst of a crisis serious decisions need to be made. If someone is unable to make decisions clearly, then different strategies may be required. Many formal tools are available for this assessment. For example, the Triage Assessment Form: Crisis

Intervention (Myer et al., as described in Myer and Conte, 2006: 968–70) has been developed, which establishes a person's functioning in relation to three domains: the affective or emotional domain, the behavioural domain, and the cognitive domain, assessing each of them on a rating scale from 1–10. This test helps to distinguish levels of functioning, and changes over time.

2. *Reassurance of safety.* While Mrs Willis is in a safe situation, in another circumstance—such as that of Melissa—you may be working with people who have been confronted with life-threatening situations, such as sexual assault, road accident, or violent incident. In trauma situations, reassurance of basic physical safety is most critical and the highest priority (Herman, 1992).

3. *Maintaining a needs and rights focus.* Despite the above comments about coping capacity, decisions are often made *for* people during a time of crisis when they knew nothing of what is being decided for them. Other people affected by crisis can remain empowered to make decisions for themselves and others. The overlooking of this range of possible responses during crisis has been a major criticism of many debriefing efforts, where people have not been allowed to act in ways they wanted to and actually might have (Crumpton-Cook, 1996). Crisis intervention skills focus on empowering the affected person to make necessary decisions in a supported environment.

4. *Validation of feelings.* As distinct from the task-centred approach, crisis intervention focuses on the intense emotional state someone may be experiencing. Mrs Willis may be experiencing a wide range of emotions. . Similarly, Mr and Mrs Stewart are experiencing a mixture of intense emotions stemming not only from their daughter's disclosures but from their multi-level feelings of responsibility for the accident. Melissa's emotions, if she is conscious and not too heavily sedated, may range from confusion to anger to pain in her feelings of abandonment over her parents' reaction. A crisis intervention encourages the **ventilation** or expression of all these emotions, if that is consonant with her physical condition. In this sense, it is connected with psychodynamic approaches; with the cathartic release of all emotions in all their complexity the first step in being able to consciously control them. Thus, listening and supporting—through probing, reflecting, and paraphrasing—is important. The listening is characterized by validating all emotions. While a cognitive behavioural approach may then move on to challenge some of these feelings, assessing them as irrational or rational thoughts or emotions, crisis-intervention approaches see this non-judgemental listening as the first step in dealing with the disequilibrium in emotions and thinking that crises create.

    The term **containment** frequently is used in relation to the ventilation of feelings and the skill of the worker in supporting the client so that the emotions are experienced without overwhelming the person. The term originates from psychodynamic understandings, so the skills of containment will be discussed in Chapter 12.

5. *Information and resource provision.* Mrs Willis has been confronted with a lot of new information. Not only will she need to support her husband in his recovery

from his fractures, but she also admits she knows nothing about dementia or of the processes involved in moving her husband to new accommodation. She has been confronted with a range of new emotions and is finding it hard to cope with their disorientating impact. Overwhelming feelings can be observed in the Stewart family, although not to the extent that they are willing to see their daughter.

Crisis-intervention strategies are 'immediate, active and directive interventions such as education, clarification, and reassurance about the normative, expectable reactions to trauma' (Gelman and Mirabito, 2005: 481) or crisis. Your knowledge of crisis and trauma, and the expectable immediate and longer-term reactions, is drawn on at this time. It may involve your making a normalizing statement like the following (apply this statement to both the Willis and Stewart family examples):

> You said you're feeling really strange, as if it's all happening around you, but you're not part of this. You may find that over the next few days, these feelings come and go, and then pass. This is a normal reaction to the distressing information you've been given.

With these skills, you are providing a psycho-educational base for your clients to understand themselves in their world. This approach is different from a more supportive or reactive approach that might be used in other situations. Here, you are actively drawing on your knowledge base to provide resources for your client to draw on.

6. *Direct influence.* In addition to the more active stance outlined in the previous section, in some instances you may use directive or influencing skills (Walsh, 2006: 282). The person may not be able to make decisions because of the overwhelming nature of the circumstances. For example, after the conversation with the doctors about Mr Willis's newly diagnosed dementia, Mrs Willis may not be able think clearly about whether she should go home, contact their children, or stay with him. In this instance, a worker might be quite directive about suggesting a plan if no priority seems to be emerging:

> How about we go and make the phone call to your children and see what they would like to do. If they decide to come in, you can wait here with your husband and meet them. If they can't come in now, we can think about how you will get home and what you might do tomorrow.

This set of suggestions sets some limits around what Mrs Willis needs to think about in the midst of her crisis. They do not take away any of her rights or disempower her, because the suggestions clearly are driven by what she wants to do. However, the suggestions contain (limit) her options to make it easier for her to come to a decision when her emotional state is high and clouding her ability to think clearly.

Maslow's hierarchy of needs was presented in Chapter 4.

In other situations, you might make some suggestions about what she could do if she is unable to make a decision. Remembering Maslow's hierarchy of needs is important in this kind of work—people in crisis often need the basics attended to, in regard to shelter, food, clothing, and communication. For example, Mrs Willis may forget that she hasn't eaten since dinner last night, and need support in ensuring these basic needs can be met.

As you can learn from the above example, the skills you employ sometimes are assertive and directive skills, in recognition of the fact that, in the disruption of life crises, people's usual coping capacities similarly are disrupted. A crisis-intervention approach acknowledges that crises are both threats and opportunities, in that new coping strategies can be introduced when usual coping strategies do not work, and thus growth and development may occur even in severely stressed circumstances (Caplan, 1990; Poindexter, 1997).

In the previous chapter we examined strategies for dealing with risks the worker encounters in the course of her or his work. Another type of risk—or crisis—is that of physical harm to the client. The Department of Justice has several tools for assessing risk specific to violent relationships and, while geared towards correctional workers, the questions are applicable to social work practice when assessing risk. One of these tools is the Aid to Safety Assessment Planning (ASAP), which is currently being used in New Brunswick and British Columbia collaboratively between Victims Services and criminal justice personnel. The ASAP (www.justice.gc.ca/eng/pi/rs/rep-rap/2009/rr09_7/p3.html) focuses on identifying risk from the victim's perspective and assists the worker in the following five-step protocol:

1. Gather the information.
2. Identify the presence and relevance of abuser and safety support factors.
3. Develop risk scenarios.
4. Work with the person (usually a woman) on her safety plan.
5. Note priority actions.

Strengths and Limitations of Skills

The skills outlined in this chapter have emerged relatively recently in human services work practice in recognition of people's immediate reactions to circumstances of trauma and crisis. In using these skills, you are aiming to provide resources to people to help them cope with immediate problems, and to find active solutions to them. These skills are less pathologizing of people's coping capacities. They encourage people to develop or regain a sense of control and empowerment as quickly as possible. The client's engagement with a supportive and encouraging worker can be a vital step, providing an ally and a resource through times of particular difficulty.

The skills within a task-centred approach are primarily task-focused, whereas crisis-intervention skills are both task- and emotion-focused strategies. Many critics fault task-centred approaches in relation to what is regarded as their conformity with a neo-liberal political agenda. As Webb (2006: 123) states:

The danger with adhering to this kind of perspective is that it can result in crude unreflective instrumentalism, in the bid to water things down to tasks, to dilute difficulty, to make things so simple that they no longer carry any depth of meaning or value for service users.

Furthermore, task-centred and crisis-intervention approaches both come under criticism for the potentially disempowered location of the client in relation to the worker. Another concern is that of the pragmatic, evidence-based nature of both approaches and their tendency towards a linear approach to problem-solving (Healy, 2005), which may be inconsistent with the world views of people who carry more cyclical notions of time and change: for example, Indigenous cultures.

Baskin (2005: 172) suggests, 'Aboriginal Peoples cannot look outside their cultures for their self-image. Aboriginal traditional values, especially in the area of relationships, carry the instructions for healing.' Baskin outlines the following steps from the Vancouver Native Education Centre for creating healthy relationships and communities:

- focusing on self-esteem and self-worth as Aboriginal peoples
- offering support
- using symbols that engage the senses and the gifts of the earth to heal, rather than only words
- teaching respect for the self, family, community, and the earth
- taking the focus away from an individualistic approach to the situation
- balancing the four aspects (psychological, physical, emotional, and spiritual) of the person, so she/he can use all of her/his resources
- promoting ways of achieving harmony and integration within.

Another consideration noted by Baskin (ibid., 174) is the circle. 'The circle implemented both culture-based and some Western healing practices (as long as these were compatible with the values of Aboriginal cultures).' Baskin describes the purpose of the circle as a safe, supportive, and confidential group forum for discussion and learning.

In some instances, task-centred and crisis-intervention skills clearly are inappropriate. More insight-oriented problems require more insight-oriented skills and understandings. These are considered in later chapters.

Chapter Summary

In this chapter, some of the key skills that are used in task-centred and crisis-intervention approaches have been introduced. The goal-setting and problem-solving skills of a task-centred approach were applied to the complex circumstances of the Ahmed family, to demonstrate how finding solutions is the focus of the work together. The emotion-and task-focused skills used with Mrs Willis and the Stewart family, illustrated the short-term, multi-dimensional emphasis of a crisis-intervention approach. These skills are primarily used in situations where communication is under time constraints. They focus on optimizing people's strengths and capacities in the face of the more extreme difficult circumstances of life.

Questions for Analysis

1. Which of the task-centred and crisis-intervention skills appeal to you? Why?

2. When would you find these skills helpful?

3. What are some of the strengths and limitations of these skills?

4. What skills would you like to develop further?

5. What cultural issues would you need to consider?

Recommended Readings

Brown, F., and J. Rainer. 2006. 'Too much to bear: An introduction to crisis intervention and therapy', *Journal of Clinical Psychology* 62, 8: 953–7.

Brownlee, K., and J.R. Graham. 2005. *Violence in the Family: Social Work Readings and Research from Northern and Rural Canada*. Toronto: Canadian Scholars' Press.

Davis, S. 2006. *Community Mental Health in Canada.* Vancouver: University of British Columbia Press.

Flannery, R., and G. Everly. 2000. 'Crisis intervention: A review', *International Journal of Emergency Mental Health* 2, 2: 119–25.

Gilliland, B.E., and R.K. James. 1997. *Crisis Intervention Strategies*. Pacific Grove, Calif.: Brooks/Cole.

Marsh, P., and M. Doel. 2005. *The Task-Centred Book*. London: Routledge.

Myer, R., and C. Conte. 2006. 'Assessment for crisis intervention', *Journal of Clinical Psychology* 62, 8: 959–70.

Tolson, E., W. Reid, and C. Garvin. 2003. *Generalist Practice: A Task-centered Approach*. New York: Columbia University Press.

Internet Resources

Australian Critical Incident Stress Association
www.acisa.org.au

Canadian Association for Suicide Prevention
www.casp-acps.ca/home.asp

Critical Incident Stress Management
www.vaonline.org/cism.html

National Center for Crisis Management (US)
www.nc-cm.org

The Task-Centered WebPages
www.task-centered.com

12 Psychodynamic and Cognitive Behavioural Skills

Learning Goals

- Identify the core skills of psychodynamic and cognitive behavioural approaches, particularly in regard to establishing the relationship between a worker and client and specific interventions.
- Understand the strengths and limitations of these skills.

Core Skills of Psychodynamic Practice

Payne (2005: 73) describes psychodynamic theory as 'based on the work of Freud and his followers, and developments of their work. They are called "psychodynamic" because the theory underlying them assumes that behaviour comes from movements and interactions in people's minds.' Payne outlines the main points of psychodynamic theory as follows.

1. Psychodynamic perspectives are an important historical source for basic social work skills.
2. Their long history means that application to different forms of practice is fully developed.
3. Recent developments in attachment theory are relevant to child care and protection and loss and bereavement.
4. Recent developments in ego psychology have influenced therapeutic work with adults, particularly in the US.
5. Psychodynamic ideas are a rich source of complex ideas for interpreting behaviour.
6. Wide understanding and study of psychodynamic theory make for good connections with other professionals and across national boundaries.
7. Lack of a strong evidence base and the use of models of integral thinking have led to criticism.
8. The historical, Eurocentric, and Jewish cultural origins of psychodynamic theory lead to victim-blaming and stereotypical assumptions about women and homosexual behaviour.

Some of the main concepts in practice are anxiety and ambivalence, coping, defences and resistance, transference and counter-transference, and relationships, which will be discussed in more detail in the chapter. To illustrate some of the key skills within a psychodynamic approach, Karen describes her work with Julia, a 40-year-old woman:

Focus on Practice

Letting the Client Take Control

Julia requested counselling because her friends had told her she was depressed. During the first and many subsequent interviews Julia revealed a complex and detailed examination of her life events through the perspective of all her family members, friends, and work colleagues. It was impossible to gain from Julia any view that she expressed alone; she apparently was incapable of identifying—or perhaps even of developing—an opinion on a subject apart from the input from others.

It became clear that her unconscious expectation of counselling was to gain further insights from yet another person into her situation. The challenge for the worker was to not be drawn into this pattern, but, rather, to reflect it back and assist her to examine the position in which she habitually places herself in relation to others. The concepts of transference and counter-transference were helpful in this instance.

A further pattern that appeared during counselling was for the client to regularly appear in a chaotic state, with a range of apparent crises to report from the previous week. Counselling sessions involved deconstructing and reframing these experiences to assist Julia to view them in a more positive light, and to restore a sense of efficacy in her own capacity to act and interpret her own experiences. Due to her long-standing habit of having others (particularly her mother) define the events in her life negatively, she found it quite challenging to break this habit and be prepared to have a hope for change.

This experience of **repetition** was challenging for me as the counsellor, but Julia began to learn how she could take control of her understanding of events.

1. What is your initial reaction to hearing about Julia and Karen's work?
2. What would you focus on in work with Julia? Why?

Notice the emphasis in this scenario is on:

- lifelong patterns of behaving and relating
- family and significant others and their impact on the client's sense of self
- conscious and unconscious motivations and drives
- parallel processes occurring in the client–worker relationship
- transference and counter-transference experiences
- working over time to address patterns of behaving, thinking, and feeling that keep repeating themselves
- developing insight and, ultimately, changes to an experience of the self as chaotic.

Each of these conceptual areas will be addressed throughout this discussion of psychodynamic skills.

Establishing and Sustaining the Relationship

The client–worker relationship is central to any work with a strong psychodynamic orientation. The focus is on the relationship dynamics (Walsh, 2006: 30). A client can resolve problematic issues from the past through experiencing a positive relationship in the therapeutic relationship or 'working alliance' in the 'here and now'. The relationship provides a 'corrective emotional experience' (McCluskey, 2002); internal working models of relationships that a client may have developed through poor earlier relationships can be influenced for the better.

The relationship becomes the vehicle for change, as issues of unconscious motivations and desires, conflicts, and anxieties repeat themselves in the client–worker relationship. The intention is that the client projects these conscious and unconscious experiences and expectations onto the therapist, hence forming a **transference**—a transfer of earlier and current significant relationships—onto the current therapeutic one. As a result: 'the client perceives the helping professional in a distorted way and brings his or her past relationships into the present relationship with the counsellor' (Corey and Corey, 2007: 67).

By developing insight over time into the transference, change can occur as these needs and desires come under more conscious control. Transference is theorized to be a part of every relationship in which people engage. In the therapeutic context, however, it is analyzed for what it tells us about ourselves and our ways of relating to ourselves, significant others, and the world around us.

Counter-transference is the parallel process that occurs for the worker, as Corey and Corey note: 'Broadly speaking, helpers may have unconscious emotional responses to a client that result in a distorted perception of a client's behaviour' (ibid.). Corey and Corey explain that counter-transference can block the neutrality of the worker. The therapeutic relationship is based on the assumption that the worker is in an objective, neutral position as a sounding board for the client. However, this assumption in psychodynamic practice increasingly is being challenged. In Julia and Karen's situation, focusing on the counter-transference would involve Karen's continually reflecting on how she feels, and what in the client's story she is reacting to. Supervision is an essential condition for such issues to be discussed and addressed.

> Remember that connections with a sense of the collective unconscious and other ways of knowing were described in Chapter 2.

The therapeutic relationship dynamic was symbolized by Jung as a series of links, an image that today we might replace with the metaphor of a complex web of relationships, as shown in Figure 12.1.

The aim of engagement throughout your work with your client is to foster a positive transference relationship so that trust and insight can be achieved. Unlike other client–worker relationships, contracting around the work is not expected to occur from the outset within a psychodynamic approach (Howard, 2006). Instead, the emphasis is on experiencing the relationship first and on analyzing what emerges in that interaction. The relationship itself is as much a focus of the work as other issues raised in the conversation.

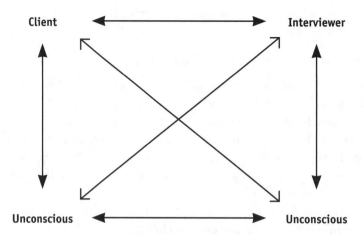

Figure 12.1 Conscious and Unconscious Levels of Communication within Relationships

Source: Jacoby (1984: 25).

The early psychodynamic view of the worker was as a 'blank screen': an objective and neutral listener onto whom the client would 'project' her or his earlier relationships that had influenced the individual's **psychosexual development**. Eventually, the impossibility of maintaining such an unnatural relationship became evident. The term 'intersubjectivity' is now used to denote the complex, reciprocal relationship between the worker and client (Gibney, 2003). Nevertheless, close boundaries are prescribed around work and the relationship, unlike some of the Indigenous practice approaches.

Psychodynamic processes are thought about in many different and, sometimes, contradictory ways. This complexity has a major impact on the types of skills that you might use. Two major schools of thought are the object relations and ego psychology approaches. The object relations approach proposes that we relate to people in the present on the basis of expectations formed by early experiences within significant relationships. During infancy, we develop internal working models of relationships based on our relationships with those around us, and it becomes necessary in adult life to explore and repair faulty unconscious object relationships internalized since infancy. How the external world is taken in and how the resultant internalizations influence psychic structure and later personality functioning are the focus of this approach (Goldstein, 1995).

Many psychodynamic theories also maintain theories of attachment at their core; that is, the infant's primary need for attachment to a caring person (Bowlby, 1984), seen to realize itself in the good object (Klein, 1962) or the holding environment (Winnicott, 1987), respectively. A mature ego develops into one that can accommodate to ambivalence and complexity in life rather than to the dichotomized concepts of 'good' and 'bad'.

Ego psychology argues that we learn a coping repertoire across the lifespan that has various strengths and deficits, and later difficulties are associated with this lifelong coping repertoire. The focus of intervention is on building **ego strengths**, where the ego is seen as 'a mental structure of the personality that is responsible for negotiating between the internal needs of the individual and the outside world' (Goldstein, 1995: xi; Walsh, 2006: 32).

Specific Interventions

In light of the above, assessment typically involves taking a detailed history and examining the following dimensions of a person's life:

- drives as related to pleasure, aggression, and mastery/competence (Walsh, 2006: 31)
- management of anxiety
- personality
- experiences across the lifespan
- defence mechanisms.

Some of the specific psychodynamic skills or techniques (Gibney, 2003; Nelson-Jones, 2006; Walsh, 2006: 40–3) you might use include the following.

1. *Promoting a corrective emotional experience.* As outlined in the previous section, the development and maintenance of the relationship over time is considered one of the most critical skills within psychodynamic approaches. This relationship enables the experience of a positive transference to emerge and for insight-oriented work to be done in a supportive environment despite the challenges the client faces on a daily basis.

2. *Offering containment.* In the previous chapter, containment was mentioned as an important skill within crisis-intervention approaches. Containment refers to 'an exquisite empathy and thoughtfulness with which the [worker] responds to the client throughout the session' (Gibney, 2003: 46). Containment enables a sense of psychological safety to be experienced, and is therefore crucial in situations of crisis. It is also crucial in Julia's situation, where she normally does not experience herself as psychologically centred and strong. Containment can be offered within the conversation; in relation to external threats; and in context.

   - *Within the conversation.* At the core, Gibney (2003: 51) describes this as relating to the fact that the client feels absolutely understood: accurately and genuinely. This, he and others argue, leads to the client being able to get in touch with her or his feelings, irrespective of the nature of those feelings. Thus, there is containment and affirmation of the client's inner-world experiences.
   - *In relation to external threats.* Through the giving of advice and direction in decision-making, the worker in many ways models adult decision-making processes and does not hesitate to advise on particular situations, particularly those of risk. In these ways, the role of 'good' parent may be enacted.
   - *In context.* Unlike other approaches, a psychodynamic approach typically is employed in a structured setting, with clear boundaries around your meeting times and space. This routine is viewed as providing 'containment' for

the anxiety of uncertainty. The certainties of this contract are considered to provide some safety and boundaries and, therefore, to provide an opportunity for the client to experience safety and boundaries in their inner world as well. In crisis situations, it is important to contain the emotional chaos through clear structuring and planning of actions. This notion of containment is similar to Winnicott's notion of a therapeutic 'holding environment' (Winnicott, 1987)—a safe, consistent environment, which is predictable in terms of time and event and surrounds.

3. *Providing interpretations, particularly through exploring internalized relationships across the lifespan.* In Julia's case, using imagery or analogy (Macnab, 1989: 101) to explore her inner objects, where she is seemingly quite articulate about her circumstances, might include reflecting to her that it is as if she has a passenger in the backseat of her car (a backseat driver) who is directing her, and what part of her 'self' this process relates to: 'Every time you're wanting to make a turn it's as if someone else is directing you.' To regain a sense of ego strength, she can begin to listen to herself as the front-seat driver and trust her own feelings and sense of knowing.

In conducting what Walsh (2006: 43) terms a 'developmental reflection', specific skills outlined in the earlier chapters are emphasized. The tendency within psychodynamic approaches is to emphasize non-directive, 'uncovering' techniques to listen her or his circumstances. The relationship, typically, is high in empathy, although a participant–observer role is strongly encouraged. Skills of interpretation, using summaries, making observations or invitations and 'why' questions are often amplified, for example: 'Earlier, you were telling me about your difficulties in finishing a project and just now you're telling me about how you're finding it difficult to leave this relationship.' Or: 'Notice that each time you talk about Brent you become quite choked up and you stop talking about him so freely as you do others.'

The timing of interpretations, however, is critical. Interpretations are usually made only in the context of well-established, trusting relationships, where they can be discussed fully in insight-oriented work.

4. *Encouraging the management of anxiety and insight into defence mechanisms.* Anxiety experiences are understood to lead to a distorting of reality, a loss of control, and inner conflict. Major anxiety in the form of trauma can lead to 'dissociation' as a defence against such severe stress. Dissociation is the separation of thinking and feeling, leading to alterations in memory, identity, and consciousness, where there can be a separating out of various aspects of the self. According to the theory, in the face of anxiety, we unconsciously use these sorts of defence mechanisms, which enable us to channel impulses 'into acceptable behaviors' (Walsh, 2006: 31).

Returning to Karen's discussion of her work with Julia: a number of areas of ego 'damage' might be assessed, including Julia's high level of disorganization both in practical terms and in emotional terms, and her high level of self-sabotage and her high level of vulnerability to the needs of others. On the other hand, in talking with Karen, it seemed she identified ego strengths that she had underestimated or not developed and was able to begin to focus on these to influence her future functioning.

A key term used in understanding change is 'resistance'. This term is originally from the **defence mechanism** of resistance, or the 'opposition to making what is unconscious conscious' (Reber, 1985: 642). It explains the unconscious process of pushing back against change in the face of potentially overwhelming anxiety.

Overall, then, some of the goals of intervention in psychodynamic approaches are to:

- free individuals and family members from unconscious restrictions and therefore establish less 'neurotic' patterns of relationship and communication
- work towards eliminating unhelpful patterns of relating
- delineate roles clearly, through establishing the fantasy compared with the reality of expectations
- find a balance of autonomy and mutuality.
- develop affect tolerance and impulse control
- restore or develop an integrated self-identity.

These goals are about expanding the person's inner capacities and his/her capacities to function in daily life.

Core Skills of Cognitive Behavioural Practice

Cognitive behavioural approaches are incorporated in many models of counselling, both implicitly and explicitly. Payne breaks down Cognitive Behavioural Theory (CBT) into two parts, which frequently are viewed in practice as one: first, behavioural models of therapy, deriving from psychological learning theories; and second, cognitive models of therapy, deriving from psychological theories of perception and information-processing (Payne, 2005: 119). Payne outlines the main points of Cognitive Behavioural Theory as follows.

1. Cognitive-behavioural work focuses on defining and addressing people's behaviours, particularly social phobias, anxiety, and depression.
2. Careful assessment and monitoring of progress often uses behavioural measurements.
3. Research evidence of effectiveness is strong and important to theory and practice.
4. The main techniques are well defined and technical, including respondent and operant conditioning, social learning and skills training, and cognitive restructuring of the person's belief system.
5. Social learning techniques, such as assertiveness and skills training, are widely used, particularly as part of group work, and are taken up in feminist practice.
6. More specific techniques are used in clinical settings where supervision and training in their use are available.

7. The use of cognitive behavioural models of practice has been controversial because of their association with politically controversial 'whatever works' standards of interpersonal control. Also controversial in the profession are 'evidence-based practice' perspectives. The proponents of cognitive behavioural models are known for their sometimes intemperate critiques—supposedly from a scientific and evidence-based perspective—of pre-existing and broader perspectives on social work practice.

8. Cautious concern about the potential for ethical problems has been raised in regard to cognitive behavioural models. These theories have been widely applied according to rigid political doctrines in Eastern countries, where scientific methods are less influential, and in countries where broad goals for the revision of society are conceived of as relevant to social work and coercive methods are permitted. (Adapted from Payne, 2005: 119–20)

In its traditional form, cognitive behavioural practice works on a model of change that sees inextricable links between feeling, thinking, and behaving. This model was represented by an 'equation' or theory of change by Ellis (1995):

$$A + B = C \rightarrow D \rightarrow E$$

where A denotes an 'activating event' or circumstance; B denotes beliefs, which Ellis describes as being initially either irrational or rational; and C denotes the consequences of the event and beliefs about it in terms of thoughts, feelings, and behaviours. In this equation, Ellis locates B as the mediating process on any event or circumstance, and the main area of focus in any intervention. D then denotes the disputation of beliefs and emotions and the attempts to establish more rational beliefs in lieu of irrational ones. Finally, E denotes the evaluation or reappraisal of both the event and beliefs about it and, therefore, the consequences should vary and change has occurred.

The basis of cognitive behavioural therapy is that in changing one dimension of a problem situation—for example, what is believed about a particular situation—change is inevitably influenced in the other dimensions, as Holly's description of her work with Craig later in this chapter demonstrates.

Turner (1986: 141) summarizes the value of cognitive behavioural practice:

The cognitive behavioural approaches all appear to share one common element; that is, they attempt to help the client to construe her problem in some other fashion, through some modification in cognitive processing, that is subsequently validated in actual behavioural assignments.

Establishing and Sustaining the Relationship

Engagement in CBT work is usually within a short-term, time-limited client–worker relationship. The relationship is understood primarily as a means to critically reflect on habits, patterns, and self-defeating behaviours. The relationship is not reflected on as a particularly significant component of the change agenda in the way that psychodynamic approaches are, as described in the previous chapter. The key focus in engaging with someone is to develop an empathic relationship in which emotions, behaviours and thoughts can be reviewed and challenged while necessary and realistic goals can be set.

Specific Interventions

Assessment focuses on a number of themes in relation to patterns of thinking, feeling, and behaving. Traditionally, the emphasis was on identifying **rational and irrational thoughts** or beliefs. Ellis and others argue that our counterproductive behaviours are sustained by the beliefs we hold onto in our everyday lives. Thus, unhelpful or unhealthy behaviours and feelings are the target of interventions.

Some of the specific skills originating from a cognitive behaviour approach include challenging self-defeating or unhelpful beliefs in the client so that the client learns to control and monitor his or her thoughts.

Challenging Self-Defeating or Unhelpful Beliefs

In earlier chapters where we have looked at the processes of assessment and goal-setting, an assumption of rational **decision-making** on the part of the client has been implied. CBT approaches have been instrumental in demonstrating the need to challenge beliefs, behaviours, and feelings in order to bring about change. Ellis and others encourage identification of the following self-defeating messages:

> I should . . .
> I must . . .
> I always . . .

These messages reflect our beliefs in behaviours that are compulsory or are absolute and, therefore, leave us without room to move. For example, we may distort beliefs about ourselves and others through catastrophizing and awfulizing (amplifying the negative consequences) or by generalizing. The reason for **challenging** these unhelpful beliefs is that more of a 'middle ground' can be reached through a 'reality check'. We may not even be aware of the place in our thinking of many of these taken-for-granted ways of thinking about the world and our behaviour. An outsider (in this case, you as the worker) may be able to hear the ways in which patterns of thinking are unhelpful cognitive patterns for the client.

Ellis identifies a number of core beliefs that he considered to be the irrational beliefs and illogical deductions responsible for creating human experiences of panic, self-blame, and self-doubt, as listed below. These beliefs have been used extensively as a starting point to explore the extent to which irrational beliefs create unrealistic expectations of ourselves and those around us.

These beliefs that Ellis considers irrational, or unhelpful, he believes can be challenged

Focus on Practice

Irrational Beliefs

Ellis's 'irrational beliefs' include the following:

- It is a dire necessity for an adult to be loved or approved by virtually every significant person in [his or her] community.
- One should be thoroughly competent, adequate, and achieving in all possible respects if one is to consider oneself worthwhile.
- Human unhappiness is externally caused and people have little or no ability to control their sorrows and disturbances.
- One's past history is an all-important determinant of one's present behaviour, and because something once strongly affected one's life, it should indefinitely have a similar effect.
- There is invariably a right, precise, and perfect solution to human problems, and it is catastrophic if this perfect solution is not found.
- If something is or may be dangerous or fearsome, one should be terribly concerned about it and should keep dwelling on the possibility of its occurring.

Source: Adapted from Ellis (1974: 152–3).

or neutralized by more rational or helpful beliefs. Fook (1993: 86) identifies resolving or tolerating conflicting beliefs and challenging false beliefs as critical strategies. These techniques are skills of reframing—of learning to think about something differently as a consequence of:

- challenging its helpful or unhelpful characteristics
- including more information into the picture of understanding
- hearing another point of view.

Controlling Thoughts: Thought-Stopping

Another central tenet of CBT approaches is that thoughts are controllable. The argument is that due to habit or a lack of conscious attention we are unaware of the thoughts, feelings, and beliefs that govern our behaviour. Strategies that combine both behavioural and cognitive strategies, such as 'thought-stopping', are used as interventions into these thought processes. In thought-stopping, the worker can interrupt the client's unhelpful thoughts during a conversation by literally saying 'stop'. Then, the client is encouraged to similarly stop his or her own thoughts when he or she becomes aware of that thought pattern. Such thought-conditioning strategies as wearing an elastic band around a wrist (to be flicked when a negative thought is experienced) are encouraged so that these automatic, unhelpful thoughts gradually come under more conscious control.

Monitoring Thoughts

Other strategies focus more on tracking unhelpful behaviours, through the use of a journal (either around specific behaviours or thoughts), for example. Below, Holly elaborates on how she worked with Craig to address this interconnection.

Focus on Practice

Using CBT Techniques

Craig is a 27-year-old man who came to see me for psychotherapy, and follow-up, due to suicidal behaviour and an underlying anxiety disorder. He is the recipient of long-term disability. Craig's mother died of leukemia when Craig was 19 years old. Craig's sister Joanne was murdered 13 years ago. He has one older brother with an intellectual disability and another brother who Craig alleges tried to molest him when the brother was eight or nine years of age and Craig was three. Craig lives alone and has a number of entrenched OCD [obsessive compulsive disorder] behaviours that he believes help to manage his anxiety, such as checking that taps are off, never having the gas turned on in the house, and washing and rewashing his hands.

Craig does not use alcohol or other substances. He does smoke cigarettes, however. He says: 'I don't drink tea or coffee or Coke because it makes my heart go too quickly.' Craig does not utilize public transport because he generally feels uncomfortable around people. He says that 'I can't get on public transport: people stare at me. I ride my bike everywhere. I haven't got on public transport for at least 10 years.'

Craig is also self-conscious of his appearance. He is typically dressed in somewhat worn tradesman's clothing and he wears woollen gloves on his hands, even on very warm days, noting this is 'because I've got tattoos'. These tattoos are from the time Craig spent in prison.

Craig notes that it takes him 60 to 90 minutes to leave the house. He has a lot of rituals to complete prior to departing. He is meticulous in tidying and cleaning behaviours—with regard to the back garden, the house, and his own body. He checks and rechecks the taps:

> I turn 'em off with a wrench because I think they're dripping. But they're not. I wreck the washers, I turn it so tight.

Specific to his self-harming behaviour Craig says:

> The voices tell me what to do. The other day I remember the voices telling me what to do: to take 5 and another 5.

And:

> I keep looking at the knife on the stove. I think about ending things.

After four weeks of talking to me, at his third outpatient appointment, Craig describes his anxiety and suicidal thought as 'like a toothache in my heart'.

What would you see as some of the possibilities for intervention with Craig?

Two interventions significantly impacted Craig's perceived level of coping, the regularity and severity of his presentations to the hospital emergency room, and his optimism.

The first was his increased role in his church community. He approached the minister about helping out, as had been discussed. He began to visit an elderly church member and another with a physical disability on a weekly basis. He would help with odd jobs, often in the garden, and in return join them for a cup of tea in their homes. Craig felt useful and the structured activity seemed to help by keeping him occupied and his thoughts for the most part off anxious preoccupations.

This intervention is about changing the outer world, through focusing on behaviours and structures that promote well-being.

The second intervention, which used more traditional CBT approaches, was the introduction of a mood journal. Craig and I converted an exercise book to a journal. Each day Craig would write down, any good thing that happened that day, and any upsetting thing that happened that day, and he would give himself a score out of 10. He would then bring the diary with him to sessions and we would discuss his week; as we were able to reduce sessions, the journal enabled him to self-monitor between appointments.

Interestingly to me, I did not recommend the daily scorekeeping at all. I once asked him—when trying to gauge the extent of his depressed mood—what he would give himself out of 10, when 'zero' was terrible and '10' was fantastic. He seemed to select this himself as a useful tool to include as part of the journal. Of course, since we were more than three months into treatment by then, he had undergone three formal assessments with me as part of the research element of the Suicide Prevention Strategy. The depression measure, BDI-II, uses 0–3 ratings, as does the quality-of-life tool; the MANSA uses a seven-point Likert scale of 25 questions. It could be that Craig found the numbering helpful for self-monitoring, or it could be, that Craig interpreted assigning numbers to things as giving them extra legitimacy.

Interesting, too, was that Craig's use of the numbers was highly subjective, so it was important to gain an understanding of his coding over time. While I would hope for a seven- or eight-out-of-ten day as a baseline for myself, when discussing what would be the score for a 'good' day Craig informed me that he was happy when he had a 'five' day. On those days he did not suffer high anxiety or feel a desire to self-harm. On a 'three' or 'four' day he would try to carry out some task in the garden or around the house, phone or visit a friend, or engage in positive self-talk. We worked out a safety plan from there whereby if he was having a 'one' or 'two' day he would call me during business hours or CATT triage after hours to talk instead of engaging in self-harm. He liked this and felt in charge of the process and that he was knowledgeable about his thought processes after all. Always, though, he required validation through my making time in the next outpatient session to read over his entries since we had last met and ask him about them.

All of these strategies actively address the ways in which thoughts, feelings, and behaviours interconnect and potentially create restrictions on the ways in which we live. In a small group or with a partner, identify the CBT thoughts, feelings, and behaviours model in the case of Craig. What did each person in your group identify? What were the similarities and differences in your group?

Strengths and Limitations of CBT Skills

CBT is often cited as the most successful form of psychological intervention. It has been found to be useful in addressing problems in a short-term, contracted way. Davis (2006: 234–5) describes behavioural techniques as traditionally being applied to persons with anxiety disorders, behavioural problems, and sexual disorders such as pedophilia, and cognitive treatments as applied to distorted thinking—irrational, unrealistic, or self-defeating beliefs and interpretations. However, the reported success of CBT is due in part to the relative ease of measuring its inputs and outputs compared with some of the more process- or insight-oriented approaches.

A major criticism of CBT approaches is that the problem is seen to be located in people's inner worlds. The major interventions focus on changing individual behaviours, thoughts, or feelings, whereas many human service workers are aware that the issues many clients are grappling with are located, or have their sources, in the outer worlds in which they live. For example, poverty can be thought about differently and behaviours can be changed in relation to it, but the essential agenda should be to alleviate poverty, not blame the individual for feeling stressed because of its effects, such as lack of adequate food, shelter, and clothing. The lack of attention to structural concerns, so often at the heart of individual experiences of stress and depression, is the major criticism of these approaches.

Psychodynamic approaches have attracted controversy in social work and psychology. Three major criticisms are made of CBT. The first is that psychodynamic approaches are inherently intrapsychic and therefore fail to address the social, structural, and cultural causes of human distress and oppression. CBT's inherently apolitical stance means that it is not a useful approach for social change; rather, it locates both the causation and responsibility for change at the level of the individual. Human service workers work constantly at the interface of the individual and the society, thus, psychodynamic approaches have major limitations in this regard. This critique is noted by Walsh (2006: 45) and others; Walsh notes that 'There is nothing that prohibits a social worker who practices ego psychology from helping clients engage in larger system change activities, but nothing within the theory itself encourages these interventions.'

The second criticism of CBT is that many of the key theories of psychodynamic approaches lack an available evidence base from which to draw conclusions about efficacy. Related to this criticism is the further criticism that the theories are unfalsifiable. The condition of the client's inner world is defined by the therapist according to an unprovable theoretical model. As the point of departure of therapy is defined within a closed linguistic system (a tautological framework), the client's progress within the model is not verifiable.

A third criticism of CBT is that psychodynamic approaches can disempower clients—through the lack of explanation to the client of the theories being used to understand that individual's inner worlds, and these theories assume the superiority of the beliefs and the authority of the therapist. Healy (2005: 57) also raises the question as to the relevance of what she terms the 'psy' (as in 'psychologically oriented') theories where the relationship is mandated. The basis of the relationship with involuntary clients may not be trust (ibid., citing Smith, 2001: 289), but a formal agreement. Yet, the assumptions about engagement in a therapeutic relationship are said to be based on trust and a positive attachment. Indeed, behavioural modification techniques can be seen as coercive, and when used with patients in mental hospitals or with prisoners in penal institutions, it can be argued that CBT violates a person's inherent civil rights. Healy also notes that psychologized approaches generally may 'limit workers' capacities to undertake responsibilities associated with decision-making in high-risk situations' (ibid., 57).

However, psychodynamic approaches are, as Healy notes, so embedded within many ways of working in the twenty-first century that their use continues despite these limitations and drawbacks. Their strength has been in providing theories of human behaviour as well as a way of understanding the client–worker relationship dynamics. They link individual agency, motivation, and coping with persons' functioning in the outer world. Psychodynamic approaches not only provide a way of understanding individual behaviour in the context of a client–worker relationship, but also behaviour and processes within organizations, groups, and families.

Chapter Summary

In this chapter, some key skills associated with psychodynamic and cognitive behavioural approaches have been explored. Psychodynamic skills focus on bringing to conscious awareness patterns of relating both to the self and to others, and beliefs from the past to understand their impact on present functioning and future expectations. Cognitive behavioural skills similarly focus on building insight into the present, and establishing more conscious control over thinking, feeling, and behaving. A major limitation of these skills is that they seek to bring about primarily inner-world change for the client. They have been criticized for failing to address the social, structural, and cultural contexts of people's lives.

Questions for Analysis

1. What dimensions of these skills appeal to you? Why?

2. When would you use these skills and when would you not?

3. What are some of the cultural assumptions embedded in each of the approaches?

Recommended Readings

Beck, A., A. Freeman, and D. Davis. 2004. *Cognitive Therapy of Personality Disorders*. New York: Guilford Press.

Brandell, J. 2004. *Psychodynamic Social Work*. New York: Columbia University Press.

Davis, S. 2006. *Community Mental Health in Canada*. Vancouver: University of British Columbia Press.

Dean, R. 2002. 'Teaching contemporary psychodynamic theory for contemporary social work practice', *Smith College Studies in Social Work* 73, 1: 11–27.

Gibney, P. 2003. *The Pragmatics of Therapeutic Practice*. Melbourne: Psychoz.

Howard, S. 2006. *Psychodynamic Counselling in a Nutshell*. London: Sage.

Payne, M. 2005. *Modern Social Work Theory*. Chicago: Lyceum Books.

Internet Resources

Beck Institute for Cognitive Therapy and Research
www.beckinstitute.org

Canadian Counselling and Psychotherapy Association
www.ccacc.ca

Canadian Mental Health Association
www.cmha.ca/bins/loc_page.asp?cid=58-85&lang=1

Canadian Mental Health Association, Ontario
www.ontario.cmha.ca

Canadian Mental Health Association, Vancouver, Burnaby Branch
http://vancouver-burnaby.cmha.bc.ca

Canadian Network for Mood and Anxiety Treatment
www.canmat.org/cme/interviews/inter_cognitive.html

Institute for the Study of Therapeutic Change
www.talkingcure.com

International Association for Cognitive Psychotherapy
www.cognitivetherapyassociation.org

Tavistock Society of Psychotherapists
www.tavistocksociety.org

13 | Narrative and Solution-Focused Skills

Learning Goals

- Identify the core skills of narrative and solution-focused approaches, particularly in relation to the establishment of the relationship between a worker and client and specific interventions.
- Understand the strengths and limitations of these skills.

Core Skills of Narrative Practice

Bitter (2009: 249) describes the narrative approach by citing Foucault:

> Foucault asserts that those perspectives that become dominant-culture narratives have to be challenged at every level and every opportunity, because their function is, in part, to minimize or eliminate alternate knowledge-positions and alternate narratives. Because of the power of dominant-culture narratives, individuals and families tend to integrate these positions as if they are the only possible ones to take—even if those positions are not useful to the individual or the family.

Narrative practice aims to understand and transform the stories people live by—individual stories as well as stories held by communities and even nations. Dowrick (2006: 57), writing about the power of story and storytelling, reminds us that:

> Storytelling is one of humankind's most basic arts and the drive to listen to and tell stories is deep in almost everyone. It's the telling of stories that allows us to explore a situation or interaction that matters to us, to make sense of it or to relive it.

Narrative approaches seek to understand the client–worker relationship and how to listen to clients' stories in particular ways. The stories are important reflections of us as individuals and/or communities but also as interior narratives that profoundly influence and maintain our lives.

For the worker, narrative techniques include skills in: listening with curiosity, posing questions that make a difference, deconstruction and externalization of client's thought patterns, the presentation of alternate stories, and assisting the client with re-authoring. As Bitter (2009: 259) explains:

> Diversity, multiple frameworks, and an integration/collaboration of the knower are all part of this new social movement to enlarge perspectives and options. For some social constructionists, the process of 'knowing' includes distrust of the dominant-culture positions that permeate families and society today. For these people, change starts with deconstructing the power of cultural narratives and then proceeds to the co-construction of a new life meaning.

Some questions to assist in exploring the real effects of culture on the person while also developing avenues for re-authoring lives may include:

1.   What influence has your culture had in your life?
2.   What challenges have you faced growing up in your culture and how have you handled them?
3.   What is significant in your life and the lives of your family and community that you feel I must know if I really want to understand you?
4.   What resources within your cultural community support you and you draw strength from in times of need? (Ibid., 261)

Establishing and Sustaining the Relationship

As a result of emerging from postmodern understandings of subjectivity and truths, narrative approaches have adopted a strong focus on the ways in which problem stories are co-created (de Shazer, 1994: xvi). Thus, the client–worker relationship provides a safe, supportive engagement in which a person's stories can be heard, witnessed, and validated. In bearing witness to a person's stories and helping to co-create new stories of strength and healing, change can occur. This approach has proven to be particularly important in coping in the aftermath of trauma experiences (White, 2004).

Specific Interventions

The agenda for change in narrative approaches focuses on understanding and re-authoring the stories we live by. Changing people's stories about their lives:

> can help to change their actual lives. Furthermore, changing these stories often involves challenging larger social stories within people's problem-saturated stories about themselves and their lives. All individual stories are social stories. (Brown and Augusta-Scott, 2007: xvii)

Thus, specific skills have emerged in relation to what is attended to in stories, and how they are explored. As in other approaches, skills in validation and exploration are used— probes, reflections, and summaries all assist to establish the dominant narratives of a person's life, both their own narratives and those that others impose on them. Narrative therapy then aims to transform the unhelpful stories, or the inhibiting and self-defeating stories, restoring (or re-storying) them with stories that are strengths-based.

Exploring the Dominant Stories

For many people, not only are their circumstances difficult, but their circumstances also are not heard by anyone. Experiences of oppression, trauma, and grief are often 'disenfranchised' from the dominant social stories—no one wants to pay attention to them or accord them legitimacy. Listening to someone's stories can be a transforming experience. And listening to one's own story allows new perspectives to form. Moore (2004: 58) notes: 'The repeated telling of a story gradually allows the pieces of life experiences to find their relation to each other.' In brief, the repetitions of a story of trauma allow the person to name and to find explanations for her or his feelings, diffusing the negative impacts of the trauma.

Some of the major skills involved in narrative work, therefore, are good listening skills: listening actively and empathically to what is being told, asking questions and summarizing along the way, and enabling the person to tell all s/he needs to tell, no matter how complex, ambiguous, or painful the story. Narrative approaches emphasize that we each carry multiple identities and roles that change and are reconstructed frequently. Listening for what is told and how it is told is the first skill in narrative practice.

Deconstructing and Re-Authoring: Externalizing the Problem

Unlike the approaches explored in Chapter 12, narrative approaches consider the problem external to the person. While the person has a narrative about the problem, its causation, and its consequences, the person is not the problem. This skill of **externalizing** the problem entails inviting the person to speak around and about the problem, but not about herself or himself as the problem. Specific questions are asked about the problem, understanding it as an issue external to the person.

Focus on Practice

Questions That Aim to Externalize the Problem

- Tell me about a time that you stood up to, said 'no' to, or resisted the problem. How was that situation handled differently?
- Have there been times recently when the problem has not played a role in your life?
- Can you think of any time in the past when the problem could have played a role in your life but it did not?
- Do you remember other times in the past when you have stood up to the problem?
- How did it feel when you stood up to the problem?
- How have you been able to keep the problem from getting worse?

Source: Brown and Augusta-Scott (2007: xxxv).

Listening for Strengths and Coping Capacities

In Heather's work with a client in a drug and alcohol service, she sets out to explore what has happened in the early days of someone's recovery, when that person has experienced difficulties, as illustrated below.

Focus on Practice

A Conversation with a Client Who Has Relapsed

Heather is talking with a client who attended one session, then missed two appointments, and has attended for a second time and has reported a relapse.

Heather: Hi Tony, why don't you tell me how the last few weeks have been going for you?
Client: Not so great.
Heather: What hasn't been so great for you?
Client: I relapsed . . .
Heather: I can see that you aren't very happy about this relapse; was it a shock for you?
Client: Nah, I always relapse.
Heather: It sounds like this is something that happens often for you?
Client: Yeah, like thousands of times, I give up . . .
Heather: What has happened in the past when you have relapsed?

Notice that rather than pathologizing the recurrence of a relapse, Heather moves on to explore this client's narrative of relapse. She invites him to explore this more fully rather than explore what he has 'failed' to do, and by becoming aware of some particular patterns of risky behaviour it opens up the way to new coping strategies. This process normalizes and validates the person rather than challenging and pathologizing the person's story.

Re-Authoring Stories through Listening for Unique Outcomes

As shown by Heather's questions above, another major skill of narrative approaches is to emphasize a time or times when the problem has not been a problem, or when ways of managing it differently have been available. This way of 'thinking again' emphasizes strengths in a person's coping and that, in some situations, the problem or the client's way of coping with it varies. This reframing of the negative experience is related to the technique of challenging some of the ways the client thinks about an experience, described in Chapter 12. The challenge to think about **unique outcomes** encourages the client to think again about how a problem dominates his or her life. Doing this involves deconstructing the dominant stories of a person's life and re-authoring new, positive, and life-affirming stories.

Re-Authoring Social Stories

Unlike the skills discussed in earlier chapters, which tend to affirm existing cultural and social realities, narrative approaches seek to challenge some of those dominant social stories. Through deconstructing and re-authoring individual or group stories, the representations of these broader social, structural, and cultural narratives can be changed, too.

Core Skills of Solution-Focused Practice

Narrative and solution-focused approaches share many skills—the use of extensive open-ended questioning around a problem, and the strategy of externalizing the problem as separate from the person in order to establish a new perspective on that person's circumstances. Both approaches step out of the assumptions of other perspectives that assume that 'there is a necessary connection between a problem and its solution' (O'Connell, 1998: 14). A number of differences, however, are evident in the two approaches. Narrative approaches are based on a very fluid understanding of the story a person lives by. Solution-focused approaches work more within a systems perspective and notions of a continuous self. 'Brief therapies are by definition solution-focused. Solution-focused therapists help clients craft fairly well-defined goals that can be accomplished in a reasonable time frame' (Egan and Schroeder, 2009: 295).

Establishing and Sustaining the Relationship

As with narrative approaches, solution-focused approaches emphasize that your relationship with your clients is a short-term, co-creating relationship. The emphasis during the listening phase of the process is to hear both exceptions and solutions to problems in daily life. The goal is 'to identify and amplify client strengths and resources' (Walsh, 2006; 208), with much of the 'work' being done by clients outside of any counselling or conversational time spent with you as the worker. Your role as worker is to stimulate a new way of thinking about problem situations, alongside your client.

Dolan summarizes the major tenets of solution-focused brief therapy as follows:

1. If it ain't broke, don't fix it. If it works, do more of it.
2. If it is not working, do something different.
3. Small steps can lead to large changes.
4. The solution is not directly related to the problem.
5. No problem happens all the time. There are always exceptions which can be utilized.
6. The future is both created and negotiable. (Dolan, 2005, cited in Bitter, 2009: 232)

A positive and rapid engagement is encouraged so that work can occur quickly—not within the context of a lengthy therapeutic relationship. A high emphasis is placed on clients' expertise and empowerment in finding the solutions they need. The emphasis in the client–worker contact is on translating that expertise and empowerment into everyday life (O'Connell, 1998: 85).

Specific Interventions

Many of the interventions are similar to those described in the previous discussion of narrative approaches. Questions are asked to explore fully the ways in which the client views her/his situation, with an emphasis on exceptions and solutions, as well as on the future.

Focusing on Exceptions and Solutions

Questions that reflect a solution-focused approach relate to the *exceptions* to problems and to their solutions, rather than to a lengthy exploration of the nature of the problems themselves. This difference in focus is the major reason for the differences in the use of skills and the emphases of the approaches described in the previous chapter. The narrative approach presumes that people have strengths and resources that have enabled them to overcome difficulties and problems at times, and that these strengths and resources are what should be amplified, rather than the potentially overwhelming nature of the problem situations themselves. The emphasis is less on insight into current behaviours, thoughts, feelings and events, and more on foresight about the future and building on a capacity to influence that future.

Focusing on the Future

Solution-focused skills are designed to orient the client towards the future, not on the past or even on the present in great detail. Asking questions about the maintenance of problem situations emphasizes the consequences of not changing and encourages the motivation to change—the realization that unless something happens, problems could remain as they are or become exacerbated, rather than diminishing.

At the heart of solution-focused therapy is the skill of the 'miracle question' (de Shazer, 1985), an open-ended question that is designed to 'enable people to pretend, to transcend the present and imagine a better state of affairs' (Manthei, 1997: 100). The miracle question was proposed by de Shazer (1994: 95): 'Suppose that tonight after you go to sleep a miracle happens and the problems that brought you to therapy are solved immediately. But since you were sleeping at the time you cannot know that this miracle has happened.' This first part of the miracle question invites the client to think that her or his difficulties could be different.

The next step is to think about how they could be different: 'Once you wake up tomorrow morning, how will you discover that a miracle has happened? Without your telling them, how will other people know that a miracle has happened?' This question can be adapted in many ways to invite people to think how differently their circumstances could or should look, and thus help set the goals for what needs to shift, even if only in the story someone lives by. Thus, the language of the questions you ask is driven by this focus on the future, and by an emphasis on possibility and change. It is an essentially positive, strengths-oriented approach to practice.

Strengths and Limitations of Narrative Skills

Narrative skills enable the client to develop a coherent but constantly evolving story about who he or she is in the changing context of the problems. Solution-focused skills enable the client to think and talk about the person she or he would like to be and how that person would like to live. They are applied in a strengths perspective so that the client focuses on positive change rather than on inescapable negativity and oppression. These skills have the potential to transform circumstances far beyond individual lives; to cause change and re-authoring of dominant social and cultural narratives.

In Chapter 14, we will explore how feminist and critical approaches adopt a strong structural and political critique, which addresses this criticism of the more subjectively located approaches.

Some of the limitations, however, are that narrative and brief-solution approaches may not provide clients the opportunity, both in relation to time and to emphasis, to explore their past and present circumstances in depth. Some critics are concerned about the lack of depth, and even the lack of understanding of or insight into the nature of personal difficulties. Particularly with solution-focused approaches, critics suggest that there is an emphasis on the positive at the expense of understanding the despair and distress.

Others question the underlying assumption around a shared strengths oriented discourse, which translates into the assumption that clients are telling socially desirable stories. However, many stories are around not-so-desirable actions and perpetrations against others, and the theory leaves unclear where these fit within an overtly positive view of human behaviour in the absence of a political, ethical, moral, or social position. Nevertheless, narrative approaches have been profoundly influential in community organizing and social action strategies.

Other critics raise cautions in relation to the extent that workers impose their personal views and dominant stories on the client (Walsh, 2006: 268)—a concern that is pertinent to all approaches in human services work. Further concerns apply to the absence of theories of human development and change in the narrative and brief-solutions methods. To what extent can stories be so subjectively located that a worker needs no basis in biopsychosocial assessments and understandings of a person's life? Bitter's (2009: 320) reply to these concerns is that '[c]ognitive-behavioural therapists approach culture as a context and a reinforcing context at that—in which thinking and behaving are enacted. For those cultures that place less emphasis on talking, expression of feeling, and intrapsychic expression, cognitive-behavioural methods seem like a welcome relief.'

Chapter Summary

In this chapter, the skills associated with narrative approaches have been discussed, including exploring dominant stories, deconstructing and challenging these stories, and re-authoring them using a strengths-based approach. The future- and strengths-focused skills of solution-focused strategies have also been examined, particularly through the use of the miracle question.

Questions for Analysis

1. What have you learned from this chapter about:
   - exploring the narratives?
   - externalizing problems?
   - unique outcomes?
   - asking a 'miracle question'?
   - focusing on personal or community strengths and resources?

2. What do you see as the key strengths of these skills?

3. When do you think you would use these skills? Why?

4. What do you want to learn more about?

5. What skills will you seek further training in and why?

Recommended Readings

Bitter, J.R. 2009. *Theory and Practice of Family Therapy and Counselling*. Belmont, Calif.: Brooks/Cole.

Brown, C., and T. Augusta-Scott. 2007. *Narrative Therapy: Making Meaning, Making Lives*. Thousand Oaks, Calif.: Sage.

de Shazer, S. 1994. *Words Were Originally Magic*. New York: Norton.

O'Connell, B. 1998. *Solution-Focused Therapy*. London: Sage.

Payne, M. 2005. *Modern Social Work Theory*. Chicago: Lyceum Books.

Russell, S., and M. Carey. 2003. 'Feminism, therapy and narrative ideas: Exploring some not so commonly asked questions', *International Journal of Narrative Therapy and Community Work* 3, 1: 67–91.

White, M. 2004. 'Working with people who are suffering the consequences of multiple trauma: A narrative perspective', *International Journal of Narrative Therapy and Community Work* 1: 45–76.

Internet Resources

Brief and Narrative Therapy Network
www.brieftherapynetwork.com

Brief Family Therapy Centre
www.brief-therapy.org

Brief Therapy Institute of Sydney
www.brieftherapysydney.com.au

Dulwich Centre
www.dulwichcentre.com.au

Hinks-Dellcrest Centre—Brief and Narrative Training
www.hincksdellcrest.org/Home/Training-and-Consultation/Brief-and-Narrative-Therapy-Training/Brief-and-Narrative-Therapy-Training.aspx

Solution-Focused Brief Therapy Association
www.sfbta.org

14 Feminist and Critical Theory Skills

Learning Goals

- Identify the core skills of feminist and critical approaches.
- Identify skills specific to the critical/feminist paradigm for establishing and sustaining a working relationship.
- Understand the strengths and limitations of feminist skills.

Core Skills of Feminist and Critical Practice

Unlike the approaches discussed in the previous chapters, feminist and critical theory approaches have an explicit lens on outer-world dimensions as the focus of their work. Many texts relating to communication and counselling skills exclude a discussion of these approaches for this reason: change is not understood to be occurring so much at the microskill or client–worker level of individual communication and interviewing. Rather, the focus of intervention is on social, structural, and cultural change. That said, however, a number of key skills emerging from feminist and critical theory perspectives are readily transferable to communication at the client–worker interface. For the purposes of this discussion, skills unique to feminist and critical theory approaches are focused on within the same discussion, rather than under separate headings.

Payne (2005: 244) provides a rationale for critical approaches:

> Critical theories question the idea of a set, continuous self and identity. Part of this has to do with language. For example, we tend to think of things as dichotomies: what we are and what we are not. However, critical ideas suggest that things can change, be contradictory and multiple: many things at once. We should see ourselves as a whole people who can develop more complexity and diversity.

In practice, this notion is centred around deconstruction, resistance, challenge, and reconstruction. In regard specifically to feminist theory, Turner (1986: 656) explains:

As our society has become more conscious of the complex and frequently unfair and unjust ways that we respond to women, and the effects it has on self-image and functioning, a growing body of relevant therapeutic theory is emerging. This theory is useful in situations when women are seeking to get a better understanding of themselves and their potential, and to find strategies to help set and achieve appropriate life, personal, and career goals.

Payne (2005: 252) provides the following practice issues and concepts.

Focus on Practice

Some Concepts for Critical Practice

Consciousness-raising (connected to the critical practice conscientization) as a strategy for stimulating awareness and change.

Reflexivity as a research tool and its subsequent adaptation as an element of practice.

Dialogic, egalitarian relationships as the vehicle of practice that values and empowers women.

Social and personal identity as the social processes by which it is formed and by which it changes is an important aspect of creating and intervening in diverse relationships.

Establishing and Sustaining the Relationship

Within feminist and other critical approaches, the emphasis within the worker's relationship with people is on establishing equality and, working in partnership, recognizing the inherent human rights each has as a citizen (Healy, 2005: 186). Another way of thinking about working with your clients is about 'becoming an ally' (Bishop, 2002). In becoming an ally or working in more egalitarian ways, your task is to emphasize the reciprocity of skills within the relationship. As Ife (1997: 150) suggests:

the critical paradigm requires that skills be shared between the worker and the 'client', that the 'client' be seen as possessing skills that are just as valid and important as those of the worker, and that each should share their skills with the other in a process of mutual empowerment and mutual education.

Within this relationship context, you remain aware that the wider social context—and its issues of sexual, racial, and class oppression and **discrimination**—is likely to be reflected. Individual client–worker relationships become the microcosm in which these power relations can be replicated. The client–worker relationship itself provides an opportunity to address power imbalances, and to name and ultimately challenge these sources of oppression. In relation to the assessment of the 'presenting problem', therefore, the personal is understood as inherently connected to the political. Thus, critical and careful attention to these dynamics is required and openly discussed throughout the client–worker contact. This approach is based on the belief that change occurs through the 'integration of personal and socio-cultural transformational processes' (Bricker-Jenkins, Hooyman, and Gottlieb, 1991: 291–2).

> Remember, in Chapter 2 we looked at the decoding process. As a worker, you are decoding the message within a feminist approach through a gender–power filter or analysis.

Most feminist and critical approaches see the relationship as a short-term resourcing role or a longer-term collaboration, rather than as a 'therapeutic' relationship. This strategy is based in the belief that individuals are dealing with the private pains of public problems and that, therefore, the solutions should be structural and political. Many models of feminist therapy, however, embrace the opportunity for both personal insight and political change.

Specific Interventions

Underlying all of the skills of any critical approach is an analysis of individual problems through a wider structural and power analysis, whether in relation to gender, class, culture, or ethnicity. Within feminist approaches, this analysis is of gender and power, and women's oppression by men specifically. Thus, you are not using different communication skills, but are using them in a particular way to focus on a particular way of understanding people and their circumstances.

Feminism exposes the glaring omission inherent in all four paradigms—that of gender analysis of women's inequality in society and of how the state contributes to women's oppression (Mullaly, 2007: 168). Consider the following example.

Susan, a recently widowed woman of colour, is facing several challenges. Susan is unable to find employment and feels strongly it is due to her visible disability, which requires her to walk with a cane. Susan feels she often is treated differently from other women and from the way she sees men being treated, for example, the length of time extended for discussion during the interview, and the wait time for an interview. Susan is uncertain how to address these issues. Susan fears that broaching her concern with a worker may cause further refusal of assistance for her and for her son, who requires daily assistance for autism. If Susan is unable to gain employment her family may risk losing their home and the required services for her child.

Practice within critical approaches draws on many of the skills we have already explored in previous chapters—the skills of questioning; of developing a story or multiple stories of the self; of understanding thoughts, feelings, and behaviours, and challenging these where necessary. Feminist and critical approaches also incorporate goal-setting processes into the work. We now explore three additional skills that are unique to feminist and critical approaches.

Three core practice skills (Bricker-Jenkins, Hooyman, and Gottlieb, 1991: 292–5) are **validation**, **consciousness-raising**, and **transformative action**. These skills lead to interventions that mobilize resources to meet basic human needs through relationships that nurture and sustain uniqueness, and the creation of validating environments.

Using Validation

To validate someone or something is to 'lend force or validity to; confirm; ratify; substantiate' (Brown, 1993: 3541). Validation, in an interpersonal relationship, affirms the 'truth' of a person's subjective experience. Thus, reflecting skills are used to affirm someone's telling of her story and her perceptions about what has occurred. Validation has emerged as an important part of the recognition that so many people's stories, and particularly women's, have been invalidated, disbelieved, or rendered invisible. Naming what has occurred is a first step in the process of work together, particularly in relation to experiences of violence, assault, and disempowerment.

Luanne is an attractive 34-year-old mother of three children. She had difficulty succeeding as well in school as her several brothers and sisters, all of whom are university graduates. She did graduate from a post-secondary secretarial course. On one of her holidays in Mexico she met Rudy, a Colombian expatriate who wanted to immigrate to Canada. They formed an intimate relationship that resulted in Luanne's first pregnancy. She helped Rudy immigrate to Canada; they married and had two more children. Rudy adapted easily to Canadian culture, has an artistic flair, and has formed a rapidly growing interior décor business supplying ceramic tile and other home decorations in ceramic and stone to builders in Toronto. They enjoy a comfortable upper middle-class lifestyle. Luanne has suspected for some time that 'things don't quite add up' with Rudy, who is physically aggressive and verbally abusive to her. Recently, he has been physically abusing their children when she was out. The morning she witnessed him striking the children she quickly packed up her important papers and clothing and toys for the children and has taken refuge with them in a women's shelter. She is very angry, very frightened, and does not know what action to take to protect her children and herself.

Some validating statements you might make in your conversation with Luanne include the nature of Rudy's cultural heritage and her courage in standing up to his abuse; her values in wanting to protect her children from such harmful practices; her courage in leaving with her children despite his threats of harm if she should ever leave him; her spirit of adventure in travelling to get to know other parts of the world; her successful transition from a social setting of very modest income to a social setting that makes more complex demands on its members; her willingness to learn what she needs to know about the legal system in order to protect herself and her children.

Your questioning, reflecting, and statement skills would focus on the wider structural and cultural dimensions of her experience, not only the personal dimensions of Luanne's self-esteem issues that made her vulnerable to an esoteric 'prize' husband to show off to her economically successful family and that made her vulnerable to him despite his overbearing, demanding, threatening, and abusive behaviours. The focus, like narrative and solution-focused approaches, is on externalizing the problem.

Encouraging a Process of Consciousness-Raising

Through validation and dialogue, your skills help your client to engage in a process of consciousness-raising, not only with your client but also in the client's wider social context. This consciousness-raising process leads to a process of liberation, which is sometimes described as spiral in nature (Bishop, 2002: 100). The process of liberation involves 'breaking the silence, ending the shame, and sharing our concerns and feelings'. The skills we use are storytelling, analysis, strategy, and action:

Story-telling leads to analysis, where we figure out together what is happening to us and why, and who benefits. Analysis leads to strategy, when we decide what to do about it. Strategy leads to action, together, to change the injustices we suffer (Bishop, 2002: 100).

Action leads to another round of reflection, analysis, strategy, and action. This is the process of liberation. Like narrative approaches, storytelling becomes an important process; thus, listening and reflecting are critical skills. Feminist and critical theories, however, in politicizing problems, also consider the naming of these issues in their wider social context as important steps in working together.

Talking with someone about her difficult relationship circumstances may lead to a wider discussion of power and gender, or power and age, so that the person comes to understand relational circumstances as emerging from wider social, structural, and cultural influences, not from the particular circumstances of her own situation. This may mean that the intervention focuses more on forming connections with others in similar circumstances, moving beyond an individual client–worker relationship and participating in transformative action, as described below.

Engaging in Transformative Action

Through the individual experience of validation and consciousness-raising, liberation from oppression comes about through transformative action. While individual counselling work might be an important step in building insight and strengths for a person, connecting in group or community work is seen as the ultimate step to recovery or adaptation (Herman, 1992; Mullaly, 2002: 173), as the problem no longer resides 'with' the person but is addressed in its wider social context.

Within this perspective, your focus as a worker is not only on the work you undertake with your clients, but also in your desire to bring about change with others in the immediate and wider context. Some examples of transformative action include 'bringing people together in order to present a petition or submission about a policy issue, or to advocate for change' (Ife, 1997: 168). Other actions include the development of groups and community activities. In Australia, for example, The Women's Circus (Liebman et al., 1997) was established in 1991, originally as a group for survivors of sexual assault, but now it includes all interested women. The Circus continues to raise awareness of women's experiences of sexual assault by reaching the wider community through its general outreach and publicity. Similarly, in North America, groups whose primary goal is to assist women in crisis—through counselling, legal support, or provision or direction to a specific service such as shelter or abortion—also are active in organizing and participating in self-empowering public demonstrations such as 'Take Back the Night' marches and vigils to commemorate specific tragic events like the Montreal Massacre of 6 December 1989.

The communication skills required for feminist and structural interventions include all of those outlined earlier—both verbal and non-verbal—enabling you to explore the story of the individual or the community that is dealing with a particular issue, to challenge where necessary particular ways of thinking and acting, to externalize the problems, and to validate and affirm people and their strengths. The skills may also include working towards linkage with, and referral to, other transformative action opportunities.

Ultimately, your focus is on collective action, however, rather than individual responsibility as the way of bringing about these resources. For example, women's groups have actively lobbied governments for the provision of refuges for women escaping domestic violence. This action requires clear communication and argument with key stakeholders. Your engagement and rapport-building skills are fundamental to these processes, as well as to your direct practice with clients.

Focus on Practice

Using Feminist Skills

Duty workers on telephone crisis lines very frequently receive calls from distressed young women who have been assaulted by a partner. These women have been hurt, are frightened, and don't know what to do—whether to leave or stay. You are the duty worker taking calls when a woman calls the crisis line. The woman speaks English but has a heavy foreign accent, making her difficult to understand. In between her phrases punctuated by sobs, she informs you she has been pushed into a dresser so that her head caught the edge of its large mirror. She also states her arms have bruises and she does not know what she should do.

1. How would you go about assessing such a situation with this woman?
2. What else would you want to know about her situation?
3. What validation skills might you use?
4. What consciousness-raising strategies would you consider?
5. Would you encourage her engagement in transformative action at all and how?

Strengths and Limitations of These Skills

The strengths of feminist skills are that they shift the focus of women's personal problems to the outer world, where so often the cause lies. They emphasize that people are both victims and survivors of these wider influences, and that through political and communal strategies, change can be achieved. Like narrative and solution-focused approaches, the emphasis is on changing the social and cultural discourses rather than regarding individuals as personally responsible and pathologizing their coping capacities. As a result of feminist discourse, radical change has been made in social attitudes and in legislation and social supports that affect the lived experience of women. The understanding and validation that a feminist critique has offered of relationships, workplaces, and family life have affected women in Europe and North America and are having an influence on the lives of women around the world.

The first and obvious drawback of the feminist approach is that it may be less than helpful or empathetic to the needs and problems of males. Even where the worker has general skills, the worker's enthusiasm for her own emphasis may provide less support and understanding than the male client needs.

The related second major criticism of feminist and other critical theory approaches is that the worker is imposing a particular world view on clients who may have a different world view. That is, the worker expects her or his lens to become the lens of the client. The dominance of Western, middle-class views in the development of many of these theoretical understandings has led to the criticism that they are themselves colonizing, polarizing, and disempowering theories, rather than theories that achieve what they fundamentally set out to achieve—equality and empowerment. Thus, as Healy (2005: 190) notes: 'A contradiction exists between anti-oppressive theorists' claim to promote dialogue in practice and their assumptions that they hold a true and correct analysis of the world.' Within the multicultural context of Canadian services, for example, significant challenges emerge for feminist workers in maintaining a particular critique of gender, power, and culture, while respecting cultural difference and diversity.

Chapter Summary

In this chapter, the skills privileged within feminist and critical theory approaches have been explored, including validation, consciousness-raising, and transformative action. Understanding your clients' experiences from a feminist and therefore critical theory perspective enables the focus to be shifted from an emphasis on individual responsibility for coping to structural solutions and strategies. Instead, the personal is deemed to be political, leading to different solutions and expectations of the client–worker relationship. Some of the challenges inherent in these skills, however, were explored in relation to the potential to replicate the very situation the perspective seeks to eradicate—disempowerment within a particular cultural community and the imposition of a particular world view and way of being.

Questions for Analysis

1. What have you learned from this chapter about:
   - how listening is influenced by feminist or critical theory approaches?
   - the nature of questions and the focus of intervention within these approaches?
   - the six specific skills primarily used within feminist and critical theory approaches?

2. What do you see as the key strengths of these skills?

3. When do you think you would use these skills? Why?

4. What skills do you want to learn more about?

Recommended Readings

Bishop, A. 2002. *Becoming an Ally: Breaking the Cycle of Oppression*. Crows Nest: Allen and Unwin.

Bricker-Jenkins, M., N. Hooyman, and N. Gottlieb, eds. 1991. *Feminist Social Work Practice in Clinical Settings*. London: Sage.

Chaplin, J. 1999. *Feminist Counselling in Action*, 2nd edn. London: Sage.

Fook, J. 2000. 'Critical perspectives on social work practice', in I. O'Connor, P. Smyth, and J. Warburton, eds, *Contemporary Perspectives on Social Work and the Human Services: Challenges and Change*. Frenchs Forest: Addison Wesley Longman Australia.

Kondrat, E. 1999. 'Who is the "self" in self-aware: Professional self-awareness from a critical theory perspective', *Social Service Review* 73, 4: 451–77.

Mullaly, Bob. 2002. *Challenging Oppression: A Critical Social Work Approach*. Toronto: Oxford University Press.

Payne, M. 2005. *Modern Social Work Theory*. Chicago: Lyceum Books.

Stoppard, J. 2000. *Understanding Depression: Feminist Social Constructionist Approaches*. London: Routledge.

Turner, F.J. 1986. *Social Work Treatment: Interlocking Theoretical Approaches*. New York: Free Press.

Internet Resources

Canadian Journal of Developmental Studies
www.cjds.ca/e/volume_26_special_issue/index.html

Canadian Women's Foundation
www.canadianwomen.org/EN/section12/1_12_1-intro.html

Canadian Women's Studies Association
www.yorku.ca/cwsaacef/research.html

Feminist Majority Foundation
www.feminist.org/research

Help Index via Domestic Violence and Incest Resource Centre
www.dvirc.org.au/HelpHub/HelpIndex.htm

Part Five | Finishing the Work

In this final part of the book, we explore the tasks involved in finishing the work with clients and the tasks of evaluation. This last chapter brings together ways of thinking about practice that are multi-dimensional and that balance a number of different tasks within the client–worker relationship. Finishing the work is the final dimension in the framework of human service work.

Part One—Framing the Relationship

- the purpose of human service work
- your value base, professional ethics, and regulatory guidelines in Canada
- your theoretical and factual knowledge.

Part Two—Forming the Relationship

- your use of self
- your organizational context
- your ongoing support and professional development needs
- meeting the people involved
- opening the communication
- active listening and working with silence
- listening empathically
- using self-disclosure.

Part Three—Focusing the Communication

- establishing the story
- forming an assessment
- goal-setting.

Part Four—Focusing the Intervention

- drawing on theoretical perspectives
- doing the work.

Part Five—Finishing the Work

- ending well
- evaluating the work.

15 | Finishing the Work

Learning Goals

- Understand how finishing the work is conceptualized.
- Describe the tasks of finishing the work with your clients.
- Analyze the challenges in finishing the work.
- Consider the ways of evaluating your work.
- Understand how an effective evaluation is conducted.

Thinking about Finishing the Work

In contrast to all the attention paid to *establishing* a good client–worker relationship, many texts pay surprisingly little notice to the process of ending it well. Your relationships with your clients will end for many reasons and in many ways, as they do in your other personal relationships. Ideally, a client–worker relationship ends when the work is done; that is, the goals agreed upon have been met and change has been able to occur or begin to occur. In some settings, the work ends because the contracted time period ends or the mandate to attend an agency is fulfilled. These endings can be anticipated and planned for as part of the overall contact.

Other endings occur in unplanned ways. The circumstances of the client or worker may change, such that the client relocates or the worker changes jobs. The relationship may end because of a poor engagement or rapport within a client–worker relationship. Clients may drift away because they are dissatisfied. In some extreme situations, the worker or client dies, through illness or suicide (Shulman, 1999: 221).

In other circumstances, your relationships with clients do not end as they are expected to. Some relationships continue over long periods of time and across different organizational contexts, particularly if you continue to work through a number of organizations within a particular field of practice. Some continue by virtue of you and the client living in the same small rural or remote community (Green, 2003; Taylor, 2004). In some instances, perhaps more controversially, client–worker relationships have become lifelong ones and are characterized more by friendship than by any professional stance (Crossley and McDonald, 1984; Stansfield, 2006). Organizational contact may not be the only context for contact, breaking down the often artificial boundary between the world of a client and his or her worker.

Focus on Practice

Different Endings?

Different endings are typified in the stories we have explored throughout this book. Remember Karen and Mark from Chapter 4?

Mark was in his thirties presenting with suicidal thoughts when he met with Karen for a first interview. His story related to the recent traumatic event of having watched as his small daughter ran across the road, was hit by a car, and dragged a long distance. His daughter had suffered multiple injuries including some brain damage, and he was wracked with guilt as well as by the trauma of witnessing the terrible event. He had left his family and the province feeling empty and hopeless.

And Nicole and Mrs B. from Chapter 6?

Mrs B. is the mother of an eight-year-old son diagnosed with a treatable but life-threatening condition. She talked with Nicole about the impact of the diagnosis on her, her son, and their family. Issues arose about subsequent contact over the following two-month period, until Nicole and Mrs B. were able to talk through their issues and expectations of each other. Mrs B. decided to continue seeing Nicole for assistance.

And David, and the client who became aggressive towards him, from Chapter 10?

David was working in a prison mental health unit, as a case manager for a client with an acquired brain injury and English as a second language. His client was charged with a serious offence and was distressed about a discussion he had with his lawyer regarding whether he should plead guilty or not guilty at court. Throughout their discussions, he became highly agitated, believing David was now accusing him of being 'guilty'. David's client started to become aggressive and threatening before storming off.

Each of these three circumstances could lead to very different endings of the worker–client relationships. In Karen's situation, through regular, supportive counselling, it was anticipated that a strong engagement and working alliance would be established over time. Karen's organization may have limits on the number of sessions she can work with Mark or she may be able to engage indefinitely with him. Each of these possibilities presents specific challenges as to how clearly an ending is contracted in their work together both at the beginning and along the way. The finishing process is likely to be a discussed, planned process in their work together.

In Nicole's working relationship she will continue to see Mrs B. throughout her child's treatment and, if the treatment is not successful, possibly through her child's dying and death. The relationship could be long-term or relatively short-term, depending on the unpredictable trajectory of the illness. Any sense of when this client–worker relationship may end could be difficult to establish.

In David's situation, the relationship did not end in this one scenario. The client returned and continued to be aggressive and threatening. David continued in his assignment as the case manager for this client until the client left the agency, but he was able to have little direct involvement with him. The relationship was crisis-driven and engagement remained tenuous. Given that a working relationship had been so difficult to establish, it was hard to think about how, why, and when it would finish. In fact, the relationship ended when the client left the agency. His client's needs were not met.

The Tasks of Finishing the Work

One of the challenges in understanding how to effectively finish the work is that there is little evaluation of what happens after it, for the very good reason that there is no further contact.

Endings, like beginnings, are important influences on the work that is achieved subsequently. We often consolidate skills and learning a considerable time beyond when we first acquire them. As Loader (1995: 38) states: 'Certainly, we "finish" counselling, we "end" a supervisory or a collegial relationship, but the development is within us, within the other, not confined to time.' Thompson (2002: 225–6) argues endings are important for a number of other reasons. First, he emphasizes the importance of working towards empowerment throughout the working relationship rather than allowing dependency, arguing that 'an unfocused, open-ended approach that loses track of ending can have the effect of undermining empowerment by increasing the possibilities for dependency developing' (ibid., 225). Second, workload management can become an issue, as the resources of any organization and worker are necessarily limited. Third, he emphasizes the need to end the labelling of someone as a client in order to end the possible stigma of the person's having been a client. Fourth, he emphasizes job satisfaction, because unfocused, uncontracted work can lead to feelings of frustration and little efficacy in working with someone. Fifth, he identifies the transfer of workers, in particular, but this can relate equally to clients moving on to other services or different workers.

What are the important tasks in ending a client–worker relationship? The following is a fictional conversation at the finishing stage of a group, as presented by Yalom (2005: 335–6), dramatizing many of the important tasks. Jakob, a group member, asks how the group facilitator is feeling, and he replies that he is tired but ready for the last group meeting that is to take place the following week.

Jakob: Okay to bring a ceremonial cake for our last meeting?
Julius: Absolutely, bring any kind of carrot cake you wish.

But there was to be no formal farewell meeting. The following day, Julius was stricken by severe headaches. Within a few hours he passed into a coma and died three days later.

This story accentuates four tasks that the worker should have in mind during a worker–client relationship about terminating that professional relationship:

- work towards a planned ending of an intervention
- manage an unplanned interruption to that ending
- participate in a ritual to mark the end of work together
- manage the evolving familiarity in the client–worker relationship.

Evidently in this example the shift from a worker-directed concern for the client has evolved to the point where the client can express concern for the worker, questioning him directly about his well-being.

Turner (2002: 205) suggests there are four major tasks associated with termination: '(1) deciding when to terminate, (2) dealing with feelings associated with ending, (3) generalizing and maintaining gains made, (4) evaluating accomplishment as service provided.' Three more essential tasks associated with termination may be asking for a **referral**, providing follow-up, and critically reflecting on the client's status and on the worker's intervention. Termination tasks differ depending on the nature and the context of the relationship: whether it has been a short-term or long-term relationship; a mandated or voluntary human service involvement; or a strong or a weak **attachment** bond.

Bitter (2009) cites two criteria for termination. 'Termination is based on effectively reaching a state in which problems have improved or have been eliminated. That is, there is no need to keep clients in therapy once they have reached the desired goals.' Segal (1991: 203) lists three criteria for termination: (a) a small but significant change has been made in the problem, (b) the change appears durable, and (c) the patient implies or states that she or he can handle things on her or his own.

Working towards a Planned Ending

At the early stage of establishing a client–worker relationship, it is important to be thinking about how the work may be ending. Will it end as a result of agency-imposed time limits, workload issues, the end of a mandate, or through the attainment of agreed-on goals? Planned endings can occur when the work is clearly contracted around any of these dimensions. It raises the question of timing of this discussion.

In some situations, you can talk with your client from the beginning of your contact as to how and when the work will end. The process of disengagement is a purpose of your work, just as the process of engagement is. From the standpoint of the client's rights and empowerment, the client should always be informed as to when and how an ending will occur. Not knowing about how and when a relationship may end creates unnecessary vulnerability, insecurity, and disempowerment, particularly when difficult or poor relationships are a prominent feature of a person's personal histories. In other situations, an ending may be planned only after the goals are more clearly established through mutual agreement. Initially, some sessions remain relatively unstructured as to the overall time frame; once the extent of work both parties wish to engage in becomes more evident the length of the client–worker relationship can be estimated. In still other situations, mentioning the inevitable ending too early in the relationship may jeopardize engagement. The early phases of most work and contact may need to focus more on building a strong engagement and rapport.

Understanding endings involves reflecting on what the intended outcomes of the work together were. For example:

- What kind of change was being worked towards and how would you know if it had been achieved?
- What are the assumptions about recovery, adaptation, or efficacy that both you and your clients have being working with?

Christine Simpson, whose daughter had been murdered and who described her relationship with her grief worker John to a newspaper reporter (Chapter 4; Stansfield, 2006: 16), saw the end of the work as relating to the following outcome: 'I still have my pain, and my anger, but I am also very happy with my life as it is.' Working towards finishing the work, therefore, involves processes of thinking about it and talking about it, ideally, well before the ending arrives. Endings mean different things for different people, depending on their age and stage, their past experiences of ending relationships, and what the significance of the work has been for them. Given that bad endings in human relationships are such a major contributor to human distress and suffering, ending a good working relationship well is one way of positively modelling the good relationship experience, even if the relationship has been a mandated one.

With planned endings, you can talk over what will be involved and what it might mean for the client and for you. Future contact and referral options can also be discussed, as described later in this chapter.

'Theorizing' Endings

How we think about endings influences what can and should happen at this point in the worker–client relationship. Each of the theoretical perspectives considered earlier has a different emphasis on the process of ending the work and whether the tasks discussed above are important. Bitter (2009: 199) notes that 'improvement in the form of movement forward is more than an acceptable end.'

Psychodynamic approaches have dominated understandings of the termination process, because of the centrality of the relationship to the goals of the work. In many discussions of the ending of a client–worker relationship or a therapeutic group, grief and sadness are identified as the dominant emotions in the finishing process. Perhaps in the intensity of therapeutic work, this reasonably can be anticipated. The goal of psychodynamic work is often the establishment or reparation of secure attachments or good inner objects, thus the focus is on ending well, having worked through both past and present feelings of loss and abandonment. Termination is a carefully planned and discussed stage of work (Walsh, 2006: 43–4).

Consistent with the psychodynamic approach, authors such as Shulman argue that **denial** is the first stage of the ending process. He proposes that there is an inevitable change in the engagement in the relationship prior to its ending, and that there may be both direct and indirect anger. Using grief theory, ending is seen as a process of mourning, 'acknowledging the client's ending feelings and sharing the worker's ending feelings' (Shulman, 1999: 209).

Sorrow and grief are not always the condition of the client, however, as it can be a time of realizing that change has been achieved and that a new phase is beginning. For many other people, the end of a client–worker relationship can be an incentive to achieve goals. The attainment of goals may mean that the relationship can end because conditions of a court order, for example, have been met. Ending can be about a client's regaining a sense of control over his or her own life, free from the scrutiny of a worker (Trotter, 2006).

Task-centred approaches are based on the premise that ending work together is positive because it signals empowerment and achievement. As Marsh and Doel (2005: 118) state: 'there is the effect which we all experience as we move towards a deadline . . . in which our mind concentrates on the coming event with increasing strength. A time limit is, therefore, motivating.'

Endings signify the achievement of clearly contracted work and the empowerment of the client to resume independent functioning. Short-term work is seen to be all that is required so that people can resume connections or establish new connections with informal social networks and their own interior resources.

Providing Feedback and Reviewing Goals

Planned endings provide an opportunity for 'systematically adding up the experience' (Shulman, 1999: 213) and identifying areas for future work if needed (ibid., 215). Where engaging in the client–worker relationship opens up the story, ending closes off and sums up the story, identifying what has been addressed and achieved.

Clearly, direct conversations with people about what has been helpful and unhelpful will provide very useful feedback about how circumstances have changed and what has been effective in bringing that about. Marsh and Doel (2005: 80) suggest a series of questions to ask in a final session as part of this review. They suggest that questions should focus on: the beginning; the problem, whether it was the correct one and whether it has changed; the agreement or the goals; how things have changed in general; and the expectations for the future.

Your review could include the following types of questions:

- Why do you think I became involved with you?
- Do you think we have worked on the right issue?
- How has the situation changed for you?
- How has the situation changed others?
- Do you think we achieved what we set out to achieve?
- What strengths can you now rely upon? How will you continue to apply these strengths?
- Do you think we could have done things differently?
- What questions haven't I asked?
- Have we explored everything?

- How near to your goals are you now?
- What do you think will happen in the future in relation to these issues? (Adapted from Marsh and Doel, 2005)

Remember the stages of change model (Chapter 1), which describes the phases of change management: pre-contemplation, contemplation, action, maintenance, and relapse.

The termination review provides an important opportunity to look at the ways in which the client will sustain the gains beyond the contact period. Reviewing what she or he will now do differently emphasizes the strengths and capacities that have been acquired. In being aware of the stages of change model, you can also talk through the possibilities of encountering future difficulties and how they may be managed. Identifying your availability for future contact is also critical if this is a possibility. This is discussed later in this chapter.

In any feedback and review process, social desirability tendencies influence a lot of the feedback we give. That is, we often give positive feedback to maintain relationships rather than provide more accurate and potentially hurtful feedback. Below, Yalom (2005: 28) suggests one form of feedback from a client who was asked to comment as to whether his worker had been effective.

Focus on Practice

Consumer Feedback

Client: [E]ventually I realized you didn't know how to help me and I lost faith in our work together. I recall that you spent inordinate amounts of time exploring my relationships—with others and especially with you. That never made sense to me. It didn't then. It still doesn't.

1. How would you feel and what would you do if your client provided this feedback to you?
2. What would you do in your interactions with your clients to try to ensure that they could talk these issues through earlier?
3. What practice skills do you need to improve?

In asking for feedback, we need to be prepared to hear both positive and negative remarks. If we are serious about a consumer perspective, we need to take all feedback on board and talk it through with the people concerned. We need to talk about these issues in supervision and critically reflect on what has occurred in specific situations. Other ways of receiving feedback include client satisfaction surveys, used in many organizations, or feedback interviews with other staff members such as managers or supervisors. An anonymous survey gives clients the option of providing critical feedback without fear of any reprisals in terms of access to the agency in the future or other personal outcomes. An opportunity to talk with a supervisor can enable clients to talk about concerns they may have about their experiences with you as a worker.

Remember the process of giving and receiving feedback, outlined in Chapter 10.

Managing an Unplanned Ending

Yalom's example of a worker's sudden death is of an interruption to a planned group ending. This can occur in practice, with circumstances equally for the client or for the worker interfering with a planned ending. In many other instances, however, the work does not finish in a planned way at all. It ends because the client departs, because of a change in the client's circumstances and/or transient circumstances, or because there is no other way to address worker ineffectiveness. Turner (2002) notes that some unplanned endings may be due to clients intentionally avoiding the ending process, due to reactions from significant others, because of conflicts, because the client is happy with the improvements but does not tell the worker, or due to factors that the client cannot control, such as a change in work schedule. Unplanned endings can be disconcerting—you can be left wondering what happened. Some strategies you can use at these times include:

- critically reflecting on your work with the client and what issues may have been influencing the decision to not return
- trying to follow up through telephone contact with your client to discuss what has happened
- sending a letter that leaves the door open for future contact, if this is possible
- fulfilling your reporting requirements in terms of the organization and duty of care to the client.

In some organizations, clients are not informed when a worker departs. Even if contact is intermittent—for example, a client comes to the hospital only twice a year for an appointment—you may want to consider whether informing clients of your departure is desirable and possible. Unplanned endings can leave people feeling unsettled, angry, distressed, or unclear about what has occurred. In some situations, this outcome is preventable and worth working towards preventing.

Potential factors in unplanned termination specific to group work are described by Turner (2002: 207) as including:

1. Feeling out of place in the group.
2. Inability to form intimate relationships with others.
3. Fear of developing problems similar to those of other group members.
4. Inability to share with group members.
5. Subgrouping problems (scapegoating, etc.).

Participating in Ending Rituals

Yalom's fictional group ends with the discussion of the making of a ceremonial cake. This sharing of food is not an uncommon gesture in the finishing of work together. Rituals in one-to-one work are similarly important. Rituals provide an opportunity to acknowledge beyond words what is taking place and what has taken place.

An ending ritual may be as simple as the review discussion outlined above, in which the ritual of closing is undertaken. Other rituals that can emerge in the ending of work together include the following:

- Creative reminders of the work can be developed, such as photos, scrapbooks, memory cards, journals, or a summary document of what has been achieved. This ensures the recognition of **continuing bonds**; that is, that a relationship can continue beyond the direct contact of your work in other forms such as good memories.
- Sharing food—particularly cross-culturally—is an important way of symbolically shifting the power imbalance to a shared power balance.
- Gratitude can be expressed through letters or cards.
- The worker/client can become involved in sharing significant milestones of the other's experience, such as attending a graduation or the funeral of a family member.
- Token gifts can be exchanged.

Each one of these gestures is a way of expressing sharing and gratitude, and symbols can remain lifelong reminders of important work that has been done together. Workers and organizations approach these gestures differently, and important choices are to be made about whether they are appropriate and empowering gestures to be supported.

Managing the Evolving Familiarity

In Yalom's group, concern is expressed by a group member towards the worker and the worker responds. This depicts a different direction of concern and attention within the client–worker relationship. Surprisingly little is written about the shifts that occur in client–worker relationships over time. Rural workers acknowledge the ongoing basis of relationship (Green, 2003; Green, Gregory, and Mason, 2006) and connection, but within the urban context it is rarely noted. It is important to emphasize the inevitable familiarity that emerges in the context of a client–worker relationship. In many instances, this continuity can lead to a curiosity and concern with someone's well-being to the point where ending the work does not occur when it perhaps should. That workers become attached to clients (and vice versa) for a variety of different reasons is inevitable, but it remains one of the less-discussed issues in practice.

The literature relating to self-disclosure we explored earlier in some ways addresses the issues of trust and vulnerability within relationships. The psychodynamic literature talks about relationship in terms of transference and counter-transference. Fiction and movies, such as *Reign Over Me* (2007) and *The Blind Side* (2009), often depict relationships that would be regarded as gross enmeshment and a violation of professional boundaries, as is true, too, in older films—*The Prince of Tides* (1991), *Good Will Hunting* (1997)—where a psychiatrist or psychologist is a central figure. They demonstrate, however, that relationships are complex and cannot be neatly compartmentalized as professional or personal.

Indigenous and cross-cultural models have increasingly challenged Western models of practice for their emphasis on the artificial boundaries between the personal and the professional. Western models have been based on a concern about the power differential and the potential disempowerment and exploitation that can emerge within the client–worker relationship, and thus authenticity and a growing trust and familiarity over time have tended to be minimized as key agents of change. Using supervision to address these issues of boundaries and appropriateness is vital so that work ends when and how it should.

Making a Referral

In many situations, a referral for ongoing or different services may be required. For example, the work may not be complete but circumstances for the worker or client may have changed. Alternatively, the worker and/or the client may realize that goals cannot be achieved within this setting and that working with someone else may be more appropriate. Ending one client–worker relationship may be about making transitions to 'new experiences and support systems' (Shulman, 1999: 218). In all of these situations, a process of referral is needed.

Referral processes have been found to be most successful when the following dimensions are attended to:

- discussion of the reason for the referral
- discussion of the process of referral
- a joint meeting with the current and new worker, if appropriate, to enable the goals to be established for continuing work
- consent of the client to speak with another worker
- the writing of reports as required.

Providing Follow-Up and Keeping the Door Open

As many of the examples in this chapter have highlighted, not all human service work occurs in the context of neat, structured sessions, nor as unique occasions. Talking about the possibility of future contact is an important step, if this contact is possible within the resource context. This involves being clear about whether the work has definitely ended, that no more contact is possible for whatever reason, or whether work can be recontracted at a later date should other issues arise.

Some of the key reflections within this process include:

- Is the client empowered to access services when and how needed? For example, can he or she see someone else if that is the preference? Can the client continue talking with you within the context of a new 'episode of care', as many organizations term it?
- How does the client reinitiate contact?
- Are there other ways in which the client can stay connected with the organization, if that is her or his wish? Many organizations have extensive volunteer networks that enable clients of the service to contribute to the organization and to others experiencing similar issues. This turn-around can be an important marker of recovery and adaptation (Herman, 1992).

In some situations, a formal follow-up after a specified time interval is part of the organization's practice. For example, where a death has occurred, some hospital workers will follow up at the time of the anniversary of the death, or invite people back to a memorial service. In some other instances, the possibility of follow-up is more complex. For example, many clients will not inform other family members that they have been in contact with services, so any attempt at reconnecting may breach confidentiality for that person.

Follow-up can provide a beneficial opportunity for the client to reflect on the intervention experiences and possible changes, and give feedback about the process. Clients can evaluate the longer-term effects of the work, as they reappraise what they have experienced since the intervention and the efficacy of the intervention. For the worker, follow-up gives some insight into the ongoing changes people have made and satisfies professional curiosity as to how things have progressed for someone. Below, a worker describes the experience of meeting a client a decade after their initial contact.

Focus on Practice

Connecting Again

I did not expect to bump into my client again. It was in another setting, where neither of us was in a work role. I was really surprised that after 10 years I still remembered so much of her situation and of the work we did together. For me, it was overwhelming to see how well she was doing and all that she had dealt with. I saw that she had survived so much. I am not sure what it was like for her to talk with me again. I think I gave her a fright, but I think she was also pleased to reconnect and to tell me about what she was now doing. We so rarely connect with people down the track and find out how they are doing.

1. What would you do in this situation?
2. What would you be curious about?
3. What do you need to keep in mind when engaging in the conversation?

The important question to ask is: Who is the follow-up for? Follow-up must first and foremost be for the benefit of the client.

Critical Reflection and Evaluation

Evaluating your work occurs in this final phase of contact in two important ways. The first is evaluating the work with the client to review his or her perceptions of what has occurred and the efficacy of that work, as we discussed above. The second is your own **evaluation** of your work in the context of all of your practice. This occurs, as Chapter 5 explored extensively, through your own critical self-reflection and your supervision.

Some key dimensions in your evaluation include, first, client perspectives, as discussed above. Second, other workers' perspectives and key stakeholders' perspectives are important. Supervision, peer discussions, and annual performance appraisals provide opportunities for you to receive feedback about your practice.

Reviewing the evidence base of your practice (Lewis, 2002) is critical, also. Supervision and your own professional development opportunities provide instances for reviewing the various sources of information you rely on. As Morris (2006: xxxiii) states in relation to social workers, they:

> need to know what interventions and services improve a client's functioning, a community worker needs to know how her or his community can work together to solve its problems and prevent other community problems, and the administrator/policy maker often just needs to know who her or his client community is.

A commitment to learning and self-reflection is essential for effective human service work.

Turner (2002: 341–2) expresses the importance of culturally competent evaluation of your work. 'Developing culturally appropriate services to diverse clients is a challenge. Demographic trends in Canadian society, such as immigration patterns and a large aging population base, mean an interesting proportion of the clients in social services, health, and mental health agencies will present social workers with challenging practice issues.' Turner suggests three main principles. The first, pertaining to attitudes and beliefs, focuses on respecting the client and the client's world view, respecting practice that is culturally important, valuing diversity, and being aware of our own assumptions and biases.

The second principle pertains to knowledge, which includes: understanding potential conflict of cultural values in practice; awareness of barriers that impede access to services for culturally diverse populations; accounting for cultural language biases; assessing information about cultural stories, family structures, natural helpers, community characteristics, experiences of discrimination, and institutional discriminatory practices; and understanding both individual and collective impacts, and creating evaluation measures that address both levels.

The third principle pertains to skills: engaging both verbal and non-verbal helping responses; assessing the impact of discrimination on the current issues; consulting a professional or person significant to the particular culture; providing service in the preferred language of the client; utilizing interpreters; adapting practice intervention; and working to eliminate clinical and social practices that are biased, prejudged, or discriminatory.

Strengths, Optimism, and Communication

While we continue to know more about experiences of change and adaptation, and the role of intervention in these experiences, much remains unknown and open to question and research. Throughout this text, we have explored many of those issues, and hope you are left with many more questions as you begin your practice. Working with people is a life-changing experience—whether that work occurs in the classroom, in the counselling room, in the corridors of a hospital, in people's homes, or in our communities.

People's lives and opportunities can change for the better as a result of interventions and resources. Oppression and adversity can be alleviated by the concerted efforts of individuals, groups, and communities. Human strength, resilience, and optimism are not only traits we encourage in the people with whom we work; they are traits we need to foster and keep alive within ourselves as workers (Mancini and Bonanno, 2006). Throughout this book, we have explored some of the ways in which those efforts can be enhanced by effective communication skills. You have been encouraged to try these skills and critically reflect on how they may be useful tools for your applied practice.

Chapter Summary

In this final chapter, we have explored how your work with people can end in planned and unplanned ways. Some of the meanings of endings have been considered, as have the skills required in managing the transition through to the end of the work together. Evaluating your work, both with the client directly and indirectly in your own supervision and reflection, has been emphasized as a critical dimension of your practice.

Questions for Analysis

1. What have you learned from this chapter about:
    - planned endings to client–worker relationships?
    - unplanned endings to these relationships?
    - the tasks of termination?
    - evaluating your practice?

2. What has been your experience of ending relationships, both professional and personal?

3. How have you felt about these various endings?

4. How will you receive feedback if the client is not happy with the work and ends it early? How may you apply the feedback?

5. What do you think are the most important dimensions of finishing the work?

6. How will you improve or add to your practice skills, based on your evaluation of your practice, to ensure continued professional development?

Recommended Readings

Klass, D., P. Silverman, and S. Nickman. 1996. *Continuing Bonds: New Understandings of Grief.* Washington: Taylor and Francis.

O'Hara, A., and Z. Weber, eds. 2006. *Skills for Human Service Practice: Working with Individuals, Groups, and Communities.* South Melbourne: Oxford University Press.

Payne, M. 2005. *Modern Social Work Theory.* Chicago: Lyceum Books.

Turner, F.J. 1986. *Social Work Treatment: Interlocking Theoretical Approaches.* New York: Free Press.

Internet Resources

Canadian Counselling and Psychotherapy Association
www.ccacc.ca/en/aboutus/associations

InfoXchange: Technology for Social Justice
www.infoxchange.net.au

Statistics Canada—Investigating Social Justice Issues
www.statcan.gc.ca/edu/edu05_0022-eng.htm

Appendix

CASW Contact Information

As a federation of nine provincial and one territorial social work organizations, the Canadian Association of Social Workers (CASW) provides a national leadership role in strengthening and advancing the social work profession in Canada. Canadian Association of Social Workers: www.casw-acts.ca

British Columbia Association of Social Workers
Suite 402, 1755 West Broadway
Vancouver, BC V6J 4S5
Tel: (604) 730–9111 1–800–665–4747 (BC residents only)
Fax: (604) 730–9112
E-mail: bcasw@bcasw.org
Website: www.bcasw.org
Executive Director: Ms Linda Korbin

Alberta College of Social Workers
#550, 10707 100 Avenue NW
Edmonton, AB T5J 3M1
Tel: (780) 421-1167 1-800-661-3089 (Alberta residents only)
Fax: (780) 421–1168
E-mail: acsw@acsw.ab.ca
Website: www.acsw.ab.ca
Executive Director & Registrar: Mr Rod Adachi
E-mail: acswexd@acsw.ab.ca
Associate Registrar: Ms Alison MacDonald
E-mail: acswreg@acsw.ab.ca
Professional Affairs Coordinator: Ms Lori Sigurdson
E-mail: lsigurdson@acsw.ab.ca

Saskatchewan Association of Social Workers
2110 Lorne St.
Regina, SK S4P 2M5
Tel: (306) 545–1922
Fax: (306) 545–1895

Manitoba Association of Social Workers/
Manitoba Institute of Registered Social Workers
Unit 101-2033 Portage Ave.
Winnipeg, MB R3J 0K8
Tel: (204) 888–9477
Fax: (204) 831–6359
E-mail: masw@mts.net
Website: www.maswmirsw.ca
Executive Director and Registrar: Ms Miriam Browne

Ontario Association of Social Workers
410 Jarvis St.
Toronto, ON M4Y 2G6
Tel: (416) 923–4848
Fax: (416) 923–5279
E-mail: info@oasw.org
Website: www.oasw.org
Executive Director: Ms Joan MacKenzie-Davies

New Brunswick Association of Social Workers
P.O. Box 1533, Postal Station A
Fredericton, NB E3B 5G2
Tel: (506) 459–5595
Fax: (506) 457–1421
E-mail: nbasw@nbasw-atsnb.ca
Website: www.nbasw-atsnb.ca
Executive Director: Mr Miguel LeBlanc
E-mail: mleblanc@nbasw-atsnb.ca
Registrar: Ms Suzanne McKenna
E-mail: smckenna@nbasw-atsnb.ca
Courier: NBASW
403 Regent Street, Suite 100
Fredericton, NB E3B 3X6

Nova Scotia Association of Social Workers
1891 Brunswick St., Suite 106
Halifax, NS B3J 2G8
Tel: (902) 429–7799
Fax: (902) 429–7650
E-mail: nsasw@nsasw.org
Website: www.nsasw.org
Executive Director: Mr Robert R. Shepherd
Registrar: Ms Joyce Halpern

Newfoundland and Labrador Association of Social Workers
P.O. Box 39039
St John's, NL A1E 5Y7
Tel: (709) 753–0200
Fax: (709) 753–0120
E-mail: info@nlasw.ca
Website: www.nlasw.ca
Executive Director & Registrar: Ms Lisa Crockwell
E-mail: lcrockwell@nlasw.ca
Courier: 177 Hamlyn Rd
St John's, NL A1E 5Z5

Prince Edward Island Association of Social Workers
81 Prince Street
Charlottetown, PE C1A 4R3
Tel: (902) 368–7337
Fax: (902) 368–7080
E-mail: vrc@eastlink.ca
President: Ms Kelly MacWilliams

The Association of Social Workers of Northern Canada (ASWNC)
c/o Geri Elkin
Box 2963
Yellowknife, NT X1A 2R2
Tel: (867) 920–4479
Fax:(867) 669–7964
E-mail: ed@socialworknorth.com
Website: www.socialworknorth.com

The Eight Steps in Ethical Decision-Making

'The model uses six "fundamental principles" for evaluating consequences of options for action and combines actions of the absolutist use of principles and the relativist emphasis on context and deliberation about consequences of actions' (Miller, 2007: 35).

Step 1: Identifying the problem or dilemma during information-gathering and consultation about the nature of the problem.

Step 2: Identifying potential issues involved in the problem in terms of rights, responsibilities, and welfare of all involved.

Step 3: Reviewing relevant codes of ethics to see if and how they apply.

Step 4: Reviewing applicable laws and regulations.

Step 5: Consulting to get other perspectives about the problem.

Step 6: Considering courses of action.

Step 7: Evaluating consequences of various courses of action using the principle framework.

Step 8: Deciding on the best course of action.

Source: Pamela Miller, Ethical Decision-Making in Social Work and Counseling: A Problem/Inquiry-based Approach. *(Toronto, Ont.: Thompson/Nelson, 2007).*

Tracking Harms's Model of Decision-Making

'The focus of this model is primarily on the goals and motivations of the participants. For each option potential obstacles for achieving are calculated within this context of goals and strategies with the ultimate objective of choosing options that minimize harm' (Miller, 2007: 34).

Step 1: Construct arguments that justify the acts or omissions of participants to try to understand their motivation for their actions.

Step 2: Determine the actual goals of the participants and the means by which they thought they would achieve those goals. Determine what their goals ought to be and what means would be best for achieving those goals.

Step 3: Identify the harm of alternative courses of action and identify to whom the harm would occur, as well as the kind and degree of harm.

Step 4: Make a judgement about what is the best outcome and what will minimize harm.

Step 5: Determine how the outcome should be achieved in a way that will produce more good than harm.

Source: Pamela Miller, Ethical Decision-Making in Social Work and Counseling: A Problem/Inquiry-based Approach. *Toronto: Thompson/Nelson, 2007).*

Holmes and Rahe Social Readjustment Scale

This Social Readjustment Rating Scale was created by Thomas Holmes and Richard Rahe, University of Washington School of Medicine, to provide a standardized measure of the impact of a wide range of common stressors: www.emotionalcompetency.com/srrs.htm.

Life Events (Past Year)	Score
Death of spouse	100
Divorce	73
Marital separation from mate	65
Detention in jail, other institution	63
Death of a close family member	63
Major personal injury or illness	53
Marriage	50
Fired from work	47
Marital reconciliation	45
Retirement	45
Major change in the health or behavior of a family member	44
Pregnancy	40
Sexual difficulties	39
Gaining a new family member through birth, adoption, elder	39
Major business re-adjustment (i.e., reorganization, bankruptcy)	39
Major change in financial status	38
Death of close friend	37
Change to different line of work	36
Major change in the number of arguments with spouse	35
Taking out a mortgage or loan for a major purchase	31
Foreclosure on a mortgage or loan	30
Major change in responsibilities at work	29
Son or daughter leaving home (i.e., marriage, attending university)	29
Trouble with in-laws	29
Outstanding personal achievement	28
Spouse beginning or ceasing to work outside the home	26
Beginning or ceasing formal schooling	26
Major change in living conditions	25
Revision of personal habits (dress, manners, associations, etc.)	24
Trouble with supervisor	23
Major change in working hours or conditions	20
Change in residence	20
Change to a new school	20
Major change in usual type and/or amount of recreation	19
Major change in religious activities (a lot more or less than usual)	19
Major change in social activities	18
Taking out a loan (i.e., for a car, TV, freezer, etc.)	17

Life Events (Past Year)	Score
Major change in sleeping habits	16
Major change in the number of family get-togethers	15
Major change in eating habits	15
Holiday	13
Christmas season	12
Minor violations of the law (i.e., traffic tickets, etc.)	11
Total	......

Scoring for the Holmes-Rahe Social Readjustment Scale:
Less than 150 life change units = 30 per cent chance of developing a stress-related illness;
150–299 life change units = 50 per cent chance of illness; over 300 life change units = 80 per cent
chance of illness.

*Source: T.H. Holmes and R.H. Rahe, 'The social readjustment rating scale', Journal of Psychosomatic Research 11,
2 (1967): 213–21.*

Drug Alcohol Addiction Abuse Assessment

The following drug alcohol assessment was created to help determine if you or a loved has
a problem with alcohol and/or drugs. If you answer 'yes' to three or more of the below
questions, then there is a chance that you or a loved one might have a problem. Please call
us right away to get help. We offer a solution that works. Recovery is an Option.

1. Do you have unstoppable cravings for drugs or alcohol?
2. While under the influence have you ever hurt yourself or others?
3. If you have caused harm to people, have you ever promised not to do it again but
   been unable to keep the promise?
4. Have people ever made comments about your drug or alcohol use?
5. Does your drinking or using negatively affect the way you perform at work or at
   school?
6. Do you drink or use drugs to numb your feelings?
7. Do you drink or use drugs because you feel insecure or self-conscious about
   yourself?
8. Have you been in trouble with the law or any other authority because of the
   amount you drink or use?
9. Have you tried to stop using drugs or drinking but found that you are unable?
10. Have you lost or damaged relationships because of the way you use drugs and drink?
11. Have you started to drink or use drugs alone because you are ashamed or be-
    cause you do not want to share what you have with others?
12. Do you feel the desire to constantly be drunk or high?
13. Have you ever been arrested for a DUI, DWI, or any drug-related offense?

14. Are you unable to have good time with people at places such as parties or clubs if you are not under the influence of drugs or alcohol?

15. Have you ever wakened the next morning after drinking or using and been unable to remember what happened the night before?

16. Do you ever tell yourself you will just have one or two drinks but find you have several more than you planned?

17. Are the people you prefer to hang out with people who use drugs and drink the way you do?

18. Have you ever stayed drunk or high for multiple days at a time?

19. Do you find that you are defensive about what people say concerning your drinking and drug use?

20. If so, do you drink and use more because they made you upset?

Source: www.gulfcoastrecovery.org/assessment.htm

First Nations Code of Ethics

The following is a *Traditional Code of Ethics* formulated by the Assembly of Manitoba Chiefs Youth Secretariat, which summarizes the most important values and teachings that are considered universal to all nations.

1. Each morning upon rising, and each evening before sleeping, give thanks for the life within you and for all life, for good things the Creator has given you and others and for the opportunity to grow a little more each day. Consider your thoughts and actions of the past day and seek for the courage to be a better person. Seek for the things that will benefit everyone.

2. Respect means to feel or show honour or esteem for someone or something; consider the well-being of, or treat someone or something with deference or courtesy. Showing respect is the basic law of life.

   • Treat every person, from the tiniest child to the oldest Elder, with respect at all times.
   • Special respect should be given to Elders, parents, teachers, and community leaders.
   • No person should be made to feel 'put down' by you—avoid hurting others' hearts as you would a deadly poison.
   • Touch nothing that belongs to someone else (especially sacred objects) without permission, or with an understanding between you.
   • Respect the privacy of every person. Never intrude in a person's quiet moments or personal space.
   • Never walk between or interrupt people who are conversing.
   • Speak in a soft voice, especially when you are in the presence of Elders, strangers, or others to whom special respect is due.

- Do not speak unless invited to do so at gatherings where Elders are present except to ask what is expected of you, should you be in doubt.
- Never speak about others in a negative way, whether they are present or not.
- Treat the earth and all her aspects as your mother. Show deep respect to the mineral, plant, and animal worlds. Do nothing to pollute the air or the soil. If others would destroy our mother, rise up with wisdom to defend her.
- Show deep respect for the beliefs and religions of others.
- Listen with courtesy to what others say, even if you feel what they are saying is worthless. Listen with your heart.

3.   Respect the wisdom of people in council. Once you give an idea to the council or a meeting, it no longer belongs to you—it belongs to the people. Respect demands that you listen intently to the ideas of others in council and that you should not insist that your ideas prevail. Indeed, you should freely support the ideas of others if they are true and good, even if those ideas are quite different from the ones you contributed. The clash of ideas brings forth the spark of truth.

4.   Be truthful at all times and under all conditions.

5.   Always treat your guests with honour and consideration. Give your best food, your best blankets, the best part of your house and your best service to your guests.

6.   The hurt of one is the hurt of all; the honour of one is the honour of all.

7.   Receive strangers and outsiders with a loving heart and as members of the human family.

8.   All the races and nations in the world are like the different coloured flowers of one meadow. All are beautiful as children of the Creator and they all must be respected.

9.   To serve others, to be of some use to family, community, nation or the world is one of the purposes for which human beings have been created. Do not fill yourself with your own affairs and forget your most important task. True happiness comes only to those who dedicate their lives to the service of others.

10. Observe moderation and balance in all things.

11. Know those things that lead to your well-being and those things that lead to your destruction.

12. Listen to and follow the guidance given to your heart. Expect guidance to come in many forms; in prayer, in dreams, in times of quiet solitude and the words and deeds of wise Elders and friends.

Source: www.manitobachiefs.com/kwyi/ethics.html

Contact: Fred Shore, Office of University Accessibility, 474–6084; fred_shore@umanitoba.ca

Kali Storm, Aboriginal Student Centre 474–8850

Aboriginal Information Series Office of University Accessibility August 2006, Number 2 kali_storm@umanitoba.ca

Core Social Work Values and Principles

The Canadian Association of Social Workers (CASW) *Code of Ethics* sets forth values and principles to guide social workers' professional conduct. A code of ethics cannot guarantee ethical behaviour. Ethical behaviour comes from a social worker's individual commitment to engage in ethical practice. Both the spirit and the letter of this *Code of Ethics* will guide social workers as they act in good faith and with a genuine desire to make sound judgements.

Social workers uphold the following core social work values:

Value 1: Respect for Inherent Dignity and Worth of Persons
- Social workers respect the unique worth and inherent dignity of all people and uphold human rights.
- Social workers uphold each person's right to self-determination, consistent with that person's capacity and with the rights of others.
- Social workers respect the diversity among individuals in Canadian society and the right of individuals to their unique beliefs consistent with the rights of others.
- Social workers respect the client's right to make choices based on voluntary, informed consent.

Value 2: Pursuit of Social Justice
- Social workers uphold the right of people to have access to resources to meet basic human needs.
- Social workers advocate for fair and equitable access to public services and benefits. .
- Social workers advocate for equal treatment and protection under the law and challenge injustices, especially injustices that affect the vulnerable and disadvantaged.
- Social workers promote social development and environmental management in the interests of all people.

Value 3: Service to Humanity
- Social workers place the needs of others above self-interest when acting in a professional capacity.
- Social workers strive to use the power and authority vested in them as professionals in responsible ways that serve the needs of clients and the promotion of social justice.
- Social workers promote individual development and pursuit of individual goals, as well as the development of a just society.
- Social workers use their knowledge and skills in bringing about fair resolutions to conflict and in assisting those affected by conflict.

Value 4: Integrity of Professional Practice
- Social workers demonstrate and promote the qualities of honesty, reliability, impartiality, and diligence in their professional practice.

- Social workers demonstrate adherence to the values and ethical principles of the profession and promote respect for the profession's values and principles in organizations where they work or with which they have a professional affiliation.
- Social workers establish appropriate boundaries in relationships with clients and ensure that the relationship serves the needs of clients.
- Social workers value openness and transparency in professional practice and avoid relationships where their integrity or impartiality may be compromised, ensuring that, should a conflict of interest be unavoidable, the nature of the conflict is fully disclosed.

Value 5: Confidentiality in Professional Practice

- Social workers respect the importance of the trust and confidence placed in the professional relationship by clients and members of the public.
- Social workers respect the client's right to confidentiality of information shared in a professional context.
- Social workers only disclose confidential information with the informed consent of the client or permission of client's legal representative.
- Social workers may break confidentiality and communicate client information without permission when required or permitted by relevant laws, court order, or this *Code*.
- Social workers demonstrate transparency with respect to limits to confidentiality that apply to their professional practice by clearly communicating these limitations to clients early in their relationship.

Value 6: Competence in Professional Practice

- Social workers uphold the right of clients to be offered the highest quality service possible.
- Social workers strive to maintain and increase their professional knowledge and skill.
- Social workers demonstrate due care for client's interests and safety by limiting professional practice to areas of demonstrated competence.
- Social workers contribute to the ongoing development of the profession and its ability to serve humanity, where possible, by participating in the development of current and future social workers and the development of new professional knowledge.
- Social workers who engage in research minimize risks to participants, ensure informed consent, maintain confidentiality and accurately report the results of their studies.

Source: Canadian Association of Social Workers (CASW) Code of Ethics © 2005, www.casw-acts.ca

Additional Resources

Addictions Resources

Northwest Territories Health and Social Services: www.hlthss.gov.nt.ca/english/
publications/manuals.asp
Canadian Centre on Substance Abuse: www.ccsa.ca
Canadian Society of Addiction Medicine: www.csam.org
Health Canada–Canada Drug Strategy: www.hc-sc.gc.ca/hecs-sesc/cds/splash.htm

Seniors and Aging

Alzheimer Society of Canada: www.alzheimer.ca/english/resources/weblinks.htm
BC Network for Aging Research: www.aginghealthresearch.ca
BC Psychogeriatric Association: www.bcpga.bc.ca
Home and Community Care Research Network: www.hccrn.com
Seniors Policy Lens: www.seniorspolicylens.ca

Mental Health

CAMH—Centre for Addiction and Mental Health: www.camh.net
Canadian Association for Suicide Prevention: www.suicideprevention.ca
Canadian Network for Mood and Anxiety Treatment: www.canmat.org/cme/
interviews/inter_cognitive.html
Mood Disorders Society: www.mooddisorderscanada.ca

Counselling

Canadian Association for Psychodynamic Therapy: www.psychodynamiccanada.org
Canadian Counselling and Psychotherapy Association: www.ccacc.ca
Canadian Group Psychotherapy Association: http://cgpa.ca
Canadian Society for Spirituality and Social Work (CSSSW) w3.stu.ca/stu/sites/
spirituality/index.html
Solution-Focused Brief Therapy Association: www.sfbta.org
The Canadian Art Therapy Association: www.catainfo.ca
The Canadian Association for Child Play Therapy: www.cacpt.com

Miscellaneous

Canadian Cancer Society: www.cancer.ca
Canadian Diabetes Association: www.diabetes.ca
Canadian Health Network www.canadian-health-network.ca/ Links with services
providers, national organizations and resources
Canadian National Institute for the Blind: www.cnib.ca
Canadian Virtual Hospice: www.virtualhospice.ca/en_US/Main+Site+Navigation/
Home.aspx
Department of Justice: The Development of the Brief Spousal Assault Form for the
Evaluation of Risk (B-SAFER): A Tool for Criminal Justice Professionals: www.justice.
gc.ca/eng/pi/rs/rep-rap/2005/rr05_fv1-rr05_vf1/d1.html

Epidemic and Pandemic Alert response: www.who.int/csr/disease/avian_influenza/phase/en/index.html

Family Care Centre: Parenting Resources, University of Toronto: www.familycare.utoronto.ca/caring_children/pr.html

Lakehead University Diversity and Anti Racism Links: aboriginalinitiatives.lakeheadu.ca/?display=page&pageid=77#LGBTQ

Northern FIRE: www.unbc.ca/northernfire

Schizophrenia Society of Canada: www.schizophrenia.ca

The Canadian National Society of the Deaf-Blind, Inc: www.deafblindcanada.ca

Women North Network: www.womennorthnetwork.ca

Glossary

active listening   All the verbal and *non-verbal skills* that affirm another person's conversation and provide a clear message that you are listening and understanding. The *skills* of active listening include the *verbal skills* of questioning, responding, *reflecting*, and *summarizing*, and the non-verbal skills of physically and psychologically attending to that person.

adversity   Events or conditions of personal, family, or community difficulty or distress.

anomie   The absence of established social norms or standards in a relationship or group of people. It often leads to a sense of anxiety and disorientation as people are unsure as to how to behave.

assertiveness   To put forward a particular point of view with the conviction that it will at least be heard, if not acted upon.

assessment   A very broad term that means different things to different professions. Assessment focuses on how people are functioning and how optimal functioning and well-being can be enhanced through the provision of specific resources for their inner and outer worlds. The type of assessment required varies according to your agency context.

attachment   The relational bond established with primary caregivers in infancy, which enables a sense of a secure base to be established within an individual's inner world. A secure attachment relationship is different from other relationships in that it provides a secure base for the infant and enables the development of a sense of basic trust; an infant seeks this relationship particularly in times of high stress.

authenticity   The quality of being real or genuine in relating to another person.

biopsychosocial-spiritual dimensions   All the significant facets of an individual that may be taken into account in a multi-dimensional approach, including the biological, psychological, social, and spiritual.

challenging   In counselling work, the process of calling into question a particular view, behaviour, or feeling; for example, challenging a self-defeating belief that someone may hold about himself or herself.

client   A person who is using human services in some way, either voluntarily or involuntarily (e.g., court-mandated).

closed questions   Questions that seek confirmation or disconfirmation of information by requiring a simple response such as 'yes', 'no', 'maybe', or 'never'.

cognitive behavioural therapy   Therapy based on the understanding that a person's difficulties emerge as a result of the interaction of thoughts, feelings, and behaviours. This therapeutic approach focuses on creating change in any of these domains, particularly cognitions, so that change in the other domains will follow.

compassion fatigue   The experience of 'a sense of helplessness and confusion, and a sense of isolation from supporters' (Figley, 1995: 12). It is understood as a trauma reaction *human service workers* may develop in response to their work with *clients* who experience grief, stress, or trauma. Unlike burnout, however, compassion fatigue can happen following a single incident.

consciousness-raising   The process of bringing to people's awareness an understanding of experiences of *oppression* and/or *discrimination*. This is the first step in liberation or emancipatory processes.

constructivist perspective A *paradigm*, in contrast to *positivism*, that does not consider that there is one objective truth or reality, but subjective positions only. The construction of the individual, family, or community is what shapes and informs 'reality'. At the extreme end of this view is the idea that 'reality' does not exist outside of these subjective perceptions.

consumer A term frequently used to describe a user of a service. As it emphasizes the notion that the *client* is making choices about services used, this term is more frequently used self-referentially and is seen to be more empowering.

containment '[A]n exquisite *empathy* and thoughtfulness with which the [worker] responds to the client throughout the session' (Gibney, 2003: 46). Containment enables a sense of psychological safety to be experienced, and is therefore crucial in *crisis* situations. Containment can be offered within a particular conversation; in relation to external threats; or in a particular ongoing relationship through offering a structured setting, with clear boundaries around meeting times and space.

continuing bonds A term coined by grief theorists to refer to the ways in which bonds can be maintained with a person who has died. This is in contrast to other grief theories, which saw the work of grief counselling to be about breaking any sense of connection with a person who has died.

conversational style The unique verbal and non-verbal communication skills we use in very particular ways depending on context, for example, under the influence of familial, peer, gender, ethnic, and regional expectations.

counter-transference Generally speaking, the reaction (conscious and unconscious) provoked in the *human service worker* by the *client*'s story and presence. Some theorists argue that this may then 'result in a distorted perception of a client's behaviour' (Corey and Corey, 2007: 67).

crisis An upset to a steady state of being.

critical incident An unexpected, stressful occurrence in which a person experiences unusually strong emotional reactions that have the potential to interfere with her/his ability to function.

Critical Incident Stress Management (CISM) A range of specific interventions offered in the aftermath of a *critical incident*, which includes *debriefing*, incident management, psycho-education, and counselling support.

critical perspective A *paradigm* based on an explicit ideological or value base and in which change is central. It is critical of the status quo, seeing *power*, conflict, and *oppression* as dominant concerns to be addressed.

cross-cultural communication Communication among people of different cultural groups that is sensitive to others' ways of living and norms as much as language differences. In some situations, this involves working with an interpreter where there are language barriers. In other situations, it involves working with a cultural consultant, who can advise on social norms and expectations.

cultural screening According to Hall, the process by which information is taken in by an individual and translated to fit the context of the individual's cultural group. If information becomes overwhelming or threatens the individual's cultural identity a cultural screen can interrupt the process as a personal safety mechanism.

debriefing A strategy that aims to reduce distress, educate, and provide support around reactions to *critical incidents*, and, if appropriate, to review workforce strategies. Debriefing provides an opportunity to emotionally *ventilate* and psychologically process what has occurred. It can occur in dyads or in larger groups.

decision-making A process of coming to a decision about a particular course of action. In counselling work, this involves a series of steps: brainstorming all the options, considering the pros and cons of each course of action, and deciding on the most manageable, realistic, and achievable option.

decoding   The process of translating, analyzing, or interpreting a message.

defence mechanisms   According to psychoanalytic thought, the unconscious patterns of response adopted when a person experiences anxiety.

denial   According to psychoanalytic thought, a *defence mechanism* that enables the individual to dismiss a particular thought or observation as untrue.

differential use of self   The ways in which you vary your *engagement* with, responses to, and focuses of your work according to the particular situation in which you are working.

discrimination   The process of recognizing differences between people or things, which then can lead to differential treatment based on these observations.

ego strengths   The strengths within a person's mental structure. The ego is seen as 'a mental structure of the personality that is responsible for negotiating between the internal needs of the individual and the outside world' (Goldstein, 1995: xi; Walsh, 2006: 32). Thus, ego strengths enable a person to cope with demands and stressors by mediating the inner and outer worlds successfully.

emotional intelligence   The conscious and careful self-management of feelings in social relationships, as distinguished from academic intelligence.

empathic highlights   The verbal *skill of reflecting* back to the *client* what you have heard in terms of how she or he feels and in relation to what, to convey that you have understood.

empathy   The 'power of mentally identifying oneself with (and so fully comprehending) a person or object of contemplation' (Brown, 1993: 808). Empathy is an active *skill*, and is about 'entering imaginatively into the inner life of someone else' (Kadushin, 1972: 52). Many argue that empathy must be expressed verbally as well as non-verbally, to demonstrate to the *client* that she or he has been heard and understood.

encoding   The process of converting information into another form. In relation to communication, it is the conversion of a thought into words and feelings into non-verbal messages.

engagement   When you as a *human service worker* enter into a positive, trusting relationship with your *client* so that your work together can occur.

evaluation   The action of assessing the process and the outcome of a client–worker relationship.

externalizing   A strategy within narrative approaches that understands the 'problem' as residing externally to the person. That is, the person is not the problem. The person is invited to explore the problem as she or he relates to it and as it influences that person's life.

feminist theory   Theoretical approach that aims to create structural change, redressing the continuing *oppression* of women within male-dominated *power* structures. Feminism locates the focus of its attention beyond the inner world of an individual, arguing that these inner worlds are influenced profoundly by the wider social and political context (Dominelli, 2002; Trevithick, 1998).

goal-setting   Setting particular actions as aims to achieve, such as changing behaviours or actions.

human service worker   Someone who provides targeted services, typically within a government or non-government agency, to alleviate human *adversity* and bring about constructive social and individual change.

invitation   A statement or a question that invites someone to talk more about their situation. Examples include the question 'Can you tell me about that?' and the statement 'Go on . . .'.

method   A 'way of doing a thing' (Brown, 1993: 1759). In the human service context, methods include individual and/or family casework or counselling, group work, community work, program and policy development, education, and research.

microskills   The building blocks of human communication, i.e., the non-verbal (nodding, smiling, etc.)

and verbal (questions, reflections, etc.) *skills* we use to influence a communication process.

minimal encouragers   The verbal and non-verbal cues we use to encourage the person to continue talking. They are minimal in the sense of not being major statements or questions or reactions—they include smiling or nodding as non-verbal minimal encouragers, or 'aha', 'oh', 'hmmm' as verbal cues.

mutual clarity   When a *human service worker* and *client* have established a shared understanding and clarity regarding a situation or issue.

narrative theory   A *theory* that places a major emphasis on how an individual constructs and relates the stories, and particularly the problem stories, of his or her life. This approach is grounded in the belief that meaning-making, through the formulation of narrative, is integral to well-being because it leads to an integrated inner state.

non-verbal skills   The cues or *skills* that emanate from our physical reactions and presence, rather than through our speech. Non-verbal skills include facial expressions, body *posture* and movements, and the use of touch.

normalizing   A *skill* of affirmation; typically, it draws on a wider pool of knowledge or experience to place a person's experience in context. Normalizing provides a useful reflection and reminder that people are not alone in their distress and difficulty.

open-ended questions   Questions that are open in the sense that they invite the *client* to provide further narrative detail. Questions beginning with the words "how', 'what', 'why', 'when', 'who', and 'where' are all typically open-ended in that they invite some kind of descriptive, expansive response, not merely confirmation of information that has been provided by the person asking the question.

oppression   The negative and often overwhelming experience of being weighed down by circumstances or being overpowered by the influence and control of other people or institutions.

organizational context   The agency in which you are located and its wider context of operation (influenced by considerations such as size, staff composition, management structures, auspice, policy, geography, and agency interconnections).

paradigm   A view often dominant among a group of people at a particular period of time that both determines and explains aspects of human society, including science, and the appropriate responses to problems.

paraphrasing   A term that describes the process of relating back in your own words what you think you have heard the other person say. Paraphrasing is seen by some to reflect 'cognitive aspects of messages rather than feelings' (Hepworth, Rooney, and Larsen, 2002: 141).

positivism   A world view that understands social reality as based on 'stable, pre-existing patterns' (Neuman, 2006: 105). A positivist *paradigm* is based on assumptions of cause and effect (Morris, 2006: 3), whereby it is possible to identify the cause of problems or difficulties and intervene to alter them.

posture   The positioning of your body as a whole, which can indicate to another person varying degrees of interest and attentiveness.

power   '[T]he possession of control or authority over others' (Brown, 1993: 2315); dominance or influence.

practice wisdom   '[T]he accumulation of information, assumptions, ideologies and judgements that have seemed practically useful in fulfilling the expectations of the job' (De Roos, 1990: 282, cited in Osmond, 2005: 891).

probes   Questions, prompts, statements, even single words (Egan, 2002: 120) used by the worker to 'examine or look into closely, especially in order to discover something' (Brown, 1993: 2362).

psychodynamic theory   A *theory* primarily concerned with the inner worlds of individuals, and how difficulties arise in functioning because of these past and present inner-world preoccupations. Thus, psychodynamic theories are concerned with human drives or motivations in relation to pleasure, *power*, conflict, and anxiety. These experiences are thought to develop across the lifespan, through various psychosocial or *psychosexual* phases.

psycho-education   Education related to psychological process; for example, in the aftermath of a *crisis*, people affected are often provided with psycho-education about what to expect by way of psychological responses in the aftermath experience.

psychosexual development   An approach that understands human development to involve an interconnected series of psychological and sexual development across the lifespan.

purpose   An intention or aim of doing something. In the context of human service work, purpose relates to the overall aim of an intervention or the reason for your professional involvement with a particular person at a particular time.

rational and irrational thoughts   The focus of *cognitive behavioural therapy*. Rational thoughts are considered helpful in that they are reality-based and enable appropriate behaviour and feelings to follow; irrational thoughts are considered unhealthy or unhelpful because they distort reality or focus on irrelevant dimensions of experience.

referral   The process of identifying another person who can be of assistance to the person and ensuring that this linkage occurs.

reflecting   A distinction sometimes made between the two types of responses—reflecting and *paraphrasing*—'while paraphrases are restricted to what is actually said, reflections concentrate upon less obvious information frequently revealed in more subtle ways' (Dickson, 2006: 171).

reflexivity or critical reflection   A process of reflection that involves a further step of turning back on oneself in a reflective process to see how your own actions perpetuate or contribute to a particular situation, and to attempt therefore to critically appraise and

adjust as necessary your own positioning within a client–worker relationship. Through a process of reflexive awareness, one of the questions we begin to ask is: 'What do I (we) do in the agency on a day-to-day basis that might contribute to the structuring of unequal outcomes?' (Kondrat, 1999: 468).

repetition   A psychoanalytic term referring to a person's tendency to remain stuck, repeating particular ways of behaving, thinking, or feeling, because these behaviours, thoughts, or feelings have not been understood and resolved.

resistance   In psychoanalytic terms, the opposition to the emergence of particular insights, memories, or repressed desires; in narrative terms, the process of withstanding particular stories being perpetuated about a person that maintain their *oppression* or particular status.

respect   '[A]ssuming the intrinsic worth of individuals regardless of their attributes or achievements' (Dowrick, 1983: 14). It involves demonstrating a positive and sometimes deferential attitude to another person's point of view and/or circumstances.

risk assessment   An *assessment* of the likelihood that certain things will or may happen, based on the currently available evidence.

self-care   Strategies about taking care of yourself, in relation to all your *biopsychosocial-spiritual dimensions* and in relation to the impact of your work.

self-disclosure   A term 'loosely defined as what individuals verbally reveal about themselves to others (including thoughts, feelings and experiences)' that is seen to play 'a major part in close relationships' (Derlega, Metts, Petronio, and Margulis, 1993: 1). While we are always revealing things about ourselves through both our verbal and non-verbal interactions, we mediate these decisions and provide some boundary around some information. Self-disclosure also can be thought of as your explicit use of your own circumstances, either past or present, within your conversations with your *clients*.

skill An ability to do something well. In the context of practice, this means having the ability to communicate or intervene successfully.

smoothing skill A communication *skill* designed to smooth over difficulties and conflict, rather than escalate a disagreement currently being expressed.

social intelligence The conscious self-management of relationships and social interactions; distinguished from academic and *emotional intelligence*.

social justice The maintenance of social rights, integrity, and fairness for individuals, families, and communities within the wider social order.

stages of change A model that understands the change process as occurring in a series of stages, within which someone can 'relapse' at any point. Developed from research in relation to addictions, the model proposes people move from a pre-contemplation to a contemplation stage, then to preparation and on to action. When change is achieved, a maintenance phase begins.

structural context The wider context of systems that influence our daily lives, such as legal, political, educational, health, and welfare systems.

summarizing The drawing together in conversation the various issues that have been discussed.

supervision The time focused on discussion of your work, your learning, and your support needs with a supervisor. For *human service workers*, a supervisor takes responsibility, typically within the context of the agency, for the workers, their learning, and their practice. A supervisor assists the workers in developing their practice and *practice wisdom* through direct modelling, support, and intervention as an experienced worker.

survival Continuing to live after some event.

task-centred A practice that has emerged from a pragmatic approach to human service delivery. It is a time-limited, contracted, and highly structured approach. Interventions focus on 'doing'—on activities either within the context of the contact itself or outside as homework (Marsh and Doel, 2005: 38).

termination The process of finishing the work and the relationship with a *client*.

theory A system of ideas that provides an explanation of a phenomenon.

therapeutic A healing influence.

transference A part of every relationship in which we engage, referring to the unconscious motivations and desires, conflicts, and anxieties that we experience in our relationships. These patterns of relationship are thought to have emerged in infancy in the context of parent–infant relationships. In *therapeutic* work, the intention is to understand these conscious and unconscious experiences and expectations in the context of the client–worker relationship, enabling the working through of earlier and current significant relationships. By developing insight into the transference, change can occur as these needs and desires come under more conscious control.

transformative action Action that creates change, often more at broader social, structural, and cultural levels than just the individual level of experience.

unique outcomes In narrative approaches, the situations when the problem under analysis has not been a problem. Exploring unique outcomes enables a focus on what helps to understand what changes the imagined problem's influence in a person's life.

validation In counselling work, the process of confirming the story or emotions of another person, so that she or he feels that subjective experience has been affirmed and understood.

values The 'generally accepted or personally held judgement of what is valuable and important in life' (Brown, 1993: 3542). Professions will often define a set of values that they regard as core to the practice of their work.

ventilation The expression and, therefore, the release of feelings, often referred to as a process of catharsis.

verbal skills Specific verbal communication processes that influence a communication in a positive and/or directed way.

vicarious traumatization A worker's reaction in response to hearing or witnessing the traumatic experiences of *clients*; similar to *compassion fatigue*, and also referred to as secondary traumatization.

violence The use of force to cause injury or harm to another person. Violence is usually thought about in its physical, sexual, and emotional forms, but others such as Mullaly (2002) have suggested that the wider social context can be responsible for structural violence; that is, the abuse of people through the failure to eliminate poverty and *oppression*.

Bibliography

Adams, R., L. Dominelli, and M. Payne, eds. 2005. *Social Work Futures: Crossing Boundaries, Transforming Practice*. Basingstoke: Palgrave Macmillan.

Adolescent Forensic Health Service. 2007. *Male Adolescent Program for Positive Sexuality (MAPPS)*. At: www.rch.org.au/afhs/mapps/index.cfm?doc_id=1150.

Al-Krenawi, A., and J.R. Graham. 2003. *Multicultural Social Work in Canada: Working with Diverse Ethno-Racial Communities*. Toronto: Oxford University Press.

American Board of Examiners in Clinical Social Work. 2004. *The Practice of Psychoanalysis: A Specialty of Clinical Social Work*. Salem, Mass.: American Board of Examiners in Clinical Social Work.

American Psychiatric Association (APA). 2000. *The Diagnostic and Statistical Manual of Mental Disorders—Text Revised*. Washington: American Psychiatric Association.

Anderson, H. 1997. *Conversation, Language and Possibilities: A Postmodern Approach to Therapy*. New York: Basic Books.

Andrews, D., J. Keissling, R. Russell, and B. Grant. 1979. *Volunteers and the One-To-One Supervision of Adult Probationers*. Toronto: Ontario Ministry of Correctional Services.

Anglem, J., and J. Maidment. 2004. 'Introduction to assessment', in J. Maidment and R. Egan, eds, *Practice Skills in Social Work and Welfare: More Than Just Common Sense*. Crows Nest: Allen & Unwin, 112–26.

Antonovsky, A. 1979. *Health, Stress and Coping*. San Francisco: Jossey-Bass.

———. 1987. *Unraveling the Mystery of Health: How People Manage Stress and Stay Well*. San Francisco: Jossey-Bass.

Arendt, M., and A. Elklit. 2001. 'Effectiveness of psychological debriefing', *Acta Psychiatrica Scandinavica* 104, 6: 423–37.

Armstrong, J. 2006. *Love, Life, Goethe: How To Be Happy in an Imperfect World*. London: Allan Lane.

Atkinson, J. 2002. *Trauma Trails: Recreating Song Lines. The Transgenerational Effects of Trauma in Indigenous Australia*. North Melbourne: Spinifex.

Bandura, A., G. Caprara, C. Barbaranelli, M. Gerbino, and C. Pastorelli. 2003. 'Role of affective self-regulatory efficacy in diverse spheres of psychosocial functioning', *Child Development* 74, 3: 769–82.

Banks, S. 2006. *Ethics and Values in Social Work*, 3rd edn. Basingstoke: Palgrave Macmillan.

Baskin, C. 2005. 'Mino-yaa-daa: Healing together', in Brownlee and Graham (2005: 170–81).

Beck, A., A. Freeman, and D. Davis. 2004. *Cognitive Therapy of Personality Disorders*. New York: Guilford Press.

Bird, A. 2006. *We Need to Talk: The Case for Psychological Therapy on the NHS*. London: Mental Health Foundation.

Bishop, A. 2002. *Becoming an Ally: Breaking the Cycle of Oppression*. Crows Nest: Allen & Unwin.

Bitter, J.R. 2009. *Theory and Practice of Family Therapy and Counselling*. Belmont, Calif.: Brooks/Cole.

Black, D., and D. Trickey. 2005. 'Children bereaved by murder and manslaughter', Seventh International Conference on Grief and Bereavement in Contemporary Society, 12 July, London.

Blagg, H. 1997. 'A just measure of shame? Aboriginal youth and conferencing in Australia', *British Journal of Criminology* 37, 4: 481–501.

Blankenship, K. 1998. 'A race, class and gender analysis of thriving', *Journal of Social Issues* 54, 2: 393–404.

Bloch, S., and B. Singh, eds. 2007. *Foundations of Clinical Psychiatry*. Carlton: Melbourne University Press.

Bluebond-Langner, M. 1978. *The Private Worlds of Dying Children*. Princeton, NJ: Princeton University Press.

Bodor, R., R. Green, B. Lonne, and M.K. Zapf. 2004. '40 degrees above or 40 degrees below zero: Rural social work and context in Australia and Canada', *Rural Social Work* 9: 49–59.

Bond, T. 2000. *Standards and Ethics for Therapy in Action*, 2nd edn. London: Sage.

Boone, M., B. Minore, M. Katt, and P. Kinch. 1997. 'Strength through sharing: Interdisciplinary team-work in providing social and health services to northern native communities', in K. Brownlee, R. Delaney, and J. Graham, eds, *Strategies for Northern Social Work Practice*. Thunder Bay, Ont.: Lakehead University Press, 45–59.

Bowlby, J. 1984. *Attachment*. London: Penguin.

Bramwell, M. 2005. 'Living with HIV/AIDS', paper presented at the Human Risk and Vulnerable Populations Lecture, University of Melbourne.

Brandell, J. 2004. *Psychodynamic Social Work*. New York: Columbia University Press.

Bricker-Jenkins, M., N. Hooyman, and N. Gottlieb, eds. 1991. *Feminist Social Work Practice in Clinical Settings*. London: Sage.

Briggs, H., and K. Corcoran, eds. 2001. *Social Work Practice: Treating Common Client Problems*. Chicago: Lyceum Books.

Brink, D. 1987. 'The issues of equality and control in the client- or person-centered approach', *Journal of Humanistic Psychology* 27, 1: 27–37.

Briskman, L., and M. Flynn. 1999. *Community Embedded Rural Social Care Practice*. Geelong, Australia: Deakin University Press.

British Association for Counselling and Psychotherapy (BACP). 2002. *Ethical Framework for Good Practice in Counselling and Psychotherapy*. Rugby.

Bronfenbrenner, U. 1979. *The Ecology of Human Development: Experiments by Nature and Design*. Cambridge, Mass.: Harvard University Press.

Brooker, P. 2001. *A Concise Glossary of Cultural Theory*. New York: Oxford University Press.

Brown, C., and T. Augusta-Scott. 2007. *Narrative Therapy: Making Meaning, Making Lives*. Thousand Oaks, Calif.: Sage.

Brown, F., and J. Rainer. 2006. 'Too much to bear: An introduction to crisis intervention and therapy', *Journal of Clinical Psychology* 62, 8: 953–7.

Brown, G. 2006. 'Explaining', in Hargie (2006b: 195–228).

Brown, L., ed. 1993. *The New Shorter Oxford English Dictionary*. Oxford: Clarendon Press.

Brownlee, K., and J.R. Graham. 1997. *Violence in the Families*. Toronto: Canadian Scholars' Press.

——— and ———, eds. 2005. *Violence in the Family: Social Work Readings and Research from Northern and Rural Canada*. Toronto: Canadian Scholars' Press.

———, ———, and P. Dimond. 1997. 'Strategies for community assessment', in K. Brownlee, R. Delaney, and J. Graham, eds, *Strategies for Northern Social Work Practice*. Thunder Bay, Ont.: Lakehead University Centre for Northern Studies, 113–28.

Brun, C., and R. Rapp. 2001. 'Strengths-based case management: Individuals' perspectives on strengths and the case manager relationship', *Social Work* 46, 3: 278–88.

Bucknell, D. 2006. 'Outcome focused supervision', in H. Reid and J. Westergaard, eds, *Providing Support and Supervision: An Introduction for Professionals Working with Young People*. London: Routledge, 41–56.

Bull, P. 2002. *Communication under the Microscope: The Theory and Practice of Microanalysis*. New York: Routledge.

Burstow, B. 1987. 'Humanistic psychotherapy and the issue of equality', *Journal of Humanistic Psychology* 27, 1: 9–25.

Butchart, A., and T. Kahane. 2006. *Preventing Child Maltreatment: A Guide to Taking Action and Generating Evidence*. Geneva: World Health Organization and International Society for Prevention of Child Abuse and Neglect.

Campfield, K., and A. Hills. 2001. 'Effect of timing of Critical Incident Stress Debriefing (CISD) on post-traumatic symptoms', *Journal of Traumatic Stress* 14, 2: 327–40.

Canadian Association of Social Workers (CASW). 2005. *Code of Ethics*. Ottawa: CASW.

———. 2005. *Practice Guidelines*. Ottawa: CASW.

Canda, E., and L. Furman. 1999. *Spiritual Diversity in Social Work Practice: The Heart of Helping*. New York: Free Press.

Caplan, G. 1990. 'Loss, stress and mental health', *Community Mental Health Journal* 26, 1: 27–48.

Carroll, M. 1996. *Counselling Supervision: Theory, Skills and Practice*. London: Cassell.

——— and M. Gilbert. 2006. *On Being a Supervisee: Creating Learning Partnerships*. Kew: Psychoz.

Cartney, P. 2006. 'Using video interviewing in the assessment of social work communication skills', *British Journal of Social Work* 36: 827–44.

Catty, J. 2005. '"The vehicle of success": Theoretical and empirical perspectives on the therapeutic alliance in psychotherapy and psychiatry', *Psychology and Psychotherapy: Theory, Research and Practice* 77, 2: 255–72.

Cech, M. 2010. *Interventions with Children and Youth in Canada*. Toronto: Oxford University Press.

Chaplin, J. 1999. *Feminist Counselling in Action*, 2nd edn. London: Sage.

Cheers, B. 1999. *Community-Embedded Rural Social Care Practice*. Geelong, Australia: Deakin University Press.

Chenowith, L., and D. McAuliffe. 2005. *The Road to Social Work and Human Service Practice: An Introductory Text*. Southbank: Thomson.

Chodorow, N. 1999. 'The anxieties of uncertainty: Reflections on the role of the past in psychoanalytic thinking', in N. Chodorow, ed., *The Power of Feelings: Personal Meaning in Psychoanalysis, Gender and Culture*. New Haven: Yale University Press, 34–65.

Chui, W.H., and J. Wilson, eds. 2006. *Social Work and Human Services Best Practice*. Leichhardt: Federation Press.

Clarke, A., S. Andrews, and N. Austin. 1999. *Lookin' after Our Own: Supporting Aboriginal Families through the Hospital Experience*. Melbourne: Aboriginal Family Support Unit—Royal Children's Hospital.

Cleak, H., and J. Wilson. 2004. *Making the Most of Field Placement*. Southbank: Thomson.

Cnaan, R. 1999. *The Newer Deal: Social Work and Religion in Partnership*. New York: Columbia University Press.

Coates J., J.R. Graham, B. Swartzentruber, and B. Ouellette. 2007. *Spirituality and Social Work: Selected Canadian Readings*. Toronto: Canadian Scholars' Press.

Connolly, M., ed. 2001. *New Zealand Social Work: Contexts and Practice*. South Melbourne: Oxford University Press.

———. 2004. *Child and Family Welfare: Statutory Responses to Children at Risk*. Christchurch: Te Awatea Press.

Cooper, M., and J. Lesser. 2002. *Clinical Social Work Practice: An Integrated Approach*. Boston: Allyn and Bacon.

Corey, G. 1996. *Theory and Practice of Counseling and Psychotherapy*. Pacific Grove, Calif.: Brooks/Cole.

———. 2008. *Theory and Practice of Counseling and Psychotherapy*, 8th edn. Toronto: Thomson Learning.

Corey, M., and G. Corey. 1997. *Groups Process and Practice*. Belmont, Calif.: Brooks/Cole.

——— and ———.2007. *Becoming a Helper*, 5th edn. Belmont, Calif.: Thomson.

Coulehan, J., and M. Block. 2006. *The Medical Interview: Mastering Skills for Clinical Practice*. Philadelphia: F.A. Davis Co.

Coulton, C. 2004. 'The place of community in social work practice research: Conceptual and methodological developments', paper presented at the Aaron Rosen Lecture, Society for Social Work Research, New Orleans, 17 Jan..

Cournoyer, B. 2004. *The Evidence-based Social Work Skills Book*. Boston: Pearson Education.

———. 2005. *The Social Work Skills Workbook*. Belmont, Calif.: Thomson Brooks/Cole.

Cox, D. 1982. *Religion and Welfare: A Study of the Role of Religion in the Provision of Welfare Services to Selected Groups of Immigrants in Melbourne*. Parkville: Department of Social Studies, University of Melbourne.

Coyne, J., C. Aldwin, and R. Lazarus. 1981. 'Depression and coping in stressful episodes', *Journal of Abnormal Psychology* 90, 5: 439–47.

———— and G. Downey. 1991. 'Social factors and psychopathology: Stress, social support and coping processes', *Annual Review of Psychology* 42: 401–25.

Cramer, P. 1998. 'Defensiveness and defense mechanisms', *Journal of Personality* 66, 6.

Crawford, K. 2006. *Reflective Reader: Social Work and Human Development*. Exeter: Learning Matters.

Crossley, R., and A. McDonald. 1984. *Annie's Coming Out*. Ringwood: Penguin Books.

Crumpton-Cook, R. 1996. 'But we have the expertise', *Psychotherapy in Australia* 3, 1: 16–17.

Cunningham, M. 2003. 'Impact of trauma work on social work clinicians: Empirical findings', *Social Work* 48, 4: 451–9.

Cutcliffe, J. 2005. 'Toward an understanding of suicide in First Nation Canadians', *Journal of Crisis Intervention and Suicide Prevention* 26, 3: 141–5.

Daines, B., L. Gask, and T. Usherwood. 1997. *Medical and Psychiatric Issues for Therapists*. London: Sage.

Dalton, D. 1993. *Mahatma Gandhi: Nonviolent Power in Action*. New York: Columbia University Press.

Davis, S. 2006. *Community Mental Health in Canada*. Vancouver: University of British Columbia Press.

D'Cruz, H., P. Gillingham, and S. Melendez. 2007. 'Reflexivity, its meanings and relevance for social work: A critical review of the literature', *British Journal of Social Work* 37, 1: 73–90.

Deahl, M., M. Srinivasan, N. Jones, C. Neblett, and A. Jolly. 2001. 'Evaluating psychological debriefing: Are we measuring the right outcomes?', *Journal of Traumatic Stress* 14, 3: 527–9.

Dean, R. 2001. 'The myth of cross-cultural competence', *Families in Society: The Journal of Contemporary Human Services* 82, 6: 623–30.

————. 2002. 'Teaching contemporary psychodynamic theory for contemporary social work practice', *Smith College Studies in Social Work* 73, 1: 11–27.

de Boer, C., and N. Coady. 2007. 'Good helping relationships in child welfare: Learning from stories of success', *Child and Family Social Work* 12: 32–42.

Delaney, R., K. Brownlee, M. Sellick, and D. Tranter. 1997. 'Ethical problems facing northern social workers', *The Social Worker* 65, 3: 55–65.

————, ————, and M.K. Zapf. 2001. *Issues in Northern Social Work Practice*. Thunder Bay, Ont.: Center for Northern Studies, Lakehead University.

Derlega, V., S. Metts, S. Petronio, and S. Margulis. 1993. *Self-Disclosure*. Newbury Park, Calif.: Sage.

de Shazer, S. 1994. *Words Were Originally Magic*. New York: Norton.

Deveson, A. 1991. *Tell Me I'm Here*. Ringwood: Penguin.

Dickson, D. 2006. 'Reflecting', in Hargie (2006b: 165–94).

———— and O. Hargie. 2006. 'Questioning' in Hargie (2006b: 121–45).

Diller, J. 2004. *Cultural Diversity: A Primer for the Human Services*. Belmont, Calif.: Brooks/Cole.

Division for the Advancement of Women. 2003. *Women2000 and Beyond: Women, Nationality and Citizenship*. Geneva: World Health Organization, June.

Doka, K. 1989. *Disenfranchised Grief: Recognizing Hidden Sorrow*. New York: Lexington Books.

Dominelli, L. 2002. *Feminist Social Work Theory and Practice*. Basingstoke: Palgrave.

Dow, B., and J. McDonald. 2003. 'Social support or structural change? Social work theory and research on care-giving', *Australian Social Work* 56, 3: 197–208.

Dowrick, C. 1983. 'Strange meeting: Marxism, psychoanalysis and social work', *British Journal of Social Work* 13: 1–18.

Dowrick, S. 2006. 'The heart of the story', *The Age*, 10 June, 57.

Dryden, W., and J. Mytton. 1999. *Four Approaches to Counselling and Psychotherapy*. London: Routledge.

Duffy, S., F. Jackson, S. Schim, D. Ronis, and K. Fowler. 2006. 'Cultural concepts at the end of life: How do culture, race, gender and ethnicity influence nursing interventions in end-of-life care?', *Nursing Older People* 18, 8: 10–15.

Duncan, B., and S. Miller. 2005. 'The manual is not the territory: Treatment manuals do not improve outcomes', in J. Norcross, R. Levant, and L. Beutler, eds, *Evidence-based Practices in Mental Health: Debate and Dialogue on the Fundamental Questions*. Washington: American Psychological Association.

DuPraw, M.E., and M. Axner. 1997. 'Toward a more perfect union in age of diversity: Working on common cross-cultural communication challenges'. At: www.pbs.org/ampu/crosscult.html.

Dwairy, M. 2006. *Counselling and Psychotherapy with Arabs and Muslims*. New York: Teachers College Press.

Dyregrov, A. 1997. 'The process in psychological debriefings', *Journal of Traumatic Stress* 10, 4: 589–605.

Edward, J. 1998. 'Psychodynamic psychotherapy after managed care', in G. Schamess and A. Lightburn, eds, *Humane Managed Care?* Washington: NASW Press.

Egan, G. 2002, 2007. *The Skilled Helper: A Problem-Management and Opportunity-Development Approach to Helping*, 7th and 8th edns. Pacific Grove, Calif.: Brooks/Cole.

———— and W. Schroeder. 2009. *The Skilled Helper: A Problem-Management and Opportunity-Development Approach to Helping*, 1st Canadian edn. Toronto: Nelson Education.

Elkhuizen, K., R. Kelleher, L. Gibson, and R. Attoe. 2006. '"Sitting on the mourning bench": Mental health workers and an elderly client', *Australian Social Work* 59, 3: 281–7.

Ellis, A. 1974. *Humanistic Psychotherapy: The Rational Emotive Approach*. San Francisco: McGraw-Hill.

————. 1995. *Better, Deeper, and More Enduring Brief Therapy: The Rational Emotive Behavior Therapy Approach*. Bristol, Penn.: Brunner/Mazel.

————. 2004. 'Post-September 11th perspectives on religion, spirituality, and philosophy in the personal and professional lives of selected REBT cognoscenti: A response to my colleagues', *Journal of Counseling and Development* 82: 439–42.

Epstein, L. 1994. 'The therapeutic idea in contemporary society', in A. Chambon and A. Irving, eds, *Essays on Postmodernism and Social Work*. Toronto: Canadian Scholars' Press, 3–15.

Esteva, G., and M. Prakash. 1998. 'Human rights: The Trojan horse of recolonization?', in G. Esteva and M. Prakash, eds, *Grassroots Post-modernism: Remaking the Soil of Cultures*. London: Zed Books.

Evans, J., and P. Benefield. 2001. 'Systematic reviews of educational research: Does the medical model fit?', *British Educational Research Journal* 27, 5: 527–41.

Evans, W., J. Tulsky, A. Back, and R. Arnold. 2006. 'Communication at times of transitions: How to help patients cope with loss and re-define hope', *Cancer Journal* 12: 417–24.

Everly, G. 2000. 'Five principles of crisis intervention: Reducing the risk of premature crisis intervention', *International Journal of Emergency Mental Health* 2, 1: 1–4.

————, R. Flannery, and J. Mitchell. 2000. 'Critical Incident Stress Management (CISM): A review of the literature', *Aggression and Violent Behavior* 5, 1: 23–40.

Falicov, C.J. 1995. 'Training to think culturally: A multidimensional comparative framework', *Family Process* 34: 373–88.

Faulkner, K., and T. Faulkner. 1997. 'Managing multiple relationships in rural communities: Neutrality and boundary violations', *Clinical Psychology: Science and Practice* 4, 3: 225–34.

Figley, C., ed. 1995. *Compassion Fatigue: Coping with Secondary Traumatic Stress Disorder in Those Who Treat the Traumatized*. New York: Brunner/Mazel.

Fisher, D. 1991. *An Introduction to Constructivism for Social Workers*. New York: Praeger.

Flannery, R., and G. Everly. 2000. 'Crisis intervention: A review', *International Journal of Emergency Mental Health* 2, 2: 119–25.

Floyd, K., and M. Morman, eds. 2006. *Widening the Family Circle: New Research on Family Communication*. Thousand Oaks, Calif.: Sage.

Folstein, M., S. Folstein, and P. McHugh. 1975. 'Mini-mental state: A practical method for grading the cognitive state of patients for the clinician', *Journal of Psychiatric Research* 12: 189–98.

Fonagy, P. 1999. 'Process and outcome in mental health care delivery: A model approach to treatment evaluation', *Bulletin of the Menninger Clinic* 63, 3: 288–304.

————. 2002. *Attachment Theory and Psychoanalysis*. New York: Other Press.

———, G. Moran, and M. Target. 1993. 'Aggression and the psychological self', *International Journal of Psychoanalysis* 74: 471–85.

Fook, J. 1993. *Radical Casework: A Theory of Practice*. St Leonards: Allen & Unwin.

———. 1999. 'Critical reflectivity in education and practice', in Pease and Fook (1999: 195–208).

———. 2000. 'Critical perspectives on social work practice', in I. O'Connor, P. Smyth, and J. Warburton, eds, *Contemporary Perspectives on Social Work & the Human Services: Challenges and Change*. Frenchs Forest: Addison-Wesley Longman Australia.

———. 2002. *Social Work: Critical Theory and Practice*. Thousand Oaks, Calif.: Sage.

Freire, P. 1996. *Pedagogy of the Oppressed*. Camberwell: Penguin Books.

Froggett, L. 2002. *Love, Hate and Welfare: Psychosocial Approaches to Policy and Practice*. Bristol, UK: Policy Press.

Freedberg, S. 2007. 'Re-examining empathy: A relational-feminist point of view', *Journal of Social Work* 52, 3: 251–9.

Furlong, M., and A. Ata. 2006. 'Observing different faiths, learning about ourselves: Practice with inter-married Muslims and Christians', *Australian Social Work* 59, 3: 250–64.

Gaita, R. 1999. *A Common Humanity: Thinking about Love and Truth and Justice*. Melbourne: Text Publishing.

———. 2004. *Good and Evil: An Absolute Conception*, 2nd edn. Abingdon: Routledge.

Gallagher, E., A. Wadsworth, and T. Stratton. 2002. 'Religion, spirituality and mental health', *Journal of Nervous and Mental Disease* 190, 10: 697–704.

Gambrill, E. 1999. 'Evidence-based practice: An alternative to authority-based practice', *Families in Society* 80, 4: 341–50.

Ganzer, C., and E. Ornstein. 1999. 'Beyond parallel process: Relational perspectives on field instruction', *Clinical Social Work Journal* 27, 3: 231–46.

Garland, C. 1998. *Understanding Trauma: A Psychoanalytic Approach*. New York: Routledge.

Geldard, D., and K. Geldard. 2005. *Basic Personal Counselling: A Training Manual for Counsellors*, 5th edn. Frenchs Forest: Pearson Education Australia.

Gelman, C.R., and D. Mirabito. 2005. 'Practicing what we teach: Using case studies from 9/11 to teach crisis intervention from a generalist perspective', *Journal of Social Work Education* 41, 3: 479–94.

George, L., D. Larson, H. Koenig, and M. McCulloch. 2000. 'Spirituality and health: What we know, what we need to know', *Journal of Social and Clinical Psychology* 19, 1: 102–16.

Germain, C. 1991. *Human Behavior in the Social Environment: An Ecological View*, 2nd edn. New York: Columbia University Press.

——— and M. Bloom. 1999. *Human Behavior in the Social Environment: An Ecological View*. New York: Columbia University Press.

Gibney, P. 2003. *The Pragmatics of Therapeutic Practice*. Melbourne: Psychoz.

Giddens, A. 1991. *Modernity and Self-identity: Self and Society in the Late Modern Age*. Stanford, Calif.: Stanford University Press.

———. 2002. *Runaway World: How Globalisation Is Reshaping Our Lives*, 2nd edn. London: Profile Books.

Gilliland, B.E., and K.R. James. 1997. *Crisis Intervention Strategies*. Pacific Grove, Calif.: Brooks/Cole.

Ginzburg, K., Z. Solomon, and A. Bleich. 2002. 'Repressive coping style, acute stress disorder, and posttraumatic stress disorder after myocardial infarction', *Psychosomatic Medicine* 64, 5: 748–57.

Gist, R., and S. Woodall. 1999. 'There are no simple solutions to complex problems: The rise and fall of Critical Incident Stress Debriefing as a response to occupational stress in the fire service', in R. Gist and B. Lubin, eds, *Response to Disaster: Psychosocial, Community and Ecological Approaches*. Philadelphia: Brunner/Mazel, 211–35.

Glintborg, B., S.E. Andersen, and K. Dalhoff. 2007. 'Insufficient communication about medication use at the interface between hospital and primary care', *Quality and Safety in Health Care* 16, 1: 34–9.

Goldberg, D. 1978. *Manual of the General Health Questionnaire*. Windsor, UK: NFER Publishing.

Goldstein, E. 1995. *Ego Psychology and Social Work Practice*. New York: Free Press.

Goleman, D. 2005. *Emotional Intelligence*. New York: Bantam Books.

————. 2006. *Social Intelligence: The New Science of Human Relationships*. London: Hutchinson.

Goodman, D. 2001. *Promoting Diversity and Social Justice: Educating People from Privileged Groups*. Thousand Oaks, Calif.: Sage.

Gordon, C., ed. 1980. *Power/Knowledge: Selected Interviews and Other Writings by Michel Foucault*. New York: Pantheon Books.

Gordon, R. 1995a. 'Contrasting trauma and Critical Incident Stress: Theory and intervention strategies', paper presented at the ACISA–ASTSS Conference, Hobart.

————. 1995b. 'Psychological effects of work related stress', paper presented at the ACISA–ASTSS Conference, Hobart.

————, D. Druckman, R. Rozelle, and J. Baxter. 2006. 'Non-verbal behaviour as communication: Approaches, issues and research', in Hargie (2006b: 73–120).

Gotlib, I., and B. Wheaton, eds. 1997. *Stress and Adversity over the Life Course: Trajectories and Turning Points*. Melbourne: Cambridge University Press.

Gottlieb, B., ed. 1997. *Coping with Chronic Stress*. New York: Plenum.

Granot, H. 1996. 'The impact of disaster on mental health', *Counselling* (May): 140–3.

Green, R. 2003. 'Social work in rural areas: A personal and professional challenge', *Australian Social Work* 56, 3: 209–19.

————, R. Gregory, and R. Mason. 2006. 'Professional distance and social work: Stretching the elastic?', *Australian Social Work* 59, 4: 449–61.

Gunzberg, J. 1996. 'Healing through meeting: Martin Buber's conversational approach to psychotherapy', *Psychotherapy in Practice* 3, 1: 33–8.

Haebich, A. 2006. *Broken Circles: Fragmenting Indigenous Families 1800–2000*. Fremantle: Fremantle Arts Centre Press.

Hall, E. 1976. *Beyond Culture*. New York: Anchor Press.

Happell, B., J. Pinikahana, and C. Roper. 2003. 'Changing attitudes: The role of a consumer academic in the education of postgraduate psychiatric nursing students', *Archives of Psychiatric Nursing* 17, 2: 67–76.

Hargie, O. 2006a. 'Training in communication skills', in Hargie (2006b: 553–65).

————, ed. 2006b. *The Handbook of Communication Skills*, 3rd edn. New York: Routledge.

Harms, L. 2005. *Understanding Human Development: A Multidimensional Approach*. South Melbourne: Oxford University Press.

———— and F. McDermott. 2003. 'Trauma: A concept and a practice across borders', *Psychotherapy in Australia* 10, 1: 32–7.

————, C. Rowe, and S. Suss. 2006. 'Family adaptation following trauma', paper presented at the Fifth International Conference on Social Work in Health and Mental Health, Hong Kong.

Harris, J. 1995. 'Where is the child's environment? A group socialization theory of development', *Psychological Review* 102, 3: 458–89.

————. 1998. *The Nurture Assumption: Why Children Turn Out the Way They Do*. Sydney: Free Press.

Hart, M. 2002. *Seeking Mino-Pimatisiwin: An Aboriginal Approach to Helping*. Halifax: Fernwood.

Healy, K. 2005. *Social Work Theories in Context: Creating Frameworks for Practice*. Basingstoke: Palgrave Macmillan.

Heath, R., and J. Bryant. 2000. *Human Communication Theory and Research: Concepts, Contexts and Challenges*. Mahwah, NJ: Lawrence Erlbaum.

Hepworth, D., R. Rooney, and J.A. Larsen. 2002. *Direct Social Work Practice: Theory and Skills*, 6th edn. Pacific Grove, Calif.: Brooks/Cole.

Herman, J. 1992. *Trauma and Recovery*. New York: Basic Books.

Hick, S. 2005. *Social Work in Canada*. Toronto: Thompson Educational.

Hobfoll, S., N. Ennis, and J. Kay. 2000. 'Loss, resources and resiliency in close interpersonal relationships', in J. Harvey and E. Miller, eds, *Loss and Trauma: General and Close Relationship Perspectives*. Philadelphia: Brunner-Routledge, 267–85.

Hollis, F., and M. Woods. 1981. *Casework: A Psychosocial Therapy*, 3rd edn. New York: Random House.

Holloway, E., and S. Neufeldt. 1995. 'Supervision: Its contributions to treatment efficacy', *Journal of Consulting and Clinical Psychology* 63, 2: 207–13.

Holloway, R. 2006. 'Looking in the distance: Spirituality in God's absence', in Moore and Purton (2006: 15–25).

Holman, E., and R. Silver. 1996. 'Is it the abuse or the aftermath? A stress and coping approach to understanding responses to adversity', *Journal of Social and Clinical Psychology* 15, 3: 318–39.

Howard, S. 2006. *Psychodynamic Counselling in a Nutshell*. London: Sage.

Howatt, W. 2000. *The Human Services Counselling Toolbox: Theory, Development, Technique and Resources*. Pacific Grove, Calif: Brooks/Cole.

Howe, D. 1987. *An Introduction to Social Work Theory*. Aldershot: Gower.

———. 1994. 'Modernity, post-modernity and social work', *British Journal of Social Work* 24, 5: 513–32.

———. 1998. 'Relationship-based thinking and practice in social work: The use of relationship', *Journal of Social Work Practice* 16, 2: 45–56.

———. 2002. 'Relating theory to practice', in M. Davies, ed., *The Blackwell Companion to Social Work*, 2nd edn. Oxford: Blackwell, 81–7.

Hubble, M., B. Duncan, and S. Miller. 1999. *The Heart and Soul of Change: What Works in Therapy*. Washington: American Psychological Association.

Hudson, C. 2000. 'At the edge of chaos: A new paradigm for social work?', *Journal of Social Work Education* 36, 2: 215–30.

Hutchison, E. 2003. *Dimensions of Human Behavior: The Changing Life Course*. Thousand Oaks, Calif.: Sage.

Ife, J. 1997. *Rethinking Social Work: Towards Critical Practice*. South Melbourne: Longman.

———. 2001. *Human Rights and Social Work: Towards Rights-based Practice*. Melbourne: Cambridge University Press.

——— and F. Tesoriero. 2006. *Community Development: Community-based Alternatives in an Age of Globalisation*. Frenchs Forest: Pearson Education.

Ignatieff, M. 2001. 'The attack on human rights', *Foreign Affairs* (Nov.–Dec.): 102–16.

Ivey, A., B.M. Ivey, and L. Simek-Morgan. 1996. *Counselling and Psychotherapy: A Multicultural Perspective*. Needham Heights, Mass.: Allyn and Bacon.

Jacoby, M. 1984. *The Analytic Encounter—Transference and Human Relationship*. Toronto: Inner City Books.

Janoff-Bulman, R. 1992. *Shattered Assumptions: Towards a New Psychology of Trauma*. New York: Free Press.

Jaworski, A. 1993. *The Power of Silence. Social and Pragmatic Perspectives*. London: Sage.

Jenaro, C., N. Flores, and B. Arias. 2007. 'Burnout and coping in human service practitioners', *Professional Psychology: Research and Practice* 38, 1: 80–7.

Jenkins, R. 2002. *Legal Issues in Therapy and Psychotherapy*. London: Sage.

Jessup, H., and S. Rogerson. 1999. 'Postmodernism and the teaching and practice of interpersonal skills', in Pease and Fook (1999: 161–78).

Jung, C. 1963. *Memories, Dreams, Reflections*. Glasgow: Collins Fount.

Kadushin, A. 1972. *The Social Work Interview*. New York: Columbia University Press.

——— and G. Kadushin. 1997. *The Social Work Interview: A Guide for Human Service Professionals*. New York: Columbia University Press.

Kessler, M., E. Gira, and J. Poertner. 2005. 'Moving best practice to evidence-based practice in child welfare', *Families in Society* 86, 2: 244–50.

Kirst-Ashman, K., and G. Hull. 2001. *Generalist Practice with Organizations and Communities*. Belmont, Calif.: Brooks/Cole.

Klass, D., P. Silverman, and S. Nickman. 1996. *Continuing Bonds: New Understandings of Grief*. Washington: Taylor and Francis.

Klein, M. 1962. *Love, Hate and Reparation*. London: Hogarth Press and Institute of Psychoanalysis.

Kleinman, A., V. Das, and M. Lock, eds. 1997. *Social Suffering*. Berkeley: University of California Press.

Kobasa, S. 1979. 'Stressful life events and health: An inquiry into hardiness', *Journal of Personality and Social Psychology* 37: 1–11.

Koltko-Rivera, M. 2006. 'Rediscovering the later version of Maslow's hierarchy of needs: Self-transcendence and opportunities for theory, research, and unification', *Review of General Psychology* 10, 4: 302–17.

Kondrat, M.E. 1999. 'Who is the "self" in self-aware: Professional self-awareness from a critical theory perspective', *Social Service Review* 73, 4: 451–77.

———. 2002. 'Actor-centered social work: Re-visioning "person-in-environment" through a critical theory lens', *Social Work* 47, 4: 435–48.

Koprowska, J. 2005. *Communication and Interpersonal Skills in Social Work*. Exeter: Learning Matters.

Kotzman, A. 1995. *Listen to Me, Listen to You*. Camberwell: ACER.

Lambert, M. 2005. 'Early response in psychotherapy: Further evidence for the importance of common factors rather than "placebo effects"', *Journal of Clinical Psychology* 61, 7: 855–69.

Laming, C. 2006. *A Constructivist Approach to Challenging Men's Violence against Women*. Melbourne: University of Melbourne.

Laub, D., and N. Auerhahn. 1993. 'Knowing and not knowing massive psychic trauma: Forms of traumatic memory', *International Journal of Psycho-Analysis* 74: 287–302.

Lazarus, R., and S. Folkman. 1984. *Stress, Appraisal, and Coping*. New York: Springer.

Leeds-Hurwitz, W., ed. 1995. *Social Approaches to Communication*. New York: Guilford Press.

Lepore, S., and J. Smyth, eds. 2003. *The Writing Cure: How Expressive Writing Promotes Health and Emotional Well-Being*. Washington: American Psychological Association.

Levesque, D., C. Cummins, J. Prochaska, and J. Prochaska. 2006. 'Stage of change for making an informed decision about Medicare health plans', *Health Services Research* 41, 4: 1372–92.

Lewis, J. 2002. 'The contribution of research findings to practice change', *MCC: Building Knowledge for Integrated Care* 10, 1: 9–12.

Liebman, A., J. Jordan, D. Lewis, L. Radcliffe-Smith, P. Sykes, and J. Taylor, eds. 1997. *Women's Circus: Leaping Off the Edge*. North Melbourne: Spinifex Press.

Lindemann, E. 1944. 'Symptomatology and management of acute grief', *American Journal of Psychiatry* 101: 141–9.

Lindsay, R. 2002. *Recognizing Spirituality: The Interface between Faith and Social Work*. Crawley: University of Western Australia Press.

Lloyd, M., and C. Taylor. 1995. 'From Hollis to the Orange Book: Developing a holistic model of assessment in the 1990s', *British Journal of Social Work* 25: 691–710.

Loader, R. 1995. 'A personal statement about counselling and an exploration of the person as counsellor', *Australian Social Work* 48, 2: 35–8.

Lohrey, A. 2006. 'Voting for Jesus: Christianity and politics in Australia', *Quarterly Essay* 22.

Lupton, D. 1999. *Risk*. London: Routledge.

Lynn, E. 1999. 'Value bases in social work education', *British Journal of Social Work* 29: 939–53.

Lynn, R. 2001. 'Learning from a "Murri Way"', *British Journal of Social Work* 31, 903–16.

McCluskey, U. 2002. 'The dynamics of attachment and systems-centred group psychotherapy', *Group Dynamics* 6, 2: 131–42.

McCubbin, H., E. Thompson, A. Thompson, and J. Fromer, eds. 1998). *Stress, Coping and Health in Families: Sense of Coherence and Resiliency*. Thousand Oaks, Calif.: Sage.

Macnab, F. 1989. *Life after Loss*. Newtown: Millennium Books.

———. 2000. *Traumas of Life and Their Treatment*. Melbourne: Spectrum Publications.

McNally, R., R. Bryant, and A. Ehlers. 2003. 'Does early psychological intervention promote recovery from posttraumatic stress?', *Psychological Sciences in the Public Interest* 4, 2: 45–80.

McNamara, M. 2006. 'Protectors need protecting too', *The Age*, 1 July, 9.

Maidment, J., and R. Egan, eds. 2004. *Practice Skills in Social Work and Welfare: More Than Just Common Sense*. Crows Nest: Allen & Unwin.

Mancini, A., and G. Bonanno. 2006. 'Resilience in the face of potential trauma: Clinical practices and illustrations', *Journal of Clinical Psychology* 62, 8: 971–85.

Mander, A., and A. Rush. 1977. *Feminism as Therapy*, 2nd edn. New York: Random House.

Manthei, R. 1997. *Counselling: The Skills of Finding Solutions to Problems*. New York: Routledge.

Marris, P. 1986. *Loss and Change*, 2nd edn. London: Routledge.

———. 1993. 'The social construction of uncertainty', in C. Parkes, J. Stevenson-Hinde, and P. Marris, eds, *Attachment across the Lifecycle*. London: Tavistock/Routledge, 77–90.

———. 1996. *The Politics of Uncertainty: Attachment in Private and Public Life*. London: Routledge.

Marsh, P., and M. Doel. 2005. *The Task-Centred Book*. London: Routledge.

Martin, P. 1997. *The Sickening Mind: Brain, Behaviour, Immunity and Disease*. London: HarperCollins.

Martyn, H. 2000. *Developing Reflective Practice: Making Sense of Social Work in a World of Change*. Bristol, UK: Policy Press.

Mayhew, C. 2000. *Preventing Client-initiated Violence: A Practical Handbook*. Canberra: Australian Institute of Criminology.

Merrett, L. 2004. 'Closure with clients', in Maidment and Egan (2004: 273–86).

Miller, J., S. Donner, and E. Fraser. 2004. 'Talking when talking is tough: Taking on conversations about race, sexual orientation, gender, class and other aspects of social identity', *Smith College Studies in Social Work* 74, 2: 377–93.

Miller, S. 2004. 'Losing faith: Arguing for a new way to think about therapy', *Psychotherapy in Australia* 10, 2: 44–51.

———, B. Duncan, and M. Hubble. 2004. 'Beyond integration: The triumph of outcome over process in clinical practice', *Psychotherapy in Australia* 10, 2: 2–19.

Mitchell, J. 1983. 'When disaster strikes: The Critical Incident Stress Debriefing process', *Journal of Emergency Medical Services* 8: 36–9.

———. 1984. 'High tension: Keeping stress under control', *Firehouse* (Sept.).

———. 2004. *Crisis Intervention and Critical Incident Stress Management: A Defense of the Field*. Ellicott City, Md: International Critical Incident Stress Foundation Inc.

Moon, J. 2004. *A Handbook of Reflective and Experiential Learning: Theory and Practice*. London: Routledge/ Farmer.

Moore, J., and C. Purton, eds. 2006. *Spirituality and Counselling: Experiential and Theoretical Perspectives*. Ross-on-Wye: PCCS Books.

Moore, T. 2004. *Dark Nights of the Soul: A Guide to Finding Your Way through Life's Ordeals*. London: Piatkus Books.

Moran, C., and M. Massam. 1997. 'An evaluation of humour in emergency work', *Australasian Journal of Disaster and Trauma Studies* 3: 1–11.

Morley, C. 2004. 'Conducting risk assessments', in Maidment and Egan (2004: 127–45).

Morley, L., and J. Ife. 2002. 'Social work and love of humanity', *Australian Social Work* 55, 1: 69–77.

Morris, T. 2006. *Social Work Research Methods: Four Alternative Paradigms*. Thousand Oaks, Calif.: Sage.

Morrissette, V., B. McKenzie, and L. Morrissette. 1993. 'Towards an aboriginal model of social work practice: Cultural knowledge and traditional practices', *Canadian Social Work Review* 10, 1: 91–108.

Mullaly, B. 2002. *Challenging Oppression: A Critical Social Work Approach*. Toronto: Oxford University Press.

———. 2007. *The New Structural Social Work*. Toronto: Oxford University Press.

Mussel, B., K. Cardiff, and J. White. 2004. *The Mental Health and Wellbeing of Aboriginal Children and Youth: Guidance for New Approaches and Services*. Victoria: Report prepared for the British Columbia Ministry for Children and Family Development.

Myer, R., and C. Conte. 2006. 'Assessment for crisis intervention', *Journal of Clinical Psychology* 62, 8: 959–70.

Nelson, D., and R. Burke. 2002. *Gender, Work Stress, and Health*. Washington: American Psychological Association.

Nelson-Jones, R. 2002. *Basic Counselling Skills: A Helpers' Manual*. Thousand Oaks, Calif.: Sage.

———. 2006. *Theory and Practice of Counselling and Therapy*, 4th edn. Thousand Oaks, Calif.: Sage.

Neuman, W. 1999. *Social Research Methods: Qualitative and Quantitative Approaches*. Needham Heights, Mass.: Pearson Education.

———. 2006. *Social Research Methods: Qualitative and Quantitative Approaches*, 6th edn. Needham Heights, Mass.: Pearson Education.

Newhouse, D.R., C.J. Voyageur, and D.J.K. Beavon. 2005. *Hidden in Plain Site: Contributions of Aboriginal Peoples to Canadian Identity and Culture.* Toronto: University of Toronto Press.

O'Connell, B. 1998. *Solution-focused Therapy.* London: Sage.

O'Donoghue, K. 2003. *Restorying Social Work Supervision.* Annandale: Federation Press.

Ogloff, J. 2006. 'Advances in violence risk assessment', *InPsych* 28, 5: 12–16.

O'Hagan, K. 2001. *Cultural Competence in the Caring Profession.* London: Jessica Kingsley.

O'Hara, A. 2006. 'The practitioner's use of self in the professional relationship', in O'Hara and Weber (2006: 46–57).

O'Hara, A., and Z. Weber, eds. 2006. *Skills for Human Service Practice: Working with Individuals, Groups and Communities.* South Melbourne: Oxford University Press.

Okun, B. 2002. *Effective Helping: Interviewing and Counseling Techniques.* Pacific Grove, Calif.: Brooks/Cole-Thomson Learning.

Ornstein, E., and C. Ganzer. 2003. 'Dialectical constructivism in clinical social work: An exploration of Irwin Hoffman's approach to treatment', *Clinical Social Work Journal* 31, 4: 355–69.

Osmond, J. 2005. 'The knowledge spectrum: A framework for teaching knowledge and its use in social work practice', *British Journal of Social Work* 35: 881–900.

Parker, S. 2006. 'Measuring faith development', *Journal of Psychology and Theology* 34, 4: 337–48.

Payne, M. 2005. *Modern Social Work Theory.* Chicago: Lyceum Books.

———. 2006. *What Is Professional Social Work?* , 2nd edn. Bristol, UK: Policy Press.

———. 2006. *Narrative Therapy: An Introduction for Counselors.* Thousand Oaks, Calif.: Sage.

Pearlman, L.A., and I.S. Macian. 1995. 'Vicarious traumatization: An empirical study of the effects of trauma work on trauma therapists', *Professional Psychology: Research and Practice* 26, 6: 558–65.

——— and K. Saakvitne. 1995. *Trauma and the Therapist: Countertransference and Vicarious Traumatisation in Psychotherapy with Incest Survivors.* New York: Norton.

Pease, B., and J. Fook, eds. 1999. *Transforming Social Work Practice: Postmodern Critical Perspectives.* St Leonards: Allen & Unwin.

Pelling, N., R. Bowers, and P. Armstrong. 2006. *The Practice of Counselling.* South Melbourne: Thomson.

Pennebaker, J., ed. 1995. *Emotion, Disclosure and Health.* Washington: American Psychological Association.

——— and R. O'Heeran. 1984. 'Confiding in others and illness rates among spouses of suicide and accidental-death victims', *Journal of Abnormal Psychology* 93: 473–6.

Perlman, H.H. 1979. *Relationship: The Heart of Helping People.* Chicago: University of Chicago Press.

Petrakis, M. 2004. 'Keeping the client safe: Complexities and clinician risk in working with the suicidal client', paper presented at the RISK (Faculty of Arts Research Student Colloquium: antiTHESIS Forum), University of Melbourne.

Pierce, J. 2007. 'Cross-cultural communication in social work practice: An interpretive descriptive approach to cross-cultural communication difficulties', MSW thesis, University of Northern British Columbia.

Pilkington, C., and S. Woods. 1999. 'Risk in intimacy as a chronically accessible schema', *Journal of Social and Personal Relationships* 16, 2: 249–63.

Poindexter, C. 1997. 'In the aftermath: Serial crisis intervention for people with HIV', *Health and Social Work* 22, 2: 125–32.

Pope, S. 2000. *Postnatal Depression: A Systematic Review of Published Scientific Literature to 1999.* Canberra: National Health and Medical Research Council.

Prochaska, J., and C. DiClemente. 1983. 'Stages and processes of self change of smoking: Toward an integrative model of change', *Journal of Consulting and Clinical Psychology* 51: 390–5.

Rakos, R. 2006. 'Asserting and confronting', in Hargie (2006b 345–81).

Ramsay, R. 2003. 'Transforming the "Working Definition of Social Work" into the 21st century', *Research and Social Work Practice* 13, 3: 324–38.

Raphael, B. 1983. *The Anatomy of Bereavement*. New York: Basic Books.

Rasmussen, B. 2005. 'An intersubjective perspective on vicarious trauma and its impact on the clinical process', *Journal of Social Work Practice* 19, 1: 19–30.

Reamer, F. 2001. *Ethics Education in Social Work*. Alexandria: Virginia Council on Social Work Education.

Reber, A. 1985. *The Penguin Dictionary of Psychology*. Ringwood: Penguin Books.

Reeves, A., and P. Seber. 2004. 'Working with the suicidal client', *Counselling and Psychotherapy* 15, 4: 45–50.

Reid, H., and J. Westergaard. 2006. *Providing Support and Supervision: An Introduction for Professionals Working with Young People*. London: Routledge.

Reiter, A. 2000. *Narrating the Holocaust*. London: Continuum.

Renzenbrink, I. 2005. 'Staff support: Whose responsibility?', *Grief Matters* 8, 1.

Resick, P. 2001. *Stress and Trauma*. Philadelphia: Taylor and Francis.

Ribner, D., and C. Knei-Paz. 2002. 'Client's view of a successful helping relationship', *Social Work* 47, 4: 379–87.

Rice, S. 2002. 'Magic happens: Revisiting the spirituality and social work debate', *Australian Social Work* 55, 4: 303–12.

Rider, E., and C. Keefer. 2006. 'Communication skills competencies: Definitions and a teaching toolbox', *Medical Education* 40: 624–9.

Rigney, D., and L. Cooper. 2004. 'Preparing for practice', in Maidment and Egan (2004: 51–68).

Robbins, S., P. Chatterjee, and E. Canda. 1999. 'Ideology, scientific theory and social work practice', *Families in Society* 80, 4: 374–84.

Robinson, M. 2004. 'Therapeutic collaboration: Bridging the gap between statutory and therapeutic work', *Australian Social Work* 57, 4: 374–80.

Robinson, R. 2003. 'Psychological debriefing: A closer look at the facts', *Critical Incident Stress Management Foundation Australia Newsletter* (special edn) 5, 3: 1–15.

———— and J. Mitchell. 1995. 'Getting some balance back into the debriefing debate', *Bulletin of the Australian Psychological Society* (Oct.): 5–10.

Rogers, C. 1967. *On Becoming a Person: A Therapist's View of Psychotherapy*. London: Constable.

————. 1980. *A Way of Being*. Boston: Houghton Mifflin.

————. 1987. 'Comments on the issue of equality in psychotherapy', *Journal of Humanistic Psychology* 27, 1: 38–9.

————, A. Ellis, and F. Perls. 1977. *Three Approaches to Psychotherapy*. Film produced by Psychological Films.

Room, G., and N. Britton. 2006. 'The dynamics of social exclusion', *International Journal of Social Welfare* 15: 280–9.

Rose, S., and J. Bisson. 1998. 'Brief early psychological interventions following trauma: A systematic review of the literature', *Journal of Traumatic Stress* 11, 4: 697–710.

————, ————, and S. Wessely. 2003. 'Counselling and psychotherapy: Media distortion', *British Journal of Psychiatry* 183: 263–4.

Roth, A., and P. Fonagy. 2005. *What Works for Whom? A Critical Review of Psychotherapy Research*. New York: Guilford Press.

Russell, S., and M. Carey. 2003. 'Feminism, therapy and narrative ideas: Exploring some not so commonly asked questions', *International Journal of Narrative Therapy and Community Work* 3, 1.

Rutter, M., and English and Romanian Adoptees Study Team. 1998. 'Developmental catch-up and deficit following adoption after severe global early privation', *Journal of Child Psychology and Psychiatry* 39, 4: 465–76.

Saggese, M. 2005. 'Maximising treatment effectiveness in clinical practice: An outcome-informed collaborative approach', *Families in Society* 86, 4: 558–64.

Saleebey, D. 1996. 'The strengths perspective in social work practice: Extensions and cautions', *Social Work* 41, 3: 296–305.

————. 1997. *The Strengths Perspective in Social Work Practice*, 2nd edn. New York: Longman.

————. 2001. 'Practicing the strengths perspective: Everyday tools and resources', *Families in Society* 82, 3: 221–2.

Salzberger-Wittenberger, I. 1970. *Psychoanalytic Insight and Relationships: A Kleinian Approach*. London: Routledge & Kegan Paul.

Scales, T., and C. Streeter, eds. 2004. *Rural Social Work: Building and Sustaining Community Assets*. Toronto: Nelson.

Schacter, D. 1996. *Searching for Memory: The Brain, the Mind and the Past*. New York: Basic Books.

Schmidt, G., and R. Klein. 2004. 'Geography and social work retention', *Rural Social Work* 9: 235–43.

———and L. Jarrett. 2000. *Mental Health and Northern Aboriginal People: An Annotated Bibliography*. Prince George, BC: Northern Interior Regional Health Board and University of Northern British Columbia Social Work Program.

Schon, D. 1987. *Educating the Reflective Practitioner*. San Francisco: Jossey-Bass.

Schore, A. 1994. *Affect Regulation and the Origin of the Self: The Neurobiology of Emotional Development*. Hillsdale, NJ: Lawrence Erlbaum Associates.

———. 2005. 'Attachment, affect regulation, and the developing right brain: Linking developmental neuroscience to pediatrics', *Pediatrics in Review* 26, 6: 204–17.

Schubert, M. 1991. *Interviewing in Social Work Practice: An Introduction*. Alexandria, Va: Council on Social Work Education.

Sciarra, D. 1999. *Multiculturalism in Counselling*. Itasca, Ill.: F.E. Peacock.

Scott, D. 1990. 'Practice wisdom: The neglected source of practice research', *Social Work* 35, 6: 564–8.

Scott, N.E., and L.G. Borodovsky. 1990. 'Effective use of cultural role-taking', *Professional Psychology: Research and Practice* 21, 167–70.

Seden, J. 2005. *Counselling Skills in Social Work Practice*, 2nd edn. Maidenhead: Open University Press.

Seligman, M. 1992. *Learned Optimism*. Milsons Point: Random House.

———, K. Reivich, L. Jaycox, and J. Gillham. 1995. *The Optimistic Child*. Milsons Point: Random House Australia.

Selye, H. 1987. *Stress without Distress*. London: Corgi.

Sharp, C. 2006. 'Towards a phenomenology of the divine', in Moore and Purton (2006: 65–80).

Sharry, J., M. Darmody, and B. Madden. 2002. 'A solution-focused approach to working with clients who are suicidal', *British Journal of Guidance & Counselling* 30, 4.

Shebib, B. 2000. *Choices: Practical Interviewing and Counselling Skills*. Neeham Heights, Mass.: Allyn and Bacon.

Shemmings, D. 2004. 'Researching relationships from an attachment perspective: The use of behavioural, interview, self-respect and projective measures', *Journal of Social Work Practice* 18, 3: 299–314.

Shulman, L. 1978. 'A study of practice skill', *Social Work* 23: 274–81.

———. 1999. *The Skills of Helping Individuals, Families, Groups and Communities*. Itasca, Ill: F.E. Peacock.

Sinason, V. 1992. *Mental Handicap and the Human Condition*. London: Free Association Books.

Smith, L.T. 2001. *Decolonizing Methodologies: Research and Indigenous Peoples*. Dunedin: University of Otago Press.

Smith, P. 1998. 'How do we understand practice? A qualitative approach', *Families in Society* 79, 5: 543–50.

Smith, R., A. Marshall-Dorsey, G. Osborn, V. Shebroe, J. Lyles, B. Stoffelmayr, L. Van Egeren, J. Mettler, K. Maduschke, J. Stanley, and J. Gardiner. 2000. 'Evidence-based guidelines for teaching patient-centered interviewing', *Patient Education and Counseling* 39: 27–36.

Smith, S., S. Thomas, and A. Jackson. 2004. 'An exploration of the therapeutic relationship and counselling outcomes in a problem gambling counselling service', *Journal of Social Work Practice* 18, 1: 99–112.

Sommers-Flanagan, J., and R. Sommers-Flanagan. 2004. *Counseling and Psychotherapy Theories in Context and Practice: Skills, Strategies and Techniques*. Hoboken, NJ: John Wiley and Sons.

Specht, H., and M. Courteney. 1994. *Unfaithful Angels: How Social Work Has Abandoned Its Mission*. New York: Free Press.

Spooner, C., W. Hall, and R. Mattick. 2001. 'An overview of diversion strategies for Australian drug-related offenders', *Drug and Alcohol Review* 20, 3: 281–94.

Stack Sullivan, H. 1953. *The Interpersonal Theory of Psychiatry*. New York: Norton.

Stansfield, C. 2006. 'The two of us', *The Age*, 23 Sept., 16.

Steier, F. 1995. 'Reflexivity, interpersonal communication and interpersonal communication research', in Leeds-Hurwitz (1995: 63–87).

Stoppard, J. 2000. *Understanding Depression: Feminist Social Constructionist Approaches*. London: Routledge.

Stroebe, M., H. Schut, and C. Finkenauer. 2001. 'The traumatization of grief? A conceptual framework for understanding the trauma-bereavement interface', *Israel Journal of Psychiatry and Related Sciences* 38, 3 and 4: 185–201.

———, ———, and W. Stroebe. 2006. 'Who benefits from disclosure? Exploration of attachment style differences in the effects of expressing emotions', *Clinical Psychology Review* 26: 66–85.

Sullivan, H. 1953. *Conceptions of Modern Psychiatry*. New York: Norton.

Swain, P., ed. 2002. *In the Shadow of the Law: The Legal Context of Social Work Practice*. Annandale: Federation Press.

———. 2005. '"No expert should cavil at any questioning": Reports and assessments for courts and tribunals', *Australian Social Work* 58, 1: 44–57.

Tamasese, K. 2000. 'Talking about culture and gender', in D. Centre, ed., *Working with the Stories of Women's Lives*. Adelaide: Dulwich Centre.

Tannen, D. 1994. *Gender and Discourse*. New York: Oxford University Press.

———. 2000. '"Don't just sit there—interrupt!" Pacing and pausing in conversational style', *American Speech* 75, 4: 393–5.

Tao, J., Y. Kang, and A. Li. 2006. 'Prosody conversion from neutral speech to emotional speech', *IEEE Transactions on Audio, Speech and Language Processing* 14, 4: 1145–50.

Taylor, S. 2004. 'Public secrets/private pain: Difficulties encountered by victims/survivors of sexual abuse in rural communities', *Women against Violence* 15: 12–21.

Thompson, N. 2002. *People Skills*, 2nd edn. Basingstoke: Palgrave Macmillan.

———. 2003a. *Communication and Language: A Handbook of Theory and Practice*. Basingstoke: Palgrave Macmillan.

———. 2003b. *Promoting Equality: Challenging Discrimination and Oppression*, 2nd edn. Basingstoke: Palgrave.

———. 2006. *Anti-discriminatory Practice*. Basingstoke: Palgrave Macmillan.

Tobin, M. 2005. 'Lost opportunity or lifeline? Women with substance use issues and their perceptions of the barriers to pregnancy care', MSW thesis, University of Melbourne.

Tolson, E., W. Reid, and C. Garvin. 2003. *Generalist Practice: A Task-centered Approach*. New York: Columbia University Press.

Tong, R. 1998. *Feminist Thought: A More Comprehensive Introduction*, 2nd edn. St Leonards: Allen & Unwin.

Trainor, B. 2002. 'Postmodernism, truth and social work', *Australian Social Work* 55, 3: 204–13.

Tranter, D., and J. Vis. 1997. 'Flexibility, sensitivity and timing: A comprehensive trauma debriefing model for the north', in K. Brownlee, R. Delaney, and J. Graham, eds, *Strategies for Northern Social Work Practice*. Thunder Bay, Ont.: Lakehead University Centre for Northern Studies, 187–216.

Trevithick, P. 1998. *Feminism and Psychotherapy: Reflections on Contemporary Theories and Practices*. London: Sage.

———. 2003. 'Effective relationship-based practice: A theoretical exploration', *Journal of Social Work Practice* 17, 2: 163–76.

———. 2005. *Social Work Skills: A Practice Handbook*, 2nd edn. Maidenhead: Open University Press.

Trotter, C. 2006. *Working with Involuntary Clients: A Guide to Practice*. Thousand Oaks, Calif.: Sage.

Turner, F.J. 1986. *Social Work Treatment: Interlocking Theoretical Approaches*. New York: Free Press.

———. 2002. *Social Work Practice: A Canadian Perspective*, 2nd edn. Toronto: Prentice-Hall.

United Nations General Assembly. 1948. *Universal Declaration of Human Rights*. At: www.un.org.

Van der Kolk, B., A. McFarlane, and L. Weisaerth, eds. 1996. *Traumatic Stress: The Effects of Overwhelming Experience on Mind, Body and Society*. New York: Guilford Press.

Veer, V. 1998. *Counselling Therapy with Refugees and Victims of Trauma*. Chichester: John Wiley & Sons.

Victorian Foundation for Survivors of Torture (VFST). 2000. *Guide to Working with Young People Who Are Refugees*. Brunswick: VFST.

———. 2004. *Towards a Health Strategy for Refugees and Asylum Seekers in Victoria*. Brunswick: VFST.

Victorian Government Department of Human Services. 2006. *Building Better Partnerships: Working with Aboriginal Communities and Organisations. A Communication Guide for the Department of Human Services*. Melbourne: Victorian Government Department of Human Services.

Victorian Interpreting and Translating Service (VITS). 2006. *We Speak Your Language: A Guide to Cross-Cultural Communication*. Melbourne: VITS LanguageLink.

Vogel, D., S. Wester, M. Heesacker, G. Boysen, and J. Seeman. 2006. 'Gender differences in emotional expression: Do mental health trainees overestimate the magnitude?', *Journal of Social and Clinical Psychology* 25, 3: 305–32.

Walsh, J. 2006. *Theories of Direct Social Work Practice*. Southbank: Thomson Brooks/Cole.

Warren, L. 2006. 'Managing the client who threatens violence', *InPsych* 28, 5: 20–1.

Weaver, H. 1999. 'Indigenous people and the social work profession: Defining culturally competent services', *Social Work* 44, 3: 217–26.

Webb, S. 2006. *Social Work in a Risk Society: Social and Political Perspectives*. Basingstoke: Palgrave Macmillan.

Weber, Z. 2006. 'Professional values and ethical practice', in O'Hara and Weber (2006: 17–33).

Weeks, W. 2004. 'Creating attractive services which citizens want to attend', *Australian Social Work* 57, 4: 319–30.

Weick, A. 1983. 'Issues in overturning a medical model of social work practice', *Social Work* 28, 6: 467–71.

Weingarten, K. 1991. 'The discourses of intimacy: Adding a social constructionist and feminist view', *Family Process* 30: 285–305.

Whitaker, R. 2010. *Anatomy of an Epidemic: Magic Bullets, Psychiatric Drugs, and the Astonishing Rise of Mental Illness in America*. New York: Crown.

White, M. 2004. 'Working with people who are suffering the consequences of multiple trauma: A narrative perspective', *International Journal of Narrative Therapy and Community Work* 1: 45–76.

Whyte, J. 2005. 'Contesting paradigms: Indigenous worldviews, western science and professional social work', doctoral thesis, University of Melbourne.

Wilkinson, K.P. 1991. *The Community in Rural America*. New York: Greenwood.

Williams, M., E. Zinner, and R. Ellis. 1998. 'The connection between grief and trauma: An overview', in E. Zinner and M. Williams, eds, *When a Community Weeps: Case Studies in Group Survivorship*. London: Brunner/Mazel.

Wiltshire, J. 1995. 'Telling a story, writing a narrative: Terminology in health care', *Nursing Inquiry* 2: 75–82.

Wingard, B. 2001. *Telling Our Stories in Ways That Make Us Stronger*. Adelaide: Dulwich Centre.

Winnicott, D. 1987. *Babies and Their Mothers*. Reading, Mass.: Addison-Wesley.

Wolterstorff, N. 1987. *Lament for a Son*. Grand Rapids, Mich.: Eerdsman.

Worden, J.W. 2003. *Grief Counselling and Grief Therapy: A Handbook for the Mental Health Practitioner*. Hove, East Sussex: Brunner-Routledge.

World Health Organization (WHO). 2003. *Constitution of the World Health Organization*. Geneva: United Nations.

Yalom, I. 2005. *The Schopenhauer Cure*. Melbourne: Scribe.

Yedidia, M.J. 2007. 'Transforming doctor–patient relationships to promote patient-centered care: Lessons from palliative care', *Journal of Pain and Symptom Management* 33, 1: 40–57.

Yip, K.S. 2006. 'Self-reflection in reflective practice: A note of caution', *British Journal of Social Work* 36: 777–88.

Yoo, S., D. Matsumoto, and J. LeRoux. 2006. 'The influence of emotion recognition and emotion regulation on intercultural adjustment', *International Journal of Intercultural Relations* 30, 3: 345–63.

Young, I. 1990. *Justice and the Politics of Difference*. Princeton, NJ: Princeton University Press.

Youssef, J., and F. Deane. 2006. 'Barriers to mental health care and opportunities to facilitate utilisation of services in Arabic-speaking communities', *Synergy* 1: 5–16.

Zapf, M.K. 1991. 'Ideology and geography: The Canadian north', in B. Kirwin, ed., *Ideology, Development and Social Welfare: Canadian Perspectives*, 2nd edn. Toronto: Canadian Scholars' Press, 656–99.

———. 2002. 'Geography and Canadian social work practice', in Turner (2002: 69–83).

Zon, A., M. Lindeman, A. Williams, C. Hayes, D. Ross, and M. Furber. 2004. 'Cultural safety in child protection: Application to the workplace environment and casework practice', *Australian Social Work* 57, 3: 288–98.

Credits

Grateful acknowledgment is made for permission to reprint the following:

Focus on Values box, page 8: The Social Work Code of Ethics, adopted by the Board of Directors of the Canadian Association of Social Workers (CASW) is effective March, 2005, and replaces the CASW Code of Ethics (1994). The Code is reprinted here with the permission of the CASW. The copyright in the document has been registered with Canadian Intellectual Property office, registration No. 1030330.

Focus on Change box, page 22: Levesque, D., Cummins, C., Prochaska, J. & Prochaska, J. (2006). Stage of change for making an informed decision about Medicare health plans. *Health Services Research*, 41(4), 1372–92.

Focus on Practice box, page 36: The Victorian Interpreting and Translating Service (VITS, 2006, pp. 19–20)

Focus on Practice box, page 66: de Boer, C. & Coady, N. (2007). Good helping relationships in child welfare: Learning from stories of success. *Child and Family Social Work*, 12, 32–42.

Focus on Practice box, page 68: Harms, L. (2005). *Understanding human development: A multidimensional approach*. South Melbourne: Oxford University Press.

Focus on Practice box, page 70: The Social Work Code of Ethics, adopted by the Board of Directors of the Canadian Association of Social Workers (CASW) is effective March, 2005, and replaces the CASW Code of Ethics (1994). The Code is reprinted here with the permission of the CASW. The copyright in the document has been registered with Canadian Intellectual Property office, registration No. 1030330.

Definition of maturity, page 76: Egan, G., Schroeder, W. (2009). *The skilled helper: A problem-management and opportunity-development approach to helping* (1st Canadian edn). Nelson Education: Brooks/Cole.

Focus on Practice box, page 94: McNamara, M. (2006, 1 July). Protectors need protecting too. The Age, p. 9.

Focus on Practice box, page 95: Figley, C. (Ed.) (1995). *Compassion fatigue: Coping with secondary traumatic stress disorder in those who treat the traumatized*. New York: Brunner/Mazel.

Focus on Practice box, page 100: Fook, J. (2002). Social work: Critical theory and practice. Thousand Oaks: Sage. Freire, P. (1996). Pedagogy of the oppressed. Camberwell: Penguin Books. Froggett, L. (2002). *Love, hate and welfare: Psychosocial approaches to policy and practice*.

Practice Exercise, page 103: Cleak, H. & Wilson, J. (2004). *Making the most of field placement*. Southbank: Thomson.

Effective engagement, page 116: Corey, M., & Corey, G. (1997). *Groups Process and Practice*. Brooks/Cole: California.

Focus on Practice box, page 146: Coulehan, J. & Block, M. (2006). *The medical interview: Mastering skills for clinical practice*. Philadelphia: F. A. Davis Co.

Initial interview, page 170: Howatt, W. (2000). *The Human Services Counselling Toolbox: Theory, Development, Technique and Resources*. Pacific Grove, Calif: Brooks/Cole.

Focus on practice box, page 182: Egan, G. (2007). *The skilled helper: A problem-management and opportunity-development approach to helping* (8th edn). Pacific Grove: Brooks/Cole.

>0t>02

Risk factors for suicide, page 179: Davis, S., (2006). *Community Mental Health in Canada.* UBC Press: Vancouver-Toronto.

Behavioural components of conflict assertion, page 188: Rakos, R. (2006). Asserting and confronting. In O. Hargie (Ed.), The handbook of communication skills. Hove: Routledge (chap. 12, pp. 345–81).

Focus on Practice box, page 197: Harms, L. (2005). *Understanding human development: A multidimensional approach.* South Melbourne: Oxford University Press.

Psychodynamic theory, page 209: Payne, M. (2005). *Modern Social Work Theory.* Chicago, Illinois: Lyceum Books Inc.

Cognitive behavioural theory, page 215: Payne, M. (2005). *Modern Social Work Theory.* Chicago, Illinois: Lyceum Books Inc.

Focus on Practice box, page 218: Ellis, A. (1974). *Humanistic psychotherapy: The rational emotive approach.* San Francisco: McGraw-Hill.

Focus on Practice box, page 226: Brown, C. & Augusta-Scott, T. (2007). *Narrative therapy: Making meaning, making lives.* Thousand Oaks: Sage Publications.

Turner's three main principles, page 254: Turner, F., J. (2002). *Social Work Practice: A Canadian Perspective.* Toronto: Prentice Hall.

Index

Schon, D., 99
Schore, A., 39, 79
Sciarra, D., 41
self-determination, 18–19
self-disclosure, 20, 65, 73, 74, 112, 124, 125, 127–31, 145, 158, 159, 196, 241, 251
Seligman, M., 18
Selye, H., 19
Sharp, C., 52, 61, 101
Sharry, J., 124
Shebib, B., 2, 14, 191–3
Shulman, L., 24, 25, 30, 60, 76, 77, 113, 127, 150, 243, 247, 248, 252
silent communication, 36–7
Sinason, V., 150
smoothing skills, 188
social self-awareness, 100–1
social variations, 34
solution-focused skills
    establishing and sustaining the relationship, 228
    exceptions and solution, 229
    the future, 229
    specific interventions, 228
Sommers-Flanagan, J, 22, 55, 59
Specht, H., 84
Spooner, W., 19
Stack Sullivan, H., 118
stages of change, 22, 23, 249
Stansfield, C., 78, 244
Steier, F., 99
Stoppard, J., 62
strength, optimism and communication, 254–5
Stroebe, M., 47
Sullivan, H, 46, 118
summarizing, 33, 131, 135, 154, 156, 157, 162–4, 199, 226
summarizing skills, 162–163
supervision, 73, 89, 94, 95, 98, 104, 104–7, 110, 111, 126, 190, 192, 211, 215, 249, 252–5
    group supervision, 105–6
supervisory relationship, 106
    confidentiality, 124
    disclosure, 125–9
    engagement, 115–17, 120–3
    finding commonalities, 119
    making initial contact, 113–15
    meeting a bereavement group, 117–18
    preparing to meet, 112–13
Swain, P., 64

Tamasese, K., 61
Tannen, D., 37, 39, 42, 49
Tao, J., 33
task-centred, 58–9
Task-centred skills, 199–201

establishing and sustaining the relationship, 198
immediate needs, 197
interventions, 198–9
Taylor, S., 87, 168, 243
The Egan Model, 182
theoretical knowledge, 55–8
therapeutic communication, 47–8
Thompson, N., 15, 21, 41, 47, 48, 52, 61, 74, 99, 105, 118, 245
Tobin, M., 177
Tolson, E., 198
transference, 60, 210, 251, 211213
Trevithick, P., 19, 43, 59, 60, 62, 82, 91, 113, 139, 143, 162, 168, 171
triads, 101–102
Trotter, C., 19, 82, 84, 121, 122, 170, 248
Turner, F., 216, 232, 246, 250, 254, 255

'use of self,' 83–89

values
    competence, 10
    confidentiality, 9
    integrity, 9
    respect, 8, 13–15
    service to humanity, 9
    social justice, 8, 16
    strengths and resilience, 19
verbal and non-verbal, 29
verbal communication processes, 33–8
Victorian Interpreting and Service, 36
Victorian Interpreting and Translating Service, 36
views and paradigms, 53–5
violence, 5, 6, 8, 14, 20, 55, 61, 69, 86, 87, 89, 94, 96, 99, 123, 130, 181, 190–3, 208, 235, 237, 239

Websites
    500 Nations, 51
    American Academy for Experts in Traumatic Stress, 111
    American Psychiatric Association and the DSM IV, 185
    Australian Critical Incident Stress Association, 208
    Australian Government-Mental Health and Well-being publications, 193
    Beck Institute for Cognitive Therapy and Research, 223
    Beyondblue National Depression Initiative, 193
    Breaking Bad News, 155
    Brief and Narrative Therapy Network, 231
    Brief Family Therapy Centre, 231
    Brief Therapy Institute of Sydney, 231
    Campbell Collaborative, 72
    Canada Drug Information, 185
    Canadian Association for Suicide Prevention, 193, 208
    Canadian Association of Social Workers, Practice Guidelines, 130
    Canadian Centre for Policy Alternatives, 72